Extraordinary Circumstances

Cynthia Cooper

WILEY

John Wiley & Sons, Inc.

ISBN 978-0-470-52830-3

Printed in the United States of America

10 9 8 7 6 5 4 3 2 1

CONTENTS

To Lance, Stephanie, and Anna Katherine the loves of my life.

INTRODUCTION

I never aspired to be a whistleblower. It wasn't how I envisioned my life. But life is full of unexpected turns.

My team and I were ordinary citizens who found ourselves facing extraordinary circumstances. In 1994, in my late 20s, I took a risk by going to work for WorldCom—then known as LDDS (Long Distance Discount Services)—establishing a start-up Internal Audit group with only two staff auditors, both of whom had virtually no prior audit experience. WorldCom was an underdog company, with an underdog CEO, headquartered in an underdog state. And while there would be many challenges, what an incredible opportunity my team and I had before us. In my first eight years, company revenues grew from $1.5 billion to over $38 billion. WorldCom transformed from a speck in the industry to one of the largest telecom companies in the world, employing some 100,000 people. We had helped grow a small regional company that bought and re-sold long distance in the South into an international behemoth that operated in over 65 countries.

Setting one record after another, WorldCom boasted what was then the largest acquisition and debt offering in corporate history. The stock price soared and investors cheered as WorldCom delivered some of the highest returns on Wall Street. The stock became the fifth-most widely held; and, in 1996, the *Wall Street Journal* ranked WorldCom Number One in return to shareholders over a ten-year period.

Bernie Ebbers, our CEO, was larger than life, a local folk hero who lived the rags-to-riches American dream. Coming from very humble beginnings, by 1999 he was *Forbes'* 174th wealthiest American. In addition to the jobs Bernie helped create, he donated millions to charity. There was even speculation that he would one day run for Governor.

Bernie grew the company quickly through acquisition. He was praised in the press as he closed one deal after another, acquiring some 70 companies in just two decades. Bernie "was an outsider, a nobody, in telecom," wrote *Network World* in 2001. "Today, he's considered one of the industry's most powerful people."

Scott Sullivan, appointed CFO at the young age of 33, was also highly respected. Wall Street regarded him as a financial wizard and a straight shooter. In 1997, with compensation of more than $19 million, he was the highest-paid CFO in the country. In 1998, *CFO* Magazine awarded him the CFO Excellence Award for mergers and acquisitions. "[Scott] walked on water," the magazine's editor said, describing Wall Street's perception of him in the late 1990s.

WorldCom became Mississippi's Cinderella story—a Fortune 500 company born right here in our state. Mississippi is the place of my birth and home of my people. Roots run deep with a love for rich fields, live oaks, magnolia blossoms, Gulf breezes, fried catfish, sweet tea and the Delta blues. But Mississippi is also poor and carries the burden of a troubled past. WorldCom was one of our greatest sources of pride, a sign that there might be better things in store for our state.

In 1997, the company announced that its headquarters would move from Jackson, the state capital, to Clinton—a suburb with a population of only 23,000, where my husband and I both graduated from high school and my parents still live. Clinton became one of the smallest towns to host a Fortune 500 company and exploded with commerce.

My nightmare started one hot June day in 2002. For a time, it seemed as if that summer would never end. I was 37 years old and the Vice President of Internal Audit. My team and I began to grow increasingly suspicious of some entries in WorldCom's books. The more we investigated, the stranger the reactions from some of our colleagues became. No one would give us a straight answer. People who helped make the entries said they didn't know what they represented, or tried to lead us in the wrong direction.

The CFO asked me to delay our audit work. The Controller insisted that we were wasting our time and should be auditing other areas of the company. The Chairman of the Audit Committee—a subset of the Board—instructed me not to ask for support for the entries, and to wait for Scott, the CFO, to provide me with an explanation.

I'd replay in my head, like a broken record, the barrage of comments I'd received—Make sure to separate emotion from business. This is nothing. You're chasing your tail. If you keep making a big deal of things, you're going to get fired. You're on Scott's to-do list; he just hasn't gotten to you yet. You're probably a decent auditor, but you don't have the expertise to be telling someone how to run their business. This is an external-audit issue, not an internal-audit issue. You can't call an Audit Committee meeting. It's not your job to be doing financial-statement auditing, and if you do, it will be low-level work that the external auditors don't want to do.

Turn off the noise, I tried to encourage myself. Don't allow yourself to be intimidated. But inside, I felt scared. My hands were shaking. My heart was pounding. Was I over-reacting? People I respected didn't seem concerned about the entries. Still, my instinct told me to press forward.

I found myself standing at a crossroads. Looking back, I would take the same path again. But doing the right thing doesn't mean there will be no cost to others, your family, or yourself.

None of us expect to find that our boss or peers have perpetrated a massive fraud. But that is exactly what happened that summer. On June 25, 2002, WorldCom announced that it had misstated its financial statements over the last five quarters by $3.8 billion, an amount that would ultimately grow to some $11 billion. The fraud immediately became an international, front-page scandal, and the lead story on news programs throughout the world. It would come to be known as the largest fraud in corporate history.

Many of us had devoted our careers, sometimes at the expense of our families and personal lives, to building WorldCom. Overnight, lives were changed forever. WorldCom once seemed unstoppable, but its fall from grace was both hard and fast. It all ended with broken trust, financial loss, and ruined careers. WorldCom filed the largest bankruptcy ever. Thousands of shareholders watched their investments evaporate; many had invested substantial portions of their savings and retirement funds in the stock. Innocent WorldCom employees lost jobs. The media jokingly dubbed the company WorldCon. Shock, disbelief, and a sense of betrayal replaced the pride many citizens, employees, and investors had felt.

How could this happen in the most respected capital market in the world? In trying to forestall and conceal the impending demise of this once-lauded company, some executives lost their way and led others astray as well. They embarked on a slippery slope—once they had begun to deceive, they did not regain their footing. Whatever rationalization was applied to the deceit, it brought nothing but ruin, the consequences of which are still felt today, and will continue to be felt for years to come.

The day before the fraud was announced, I was a private citizen. The day after, I became a public figure. I never contemplated being thrown into the spotlight and was completely unprepared. FBI agents suddenly appeared in my office. Members of the press were walking door-to-door in my neighborhood. Congress, Department of Justice prosecutors, and SEC officials were calling for interviews. I was an ordinary citizen who, like most people, preferred a private life, but I had stepped over some "invisible line" and become a whistleblower. Though I didn't know it at the time, whistleblowers often experience negative repercussions. I would quickly learn first-hand what that meant.

I've tried to tell the story as I saw it, felt it, and lived it. I once hoped I could eventually put these thoughts and events away for good, and feel a sense of peace again. Now, I know what happened will always be a part of me, but my attitude toward it has changed, and sharing the story with others has helped me to heal. I've been passionate about completing this book because I believe there are valuable lessons that can be passed on to the next generation. I have finally found that place of healing and peace. But it has been a long journey.

ACKNOWLEDGMENTS

I couldn't have written this book without the encouragement of my mother Pat Ferrell, and her insistence that this was a story worth telling because it could help others faced with tough choices. My husband Lance was an unwavering source of strength for our family during the most trying times. Lance and my two daughters Stephanie and Anna Katherine have been exceedingly understanding about the time and dedication writing requires. ("How many more pages before you can play?" my six-year-old asked regularly.) My sister-in-law Rachel Ferrell and my father Gene Ferrell have worked countless hours helping to research and edit, and my brother Sam provided much-needed encouragement throughout. Each is a blessing, and I could not have done this without them. Thank you to each of my friends and family who took time to provide honest feedback on the manuscript.

Thank you to Sheck Cho, the Executive Editor at John Wiley, for believing in this book, for his friendship and guidance, and for truly making me feel like part of the Wiley team. I am indebted to him. Charles Cannada and Steve Dobel shared their career experiences at WorldCom, adding significant dimension to the book. My editor Boris Fishman also brought tremendous talent and enthusiasm to the project, and I am grateful to him for his patience, his ability to sculpt the manuscript, and for teaching me so much along the way. Senior Production Editor Natasha Wolfe worked long hours to put the final polish on the manuscript. My agent Lloyd Jassin and attorney Eric Brown helped me through the complexities of the publishing world. Thank you also to attorney Mike Massey for encouraging me as I wrote this book and for his valuable input and sound advice. I'm also indebted to Kristen Green and, at Wiley, Associate Director of Publicity Jocelyn Cordova-Wagner and publicist Evelyn Perez, who have worked tirelessly to promote the book.

Thank you to each of the former internal auditors at WorldCom for your incredible fortitude during WorldCom's darkest hours. I'm grateful to Elaine Saxton, Lisa Smith, Glyn Smith, Jon Mabry, Stacy McEachern, and Dean Taggart—former directors of the Internal Audit Department— for their friendship, input on the manuscript, and for holding steady in the face of enormous adversity. Elaine—the last internal auditor left in Clinton, the one who "turned out the lights"—for the entire team, thank you for persevering to the end. Tonia Buchanan, Gene Morse and Glyn Smith each played a pivotal role in identifying the fraud at WorldCom. I also would like to express my appreciation to Glyn for his steadfastness throughout the ordeal. This was truly a team effort.

Denny Beresford, Professor of Accounting at the University of Georgia, and WorldCom Audit Committee Chair during the company's restructuring, encouraged my team during some of the most difficult times. He also provided encouragement and invaluable input on the manuscript.

Professor Parveen Gupta, Chair of the Department of Accounting at Lehigh University, who first introduced me to Sheck Cho at John Wiley, and Professor Glenn Sumners, Director of the Center for Internal Auditing at Louisiana State University have both put in a great deal of time advising on the book. I am extraordinarily grateful to each of them for their guidance and friendship. Thank you also to the many educators across the country who have supported my team and encouraged me to share this story with students and professionals.

I'm grateful to my pastor Chip Henderson for helping me keep perspective about what truly matters and for sharing such essential life lessons. Thank you to my attorney Bob Muse and his colleagues Bill Corboy and Ron Kovner for their friendship and wise counsel and for helping me navigate the tangle of FBI agents, trials, depositions, and congressional hearings. Thank you also to Tina Bedwell, Bob Cooper, Vickie Cooper, Marianna Finch, Susan Izenson, Patrick Kuhse, Phyllis

Massey, Amanda Ripley, Coleen Rowley, Sherron Watkins, and my Aunt Rachel Shepherd for their time and suggestions.

Thank you to Joe Wells, founder and Chairman of the Association of Certified Fraud Examiners, for his support and advice, and the significant contribution he has made to educating the public on white-collar crime and promoting fraud prevention and detection. I'm also indebted to Joel Kramer of MIS Training Institute and the late Bill Bishop of the Institute of Internal Auditors who reached out to offer encouragement during the WorldCom aftermath. Thank you to the management team at the Institute of Internal Auditors for their leadership and promotion of internal audit as a profession. I am also appreciative of the many other professional associations that have offered support, including the Association of Certified Fraud Examiners, the American Accounting Association, the American Institute of Certified Public Accountants, and the Information Systems Audit and Control Association. Thank you to the staff of the G. Chastaine Flynt Memorial Library where I spent many hours researching and writing.

So many people, some of whom I have never met, took the time to call or write letters of encouragement during some of the most difficult times. To each of you: Thank you for your kind words. They meant a great deal and helped sustain me during those days.

CHAPTER I

A Dark Cloud

People don't wake up and say, "I think I'll become a criminal today." Instead, it's often a slippery slope and we lose our footing one step at a time.

It's the end of summer 2001. White linen tablecloths blow in the warm breeze of the evening. Candles glow softly throughout the backyard and patio. The weather is unseasonably gentle, a break from the usually sultry Mississippi humidity.

My husband Lance and I are at the home of David Myers, the WorldCom Controller, who oversees the accounting department. We're attending a shower for Scott Sullivan, the company's Chief Financial Officer, and his wife Carla. Recently, they adopted a beautiful baby girl, their only child and the reason for our celebration. Carla has been in and out of hospitals, battling diabetes, and has come close to death several times. Many of us know about her struggles with her health. The office has been buzzing with excitement at their good news.

Some 20 people have come together at David's home—executives reporting to Scott and spouses, as well as Bernie Ebbers, our CEO, and his wife Kristie, who are helping to host the shower. The Myers home is beautifully decorated, reminding me of one of the fine homes in *Southern Living*. Lance and I admire each room as David takes us on a tour, excitedly telling us about the changes he and his wife made after moving in. "We're trying to move Jack from his crib to the big bed," he says, pointing to his son's crib, still sitting in his room.

Scott and Carla are showing off their baby girl. With plump rosy cheeks, she looks like the perfect Gerber baby. We watch as they take turns feeding her a bottle. Scott, the man known as intensely serious at work, is suddenly very nurturing, almost giddy.

Only a few months before, Lance and I were also blessed with a beautiful baby girl, and I've just come back to work from maternity leave. Since our babies are only months apart, it's been fun to talk to Scott and Carla about how our girls are growing, especially because Scott and I usually talk only about business. For my daughter's birth, they gave us a small doll wearing a beautiful pink dress with smocking across the collar. It sits on a white shelf above my daughter's bed. And Carla recently brought her daughter to the office wearing the dress Lance and I had given her.

Everyone ambles about, visiting and sampling the hors d'oeuvres. The tables scattered about the lawn overlook a beautiful lake. After dinner, we stand in a large circle on the back patio. The men smoke cigars and guests take turns telling humorous stories about old times. In typical fashion, Bernie Ebbers chews on an unlit cigar and occasionally throws out one of the one-liners he's famous for, making everyone laugh.

The atmosphere is full of warmth and good-hearted banter, but an unseen cloud hangs over this seemingly perfect picture. Within two years, with the exception of myself and one other guest, every employee present will be gone from the company. Three will be criminally indicted for financial-statement fraud, and I will be thrust into the center of a storm.

That night reminds me that numbers and accounts are only part of what hung in the balance. What happened touched real people: The man who lost his children's college fund, the elderly lady whose life savings disappeared, the employee living paycheck to paycheck and struggling to find another job. It also affected the families of those involved in the wrongdoing, who, on an emotional level, would endure the pain and serve prison sentences along with their loved ones. So happy and full of life at the dinner party, the faces of Kristie, Carla, and David's wife

Lynn—the spouses of three of the men indicted—will soon show only pain and sorrow.

The Slippery Slope

> Sow a thought, reap an action; sow an action, reap a habit; sow a habit, reap a character; sow a character, reap a destiny.
>
> —Scottish author Samuel Smiles

It's October, 2000, a year before the dinner party. The accounting team at WorldCom has just closed the company's books for the third quarter. David Myers is shocked by the numbers. Line cost expense—what the company pays to lease telecommunications lines and to originate and terminate telephone calls, its single largest expense—is too high by hundreds of millions of dollars, driving earnings well below Wall Street expectations. Someone must have made an error. But where?

David is a Mississippi boy who's done well for himself. Tall with a slim build, he played basketball in high school and earned a degree in accounting from the University of Mississippi in Oxford. He started his career in public accounting with Ernst & Whinney (now Ernst and Young), one of the country's most prestigious firms, and then moved into industry with Lamar Life Insurance in Jackson, the state capital. Hard-working and friendly, David quickly moved forward professionally.

Things have been going well for him. He's happily married with three children, two from a previous marriage. In his early 40s, David has been able to achieve some financial security for his family. By working hard and putting in long hours, he's moved up the corporate ladder to Senior Vice President, commanding an annual salary close to a quarter of a million dollars. As the Controller, he reports directly to Scott Sullivan, the Chief Financial Officer, and has hundreds of finance employees under his charge.

David joined WorldCom in 1995. In his first years with the company, the stock soared. By 1999, when the stock hit a record high, his stock options were worth over $15 million. David has received some $700,000 in pre-tax profit by exercising his options. He and his wife moved into a lake-front home in an upscale neighborhood, and purchased a home for his wife's parents, but David has held the remainder of his options.

Now that potential wealth seems at risk of evaporating. The high-flying bull market of the 1990s is on a fast downhill slide. The Internet stock bubble that burst in March, 2000 is about to be followed by a less publicized but much larger and more devastating collapse: Telecom. The entire sector is in disarray, but many in the industry believe the problems are temporary. Still, the figures glaring back at David are far worse than expected. Are the numbers he sees an error or a train wreck in progress?

David isn't looking forward to presenting such bad news to his boss Scott Sullivan, especially since he has no idea why the numbers are so abysmal. But he knows he can't put it off. WorldCom soon has to release its quarterly earnings to the public. He walks through the halls joining the building where the accountants work with the one housing the executive suite, where Bernie and Scott have large adjacent corner offices. As he walks through the double glass doors to the suite, he sees the lighted bookcases he's seen so many times on his way in, filled with company memorabilia Bernie has collected over the years, including items marking each acquisition.

David takes a deep breath and walks into Scott's office. The glass windows taking up the entire wall behind Scott's desk provide a beautiful view of the small man-made lake, fountain, and walking trail below. But David is in no mood to admire the view. He might as well get right to it: The numbers are bad. He can't explain why. His department has checked and re-checked them. The accountants can't find any errors.

Scott isn't happy. This is unacceptable news. Surely, someone made a mistake. David is sent back to his office to go through the numbers again, or do whatever it takes to find and fix the errors. He asks several of his accountants to retrace their steps, but even the second time around, they find no mistakes. He returns to Scott with the news, but Scott still refuses to accept the numbers, insisting there's a mathematical mistake.

Management is now only days away from having to release financial results to the public. Scott and David know that if they report these results, WorldCom will not meet the earnings guidance executives previously issued. The stock price will get hammered, and analysts will downgrade their opinions, which could send the company into a downward spiral. And WorldCom depends on its high stock price to acquire companies.

The pressure is intense and building every hour. What are we going to do, David asks Scott. Scott is at a dangerous crossroads. He rationalizes that the cost of telling the truth is too high. In any case, there must be an error, he thinks, and it'll surely correct itself the following quarter. Change the numbers, he instructs David. Reduce line-cost expense so that the company can meet earnings guidance. "While [Scott] didn't believe that this was the right and appropriate thing to do," David later recalled, he said "this is what we needed to do at the time."

Scott's instructions are stressful for David. But David has always felt loyal to his boss, so he, too, rationalizes. This will be temporary. There must be an error. Scott is sure of it. Either way, WorldCom is just going through a tough time. The industry will soon turn around.

To change the financial statements, David will have to pull several of his mid-level accountants into the plan. David and Scott are at high enough levels in the company that they don't actually make accounting entries in the system. The trusted inner circle will have to grow.

David decides to relay Scott's message to his right-hand lieutenant, an accounting director named Buford (Buddy) Yates. David trusts Buddy. They've been friends for many years, having worked together at Lamar Life. Buddy joined WorldCom in 1997. With a stocky build and gray hair, some say he can be like a bulldog—he isn't afraid to speak his mind and doesn't mince words, turning gruff at times. This time is no exception. Buddy can't believe what he's hearing. Is Scott really serious? Very much so, David tells him.

David then turns to Betty Vinson and Troy Normand, two mid-level accountants who report to Buddy and play a key role in compiling the financial results. They'll be able to analyze the details, help decide which specific accounts to adjust, and physically make changes in WorldCom's accounting system.

Like Buddy, Troy and Betty are extremely uncomfortable with Scott's request. This is beyond tweaking—to meet earnings expectations, they'd have to make adjustments in the hundreds of millions of dollars with no support and only the hope that the problem would correct itself. They're feeling upset and pressured, but there's little time to think things through—the company has to release its earnings to the public. All three are their families' primary breadwinners. Not following orders could mean losing jobs that aren't easily replaceable in Jackson, Mississippi. Begrudgingly, they decide to go along with the plan—this once.

The three split the work load. Buddy and Troy work on one side of the accounting entries, deciding which liability accounts can be reduced. Betty works on the other side, doing the same for expense accounts.

Because there are estimates in accounting, especially during acquisitions, companies sometimes overstate liabilities and expenses. This has to be corrected once the exact numbers have been determined, though some companies choose to leave them in place, creating what's known in accounting, disapprovingly, as rainy-day "cookie-jar reserves." These are the accounts that Betty, Buddy, and Troy are drawing down, but they don't have a legitimate business rationale. They're just drawing down reserves by whatever amount is necessary to meet earnings. "I just really pulled some [accounts] out of the air," Betty will recall.

Once the changes have been made, David takes Scott the adjusted financial statements. Now they're exactly what the boss wants to see, but David is worried that his accountants may jump ship. Both Betty and Troy have told him that they're contemplating resigning from the company. Buddy is also growing upset. They love their jobs and have been devoted to WorldCom, working long hours and often taking work home to continue through the night—whatever it took to get the job done. But now, it seems, they're being forced to walk away.

Scott offers a solution—the company will reduce earnings guidance going forward so that, in the future, no one will have to make bad entries. David is relieved to hear the news. He asks Scott if he would mind personally reassuring the three accountants. Hearing it from someone so senior to them may make a difference.

Scott agrees to meet with the accountants. Buddy doesn't attend, but Betty and Troy are anxious to hear what Scott has to say. When they arrive at his office, he invites them to sit in the executive seating area in front of his desk. Employees usually sit around the large conference table, but the sofa and chairs make for a homier, more intimate setting.

Scott knows all too well what's at stake, and he pours it on thick and heavy. He appeals to their loyalty. He flatters. He assures Betty and Troy that the false entries were a one-time thing, since earnings guidance will be lowered. He thanks them for their hard work and apologizes that they had to do this. In any case, he still believes that the numbers in the initial statement were simply wrong and will correct themselves come next quarter.

"This is a situation where you have an aircraft carrier out in the middle of the ocean and its planes are circling up in the air," Scott tells the two accountants, according to David's recollection, "and what you want to do, if you would, is stick with the company long enough to get the planes landed to get the situation fixed. . . . Then if you still want to leave the company, then that's fine, but let's stick with it and see if we can't change this."

Troy tells Scott that he's "scared" and doesn't want to find himself "in a position of going to jail for [Scott] or the company." Scott "said that he respected our concern," Troy would later recall, but that "we weren't being asked to do anything that he believed was wrong . . . but that if it later was found to be wrong, that he would be the person going to jail, not me."

As Troy and Betty discuss the meeting on the way back to their offices, Troy wonders if maybe he's making too much out of this. After all, Scott's very smart and highly regarded. He must know what he's doing. Still, in the end, he and Betty decide that they don't feel any more comfortable. Not wanting to be pulled any further into Scott's scheme, they think about resigning.

On October 26, 2000, the same day that WorldCom issues a press release announcing the third quarter financial results, Troy writes a formal letter of resignation addressed to Buddy and David: "Due to the circumstances surrounding the third quarter 2000 close, I feel I have no choice but to resign. I have chosen not to participate in the recommended course of action and have also decided not to take any future risk."

Betty composes a similar letter. "Dear Buddy, this letter is to serve as notice of my resignation from WorldCom effective today. The actions proposed regarding quarter close entries has necessitated this action. If needed, I can assist with any transition issues that may arise. My income situation is such that I request we . . . work out an equitable arrangement regarding some sort of salary and benefits continuation until I can obtain other employment, because I feel that upper management has forced my decision surrounding my resignation. This is not the course of action that I prefer, but feel I must take. It has truly been a pleasure working for you."

Betty and Troy decide to hold their letters to see if the company will lower earnings guidance as Scott promised. On November 1, 2000, five days later, WorldCom sends out a press release lowering future guidance. Scott has kept his word. But will the revised guidance be low enough to keep them from having to make these types of entries again?

Day after day, their letters unsent, outside pressure begins to weaken Troy and Betty's resolve. "Me and my wife had lost a set of twins in early 2000," Troy would explain. "Subsequent to that—I was the only income earner in the family. [Then] she had a miscarriage, and . . . soon thereafter she got pregnant once again. And I was scared to leave as the sole provider of my family." Doubts begin to grow in Betty's mind too. She's also the primary breadwinner. She has a young daughter and is worried that, in her mid-forties, it will be tough to find a comparable position. "I thought about it for a while, and I believed what Scott said, that this would be a one-time thing, go ahead and get through it," she later recalled. "I liked my job. These quarter close entries were so much removed from what I did every day, I liked the people I worked with, and I really wanted to stay there."

As 2000 draws to a close, David and the accountants discover bad news: Scott's prediction that the problem would reverse itself in the fourth quarter hasn't come true. What's worse, the new lower guidance still isn't enough to prevent doctoring the results. Once again, the four accountants find themselves forced to choose—blow the whistle and come forward with the truth, resign and say nothing, or make the entries and hope things will turn around next quarter.

Once again, Troy and Betty search the company's books for liability accounts they can reduce to offset the higher-than-expected line costs and lower-than-expected earnings. But such accounts are nearly depleted by now; this is the last quarter they can draw down excess in liability accounts to meet earnings. If the telecom market doesn't make a drastic change for the better in the first quarter of 2001, Scott will have to come up with a new plan. Surely things will turn around by then and this will be the last quarter they're asked to make unsupported entries.

But the end of the next quarter shows this was wishful thinking. The expected turnaround is nowhere in sight. Since the previously lowered accounts no longer have any excess amounts to draw down, Scott instructs his staff to employ a new scheme—count the excess line costs as capital assets instead of expenses. The cost of capital assets, like facilities and equipment, is written off over a much longer period than the cost of operational expenses like these line costs, which must be expensed in the month they are incurred. Scott's plan will spread the costs over a much longer period, buying the company time for a turnaround.

As quarters pass, the accountants commit themselves further and further to a path of deceit. Almost a year has passed since Betty and Troy wrote their resignation letters. Still, the letters are unsent. Each quarter, David and his three accountants hope for better news, but the telecommunications sector continues to deteriorate. At home, life goes on with husbands, wives, and children, and, at times, the accountants can focus on other things—the parts of their jobs they love, their children's activities. But still, shelved in a corner of their minds, their actions weigh heavier and heavier, taking a physical and emotional toll. Buddy eventually visits an attorney to discuss his options, but ultimately doesn't take any action. Betty struggles to sleep and begins losing weight.

It's October, 2001. David is reviewing the company's results for the third quarter. Things are getting worse, not better. For the first time during David's tenure with the company, WorldCom is not making a profit.

"Scott, how are we going to stop this?" David asks, desperate for a solution.

Hearing no good answers, he realizes in his heart that, for the foreseeable future, nothing will change. He has begun to feel deeply depressed. He withdraws and becomes distant from his family, and no longer wants to go out and visit with friends.

Eventually, David starts thinking of taking his own life. Maybe it would be better to just end it all, he thinks. He punches the accelerator of his BMW to see how much speed it will take before spinning out of control. He watches the speedometer rise to 80, 90, 100, 115 miles per hour. But he always takes his foot off the gas pedal. It's no good. Taking his life is not the answer to his problems.

David's increasingly dark moods have not gone unnoticed by his wife Lynn. As they look out over the calm lake behind their home, the scene is peaceful, but Lynn is tense. She's been watching her husband, the man she adores and loves deeply, suffer under the extraordinary stress of his job. David hasn't told her what's going on at work, but a wife can tell when something is terribly wrong. She misses the old David. She and her son need him to come back.

"You're somewhere else," she says. "We have a baby. You work all the time. Why not quit?"

David tries to comfort her. He explains that he can't quit yet, but he doesn't share with her the real reason for his distress. With Lynn's encouragement, David finally goes to see a doctor and begins taking an antidepressant. It helps his moods, but it can't fix the source of his anguish.

David ponders various options, but there seems to be no good way out of his dilemma. It's too late to quit. He's already participated in the deception; if it ever comes out, the road will lead back to him. He still feels loyalty to Scott, and an obligation to Buddy, Betty, and Troy, whom he's talked into seeing this through. His team depends on him. He can't just leave them to deal with this.

Plus he has a wife and baby to support. His $240,000 salary would be virtually irreplaceable in Jackson. If things turn around, maybe, down the road, he can leave. Then he can start a new life, maybe go into business for himself, and finally be free of all this. But the slippery slope leaves few options.

CHAPTER 2

Graduation Day

It's 1982. I carefully place my high-school graduation gown on the bed I've slept in for the past 15 years. My room looks much the same as it has since I was a little girl—pink-and-yellow-tulip wallpaper and a small single bed with white spindles across the headboard.

I place the gold ribbon, "Honors" embroidered across the front in bold black letters, around the collar of the gown, lay it flat, and admire the ensemble for a moment. The gold ribbon strikes a sharp contrast against the bright red of the gown.

After stepping into the gown, I move the cap and tassel back and forth on my head until they're perfectly situated, hang the ribbon around my neck, and smile as I look at myself in the bathroom mirror from every angle. Satisfied, I take off the gown and lay everything out on my bed just as carefully the second time, as snapshots of the past roll across my mind.

My guiding lights, the people who have had the greatest influence on my life, were neither famous nor powerful: My parents; Nannie Ferrell, my grandmother; my church pastors; my youth minister; my high school teachers.

My father, Gene, spent a lot of time with me when I was growing up. I loved to play games with him—everything from ping-pong to Jacks to card games like Go Fish. Each time we started, he would tell me the same thing. "I'll play, but you need to know: I've never lost a game of Go Fish," or whatever game we were playing that day.

"Yes, you have!" I'd say, laughing.

"No, never lost a game," he would assure me. Then, often, I'd win. "That's the first game of Jacks I've ever lost!" he'd say, pretending to be totally surprised.

"My daddy is the tallest man in the world," I bragged as a young girl. I was so disillusioned when I first saw one of my father's friends standing next to him in our kitchen. He looked twice as tall as my dad. Concerned, I sought out my mother. "He's bigger than my daddy," I whispered in disbelief.

In high school, it was my dad who made sure I had plenty of gas in the car, reminded me to buckle my seatbelt, and sat up late in our living room waiting patiently until I arrived home safely from a night out with friends.

He is a cherished guardian, friend, and advisor, and will remain so throughout my life, especially during the dark times waiting for me. From a young age, he's the one I turn to for advice when I'm looking for answers. "Why do bad things happen to people?" I asked him when a close friend of the family became very ill. "We all face adversity," he said. "Some of us will have to walk through doors of difficulty others won't, but we all have our doors." And when I reached those challenges in my own life, he urged me, "stay close to God."

As for my mother, she was the first-born in her family, so she was the leader of her band of four siblings. Family lore has it that she was daring and fearless as a child, a tomboy who was the one her brothers and sister counted on to fight off the neighborhood bullies. She was a free spirit, sometimes to the point of mischief, putting soap in the teachers' coffee pot or persuading her friends to go skinny-dipping in a nearby lake. Her favorite pastime was to climb the huge oak tree behind the playhouse in her backyard. She'd say the tree had been wrought by the hand of God and bequeathed only to her, the tomboy Patsy Lee. You could see the whole world from the top of that tree, but the most fun was to climb as high as possible and ride the short, thin limbs with the winter wind. If a hard storm was blowing, it was better than any ride at the state fair.

The climbing came to an end after Nannie Nola, my maternal grand-mother, looked out the back window in horror one day to find her Patsy Lee happily blowing back and forth in the middle of a winter storm. It's completely safe, my mother tried to assure her. She'd already done it more than a dozen times! "Well, you better never do it again," her mother said all the same. Fortunately, my mom survived her childhood adventures with just a few bumps, bruises, stitches, and one broken arm.

My mother tried to guide my brother Sam and me from the time we were little. Sometimes, it seemed as if she was sitting in wait for teachable moments. She especially worked to build our self-confidence, to impart the value of perseverance. Don't be discouraged. Press on. Don't give up. Keep your chin up. Fight the good fight.

"Don't ev-v-ver allow yourself to be intimidated," she would say, drawing the word out in her heavy Mississippi accent, after we told her about someone bullying us at school. As much as any advice she gave, this was the lesson that helped me push through my fears and find my courage when I needed it most.

"People don't always think about the consequences of their actions," she would say. "Think about the consequences of yours. I've seen too many people ruin their lives."

The words "I love you" came easy and often in our home. We told each other when we left the house, hung up the phone, and before we went to sleep. Our parents were our biggest cheerleaders, the first to praise our accomplishments and comfort us in failure, always listening to us when we needed to be heard.

They volunteered to head the Parent Teacher Organization, chaper-oned school dances, and came to hear my violin screech at school orchestra concerts. They were on the sidelines at Sam's soccer games, watching him streak down the field, nimbly dribbling the ball around defenders. They were at the finish line the day Sam came barreling around the corner on the final stretch of an elementary school race, only to be passed by one racer after another. Usually, he won, but this time he hadn't paced himself, and my mother sat on the ground with him as tears streamed down his cheeks.

In our home, "roots and a sense of place are important," my mother would say. Even though no one in the family cared much for ambrosia—a combination of coconut, oranges, and pineapples made by Nannie Ferrell, my paternal grandmother—we knew we'd be forced to partake each Christmas. "We have to have ambrosia," my mother would remind us. "It's tradition."

My mother keeps pictures of extended family throughout the house, and thirty albums to hold the rest of her photo collection. She holds tight to family heirlooms—doilies crocheted by great-grandmothers, the old wooden rocking chair where my grandfather was rocked as a baby, hand-made Christmas tree ornaments commemorating special occasions, and an old Victorian secretary, the only piece of furniture salvaged from a fire that destroyed my great-grandmother's home. While I have difficulty remembering the history of each heirloom, she can recite the backstory no matter how many "greats" are attached to whatever grandmother or grandfather once owned it.

My parents often saved any extra money for books, classical music, and symphony and ballet tickets. They were determined to expose us to the arts. My mother loved to play classical music on the stereo. As a child, Sam jumped from sofa to coffee table to armchair, toy sword in hand, chasing the French out of Russia together with Tchaikovsky, the "1812 Overture" blaring in the background.

When he was four, my parents taught him to play chess. Within a year, he had no competition in the family. Like my parents, Sam loved art, literature, and classical music. He had a gift for drawing, writing, and piano composition. I, however, was always the odd person out, pre-ferring the practical and concrete. While they were listening to classical music, I was more inclined to be figuring out how much to charge for each cup at my lemonade stand.

On occasion, the family gathered in the den for a poetry reading. ("Why don't we go to Cynthia's house and listen to classical music while her parents read poetry?" my high-school friends would tease.) "Two roads diverged in a wood," my mother would say in a deep voice imitating Robert Frost reading "The Road Not Taken," "And I, I took the one less traveled by, and that has made all the difference." My dad had a different style, theatrically moving around the room and racing through Edgar Allan Poe's "The Bells" as Sam and I laughed in the background:

> From the bells, bells, bells, bells
> Bells, bells, bells
> From the jingling and the tinkling of the bells.

Real Friends

When I was in 3rd grade, the insurance company where my father worked promoted him to district manager and my family moved from Jackson, the state capital, to Tupelo, the small town in northern Mississippi where Elvis was born in a two-room shotgun house. Tupelo sat at the bottom of the ocean in prehistoric times, and later was Chickasaw Indian territory, so the enterprising adventurer had many treasures to find. My friend Sandy Lacks and I scoured the neighborhood. Proper exploration required sticks long enough to push through the brush behind our houses. Each hunt turned up broken sea shells, and it wasn't unusual to find an old flint arrowhead or two.

We were usually looking for the perfect place to build a fort—only girls allowed, of course. If the boys tried to bother us, we were forced to push back the intruders with dirt clods. The underground culverts that ran behind our neighborhood led us near the front door of the local drugstore, where we happily spent our dimes on bags of candy.

Like my mother, I was a bit of a free spirit and somewhat single-minded. But my actions were often tempered by my father who was always cautioning me: "You need to be careful. A flash flood can come out of nowhere and wash you through the culvert at any moment." Even though Sandy assured me this wasn't going to happen, after my dad's warning I wouldn't take a trip to the drugstore without a precautionary look to make sure there wasn't a dark cloud in the sky. Even when there wasn't, I'd walk as fast as I could, still afraid we might be carried away by a huge surge of water.

During the 4th grade, Sandy showed me what it really means to be a friend when one of the more popular girls in my class decided she didn't want to play with me anymore. She didn't give a reason, and I couldn't figure out why. She told the other girls in our class that they couldn't be in her club if they dared to play with or even speak to me.

For me, the ordeal was traumatic. For several weeks, I returned home in tears. My parents were beside themselves. One day, my mother made a poster and hung it on my bedroom door: "God made you special," it said beneath a picture of me. "There's no one on Earth exactly like you." She even called the little girl to our house to explain how much this was hurting my feelings, but that only made it worse. The girl told everyone in our class. The next day in the cafeteria, she told all the girls to leave my table and sit with her. One by one, they got up and moved. All but one—Sandy. As they continued to call her name, I pleaded, "Please don't leave me, Sandy." "I promise I won't," she said.

"Remember how sad this made you feel," my mother said to me. "Make sure you treat other people the way you would want to be treated. When you are unkind, you can't go back and change the hurt."

There's A Fiddler on the Roof

That same year, two music teachers named Mr. Woodward and Mr. Holland moved to Tupelo to start a public-school orchestra, introducing hundreds of students to music. After Mr. Woodward came to our classroom to demonstrate the difference between a cello, a viola, and a violin, I really wanted to sign up for orchestra. I also wanted to take dance and gymnastics, but I knew gymnastics was out of the question: "You might fall and break an arm or leg," my father, master of the worst-case scenario, warned.

So I decided on the violin. My parents paid a monthly fee to rent one. I walked a little taller carrying my violin case and often performed my own version of "Twinkle Twinkle Little Star" for my parents, who applauded and requested encores.

Mr. Woodward and Mr. Holland couldn't have been more different. Mr. Holland was mild-mannered, soft-spoken, and gentle. Mr. Woodward was passionate and emotional. If the orchestra hit too many sour notes during practice, he was liable to storm off the stage, his baton flying in the air, leaving us staring wide-eyed at one another, wondering whether we'd have to proceed conductorless. I adored both, and they became mentors to me.

Once, after watching *Fiddler on the Roof*, my mother allowed me to climb to the top of the house with my violin, where I played my heart out for the entire neighborhood. "Come down before your father gets home!" she finally called. "He'll have a heart attack if he sees you up there."

After playing the violin for years, I had only briefly held first chair at summer orchestra camp when my parents delivered the terrible news: We were moving to Clinton, a suburb of Jackson. My father had high hopes for a small print shop he planned to open there with one of his high school friends. I wasn't happy at all about leaving, but you don't get a vote in the matter when you're 12.

The first people I called were my violin teachers. They had a strong influence on my young life, giving me an opportunity that expanded my horizons and helped build self-esteem.

A Lady Called Lillian

After a year, Clinton started to grow on me. The quintessential all-American town, it's little more than a close-knit hamlet, a sleepy Southern college town of 23,000 where you're always likely to run into someone you know at the local stores, and where, in the summer, everyone comes together at the grand July 4th celebration to watch local talent sing and dance, eat hamburgers and hot dogs, wave the American flag, and lie under the stars as fireworks light up the sky. My friends and I walked to school, to the park for tennis, and to swim at the YMCA. On Friday nights, we went down to the skating rink, hung out at the Dairy Queen, or played basketball in the Baptist or Methodist church gyms.

Moving to Clinton also brought me much closer to my paternal grandmother, Lillian Ferrell, or Nannie Ferrell, as I called her, as she lived in Jackson, only twenty minutes away. "Always remember, you come from a long line of strong women," my mother would say, telling me stories about my grandmothers and great-grandmothers, and Nannie Ferrell is no exception. She has had a tremendous presence in my life and a positive influence on everyone in our family. She is our spiritual matriarch and a rare soul from whom I've never heard an unkind word.

A widow in her 70s, Nannie Ferrell helped raise my brother and me, picking us up from school while our parents were working, helping to clean the house, and making the evening meal. She had a head full of gray hair and a heavy foot on the gas—a dangerous combination. Sam and I held on for dear life as she weaved in and out of traffic. "I *declare*, why is everyone creeping along?" she'd say.

I loved accompanying Nannie to Parkway Baptist Church, which she and my granddaddy had attended for more than 40 years. On her wall at home, Nannie kept a photograph of my father as a chubby-butterball Baby Moses in a church program. "Your grandfather helped build this church," she always reminded me. "He was one of the first deacons. Here is his name engraved on the cornerstone," she'd say with pride, pointing to the old sanctuary, built in 1942. When I was a young girl, she'd unwrap the peppermint Life Savers that kept me quiet through the service. I could go through half a roll by the time Brother Bill wrapped up his sermon.

When I spent the night at my grandparents' as a child, Nannie Ferrell would tell me her childhood stories to help me fall asleep. "Have I told you what my father used to tell my sisters and me?" she would ask. She had, but she would tell me again, smiling as she remembered.

"'I don't have much to give you, but I have given you a good name. Always protect it.' That's what our father, who was named Sam like your brother, would tell the seven of us, three brothers and four sisters."

"So always protect your good name. And tithe. Give a tenth of what you make back to God and then save a tenth."

She would reminisce about riding in a horse-drawn buggy, her father's prohibition on his daughters leaving the house without stockings, and meeting granddaddy, over whom she towered by a full head. Without fail, each evening ended with Nannie Ferrell taking her Bible from the nightstand. "Let's read from the Bible."

"Oh, do we have to?" I'd ask sometimes, when I was too young to fully understand the reading, especially from her King James version, with all its "thees" and "thous."

"Yes, let's read just a little bit. I always read from my Bible at night." As she read, I listened. Many of the verses resonate to this day: "Be kind and compassionate to one another...." "Love your neighbor as yourself." "Do to others as you would have them do to you." "Love is patient, love is kind."

One of my favorite Bible stories was Jesus telling the parable of the Good Samaritan. Seeing a man robbed and beaten on the side of the road, a priest and a Levite cross to the other side and keep going. But a third man, a Samaritan—at that time, of more humble social standing than the other two—pauses, tends to the traveler's wounds, carries him to the next town on the back of his donkey, and pays an innkeeper to care for him.

Nannie has come to remind me of the Good Samaritan. She's often the first person people call when they're in need. She visits the elderly, helps people who are struggling financially, takes people into her home, sits with those who are terminally ill, and drives friends to the doctor. As my father says, "She has held more grieving hands than anyone I've known."

A Job Well Done

It was Nannie who helped me find my first job. I was 14. Despite hard work and long hours, the print shop my father had opened was struggling. I could see the strain he was under and wanted to help. One afternoon before my parents came home from work, I asked Nannie Ferrell if she'd drive me around town to look for a job.

"Well, I don't think you're old enough," she said. "I think you have to be 15."

"I'll find someone to hire me," I insisted. Finally, she agreed.

"Stop here," I said each time I spotted a potential employer. We paid a visit to almost every business we saw, from a paint store to a Kentucky Fried Chicken. Nannie waited patiently at each stop while I went in and quickly returned with the same bad news—"no" again. It was starting to seem as though she may have been right about my age. Everyone said I was too young, or they didn't need help. It was discouraging, but all I needed was one person to say "yes."

After several days of rejections in Clinton, I ventured to the mall in Jackson. There, I finally had a turn of luck, landing a job at Morrow's Nut House, a small shop that sold candy and nuts. My friends loved to give me a hard time about the name. "How are things going for you at the Nut House?" they'd joke.

As my mother tells it, I started working in kindergarten. Thinking my tricycle no longer suitable now that I had turned five, I wanted a bike. "We can't afford a bike just yet," my mother explained. But I knew how to solve the problem. Late one afternoon, my mother glanced out the window to find me in the front yard, water hose in hand, carefully washing my tricycle.

"Cindy, what are you doing?" she called.

"I'm washing my tricycle so I can sell it and buy a bike."

Next, I asked my parents for their old magazines. After going door to door selling them to neighbors, I gave the change to my dad, certain I had made enough to cover a new bike. Not having the heart to turn me down, my parents found a way to buy me a brand-new, shiny, purple bike. It was perfect—except for the training wheels. I insisted on taking them off the first day, only to find myself wobbling down the street until I crashed into the curb.

In 3rd grade, I moved on to a more lucrative venture: flower stickers. I cut them out of old contact paper that my mother had left over from lining the kitchen drawers, and sold them at school, five cents for a small one, ten cents for a large. It was a great business until my teacher noticed that everyone's books were covered with flowers but they had no milk money. I was shut down.

At fifteen, I graduated from the candy store and moved to the big leagues—McDonald's. But I quickly had my fill of hamburgers. The next year, I took a job as a clerk at Howard Brothers, a regional discount store in Clinton. Eunice and Cena, two young women who worked there full-time were already adults, and seemed to know everything down to the exact location of every stick of deodorant and fishing lure. I was the kid sister who drove them crazy with questions about prices and product locations. "You ask too many questions," Eunice would say, in mock aggravation that I was interrupting while she restocked the shelves. (She was right, too. My parents had the same look when I would interrupt a conversation to inquire about the finer details.)

The high-school graduation ceremony is now only a few days away. I'm especially excited to wear the National Honor Society Ribbon. Much to my surprise, my teachers have selected me to receive a scholarship for Most Outstanding National Honor Society Student. Usually the award goes to the Honor Society President or an officer, but I'm only a member. "One reason we selected you was because you volunteered for the jobs no one else wanted to do," my teachers, Ms. O'Brien and Ms. Calvert, told me. I never thought of it that way, but I suppose people weren't exactly lining up to take some of the jobs I volunteered for, like cleaning the football field after each home game.

There were times when I dreaded organizing a team to clean the empty cups and food left behind by the good citizens of Clinton, as it usually required pleading and, when that failed, imposing on my best friends to help. Once we were done, looking across the stadium, the bleachers once strewn from top to bottom with litter, and seeing it spotless, ready for the next big game, gave us a sense of accomplishment. The process would start again next Friday night, as the mighty Clinton Arrows tore through the red, black, and white banner held across the end zone by our cheerleaders, leaving it ripped to shreds. This week, looking down at the graduation gown on my bed, I'm proud that I helped clean the field.

I also wonder what my future will hold. I know I want to go to Mississippi State University, 160 miles from Clinton, but I don't have the foggiest idea what to major in. I'm excited and apprehensive to go off on my own.

There has never been a question about whether I'll be going to college. Neither of my parents have a college degree, but they're determined to give my brother and me the opportunity for a higher education. "A college degree will open doors," my mother has told me for as long as I can remember. They encouraged me to save pennies for college when I was a child, and I continued to save throughout high school.

"I've always had to work for peanuts," my mother, who went to secretarial school after high school, would tell me. "If you're going to work, you might as well make decent money. I want you to get a college degree in a specialized field where you'll be able to make the same money the men make. There may come a day when you have to support yourself and your children. I want you to always be able to stand on your own two feet."

But not everyone in my family agrees that college is a worthwhile investment for a girl. "You're wasting your time and money sending Cindy to college," my maternal grandfather told my mom. "She'll just get married and have babies." Of course, my grandfather comes from a different era. He married my grandmother Nola (after whom I am named Cynthia Nola) in the 1930s, when she was just 16. Nannie Nola only finished nine grades, giving birth to my mother, the first of five children, when she was 18. My grandfather's remark upset me, but made me want to continue my education only more. "That really makes me mad," I told my mother. "I'll prove him wrong."

"Education is never wasted," she reassured me. "If I can only afford to send one child to college, it will be my daughter," she added, reasoning a man would have a better chance of making it financially without a degree.

I may not know what specialized field to choose in college, but one thing is for certain—I don't want to disappoint my parents. They were high-school sweethearts who married when my mother was only 18 and my father just shy of 20. I know all too well the sacrifices they're making to educate me, as they live paycheck to paycheck, sometimes rushing around town to pay the utility bills so we won't be cut off. Sometimes they make it, sometimes they don't, and we find ourselves for a time without phone, power, or water.

Whatever my father makes goes to provide for our family. He's always the one who does without the longest. I remember seeing him put cardboard in his shoes once to cover holes he'd worn into the bottom. This worked fairly well until it rained. "He has to remember to keep his feet down when he's sitting with other people," my mother said, teasing. My mother wore the same few dresses to work week after week. I told her the material was worn. "I don't care. It doesn't bother me," she said.

I manage to pull myself away from my graduation gown to tromp around Clinton with friends before our class is scattered across the country. I'm still out when my mother comes home from work. Exhausted from a long week, she makes her way down the narrow hall to her bedroom, hoping to rid herself of high heels and pantyhose. As she passes by my room, she grows still. Seeing my graduation cap and gown for the first time brings a rush of emotion. For her, my accomplishment represents much more than the mere achievement of a goal. She knows this is not only a new beginning for me, but also an end. She knows that even though I'll come home some weekends and summers, our family won't be the same. She recalls a poem she wrote when I was seven, "Stay Awhile Longer," which still hangs in the hall just outside my room.

While my mother feels tremendous pride, she can't help feeling sadness. It's an emptiness only a mother can feel when one of her children finally leaves the nest she has so carefully built. There's no fighting back the tears as she sits down on my bed, picks up the Honors ribbon, and pulls it close to her chest. No one watches but the pink and yellow tulips she hung on the wall for me so long ago.

Stay Awhile Longer

Little girl. Little girl wait for me,
Crawling and toddling, walking and running,
With golden hair blown in the breeze.
Mama and Daddy, I'll be right back.

Red and yellow and blue and green,
Masterpieces in finger-paints.
A-B-C and on to CYNTHIA.
1-2-3 and 2+2 is 4.

Tea-parties, Kool-Aid, cookies, and chips,
Grown up lady in mama's long dress.
Tiny feet lost in a pair of high heels.
Little girl, stay. Stay awhile longer.

First came one and rushed into seven,
Leaving me wanting more of the same.
Autumn into winter, spring into summer,
Changing the years and my little girl.

Playfully to kindergarten, timidly to school,
Entering a world I share only in part.
Life expanding out, and out still again.
Little girl. Little girl wait for me.

Pat Ferrell, September 1971

CHAPTER 3

New Beginnings

It's 1983. A Tennessee native named Murray Waldron kneels down to pray in his Tupelo, Mississippi motel room. "My life hadn't been what it should have been, and I told the Lord to take control of it," he will later explain. "When I got up, I felt the world had been lifted off my shoulders. The next day, I started putting some numbers together . . . I knew I was onto something really big that could only happen with the Lord's blessing."

The business idea that has Murray on fire is a telecommunications company that will resell long distance. For years, AT&T has had a monopoly on long-distance and local phone service, but a government antitrust suit has forced its break-up. To increase competition, "Ma Bell" AT&T will have to divest its local phone business to seven spin-off companies that will come to be known as "Baby Bells." Each will sell local service—but not long distance—in a different region of the country while AT&T will have to stick to long distance, where it will compete with two existing carriers, MCI and Sprint.

The architect of the settlement was William Baxter, the head of the Department of Justice's antitrust division, who felt the separation of long distance and local would create greater savings for consumers.

In addition to giving up local service, the settlement requires AT&T to lease its long-distance lines to resellers at sharply reduced rates. It's a monumental change in the way the industry works. Entrepreneurs and opportunists across the country are charging out of the gate in search of fortune. Mom-and-pop long-distance resellers are beginning to dot the landscape across America, ushering a brand-new industry into existence.

Murray has very little telecom experience. He's worked at a used-car lot and was once in the grocery business. But currently he's selling accounts for a Tupelo sister company of a Tennessee-based long-distance reseller called, simply, The Phone Company (TPC). Murray's business plan is simple—buy minutes from AT&T wholesale and resell them at a higher rate, primarily to customers in the South. He's so excited that he's decided to share his idea with William Rector, a friend from Tennessee. William likes the idea. He wants in on the deal, and the two begin debating where to locate the business. They finally decide that Hattiesburg, Mississippi, 90 miles southeast of Jackson, is the perfect spot—a "hub city" that has easy access to major cities like New Orleans and Jackson.

A visit to the Hattiesburg Chamber of Commerce reassures them: Though resellers are popping up all over the country, no one has hung out a shingle in Hattiesburg. But they still haven't thought of a name. Sipping tea at a Hattiesburg diner, they scrawl potential names on a napkin, rejecting one after another. At wit's end, they ask their waitress if she has any brilliant ideas. Between serving hot plates and pouring coffee, she takes a pen and writes on a napkin, in an act that will become the stuff of legend: LDDC, for Long Distance Discount Company. Sounds a heck of a lot better than any of our choices, the two friends decide. They tweak the suggestion by changing Company to Services, but the rest stays the same. And LDDS, the predecessor to WorldCom, is born.

With a name, location, and business plan, only one thing is missing—capital. It will take $650,000 to get the business going if the partners want to purchase a sophisticated call-routing switch. Murray thinks he knows someone who may be able to help—Bill Fields, a financial planner he met in Tupelo.

Bill likes the idea as well and agrees to put out some feelers. He calls David Singleton, an investor in Brookhaven, Mississippi, he's worked with before. Initially, David is skeptical about starting a new business in a sector that's been controlled by AT&T for so long. "There was not that kind of money around in my world, with people who could afford to take real risk," he will explain. But he has just seen a news report on the opportunities in the long-distance market. "I didn't fully understand what [Bill] was saying, but I trusted him."

In turn, David decides to get in touch with an old friend from his prayer group at Brookhaven First Baptist Church, a local businessman who owns several motels that have done well. David has worked with him on several deals and respects his business judgment. His friend's name is Bernie Ebbers.

It was the early 1960s when Bernie Ebbers first made the journey south to Mississippi, thousands of miles from his home in Canada. While he would become one of the wealthiest people in America, business was the last thing on his mind at the time. Accepted to play varsity basketball for Mississippi College—a small Baptist college in the heart of downtown Clinton—he was pursuing his dream of graduating with a degree in physical education and becoming a coach and schoolteacher.

Bernie was moving to the poorest state in America, but he'd already seen plenty of hard times. Born in Edmonton, Alberta, Canada in 1941, Bernie was the second of five children. His father worked as an auto mechanic, and the family often struggled to make ends meet. There was no running water until Bernie was four. "We didn't have much," he will remember. "If my dad had a few dollars left in his pocket at the end of the month, we would go out and eat hamburgers as a family. I remember the most exciting Christmas for me was the year my sister received a deck of Old Maid cards and I received a deck of Animal Rummy cards."

Bernie had lived in the States before. When he was six, his family had moved to California, and then to western New Mexico, where they lived on a Navajo reservation. Bernie's father worked for a reservation hospital and at a boarding school for Native American children, which Bernie attended from 6th to 10th grade. In the summer, Bernie worked for the school's maintenance department. "Our work ethic came from our father," his brother Jim Ebbers will say. "Dad always provided for us very well, worked hard and gave us what we needed."

When his parents moved back to Edmonton, an oil and gas town in the Canadian Rockies, Bernie signed up to play on the Victoria Composite High School basketball team, where he started as a forward. At 6′4″, he had long arms and a lanky frame that seemed made for the sport. On the team, Bernie made a new friend in a fellow student named Brent Foster, who was Bernie's back-up at forward. He also found a mentor in the team's coach, John Baker.

After graduating, Bernie tried his hand at college, majoring in physical education, but his grades were poor. Intelligent but rarely applying himself, he dropped out of school twice, once at the University of Alberta and later at Calvin College in Michigan. Unsure of his direction, he floundered between jobs—bread and milk deliveryman, bouncer at a local bar—none of which brought him any closer to figuring out what he wanted to do.

It was the guidance of his basketball coach John Baker that helped him get his life back on track. Coach Baker told him to stop throwing his life away and offered him a new direction—a job coaching a team of 10th- and 11th-graders at a new school in Edmonton. Coach Baker was also advising Bernie's friend Brent to enroll in college. Baker, who was attending graduate school at the University of Washington, once took Brent along to show him the campus. While waiting in a bank lobby for his coach to make a currency exchange, Brent came across a Mississippi College brochure that someone had left behind. The place seemed exotic, and the tuition was affordable. He decided to apply, and received a basketball scholarship.

Back in Edmonton, Bernie accepted the job his coach had offered, but after working with the team for a year realized that he wanted to return to school to pursue his goal of becoming a teacher and coach. After hearing how much Brent liked Mississippi College, Bernie and another friend named Dave Prins decided to enroll there themselves.

That fall, the three friends—Brent, Dave, and Bernie—took turns driving the more than 2,500 miles from Canada to Mississippi. With the below-freezing temperatures and the Canadian Rockies behind them, they were entering a world very different than the one they had left behind. Bernie was all too glad to leave the odd jobs and cold weather. "Delivering milk day to day in 30-below-zero weather isn't a real interesting thing to do with the rest of your life," he would later explain.

The college in which Bernie and his friends enrolled is rich in history. Founded in Clinton in 1826, Mississippi College is the oldest four-year college in the state and the second-oldest Baptist college in the country. It is also the first co-educational college in the United States to have graduated a woman. A religious institution in the heart of the Bible Belt, it requires students to take classes in Biblical studies and to attend chapel services.

Clinton, named after DeWitt Clinton, the former Governor of New York, was only one vote shy of becoming Mississippi's capital in 1829. The college and surrounding area figured prominently in the Civil War. Union General William Tecumseh Sherman once set up his headquarters in Clinton. In the heart of the campus, the top floor of Provine Chapel, built in 1860 and cited as one of the nation's best examples of Greek Revival architecture, was converted into a Union hospital. The chapel's basement was turned into a stable for Union horses, which outraged many in Clinton. In the end, the small chapel was one of the few buildings spared by Sherman.

Clinton was like a hinge between Jackson and Vicksburg, the two Mississippi cities General Ulysses S. Grant considered strategically critical. Jackson, in the center of the state, was a Confederate stronghold. Vicksburg, in western Mississippi, was the South's Gibraltar—the Confederates' last open supply line on the Mississippi River. Losing Vicksburg meant losing the Civil War. Back and forth through the small town of Clinton Generals Grant and Sherman marched their troops to the Battles of Jackson and Vicksburg.

Leaving General Sherman to destroy Jackson, Grant moved through Clinton to Vicksburg. For 47 days during the spring of 1863, Vicksburg was under siege by Union troops. For protection, residents moved inside caves dug into hillsides. Completely cut off from food and supplies, they began suffering disease and starvation. On July 4th, the city finally fell to General Grant. The loss of Vicksburg was thought by many to be the death knell of the Confederacy. Until after World War II, the city refused to celebrate Independence Day.

After winning the Battle of Vicksburg, Union troops again made their way through Clinton, returning to Jackson for a second time. Under the command of General Sherman, this time they left little of the capital city standing. Sherman submitted the news to Grant: "Jackson will no longer be a point of danger. . . . The inhabitants are subjugated. They cry aloud for mercy. The land is devastated for thirty miles around." People took to calling the city Chimneyville, as brick chimneys were the only consistent feature left dotting the landscape once Sherman was through torching Jackson.

Because of the complete devastation, Mississippi and other southern states were thrown back economically. Since the country had no Marshall Plan—the plan after World War II to help Europe recover from the war—to rebuild the devastated South, recovery was exceedingly slow. The Mississippi that Bernie encountered in the 1960s often ranked last of the fifty states in everything from health care to education. While, in the nineteenth century, the northern states established industry, Mississippi—where cotton was king—continued to rely heavily on agriculture, like other states in the Deep South. Yellow-fever epidemics, the Civil War, the challenges of Reconstruction and the Great Flood of 1927 also stifled progress. As late as 1900, Jackson, the state capital, had less than 8,000 residents.

By the 1960s, Mississippi College showed few of its scars from the war. Red brick buildings sat atop rolling hills surrounded by azaleas, magnolias, and towering oaks. A lone monument commemorated the

Mississippi College Rifles, a group of 104 students who formed Company E of the 18th Mississippi Regiment in the Confederate infantry. They fought at Manassas, Leesburg, Richmond, Chickamauga, Sharpsburg, Chancellorsville, and Gettysburg. Only eight came home. They were with General Robert E. Lee at Appomattox when he surrendered to General Grant.

Just as his high school coach had been a mentor, James Allen—Bernie's college coach—also had a significant impact on his life, taking Bernie under his wing and helping him find a basketball scholarship to cover tuition. It was a good thing, too, considering Bernie had little more than a pair of jeans and a few dollars to his name when he arrived at school. The coach also had a major influence on Bernie's faith. Once, when Bernie questioned something said by the preacher at the First Baptist Church across from campus, Coach Allen "told him, 'Boy, shut that door,'" college dean Van D. Quick later recalled. "Coach Allen pulled out an old Bible and led [Bernie] to a salvation experience." Bernie would refer to this experience as his "last chance," to set his life straight.

Bernie's basketball career went well until an incident the summer between his junior and senior years. On the way back to Mississippi from Canada, Bernie and a friend ran out of gas in Michigan, "in a tough part of town," as Brent Foster will recall to Lynne Jeter, a *Mississippi Business Journal* reporter and the author of *Disconnected: Deceit And Betrayal at WorldCom*. "[They] walked up to a bar to ask where the nearest gas station was and things turned ugly. These guys chased them down the street and one guy threw a bottle at Bernie. It hit him on the Achilles heel and severed it completely, ending his basketball career."

Though he could no longer play basketball, Bernie was determined to complete his education. In his third try at college, he had managed to keep his grades high enough to remain in school. To make up for Bernie's lost sports scholarship, Coach Allen helped him get a job coaching the college's junior varsity team.

"We didn't have a very good basketball team, but we sure did have a good time," Brent, who helped Bernie at practice, will recall. "Bernie did a darn good job coaching that group of guys, too." "He enjoys being in charge," Bobby West, one of the players Bernie coached, will remember. "He has always had plenty of nerve [and] he dared anybody not to like it. The night before cuts, I can remember going to his dorm room . . . to find out if I was going to make the team." Bernie would string Bobby along as if he wasn't sure. "He got the most out of that, and then told me to get on out, knowing all the time I was going to make it."

While Bernie was aggressive in basketball, he was shy off the court. "Bernie was painfully shy, especially around girls," Brent Foster will say. "In high school, he would certainly not have been classified as a Casanova. . . . We were more interested in playing sports. That was basically what our life was all about, to the detriment of all other things, including our social life." Bernie pushed through his introversion when he met and began dating Linda Pigott, a fellow student from Magnolia, a small Mississippi town near the Louisiana border.

In 1967, he graduated with a Bachelor's of Science in Education. While his friends eventually decided to move back to Canada, Bernie resolved to stay. He had fallen in love with the place, and with Linda. The only way he'd ever leave is "in a box," he would take to saying. That December, he and Linda married. Together, they would raise four daughters—Treasure, Faith, Joy, and Ave—two born to them, one adopted, and an Indonesian girl they'd raise from childhood.

Bernie came of age at a tumultuous time for the country. The Vietnam War was in full thrust, and the antiwar protests and civil rights movement were at their height. In 1962, Deputy Attorney General Nicholas Katzenbach had led federal troops to Oxford, Mississippi to protect James Meredith, the first African-American admitted to the University of Mississippi, as he attempted to register. The next year, Medgar Evers, the Mississippi civil rights activist, was tragically gunned down in his driveway.

The year Bernie graduated from college, I turned three. Just months before, my grandparents, mother, and I had stood on a tarmac watching in silence as the plane carrying my Uncle Jim to Vietnam became a speck on the horizon. He was only 18. "Our circle may be broken," my grandmother said, staring into the sky. "Maybe not," my mother comforted.

Uncle Jim would come back alive. The circle would not be broken. Despite his youth, he'd already experienced the horror of war, contracted malaria, and been wounded by shrapnel. He weighed 98 pounds, a fraction of the young man who had left just a few years earlier. But like so many of our war veterans, he never completely came home. A part of him remained in Vietnam with those who never returned, and it would be thirty years before he felt that his country had truly welcomed him home.

Soon after graduation, Bernie started a job coaching baseball and teaching science to 7th and 8th graders in the small country town of Hazlehurst, 30 miles south of Jackson. A community of less than five thousand, many of its residents living below the poverty line, Hazlehurst was known as the birthplace of the famous blues singer Robert Johnson, remembered in legend for selling his soul to the devil at a Mississippi crossroads in exchange for his preternatural guitar skills.

In the summer, Bernie coached a Little League baseball team. As Hazlehurst was too small to form teams, he took his boys to Brookhaven, one town over. There he met Lamar Bullard, the coach of another team. After a summer of competition, the two men developed a rapport, and Lamar offered Bernie a job. The garment factory Lamar's family owned in Brookhaven, which made winter jackets and pants, needed a warehouse manager.

After only a year, Bernie quit his job at Hazlehurst High School and accepted Lamar's offer. Bernie did well at the garment factory and was given increasing amounts of responsibility. But after six years, he decided it was time to move on. He would later explain that he left because the factory sales manager was asking him to lie to customers about delivery dates for factory products.

Looking in the newspaper one day, Bernie saw an ad: "18 motels for sale." He had been thinking about taking on a small business of his own, and was considering buying a store called the Slack Shack, which sold men's pants. But the motels won him over. Managing a motel doesn't require specialized technical skills, he thought. Maybe I could do it. Inspired, Bernie decided he wanted to buy The Sands, a 40-room motel and restaurant popular with oil-rig workers in Columbia, a southern Mississippi town of less than two thousand families. First, though, he had to cobble together the money. He borrowed, cashed in his wife's certificate of deposit (CD), and obtained a loan from a garment-factory friend who took out a second mortgage on his home to help Bernie.

Bernie and Linda managed the business together, living "like a band of gypsies in a two-bedroom house trailer" behind the motel, as Bernie would later describe it. They put in long, hard hours. Linda coordinated the maids, cleaned the rooms, and saw after the laundry. Bernie ran the motel and mowed the grass. He also did everything he could to keep his operating costs low. "[W]e kept track of what supplies we put in the room," he later recalled, "we would know how much the soap cost was per rented room . . . we knew how much towels cost per rented room. . . . I handed out the towels at the front desk when the people checked in and required them to bring the towels back when they checked out and charged them [if any were missing]."

"I stayed there once," Charles Cannada, who would become World-Com's Chief Financial Officer, will recall. "It was the worst hole-in-the-wall motel I've ever stayed at in my life."

"I remember driving down to see Bernie . . . and he was telling me about slicing tomatoes for [the hotel restaurant]," Brent, Bernie's college friend will say. "I remember him saying, 'You have got to slice tomatoes this [thin] because that's where a lot of your profit is.' From a business point of view, he really started to evolve from that kind of beginning."

Eventually, Bernie decided that the restaurant wasn't his strong suit and closed it. But he enjoyed managing the motel and wanted to expand. After pulling in several investors he met through church connections, Bernie bought two more small motels. In 1978, he sold The Sands and moved back to Brookhaven, where he and his wife built a Best Western motel—with over 60 rooms, a step up for the fledgling hotelier.

By 1983, Bernie owned an interest in seven motels. And he might have been managing them for many years to come were it not for the call from David Singleton, his friend from prayer group, about an investment opportunity in a small telecommunications start-up.

Bernie is engrossed in his motel ventures, but tells David he'll hear out Murray Waldron, the man who came up with the long-distance resale idea. Who knows, it could turn into something. They're scheduled to meet at a Days Inn in Hattiesburg, but as the meeting approaches, Murray's friend William Rector backs out of the deal. Meanwhile, Bernie has read that AT&T is going to muscle aside all the resellers, so he, too, is uncertain about the resale industry's prospects. But David insists. "You owe it to me after the money I raised for your motels to get in the car," he tells Bernie. "At least let's go see what the guy's got to say. And let's penetrate the numbers. . . . But don't say no when you haven't even talked to the guy." Reluctantly, Bernie agrees.

Bernie doesn't know the first thing about telecommunications, but at the meeting, he notices something he likes in the business plan. It predicts that the business will quickly generate positive cash flow, and cash is exactly what he needs to grow his motel business. Bernie's already a self-made man, with a net worth approaching $3 million, wealthy and successful by most people's standards, but his assets are illiquid, tied up in motels. "Motels don't generate a lot of cash flow, and we were hoping to take the cash that was generated out of the telephone business and buy more motels," he would later explain.

By the end of the meeting, Bernie is on board. He doesn't have enough capital by himself, so he turns to his three motel-business partners. They're willing to help out—after all, Bernie's motel recommendations have paid off well. But like Bernie, their money is tied up in the motels. So, they decide to co-sign a $650,000 loan against the equity in the motels with a bank in Brookhaven. It's a mountain of risk, but it seems worth it. So far, Bernie has had the Midas touch.

For their capital, the four investors receive a business plan and, for $450,000, a telephone switch to route customer calls. Even though they're the ones incurring the financial risk, each receives only 14.5% of the initial shares. The rest is split between Murray, the man who came up with the idea; Bill, the Tupelo financial planner; David, who found Bernie; and several others who will help start the business. Making a few phone calls to put the deal together has paid off especially well for Bill. He receives 17% of the shares, more than anyone else, and agrees to be Chairman of the Board. Though Bernie is the one who rustled up the capital, he has no interest in playing an active role in LDDS—he's busy managing and acquiring motels.

While Bernie and his friends are consumed with their new venture, I'm embarking on my freshman year of college. The only thing I know about telecommunications is how to talk to my friends on the phone—for hours and hours.

I'm also launching my new summer job as a waitress at the Golden Corral, a steakhouse in Clinton. Most of the other employees are career waitresses. The best of them carry six plates at a time, one in each hand while the others line each arm up to the shoulder. I, on the other hand, with my small hundred-pound frame, can manage only one in each hand, my left hand shaking under the massive weight all the way from the kitchen to the table. If the tea pitcher is too full, my hand shakes as I pour, sometimes leaving my customers with more than a full glass.

For a while, I work 40 hours a week. But then, I notice that my hours are cut back dramatically. Week after week, I'm disappointed to see fewer and fewer hours until, at last, I'm scheduled to work only two hours a week. I approach the manager several times to ask for more work, but he explains that business is slow and first consideration has to go to the career waitresses.

Meanwhile, I ask my dad to buy me some weights so I can bulk up in order to carry more plates. After weeks of lifting dumbbells and squeezing hand grips, I finally manage to carry two plates in my right hand and one in my left without any shaking. Each week, I put on my polyester brown skirt, brown plaid shirt, and brown head scarf—"that tacky little uniform," as my mom puts it—and go in to work my two hours, usually during a slow part of the day. Sometimes, if I'm lucky, I get a last-minute call to sub for someone who can't make it.

Then, toward the end of the summer, my hours go back up to 40. On my way out one evening, the manager stops me. "You were the worst waitress I ever hired," he says. "I did everything I could to get you to leave and you just wouldn't quit. Now you're one of the best waitresses I have."

While my skills as a waitress have improved, I've been struggling to find that "specialized" college major my mother keeps talking about, one that I not only like, but will pay well. I started out in public relations, but wasn't sure it was a good fit, and the salaries are generally lower than in other fields. Then I tried math. I took every advanced math class in high school. There was only one other girl in my high-school calculus class of 30, and I had scored fourth-highest in our school on a standardized test given to advanced math students. But I found pure math unexciting, and what would I do with a math degree other than teach or become an actuary, neither of which appealed to me.

In the second half of my sophomore year, I decide to take several business courses, among them an accounting class, which I enjoyed in high school. It seems to be refreshingly black and white—one plus one equals two. This is something I can do. After finishing the semester and evaluating the potential compensation for accountants, I finally settle on it as my major. I can still use my math skills, and, from what I can tell, accounting can be a stepping stone to higher-level positions in the business world. I'm determined to try to work my way up the corporate ladder. I want to make sure I can achieve what my parents have worked so hard to make possible for me.

By the spring of 1985, less than two years after going into business, LDDS is faltering. Two of the investors have already tried to manage the business, but neither could turn things around, and the company is now losing about $25,000 a month. Finally, the bank informs LDDS that it has no more credit. Things are so bad—the company needs more capital just to keep operating—that the investors agree they're willing to walk away with the losses if they can just find someone to take over their bank note. Other than that, there's only one hope—Bernie. He doesn't have telecommunications experience, but the LDDS investors think he has business savvy.

LDDS is about $1.5 million in debt when the board asks Bernie to take over as CEO. He's reluctant to accept the position, but eventually agrees—he has a substantial investment at stake. He'll split his time between the motels and LDDS. "My vision was simple," he would later explain. "I planned to get our profits up, hoping somebody would buy us."

The way Bernie sees it, there are three main parts to the company—sales and marketing, technology, and accounting. He isn't trained in engineering or accounting, so he decides to hire outside help for those. As he studies the business, Bernie comes to understand that in order to survive, he must find a way to lower what LDDS pays to resell a phone call. His strategy is to gain economies of scale by building larger customer bases. But the company is on life support—using the sales force to expand the customer base will take too long. To move quickly, he'll mimic the strategy he's followed with his motels—growth through acquisition. Bernie will become a reseller consolidator, buying companies with telecom traffic close to LDDS's, since a larger volume of calls in close proximity permits lower costs.

Bernie uses the small amount of cash LDDS is generating to make his first acquisition, a small bankrupt reseller in Jackson, Tennessee called The Phone Company—the very same company where Murray Waldron was working when he came up with the idea for LDDS. Though TPC's finances are a mess, it still has a considerable customer base. In just six months, the plan yields results: Bernie has turned monthly losses into profits. In fact, he's so successful that he postpones his initial plan to sell the business.

But this is only the beginning for Bernie. "It just kept on growing and getting bigger and bigger and bigger," Murray Waldron later recalled. "It was a great feeling. I mean, you talk about an old country boy's dream? This was a dream, I'll tell you."

Bernie will prove to be one of the most audacious CEOs in business history. In less than 20 years, he will lead the company through some 70 acquisitions on his way to becoming the man *Business Week* will one day call the "Telecom Cowboy."

CHAPTER 4

Hotlanta

It's 1987. I've completed my undergraduate work in accounting at Mississippi State and will soon receive a Master's in accounting from the University of Alabama in Tuscaloosa. Again, not everyone in my family supported the idea of an advanced degree. Graduate tuition isn't cheap, and my parents have another child about to enroll in college.

"An undergraduate degree is all she needs," my father had said, but, again, my mother refused to budge.

"No, you're wrong. A graduate degree will open more doors for her. She's studied hard and deserves to go to graduate school."

"You get that graduate degree," my mom told me. "I'll cash in my 401(k) savings to help pay for it. Your education is more important to me than retirement savings."

I've studied hard and kept my grades high. It's close to graduation and the "Big Eight," the country's largest public accounting firms—Arthur Andersen; Arthur Young; Coopers & Lybrand; Deloitte, Haskins and Sells; Ernst and Whinney; Price Waterhouse; Peat Marwick Mitchell; and Touche Ross—are coming to the University of Alabama to interview accounting students. Working for one of these firms is a calling card that tells someone you have a strong foundation, that you made the cut after a competitive recruiting process.

Most of the top students will try to work with the Big Eight or a large regional public accounting firm at least for a few years even if they don't plan to make it their long-term career. It's considered paying your dues— the experience a young staffer can gain is invaluable and can "open

41

doors," as my mother says. The firms are a talent pool for corporations, which like to see Big Eight experience on a resume. I'm interviewing with the audit divisions, which conduct annual audits of their clients' financial statements to ensure they abide by generally accepted accounting principles.

Everyone knows the first several years as a Big Eight auditor will be grueling. Staff auditors tend to work incredibly long hours. You don't leave until the team goes home, even if it means working until three in the morning. Throughout the 1980s, the turnover rate in public accounting is high. The firms' hierarchies are sometimes likened to inverted funnels: Lots of lower-level staff are needed, but very few stay long enough to make partner.

Some of the firms are thought to have a "churn and burn" mentality. In the spring, after accounting firms finish auditing their clients' financial statements for the previous year, they expect some of their young staffers to leave, thereby avoiding over-staffing during the slow season. If a firm over-hires or too few people resign, it may force a reduction through lay-offs.

After the firms interview students on campus, each invites a winnowed pool of potential hires to an "office visit" for wining and dining. The recruiting process is competitive, but I remain hopeful. I've kept my grades high enough to graduate with honors. I've been working toward this moment for many years—my first full-time professional job.

Because I don't want to miss class, I can't afford to go back and forth between Birmingham and Atlanta, where the firms have their nearest regional offices, for too many interviews. In my opinion, you can't go wrong with any of the Big Eight. I decide that if I get an offer I'm happy with early in the process, I won't continue to interview. Ernst and Whinney and Price Waterhouse are two of the first to visit campus. I want to move to a larger city with more career potential, so I've asked to visit Ernst and Whinney at its Birmingham office and Price Waterhouse in Atlanta.

I have a great office visit with Ernst and Whinney and receive a job offer. I thought my Price Waterhouse interview went equally well, but I don't get invited for an office visit. I'm disappointed—it's regarded as one of the "blue-chip" accounting firms. I decide to call John Shevlin, the head of Human Resources there. I want to reiterate my interest and make sure he knows I passed three parts of the Certified Public Accountant (CPA) exam while still an undergraduate at Mississippi State. I'd forgotten to mention that in the interview. Maybe it'll make a difference. All he can do is decline a second time.

The extra effort pays off. John calls back several days later and invites me to visit Atlanta with students from other universities.

My visit to Atlanta is going well so far. I like the people I've met and Atlanta seems like an exciting place, though it does feel a bit overwhelming compared to the small towns where I've lived all my life. After a day of office meetings, the students are invited to a cocktail reception. "Can I get you a drink?" the waiter asks. I've had alcohol only a few times in my life.

"I'll have a White Russian," I say, calling out the first drink that comes to my mind. I had one in college.

"What? That's not a good business drink," the recruiter standing next to me says, laughing at the choice.

"Oh, what do you recommend?" I say, wondering if my drink choice is going to cost me my job offer.

"Try a vodka tonic with a twist of lime."

I barely sip the bitter vodka, which tastes like I imagine rubbing alcohol would—definitely an acquired taste, I think.

Soon after returning to Tuscaloosa, I receive an offer from Price Waterhouse. My eyes scan for the starting salary: $26,000. Wow. I can't believe they will pay so much! After debating the two offers, I accept the Price Waterhouse position. Location is the deciding factor—I want to try living in a faster-paced environment. Besides, Atlanta is likely to have more career opportunities.

Within weeks, I receive a second letter from Price Waterhouse, increasing my starting salary to $31,700—the firm is changing the way it pays employees for overtime, and salaries are being adjusted to compensate. I really can't believe my luck.

Soon after graduation, I begin planning my move. I've rented an apartment in Atlanta with Julie Warner, my graduate-school roommate, who's going to work for Arthur Andersen. We're both beside ourselves with excitement. We want to pay someone to move us to Atlanta—Julie's from Port Gibson, Mississippi, about 50 miles southwest of Clinton—but Julie's very petite mother has assured us that she can drive the large U-Haul.

My father is out of town on business, but with my brother's help, the ladies spend a day loading the truck. Finally, we're ready and say our goodbyes. But the truck hasn't even reached the end of the driveway before we run aground, the left wheel dangling helplessly above a small drainage ditch. We spend the afternoon looking for a professional driver. I hope this isn't an omen of some kind.

At last, we make it out of the ditch, drive to Atlanta, and move into our apartment. Julie has convinced me that I must buy expensive suits for the new job. Since I don't have any money yet, I'm running up quite a tab on my new credit cards, but on my first day of work, my conservative grey and navy suits, starched white shirts, and bow ties blend in perfectly with the other auditors.

Everything goes well my first day until I leave the downtown office and inadvertently run a red light, getting a ticket. Having bought my first car only recently—after my grandmother offered to help with monthly payments, I talked down a used-car salesman named Curly on an old Buick Skyhawk—I'm nervous driving the interstates here. It's quite a change from Clinton and Tuscaloosa. One wrong turn in Atlanta, and it takes forever to get going in the right direction again.

I survive my first year in Atlanta, but everything about it—the size of the city, the traffic, the new job, being on my own—involves an enormous transition. At work, my reviews are good and getting better with each engagement; the last two were "exceeds expectations," and I've just received a very good raise. I've also started dating someone. Tom is an auditor at Price Waterhouse as well. There's been so much to learn in my new career, but, finally, I'm starting to feel like my feet are firmly on the ground.

Apparently, you can spot an auditor a mile away. Some of our clients joke that we all look alike in our starched white shirts and dark suits, as if we have been punched out with a cookie cutter. My peers and I often sit elbow to elbow, piles of papers around us, in a tight conference room at a client's office. Sometimes it seems as though the client provides us with the smallest, most uncomfortable space possible. Maybe this is so we won't stay too long, my friends and I joke.

Today, we're lucky, as the room we're working in isn't so small. It's after lunch when I receive a phone call from John Shevlin, the head of Human Resources.

"I need you to meet me at the Galleria office at 5:00," he says curtly, referring to a company office in northwest Atlanta.

"Okay," I say. "Is something wrong?"

"I just need you to meet me at 5:00," he says before hanging up.

I look up to find everyone staring curiously, so I tell the other auditors about the call. They try to reassure me and settle back into their work, but I just keep staring at the numbers in front of me. Have I done something wrong?

The afternoon takes forever. Every time I look down at my watch, the minute hand is moving slower and slower. I leave work early and drive across town to the Galleria office, only ten minutes from where I live. The closer I get to the front door, the quicker my heart beats. When I walk into the small bullpen where staff often gather, all the chairs are taken. I'm surprised to see many of my friends, who also started a year ago. Tom is here, too. Surely this many people haven't done something wrong.

Some are sitting, others standing and fidgeting, but each one has the same long face. It feels as if I've just walked into a funeral parlor, the hushed, hesitant whispers coming to a stop when I enter.

"What's going on?" I ask.

"We're all getting laid off," someone says.

"You've got to be kidding." I look around, hoping it was a joke, but no one laughs.

Eventually, I manage to sit down and process the news. I'm completely confused. My performance reviews have been strong. There must be an error. I've been working here just over a year. Maybe they don't know that the reviews on my last two engagements were "exceeds expectations." How could I have gotten such a good raise only a few weeks ago if they were planning on laying me off?

An employee walks out of John's office; another is called in. This goes on throughout the late afternoon; some walk out crying. The remaining auditors try to comfort colleagues as they come out, but no one is in the mood to talk. Each tries to leave as quickly as possible. Whatever it is, I'm not going to cry, I tell myself. Tom comes out and tells me he lost his job. Like everyone else, he seems a bit shaken.

Finally, my name is called. I listen intently as John explains that the firm regrets having to lay off employees. The Atlanta office has recently lost some key clients and is over-staffed. I hurriedly tell him about the strong performance reviews I received on my last engagements, but he stops me.

"This has nothing to do with performance," he explains.

"Are you sure these good evaluations won't make a difference?" I ask.

"No. Performance reviews weren't a factor. If it makes you feel any better, Wayne Jackson tried to save your job." Wayne is a well-respected senior manager who helped recruit me at the University of Alabama. It does soothe my ego to know someone went to bat for me.

I, too, leave the office in a hurry. But I don't cry. I won't do that. Not here. That evening, Tom and I, along with several colleagues, meet at a local restaurant. A friend who was lucky enough to keep his job buys me a beer, but it doesn't make me feel any better. We try to make sense of the layoffs. The real estate group where Tom and I both worked was hit hard due to loss of clients. I also hear through the grapevine that recently hired employees with graduate degrees were at higher risk of lay-off because the same work could be done by auditors with under-graduate degrees for lower salaries. If true, it's frustrating to think I've spent all this time and money getting a graduate degree only to have it work against me when lay-off time comes. Logically, I understand this is just business, but, nonetheless, I feel terrible, as if I've failed in some way.

The truth is that I also have a good old-fashioned case of embarrass-ment. In high school and college, I worked hard to keep my grades high. I've set goals, and losing my first job at 22, right out of college, wasn't part of my plan. Later that evening, I call home. "Life is full of curves and hardballs," my father comforts after hearing me out. "You have to try to deal with them and move on."

"Pick yourself up and dust yourself off," my mother says. "Chin up. I have no doubt you'll find another good job."

I don't really want to deal with curves and hardballs or dust myself off. I think I'd rather just sit and feel sorry for myself, at least for a day or two.

I do let myself have a good cry, but that's all—now, it's time to move on. My salary hasn't made me as rich as I thought, and, after running up my credit cards to buy clothes for work and a mattress, which sits on my floor without a bedframe, I'm living paycheck to paycheck. Having left the apartment I shared with Julie, I'm paying rent by myself, and the severance money will be gone in just a few weeks.

When I was six, my father took me to a carnival at a local shopping center parking lot. There were lots of rides for children, but I wasn't satisfied. I wanted to impress Dad. "I want to ride that big Ferris wheel," I told him. "I want to ride it by myself."

As I craned my neck to see the red cages tumbling over themselves in the air, I secretly hoped my dad would say no. But he didn't.

"Are you sure?" he said. "It's awfully big."

"I'm sure," I said confidently, though I was terrified. As I stepped into the cage, the carnival man locked the door, and I knew there was no turning back. I gripped the bar in front of me tightly, looked straight ahead, and hunkered down. Throughout the ride, I never looked any-where but directly in front of me, struggling to be brave.

Living here in Atlanta by myself, with no family and few friends, has made me feel a bit like that little girl, gripping the bar too tightly. Maybe coming here was too much for me.

I send my resume to the other Big Eight accounting firms in town. I don't want to risk their getting lost in the shuffle, so I begin to network, trying to reach Human Resources directors and audit partners. While Price Waterhouse said this had nothing to do with performance, I'm concerned that the other firms may be hesitant to hire someone who's been laid off. I decide to give them a copy of my reviews. "Cynthia demonstrated that she is ready to accept increasing responsibility," one reviewer wrote.

I soon have an interview with Coopers & Lybrand, though I don't have a good feeling about it. The chemistry doesn't seem right. Soon enough, I find out that my hunch was right—no offer.

I have another interview with a partner at Touche Ross. He can be gruff, I've been warned, and, indeed, he's quite abrasive during the interview, but I had to go for it—I really need a job.

Several days after the interview, the partner calls and extends an offer. I'm thrilled, but have one more interview with Deloitte, Haskins and Sells later in the week. This is an important decision, and I don't want to rush. Because I didn't interview with every firm when I was in college, I feel like I owe it to myself to be more thorough this time. But when I ask if I can have a few days to consider the offer, the partner seems offended.

"No," he barks. "You should be able to tell me right now whether or not you want this job."

I'm taken aback. "I can't have just a few days?" I ask pleadingly.

"No. You're a marginal candidate anyway," he snaps.

"Marginal candidate." Marginal means "not very good," "barely made it under the wire." Am I really marginal? I don't think I want to go to work for someone who thinks I'm marginal.

"Well, thank you for the offer, but I think I'll have to decline."

"Fine," he says, hanging up the phone without saying goodbye. I sit at my kitchen table crying. I know I've got to get some tougher skin if I want to survive in the business world. Chin up.

Finally, I have my interview with Deloitte, Haskins and Sells. This is my last interview before it's back to square one.

The people are friendly and down to earth. One of the things that surprises me is that so many women—at least compared to other firms I've seen—have moved up to manager and partner. The Atlanta office alone already has several female partners. In college, I never considered the number of women in management as a factor, but now I think it's an important consideration, along with what client engagements I might get to work on. When I started at Price Waterhouse, I didn't state a preference and ended up in the real-estate group. This time around, I know enough to ask if I can work on public company audits, which is what really interests me.

An assistant in Deloitte's Human Resources department calls several days later, but, again, it's bad news. "We appreciate you interviewing, but aren't going to be able to extend an offer."

I'm completely deflated. If I don't find another job soon, I may have to take out a loan. I suppose I can also pack it up and move back in with my mom and dad, but I really want to make it on my own.

Early the next morning, my phone rings. This time, it's the head of Deloitte's Human Resources department. "We're excited about extending you an offer," he says.

I'm grateful, but confused. "I received a call just yesterday from someone saying you weren't going to be able to extend an offer."

"Oh, no. There's obviously some kind of mistake." Whatever the mistake, I'm relieved and excited.

Several weeks after settling into my new job with Deloitte, Wayne Jackson, the senior manager at Price Waterhouse who had tried to save my job, calls. "I wanted to tell you how sorry I am about what happened and make sure you found a good place to land," he says. "Some of the professors at the University of Alabama called and let me have it about you being laid off." Twenty years later, I still remember the kindness of his call.

CHAPTER 5

The Turnaround

This may sound hokey to a lot of people, but I feel just as called to this work as a preacher is called to his work.

— Bernie Ebbers

It's the summer of 1986. A young man named Charles Cannada has just received a promotion to audit manager with Arthur Andersen in Jackson, Mississippi. Soon after, his cousin Barry, who works for Butler Snow, one of the largest law firms in the state, approaches him with a potential engagement. Barry represents a group of men from Brookhaven, Mississippi, who have invested in a pineapple farm in Costa Rica and are looking for an auditor to fly down and do some accounting work.

Charles certainly wants to reel in new business for his employer, but he's a new manager and doesn't have the authority to approve client engagements. And the sole partner in Arthur Andersen's small Jackson office is on a three-month sabbatical. Charles decides to turn to the New Orleans office, for which Jackson is a satellite. The pineapple business doesn't amount to much, but since it's the slow summer season, an audit partner there agrees to let Charles and the Jackson auditors perform the work. It's a giveaway job—the fee is $5,000—but the fact that Charles has retained a client is rare for someone at his level.

By August, Arthur Andersen has completed its work in Costa Rica. Charles and his cousin are driving an hour south on I-55 to Brookhaven, where the pineapple farm investors have invited them to sit in on an all-hands meeting. It's another scorching Mississippi summer. The pavement has buckled in places from the heat, and Charles and his cousin veer across the interstate to avoid the bumps. In one spot, the concrete looks to be jutting half a foot out of the ground.

As Charles sits at the conference table listening to the men discuss the farm's prospects, he notices "this one guy sitting at the end of the table . . . ripping everyone a new one. I thought, This guy's a jerk, but he's the only one at the table who has a clue about what's going on." Charles is wondering who this man is, wearing cowboy boots and giving everybody what for. He's about to find out.

After the meeting, Bernie Ebbers leaves the head of the table and approaches Charles with an opportunity that has nothing to do with pineapples. At 6'4" plus the cowboy boots, Bernie towers over Charles as they talk. "He said, 'The CEO tells me you did a nice job on this account,'" Charles will recall. "'I have this little telecom company I'm thinking about taking public and we are going to need some accounting services.'" It turns out most of the pineapple investors have also invested in Bernie's motels, as well as in LDDS.

Charles is excited. He's only 27. LDDS seems like a decent, if small, company, and winning its business would be quite a feat for someone who's just become an audit manager. Before he can accept the engagement, however, Charles has to talk another New Orleans partner into going with him to Brookhaven to meet Bernie. They arrange to speak with Bernie at LDDS's office, in a refurbished home just off the interstate. When they meet, Bernie explains that he needs audits completed on three years of LDDS financial statements in preparation for taking the company public. The partner likes what he's hearing. Certainly, it has more potential than pineapples. Arthur Andersen agrees to do the work for some $30,000 in fees.

LDDS' 1986 revenues are $8.6 million, with a profit of around $900,000. Bernie has yet to hire a CFO, so Charles and his staff pore over records with LDDS's Brookhaven bookkeeper. The books seem to be in good order, and the audit goes off without a hitch.

As 1987 opens, Bernie is eager to continue with his strategic plan of buying long-distance resellers. He has his eye on Telemarketing

Communications of Mississippi (TMC), a franchised reseller in Jackson. But LDDS is out of capital. Bernie has already tapped out his Brookhaven network—the initial investors have even signed notes for additional loans, but now the well has run dry.

The board doesn't want to invest any more capital or incur more debt, but Bernie's not afraid to take the risk. He has a vision for the company and decides to put up the money personally. "Bernie took a big risk and mortgaged everything he had to buy TMC outright," an early investor later explained. "That's when [he] got way ahead of everybody else with the most stock. And rightly so."

Bernie's risk-taking pays off and he closes the TMC deal, which gives him an opportunity to approach other TMC franchise owners across the country. In 1988, he contacts John Porter, an Atlanta-based entrepreneur who owns several TMC franchises with extensive reach in states like Indiana, Kentucky, and Arkansas, which are contiguous to LDDS's current operations, a critical factor to economies of scale and Bernie's buying philosophy.

Initially, John isn't interested in selling. He has big plans to take his company public and has been working with investment bankers for months. If all goes well, he'll make millions in profits. Why in the world would he sell now? And why would he give up the opportunity to run his own company?

Bernie and John meet in an Atlanta restaurant, each with an investment banker by his side. LDDS is way too small for any of the Wall Street firms to give Bernie the time of day, but the Breckenridge Group, a boutique Atlanta mergers-and-acquisitions firm, has agreed to advise Bernie.

Bernie is doing some fast talking to convince John that he's better off selling and taking a combination of LDDS stock and cash for his company. It's a tough sell. Seeing that the deal is going nowhere and feeling that John's investment banker is slowing progress, Bernie changes tactics.

"I'd like to talk to John alone," he says, according to Charles. Immediately, Bernie's investment banker rises to leave the table.

"I'm not leaving," John's banker replies.

"Does this guy report to you or what?" Bernie challenges John, who asks his advisor to give them a few minutes.

Bernie is keenly aware that there's more to buying companies than simply making the right offer. Always, there are the more subtle psychological factors. Bernie decides to offer John the position of Chairman of the Board. "I'll run the company, and you can do all the wining and dining," Bernie says.

Within 30 minutes, John agrees to scrap his plans to go public. Bernie seals the deal with a gentleman's agreement: John will take a combination of 40 % LDDS stock and 60 % cash in addition to becoming Chairman of the Board.

It's a title that Bernie will never hold during his tenure at the company. Instead, he'll continue to use the Chairman position and board seats as leverage to appease top decision-makers at companies he targets for acquisition. "You run into a lot of CEOs, heads of companies, whose egos wouldn't fit in this room," Bernie would later explain. "One of the things I do that's effective is I don't play like I have an ego. A lot of deals go bad because of social things [like] who's going to report to whom, who's going to have what title. I'm willing to accommodate them, give them the position they need."

"Bernie made a lot of decisions based on not losing people even though it may not have been in the best long-term interest of the company," Charles will say. "I guess he had to do that [to close deals]."

At the same time, though the company being acquired typically appoints some board seats, Bernie always makes sure to personally choose the majority. Acquisitions often begin with stormy relationships. "When new board members initially joined, there was always contention—an *us* versus *them* mentality," Charles will say. "Bernie and John Porter initially had contention. It usually took about a year or more to come together. But after a while, as the board members began to make money in their stock, they decided they liked Bernie, and *they* became *us*."

Because the board is being assembled with executives who receive LDDS stock for their companies, many board members will have significant assets tied up in company stock.

It's August 1989. For several years, Bernie has wanted to take the company public. He's been able to use LDDS's privately held stock to purchase companies, but being public means more liquidity and, hopefully, a higher premium on LDDS stock as it begins to trade on the open market. A higher stock price means more currency to buy resellers.

He's talked to a few regional investment banking firms, but the stars haven't aligned. Now he sees an opportunity. Not surprisingly, he wants to bypass the headaches and regulatory hurdles of taking LDDS public through its own initial public offering (IPO) by purchasing a company that's already public. Buying it will instantly result in LDDS trading on the NASDAQ stock exchange.

Advantage Companies, the acquisition he has in mind, is a mish-mash of businesses, including several hotels, a publishing house, and a long-distance reseller offering services primarily in Tennessee. The long distance part of the business was a side-line for the executives who started the company, but, it will turn out, a lucky one: The company is struggling financially when Bernie comes knocking.

To make the deal happen, Bernie agrees to keep the hotels, which are run-down and inoperable. The Advantage owners agree to accept an all-stock offer for the company, allowing Bernie to conserve cash. "The worst part about these small acquisitions is the clean-up," Charles will say. "How do you unload a couple of shut-down hotels that nobody wants?" Eventually, Bernie manages to sell them. Advantage's former CEO keeps the publishing arm, and Stiles Kellett, its Chairman of the Board, receives millions of dollars in LDDS stock as well as a long-time seat on the LDDS Board and Compensation Committee.

By 1989, LDDS has grown revenues to more than $100 million. One CFO has already come and gone, burned out by having to work on one acquisition after another. This time, Bernie turns to Charles Cannada.

The offer isn't a surprise to Charles—he and Bernie have developed a good rapport—and he accepts immediately. Becoming CFO of a public company at 30 is an incredible achievement, not least because Bernie has offered Charles a few thousand stock options along with an $80,000 salary, significantly higher than what he's currently making as an auditor. Charles will have to work for a year to qualify for any significant options, but if LDDS keeps growing and Charles receives more options, he might be able to make far more with stock than he would from his salary.

Charles is a seventh-generation Mississippian whose father and grandfather were cotton and soybean farmers in Edwards, just west of Jackson. Each summer, he worked alongside his father and brothers in the hay fields stacking hundreds of bales on long trailers and then unloading them in the barn. Covered with one too many ant bites and drenched with sweat in the sweltering heat, Charles decided not to follow in his father's footsteps. "I'm getting an air-conditioned job," he told his older brother. "I don't care what kind, but it's going to be inside."

While his older brother continues to run the family farm, Charles is working in an air-conditioned building as Bernie's right-hand deal guy. When it comes to completing acquisitions, their formula is simple. Charles has a one-page form he completes for potential candidates. LDDS will buy only companies that add to earnings per share. With a combination of cash and stock, Bernie will pay the resellers they target six times their monthly revenues—half upfront and half once the investment has proven itself. This insulation frees LDDS from having to spend too much time beforehand on due diligence—analyzing the company's books before an acquisition.

It's the spring of 1990. In the past, LDDS has been forced to turn to Heller Financial—a venture-capital-type lender out of Chicago—to obtain loans. But borrowing from Heller has proven expensive because LDDS has to give Heller warrants—the right to buy shares in the company at a specified price—to get a more reasonable interest rate. Commercial banks don't like to make high-risk venture-capital-type loans, especially to start-ups without a long track record. Plus LDDS is playing in an industry dominated by giants like AT&T and littered with failed start-ups.

But LDDS is gaining credibility, and First Chicago Bank recently consolidated the company's outstanding debt under a revolving line of credit that allows LDDS to draw down funds as needed. But only months after the credit facility is finalized, the coffers are empty—LDDS has maxed out borrowing for acquisitions.

To avoid going back to First Chicago so quickly, LDDS wants to raise capital by placing a $50 million convertible note—which gives the holder the choice to convert the debt to stock at a future date, a windfall for the lender if the company's stock does well—and has several regional investment banks lined up to help. But as Charles makes his way around the country on a "road show" to generate investor interest, the first Gulf War begins. In the midst of war, investors have little interest in loaning cash to a start-up. The deal falls flat, and Charles comes home empty-handed. Once again, he appeals to First Chicago, and the bank agrees to increase LDDS's revolving line of credit—giving the company access to another $50 million—by organizing a syndicate of some 15 banks to spread the risk.

Bernie wastes no time putting the borrowed funds to use. So far, he's acquired mainly in the Southeast, but now he wants to expand to the Midwest and Southwest. In late spring, within weeks of each other, LDDS makes offers for three resellers—Omaha-based MidAmerican Communications, which is owned by an Australian company in bankruptcy; Austin-based National Telecommunications; and Charlotte-based Phone America. The Phone America executives refuse to accept stock, and persuade Bernie to pay $20 million in cash for the company. The other two resellers want cash, too, but there's no way LDDS can manage the price tag for all three deals—around $100 million—if it pays all-cash. After much haggling, Bernie convinces the MidAmerican and National Telecommunications sellers to take a combination of cash and stock.

By the time the Phone America deal closes, in May, LDDS' stock price has gone up dramatically. " 'I can't believe your husband wouldn't take stock,' Bernie tells the wife of one of the owners, waving his cigar, according to Charles. 'You would be twice as rich today if he had.' [The woman's] face lit up. She looked at her husband and said, 'You've got to be kidding me. Is that true?' 'I'm afraid so,' her husband said, kind of sheepishly."

But the executives of MidAmerican's Australian parent company still have no interest in LDDS stock, so they dump hundreds of thousands of shares. To handle the sale, they turn to Paine Webber and a little-known analyst named Jack Grubman, who will hustle the Street to build interest. The stock has to be sold at a discount to incentivize buyers to purchase so much.

The MidAmerican parent-company executives might not believe in LDDS, but Bernie has nothing but confidence. He approaches the employees who report directly to him with an idea. "We're going to personally buy as much of this stock as we can from PaineWebber," he explains, according to Charles. It's an extraordinary opportunity to buy the stock below market value. "We'll all open accounts at Paine-Webber. You each buy as much as you can afford and want on margin"— the amount an investor can borrow relative to the value of his or her investments—"and I'll transfer extra margin from my account to yours." Between his and Bernie's margin, Charles doesn't have to personally put up any cash—a good thing because he and his wife don't have extra funds to invest.

Jack Grubman is impressed by Bernie's aggressive style. It's a big vote of confidence when insiders buy their own company stock. Several LDDS executives take advantage of the discounted price, with Bernie guaranteeing the risk, and the gamble pays off. In just six months the stock has gone through the roof. For Jack Grubman and Bernie Ebbers, this is the start of a long and lucrative friendship. Years from now, Jack will play a critical role in the rise of the company.

While Bernie holds on to his stock, Charles, who's watching his profits increase day by day, pulls the trigger after six months, making $100,000. "It was the first time my wife and I ever had any cash in our pocket," he will explain. "I decided to buy her a brand new [Chevy] Suburban. It had everything they offered at the time—customized bucket seats in the back for the kids, a built-in VCR, a cell phone."

It will be a sale his boss makes sure he never forgets, making a tradition of calculating the car's effective cost to Charles in front of employees, shareholders, and analysts as the LDDS stock continues its climb. At the stock's height, the car will have effectively cost Charles more than a million dollars. "He used it all in fun and good humor to convince people our stock was a good deal," Charles will remember. But he'll have no regrets. "My wife and I enjoyed the heck out of that car."

Bernie's philosophy is to appeal to customers through discount prices and a personal touch. LDDS doesn't do any telemarketing, and advertising is minimal. While those approaches might be effective with individual consumers, Bernie thinks they're less effective with the small-business market LDDS targets. Instead, he sends LDDS sales reps on personal customer visits and ensures that support staff are geographically close to their customers. After an acquisition, field executives personally visit every major new account.

The company has had a decentralized management approach since its inception. Bernie hires an executive to oversee each state's entire operations; that executive is responsible for integrating newly acquired companies in the state. Each state has its own support staff: Sales, billing, credit and collections, customer service. Meanwhile, executives in the field have end-to-end responsibility over every aspect of customers' accounts, which enables them to react swiftly to competitive challenges.

Bernie's approach has allowed the company to move quickly, but decentralization and growth through acquisition are resulting in operational inconsistency. Each purchased company and each state use different billing systems, processes, and procedures.

Because of the recent purchases, Bernie has decided to move to a regional approach, with eight executives overseeing multiple states, but the regional heads are becoming overwhelmed by the lack of standardization, especially in billing. "We were running loose with systems. It was difficult to manage," Charles will recall. To help standardize customer billing, Bernie decides to outsource it to EDS, the Texas company started by Ross Perot, which allows LDDS to continue focusing on building the company. As Bernie tears through acquisitions, EDS is there to migrate customers to the new billing system.

By the end of 1991, the company has once again burned through its line of credit for acquisitions. In what will become an annual routine, Charles must go back to the bank to negotiate additional loans. LDDS's revenues for the year exceed $700 million, more than 80 times higher than annual revenue only five years ago. The executives reporting directly to Bernie—a close-knit group proud of its accomplishments and intensely loyal to their boss and the company—pool money to buy him a Christmas present: a vintage Corvette Stingray. He's made most of them successful beyond their wildest dreams, and they want to do something to thank him.

CHAPTER 6

Coming Home

A million thoughts race through my mind as I drive the lonely stretch of I-20 from Atlanta to Mississippi with my two-year-old daughter in the back seat of the ancient beige Buick Skyhawk I bought in graduate school. Thumbtacks hold up the headliner. The car is on its last leg, and I'm just praying it carries us all the way to Clinton.

It's 1992. I've earned a graduate degree, passed the CPA exam, and moved forward with my professional career, but my personal life seems to have taken on the lyrics of a bad country song. I've failed. Tom and I got married, but the marriage is over. And while I now see that I rushed into a relationship that was destined to fail, we do have a beautiful daughter. Stephanie and I are coming back to Mississippi to move in with my parents. I found it too difficult to be a single mother in Atlanta, with none of my family nearby for moral support.

I'm anxious about supporting myself as a single parent. What if I can't find a decent job in Mississippi? I don't want to be a burden to my parents, who are now in their fifties. They've raised their children and are supposed to be enjoying time to themselves. Isn't playing with your grandchildren and then sending them home with their parents the best thing about being grandparents? Having a toddler underfoot surely will turn their life upside down. And how will I manage having Mom and Dad in the middle of my life after being on my own for ten years?

As I scan the radio for a decent song, a part of me wants to seal off the failures and disappointments of the last several years, but my mind can't keep from retracing my time in Atlanta.

Tom and I purchased a nice home in the Atlanta suburbs soon after we married. The commute was longer to the office, but it was worth it. I loved my work at Deloitte. Partners and managers were requesting me to work on their audit engagements, so that I ended up with some of the office's most coveted public-company clients: RJR Nabisco, the conglomerate that had just gone through the largest leveraged buy-out in history; T^2 Medical, a home health-care company that was one of the country's hottest fast-growth businesses. The hours were often grueling, but I was up for whatever it took.

While being laid off from Price Waterhouse felt traumatic at the time, I had come to look on it as a valuable life lesson—to be successful, you have to be willing to take risks and expect some set-backs along the way. In the end, the process had moved my career forward even more quickly by allowing me to experience first-hand the different operations and cultures of two prominent Big Eight accounting firms. Between Deloitte and Price Waterhouse, I'd worked on clients in industries as diverse as cable, insurance, oil and gas, entertainment, health care, real estate, printing, and manufacturing.

One of my most significant challenges in Atlanta had been to figure out how to juggle a demanding career that required extremely long work hours with being a mother. By the ninth month of my pregnancy, I had gained a detailed appreciation for what pregnant working women go through. I felt an obligation to keep up with my colleagues—most of them young and single—and managed well until the last few weeks before delivery. I could no longer hide how exhausted I felt. I was enormous. I waddled back and forth when I walked. I couldn't see my own feet anymore, or even pull up those aggravating maternity pantyhose. Sometimes, I skipped lunch and rested on the day beds in the nurse's station at the client office where I was working at the time. Some days, I even dared to go home on time. I was starting to wonder how I would manage my career and a baby. It seemed that the colleagues who were married with children had a spouse who stayed home or had hired a full-time nanny.

I also experienced more than a few misadventures with obstetricians. Since I didn't know any in Atlanta, I randomly chose a doctor from my insurance plan's pre-approved list. One name looked just as good as the next. But the first doctor I visited had a terrible bedside manner, so I chose another. When Tom and I arrived at the second doctor's office, the place was run-down and dirty. One of the ladies next to me said she'd heard that this doctor had been criticized for being "quick to use the knife," performing Caesarean sections on a high percent of his patients. "Why would he do that?" I asked. "He does it because it takes less time," she said. "This way he can get patients in and out more quickly." That's all I needed to know.

For the third time, I randomly selected a doctor from the list. This one seemed nice enough. He also appeared to be cautious, which was reassuring, though he kept sending me to the hospital for monitoring because he was convinced the baby's heartbeat was slowing. Each time I rushed to the hospital, worried, but the monitors showed no problem.

"Do you know whether you're having a girl or boy?" one of the hospital attendants asked during one such visit, late in my pregnancy.

"I don't know. They couldn't tell on the sonogram because of the way the baby was turned."

"Do you know about the accident your doctor was involved in?"

"No, what?" Concerned, I raised my head from the table.

"I'm not supposed to tell you, but I'm going to anyway," she whispered. I listened intently as she told me a terrifying story of some serious complications during a circumcision the doctor had performed.

"Oh my gosh." I was horrified. It sounded like something out of a bad movie.

I started to wonder how this insurance plan selected the doctors on its pre-approved list. I wanted to change doctors again, but I was so close to my delivery date that I felt like I couldn't. I decided that if I had a girl, I wouldn't have to worry; and if it was a boy, well, I simply wouldn't let him perform the circumcision. I would cross that bridge if I came to it.

Finally, the guessing was over. After 18 hours of labor, I delivered a healthy baby girl into the world. It had been an ordeal. To ease the pain, the hospital anesthesiologist had given me an epidural, but it also stopped my contractions. My doctor could have given me medicine to restart them, but he had vanished from the hospital altogether—to run errands for his upcoming wedding, my mother was convinced. Finally, he returned and gave me the medicine.

We named my daughter Stephanie Nola in honor of my maternal grandmother. Tom was elated. My father-in-law, who had two sons, picked up Tom's mother in his arms and twirled her in a circle: "Well, darling, we finally got our little girl!"

I'd developed a fever at some point, so the hospital staff immediately wheeled Stephanie away as a precaution. My doctor returned early the next morning.

"Well, I'm discharging you," he said matter-of-factly. "You're fine to go home."

"What? I've just been in labor for 18 hours. I'm supposed to stay at least one more night."

"No. You're fine to go home today," he said in an unfriendly tone. "It's people like you who run up the insurance costs in this country."

Tom was livid when he heard the news, but I just told him to come pick me up. I wanted no more of this doctor. While I was waiting for Tom, the nurse rolled in a small bassinet. I stared in disbelief. Stephanie was so beautiful, an awesome wonder.

I tried to pick her up, but her head began to wobble. I maneuvered my hands to try from a different angle, quickly glancing around to make sure no one would see. I realized that I didn't even know how to hold her. Finally, I called the nurse, who showed me how to do it. And so we sat, just the two of us, Stephanie and me.

At home, I started settling into being a new mother and was starting to face an internal battle I had heard other new mothers talk about. I would have loved to stay home with Stephanie for a few years. But I'd also set career goals. I'd been following them since high school—keep my grades high, select a field that was not only enjoyable but well-compensated, get a graduate degree, pass the CPA exam, go to work for a prestigious firm. Now that I'd come this far, I felt like I couldn't just stop—after all, wasn't that why my grandfather thought my education would be a waste of money?

The manager on one of my Deloitte clients soon called to see when I planned on coming back. If I couldn't come back within four weeks of delivery, he'd have to put someone else in my place on the T^2 Medical audit. I assured him it was no problem. Even though I didn't feel ready when the time came, I kept my commitment.

I had recently made senior auditor and Tom had moved into investment banking—both were career advances, but we were still young and expected to pay our dues by working long hours. Thankfully, Tom's mother was keeping Stephanie during the day, but Tom's parents lived an hour away. With the Atlanta traffic and long hours, we often got home late in the evening and it was always a debate as to who could leave work earlier to pick up Stephanie. Something had to give.

Fortunately, a high-level finance position reporting directly to the CFO opened at T^2 Medical, my Deloitte client. Maybe the balance I was looking for would be easier to find if I could go to the same place every day and have predictable hours. T^2 was growing rapidly through acquisitions. The new CFO had managed the entire finance organization—payroll, accounts payable, accounting—as Controller until his promotion, and was now looking for someone to take over his old position.

I decided to apply. By this point, I had enough experience to know to ask for stock options as part of the compensation package. When I was auditing public companies, my work included reviewing stock option programs. I had seen their power first-hand, something I didn't understand fully when I graduated from college. It was an eye-opener. Executives with public companies that were growing and reporting strong earnings rarely created great wealth through salaries. They did it by owning stock and options in their companies.

However, I didn't know the first thing about how to negotiate compensation. It wasn't something they taught in college. But one thing was for sure: If I didn't learn fast, I could end up with a lower offer. At a bookstore, I tried to brush up: Don't be the first to put your cards on the table, or you may lose money. Get the employer to first give you the salary range he or she is willing to pay. Repeat the range several times slowly, staring at the floor with a look of disappointment. If the range is acceptable, explain that with your experience you need at least the top of the range.

During my interview, I used the recommended techniques. I decided to lock in the salary range before discussing options, so they wouldn't be used as a reason to offer a lower salary. But I was having trouble getting the CFO to give me the salary range. He wasn't following the script. He kept asking what it would take to hire me. I didn't remember any books giving advice on this scenario. So I kept repeating, "Well, what's the range you'd be willing to pay for this position?"

We went back and forth with this routine several times. It was starting to get awkward. But finally, he came out with it—"$45,000 to $50,000." Fifty thousand dollars was much higher than my salary at the time and more than I expected him to say, but still, I restated the figures slowly, as recommended. Then I asked for the top figure and repeated the negotiating process for options.

Several days later, a formal offer arrived. My trip to the bookstore proved lucrative, as T^2's offer was for the top of the range, plus options. At 25, I was given a large corner office with floor-to-ceiling windows on two sides that overlooked a beautiful wooded area. My boss gave me several laminated plaques to hang on my wall—*BusinessWeek* and *Forbes* cover stories in which T^2 had been lauded. Just outside my office sat a team of finance employees who reported to me. This was the opportunity of a lifetime. I would gain experience far beyond my years in terms of knowledge and management skills.

So far, I'd only seen the corporate world from an auditor's perspective. I used to audit management. Now I was management in the middle of a fast-moving, chaotic environment. Every month, my team and I had to close the books for over a hundred subsidiary companies while juggling all of the other finance functions. Once we completed the task, it was time to start the same process for the next month.

T^2 had experienced explosive growth. In 1990, it was 8th on *Forbes'* list of the 200 best small companies in America. But the accounting department was too thinly staffed to handle the workload, and most of the finance employees were bookkeepers without much accounting experience. Very soon my hours at T^2 came to resemble those in public accounting. At least in public accounting auditors were allowed to take time off between engagements to make up for the longer hours. Here, we consistently worked the long hours with less time off. I had jumped from the frying pan into the fire.

My boss, the new CFO, was pleased with my work, giving me a raise soon after I started. But he seemed to have trouble letting go of those details he had hired me to take over. At times, he even acted like a staff accountant, personally closing the books, completing bank reconciliations, and manually writing accounting entries. He even required my team to regularly make accounting entries for pennies—everything must tie out to the cent, he insisted. My employees strained at having two people issue instructions.

I probably could have handled the pressure of the work environment better if things were going well at home, but they weren't. My marriage was struggling. In fact, I wasn't sure it was going to work at all. And I realized that my work situation wouldn't improve even after well-meaning dialogue with my boss. With disarming honesty, he confessed that he just couldn't leave the day-to-day operations alone, much as he tried. So I decided to take a break from the corporate fast track to sort out my personal life and spend more time with Stephanie.

At home, I was finally forced to face the reality that my marriage was not going to work out. I've heard it said that we all have a God-shaped vacuum, an emptiness and longing that only He can fill. I had wanted to believe that a long-term relationship would make me feel more secure, especially in a sprawling city where I sometimes felt vulnerable. Tom and I had tried marriage counseling, but without success. Even though I was married and had a two-year-old child, I'd never felt more alone.

Early one morning, I waved the movers into the driveway. With half our belongings, Stephanie and I moved to an apartment in Atlanta. The first night there, I snuggled her close, as much for my benefit as hers. All around me were halves: half a home, half a marriage. I stared at the ceiling for hours, waiting for sleep to take me. The next morning, Stephanie laid her head on the couch sadly, and said, "Where are we, mommy?" I thought she would be too young to understand what was happening, but I had been wrong. It was my first day as a single parent and I had no idea what lay ahead.

I had moved to Atlanta just five years before, wanting to experience life in a large metropolitan city. From a career perspective, I'd built a strong resume. But for all my plans, they hadn't worked out the way I'd hoped. My years in Atlanta had been a roller-coaster—moving, starting a new career, getting laid off, getting married, having a baby, buying a house. But my life was about to dramatically change course once again.

After only a few months in our Atlanta apartment, Stephanie and I are moving to Mississippi. I glance in the rearview mirror at her, resting peacefully in her car seat. What a blessing she is. My mother was right when she said, long ago, that nothing can compare to the joy of having children. I worry about how Stephanie will adjust, and feel guilty that she won't grow up with two parents as my brother Sam and I did.

As the Appalachian foothills disappear, Atlanta and Birmingham recede and I know home is close when the land flattens out and my car begins to ride the blacktop like a wave because of the Yazoo clay underneath.

I'm told there's only one place in the world suffering from the Curse of Yazoo Clay: Mississippi. Like a sponge, the clay earth expands with moisture and then contracts in dry seasons. It meanders in veins, skipping one yard and striking the next, damaging many of the homes in town. Some of my parents' neighbors have paid thousands of dollars to have mud pumped under their homes to level the foundations, but it's a losing battle. With time, cracks have appeared in my parents' walls too, promptly caulked by Dad while Mom cheers him on. "Marvelous," she always says. "It's hardly noticeable." The walls continue to crack, and the corners of the house have sagged. It feels like a downhill walk from the kitchen to the back bedroom.

It's comforting to return to the green of Mississippi and my childhood home. Being here is like pulling up a favorite cozy blanket, like slipping on a pair of old shoes that fit perfectly through the wearing of time. Any time I travel to other parts of the country, I know I'm back home when the humidity, so heavy it hangs in the air, hits me in the face, making it difficult to breathe. The wet heat will keep your skin looking younger, the theory among Mississippi ladies holds. Personally, I'd be all too happy to take on a few more wrinkles if it meant different weather, but still, the feel of home is sweet.

I know I'm home when people say they're "fixin'" to do something, or when children address adults with a "Yes, Sir," or "No, Ma'am," followed by "Miss" or "Mr." and the first, not last, name (Ms. Phyllis, Mr. Mike). And the names are often double—Mary Katherine, Emma Grace, Sarah Beth.

I won't hear "you guys," but "y'all." My mother will make some fried green tomatoes, and every restaurant will have sweet tea, the only way many people in the South drink it—the sweeter the better. For Thanksgiving, we'll have dressing made with buttermilk cornbread.

I know I'm home when "there's a church on every corner," as a friend visiting from New York once put it; when the downtown skyline is a miniature of those in major cities; when the hustle disappears and the pace of living calms. People even speak more slowly, drawing out each word as if they're savoring the last sip of a favorite drink. One-syllable words often become two. And that old-fashioned, somewhat aristocratic Southern accent still survives, the one that has little use for the letter "r," turning "water" into "watah."

A Place to Heal

As I pull into my parents' driveway exhausted, my mother comes out the back door to greet us. "You'll be okay," she reassures me as we embrace. "You come from a long line of strong women. Life may knock us down, but we don't stay down, and neither will you," she says, repeating the encouragement I've heard from her so often. Strong is the last thing I'm feeling, as I battle the misery of constant nausea. "Chin up, chin up," my mother says. "Cry your tears and then you have to throw the tissue away and move on."

To distract me, my mother tells me funny stories as we sit at the kitchen table. My parents are caring for elderly relatives who have no one else for help—Nannie Ferrell, my father's mother, and Uncle Mac, who is related by marriage. They live in two different nursing homes, which means that my parents have to run back and forth.

In his late 80s, Uncle Mac is a small, frail slip of a man who has Parkinson's disease. My mom tells me that he called her from the nursing home. "'I want you to bring me my gun,'" she says he told her, imitating his grumble. "'Someone keeps coming in and taking my chocolate Kit-Kats. This place is full of undesirables.'" My mother thinks she'll load him up with extra chocolate instead. "Now you have plenty to share," she tells him.

Later, Great Aunt Debbie, my father's aunt, has to move to a nursing home as well. Always the pistol, she soon decides to never bother with bathing again. "This is the third time the staff has asked us to come to the nursing home," my mom says when she returns. "They say if this keeps up, she won't be able to stay."

"Did you get her to bathe?" I ask.

"Yes, finally, but I wouldn't say it went well. I said, 'Aunt Debbie, the nurses say you're not cooperating with them—they're getting mad at you.'"

"Well, I'll slap the fire out of them if they try to touch me," Aunt Debbie said adamantly.

"Mama, you've got to get everyone together under one roof," I will urge. "This is running you ragged." At last, the three are together in the same nursing home, and caring for them becomes much less hectic.

As for me, my mother's pampering gradually shifts to gentle exhortation. "Let's go for a walk around the block," she says one day. "It's chilly, but the sun is shining."

"No, I don't want to," I say, still feeling listless.

"Oh, come on. We'll pull Stephanie in her wagon, and when we get back we'll sit on the kitchen floor and have a tea party. It'll be fun."

I put on my coat and bundle Stephanie. And thus the healing begins— one foot in front of the other, I walk into my future pulling a small red wagon with a bright-eyed, laughing child.

CHAPTER 7

Building A New Life

I know the Mississippi job market will be tight, but maybe I'll get close to my former salary. Soon after moving in with my parents, I hit the pavement, but there are fewer job advertisements than I expected. Replying to ads and even using a recruiter isn't likely to result in a decent position—I'll cold-call companies just like I did after being laid off in Atlanta. Companies often have unadvertised openings.

I've been away from Mississippi so long that I no longer have a network of contacts, so I draw up a list of the most significant companies in our area, and dial the main number for each, asking for the chief financial officer. I'm also trying managing partners at large accounting firms to see if their clients have openings. Though I manage to overcome the initial awkwardness of cold-calling, for weeks I don't have any luck. It feels like déjà vu: This is the same thing I went through in Atlanta, but I know rejection is a natural part of the process.

Finally, I receive a second interview for an accounting position with a prominent real-estate investment company. "We'd like to offer you a job," the CFO says, smiling widely. "The starting salary will be $19,000." I don't really hear much after that. I'm too shocked to receive an offer so far below even my starting salary after college. I decline, determined to hold out for a better offer. Thankfully, I have the luxury of doing so because I'm living with my parents.

"There are two telecommunications companies in town that are really starting to take off," my father says one day. I'd love to work for a growing public company, and my father thinks that both are. "One is called LDDS, and the other SkyTel. You should send them both a resume."

I've never heard of either. After asking around, I learn that LDDS, in Jackson, sells long distance, and SkyTel, also in the capital, sells wireless pagers. I've had some communications experience—one of my audit clients at Deloitte was one of the largest cable companies in the country—so I decide to give both a try.

After calling LDDS's reception desk to find out the CFO's name, I try him.

"Charles Cannada," he answers the phone. I'm surprised to get him directly and introduce myself. He's familiar with the companies on my resume and likes the fact that I have public accounting experience and worked for T^2, another fast-growth public company.

"If I don't find a job soon, I'm going to be in the bread line," I joke.

Charles is friendly and seems genuinely interested in helping me. "Fax me your resume, and I'll see what I can do," he says. "I don't have a permanent position, but we might need some temporary help in the accounting department."

Charles forwards my resume to Brenda McGraw, the Controller managing the accounting department, who soon calls. "We'd like to hire you as a temporary contractor to do some data entry work," she says. "We can pay $12.00 an hour."

It's another disappointing offer. I'm grateful that Charles has gone out of his way to find a position for me, but data entry isn't what I was hoping for. Still, everyone I talk to has good things to say about LDDS. It seems to be going places, and it's not as if I have so many choices in Jackson. And who knows—if I prove myself, I might get a full-time position.

It's my first day on the job. After introducing me, Brenda escorts me to my new work space. I'm standing in front of an old metal desk sandwiched in the walkway between two cubicles. It looks like it's been banged with a few hammers.

"I'm sorry. This is the only space we have right now." The accountants around me are laughing, apologizing that there is no more room. Either LDDS doesn't want me to stay too long or it's bursting at the seams with growth. I take their joking in stride. Be happy to have a desk and be working again, I tell myself. Be thankful for the blessing.

In general, having no space left is a good sign. "If we'd ever dreamed we would get where we are now, we probably would have left [Jackson]," Bernie will later say. "But as you grow with each acquisition, you make decisions and somewhere along the way we decided to stay. It's worked out."

LDDS is growing quickly, but it's small enough to retain a strong spirit of camaraderie. I'm meeting new friends, and staying busy helps me keep my mind off the divorce. The company is also so young that the organizational structure is relatively flat, unlike what I saw with some clients in my public-accounting days. Charles is approachable and friendly, often walking through the accounting group and chatting with staff. And the CEO wears bluejeans and boots.

I've never met Bernie—that's the way everyone refers to him, from the mailroom to the highest executives—but after working here only a few weeks, I see him in action. He has a dominating presence. He's the king, sometimes feared, but usually admired, and held in the highest esteem. Each month, the accountants meet with him, and he drills them with questions.

Brenda has invited me to sit in on this month's meeting. Everyone sits and chats as they wait for Bernie to arrive, but clearly the accountants are tense. Each one keeps the books for one or more of the small companies LDDS has acquired; for days, they've been poring over their regions' results, trying to anticipate Bernie's questions. I had a front-row view from my desk as they called people in the field to ask why they were over or under budget on items like office supplies. Inevitably, the staff tell me, Bernie asks questions no one can answer or even anticipate, and someone is always caught flat-footed in front of the group. "Who will be in the hot seat today?" they joke.

After all the talk about hot seats, I think I'll sit toward the back of the conference room, where the seats are more comfortable. I just want to be a fly on the wall. When Bernie comes in, a hush falls over the room. He takes a seat at the head of the table. Each accountant takes a turn explaining the month's results, and, as promised, Bernie throws several curve balls. If a division is over budget for the month even by a few hundred dollars, Bernie might ask why, even if it's on track or under-budget for the year.

There's a bit of tension, but then it's over. It isn't typical for the CEO to sit in a meeting with staff accountants and ask about airline travel and how much is being spent on desks in a particular state, but I suppose it goes back to the way LDDS has grown. Bernie's been here from the start. Maybe his vigilance is one of the reasons the company is so successful.

I'm amazed at how fast the company's growing. Management is looking to lease more office space and may buy its own building. The company is in the middle of an acquisition. From what I hear, this is only one of many to come. My co-workers are putting in long hours. If the company offers me a full-time position with a decent salary, I'd certainly consider it. I've never had a professional job that didn't require overtime. It would be difficult as a single parent, but my mother has volunteered to keep Stephanie when I need extra time.

Still, I want to keep looking for a management position. One of the senior accountants, who is my equal in experience, says LDDS pays very low salaries; she's making less than $20,000. I'm shocked, but then again, maybe I shouldn't be, considering that the employees joke that the CEO chastises them for overspending on items like pencils and notebooks.

I've gotten to know Charles, the CFO who helped me get this job. With wavy hair brushed straight back and stylish preppy clothing, he reminds me of a fraternity boy, which he was at Ole Miss. Most accountants I've met tend to be introverted and reserved, but Charles has a charismatic charm, an electric smile, and a gregarious personality. I'm always glad to see him. He takes the time to chat, usually says something witty, and asks how things are going. Fine, I want to tell him—except that I'm making $12.00 an hour and sitting in the middle of an aisle.

No Strings Attached

It's early in the evening when I answer a phone call that will again change my life. "You'll never guess who this is," the man on the other end says. "This is a voice from your past." I play the game and guess several times, incorrectly. "It's Lance Cooper," he finally says.

I'm more than surprised to hear from Lance, my good friend from high school. An athletic, charming guy, he was always tapping me on the shoulder in Mrs. Peevey's 9th-grade algebra class instead of letting me focus on $a^2 - b^2 = (a + b)(a - b)$. He had dark eyes and dark-brown hair parted down the middle in what would later be called a zipper cut. He had just moved from Birmingham, Alabama, after his parents had divorced.

Mrs. Peevey's patience had quickly run out and I found myself being moved to the other side of the room. I wondered why she moved me if he was the one who wouldn't stop talking? I felt a rush of excitement when, several weeks later, a flower deliveryman appeared at my door with one very beautiful rose. Who in the world would send me a rose? The card had a message from Lance. It was the first flower I'd ever received from a suitor.

Lance was outgoing and made friends quickly. He loved to drive me crazy by squeezing my hand over and over, exclaiming "Hi! I'm Lance with the heart foundation." I was more serious—too mature, I thought, for Lance's cornball jokes—though I did tease him about being voted Mr. October in the school calendar our junior year. He played baseball, started on the football team, and led many school activities. Teachers loved him because he was an athlete who kept his grades up.

We served together on the student council, helped decorate the gym for prom, and recycled cans and paper for school fundraisers. There were even pictures of the two of us together in the yearbook. But we never dated.

It's great to hear from him and catch up. Last I heard, he was a cheerleader at the University of Southern Mississippi in Hattiesburg, and graduated with a degree in computer science. He says one of our mutual friends told him that I had gotten divorced and moved back home. "I wanted to see if you'd like to get together for lunch next week," he says.

I don't want to date anyone right now. Besides, I've always viewed Lance as a friend, my old buddy. But I suppose lunch will be harmless, not really like an official date. I accept the invitation, thinking I'll go this once.

I also mention that I have a daughter who is almost three. In case he does think this is a real date, that should scare off a single guy who's never been married. But it doesn't. He says he'd like to meet her.

As the day of our lunch approaches, I start to get cold feet. I don't want to hurt Lance's feelings, but I just don't want to go. I dial his number, but hang up before the phone rings. Oh, I wish someone else would call him for me! I finally get up the nerve to call the night before lunch.

"I really appreciate you asking me to lunch but I don't want to go out with anyone right now," I explain.

"That's okay. I understand," he says. "But if you ever just want to get out, give me a call."

"I will," I say, though I don't intend to call. I'm relieved to get out of the date.

The next evening, the phone rings. To my surprise, it's Lance. I thought I'd never hear from him again, but he doesn't seem to give up easily.

"Glen Jones is getting married. He and his fiancée are having an engagement party this weekend," he says. "There should be a lot of people we graduated with. Why don't you come with me?"

I can't believe he's being this persistent. I'm amused and flattered. I've turned him down twice. He knows I'm divorced and have a small child, but, still, he's back at the door.

"Oh, come on. You'll have fun. No strings attached," he promises, making me laugh. "No strings attached" sounds good. And it would be great to see Glen, our old friend from high school. Maybe it will be fun to go out this one time.

This time, I keep my end of the bargain, but something unexpected happens. I have the most fun I've had in years. We see friends we haven't seen since high school and catch up on old times, laughing and reminiscing. I feel like a bird let out of a cage. Maybe I'll go out with Lance one more time.

The Other Telecom Company

It's September, 1992. After several months at LDDS, I've forgotten about the resume I sent SkyTel, Jackson's other growing telecommunications company. They've called me to interview for two positions, in Finance and Internal Audit.

At first, I'm reluctant to apply for Internal Audit. External audit is more established because public companies have been required by law to have an annual audit since the Securities Exchange Act of 1934. But there's no law or requirement that a company even have an internal audit function. Unlike their external counterparts, internal auditors are usually employees of the companies they audit. Some companies choose to have only a small, token group, others none at all, and others outsource the function altogether, sometimes to the same public accounting firm performing the external audit. My impression is that internal audit groups struggle for support, staffing, respect, and to keep their departments from being outsourced. During my three years in public accounting, I don't remember even meeting anyone from a client's internal audit department. In college, external audit seemed to get all the glory. My professors promoted it. Mike Morgan, LDDS's internal auditor, seems to like his job, but he has done barely any internal audit work because he's been so busy working on acquisitions.

"Our department was like the elephant graveyard," one chief internal audit executive of a major public company will later tell me. "People who weren't a good fit for any other area or were in their final career days were moved to Internal Audit." He added that his company's CEO eventually outsourced the entire department after hearing unwelcome internal-audit results.

Still, I decide to at least go on the interview. I'm surprised. Of the two available positions, it's the one in Internal Audit that sounds far more interesting. I'm intrigued by what Terri Hudson, who directs the department at SkyTel, tells me about her group. A number of her previous employees have used Internal Audit as a springboard to higher-level positions in other parts of the company. And it sounds like a job that will allow me to build on the skills I developed in public accounting.

External auditors have a more focused mandate—to audit a company's financial statements to ensure that they are in accordance with generally accepted accounting principles. Terri's group has a broader range of tasks, including operational audits (reviewing internal controls as well as the effectiveness and efficiency of operational processes and procedures) and systems audits (testing, for example, to ensure that access to critical system data is well-controlled). The goal is to increase audit coverage of the higher-risk areas of the company while minimizing any duplication of effort with the external auditors.

SkyTel offers me a permanent position with a good salary and health insurance. I debate whether to take the bird in the hand or wait for the one in the bush with LDDS while I'm sandwiched between two cubicles with no insurance benefits.

I decide to play it safe and leave my $12 an hour job. Today is my last day at LDDS. I stop by to say goodbye to Mike Morgan, the Internal Audit manager. We've become friends during my brief stint, and he's mentioned that his long-term interest is in acquisitions, not Internal Audit.

"Will you keep me in mind for your position if you decide to do something else?"

"I'll do it," he promises.

It doesn't take me long to realize that SkyTel and LDDS have very different work environments. Although both are entrepreneurial telecom companies, SkyTel is growing more slowly through internal evolution rather than via acquisitions, making the pace of work here dramatically more relaxed.

Company culture depends on many factors—size, whether it's public or private, how regulated the industry is, whether the company is growing through acquisition or from within. But nothing matters more than the tone set at the top. John Palmer, the founder of SkyTel, is a polished, refined man who wears fine suits, has a keen interest in art, and is flexible about employee spending. Bernie, on the other hand, prefers to be riding his tractor and working the land in his spare time. He walks the office in bluejeans and boots, and is tight with the purse strings, seeming to chase pennies. While expensive artwork and antiques line the halls of SkyTel, LDDS makes do with a folding table in the conference room. No one here jokes, as they did at LDDS, that you have to get the boss's approval to buy a pencil.

But compared to LDDS, SkyTel is much more formal and hierarchical. At LDDS, the CEO and CFO sit in on monthly meetings with staff-level accountants. SkyTel's top executives aren't nearly as visible; people at high levels seem inclined to limit dealings to others at their level or above. LDDS's relatively flat organizational structure and informal hierarchy means that you might get a call from the man at the top himself if he thinks you bought something unnecessary.

My uncertainty about internal audit quickly vanishes. I learn more about the Institute of Internal Auditors—the organization that sets best-practice standards and promotes the profession—and what it's doing to move internal audit forward. And Terri manages a progressive group, keeping up with the latest trends. It's allowing me to learn many aspects of the business quickly and network with more senior executives at a young age.

The internal audit environment is quite different from public accounting. External auditors have accounting backgrounds, but internal auditors often have more diverse training. I've gotten to audit and learn about a wide array of departments: engineering, marketing, billing, inventory, customer service, sales, commissions, pricing, information technology. I like the variety; there's less repetition than in external audit. I'm still using my finance skills, but in a far wider context. I start to think of internal audit as the best-kept secret in corporate America.

And Terri will become the most influential female mentor and role model in my career. Other than a few audit engagements in public accounting, most of the people I've worked for have been men. In addition to teaching me a great deal about internal audit, Terri will shape my perspective as a woman executive. I'm aware of her influence at the time, but it will be years before I fully appreciate her impact.

Terri is paving the way for many women at the company. She will break through the glass ceiling to levels few women have achieved, moving from director to vice president and, ultimately, to CFO. Along the way, she will reach out to help others succeed.

Terri built SkyTel's internal audit group from the bottom up with just a few staff auditors. There have been battles to fight and executives to convince, but with time, hard work, and determination, she has proven the value of her group and earned respect.

I've heard that women are more hesitant than men to ask for promotions or raises. Not so with Terri. She's assertive, makes her career aspirations known, and asks her boss for what she feels she and her staff deserve. Nothing has been handed to her.

I'm also learning how diplomatically she maneuvers through sticky political situations. Internal auditors are on a tightrope. By definition, audit reports tend to cause tension and disagreement. Some executives don't take kindly to being evaluated by another group and having the results forwarded to the company's management and Audit Committee.

And then there are those times when diplomacy won't work. I've been confronted by some inappropriate remarks, but nothing like what Terri experiences the week the CFO assigns her to act as liaison to a consulting partner with an external firm. After speaking to the partner on the phone for the first time, Terri walks into my office, shuts the door, and sits down. I can tell by the look on her face that something isn't right. She's unnerved as she relates what happened when she spoke to the consultant about picking him up at the airport.

"I told him 'I have red hair so you can't miss me,'" she says. "He said, 'And I bet you've got a great body to go with it.'" Shocked, she was caught off-guard, and let the remark pass. She's uncomfortable about having to work with the man, but the CFO has personally told her this is an important project.

"Am I overreacting?" she asks, looking at me in disbelief.

"No. That's definitely an inappropriate thing for him to say to you," I say.

"Maybe it'll be fine," she says. "Let's just see how it goes."

When the consultant arrives, Terri asks one of the other audit managers and me to sit in on the meeting until it's clear that he's going to conduct himself appropriately. I catch myself glaring at him a few times. The first day goes fine; feeling a bit better, Terri decides to work alone with him the next day.

The following day, she sits across from him, but soon he moves to her side of the table, supposedly to look at the document she's reviewing. " 'Why don't we go to my hotel room to finish our work?' " she'll tell me he said. " 'It's quieter, and I have a conference table in my room where we can work.' "

Horrified, Terri asks him to leave. Initially, the man thinks she might be joking, but she's not. Humiliated, he quickly gathers his things and heads for the door. He's thrown off the premises and sent to the airport. Terri now has to break the unfortunate news to her boss, who is equally shocked. He notifies the external firm, and the consultant's behavior has career-limiting consequences.

CHAPTER 8

King of the Resellers

A Game of Leap Frog

It's the summer of 1992. While I'm building my career at SkyTel, Bernie is expanding LDDS's reach to resell long distance in 27 contiguous states, strategically moving from the Southeast to the Southwest and Midwest. For all his work, though, LDDS is still just one of hundreds of resellers. The reseller sector is a gold rush—LDDS and other companies are racing to consolidate the industry, and so far, these "consolidators" are similar in size. No one's broken out of the pack yet, but that is about to change.

While Bernie continues to tell close associates that the long-term strategy is to sell LDDS, in fact he's not ready. He's planning another, ante-raising acquisition for ATC, a well-established Florida consolidator that has acquired its own way to a large customer base across 26 states and more than $350 million in annual revenues. In a purchase valued at $850 million, ATC shareholders will receive LDDS shares in exchange for their ATC stock.

ATC has come under investigation by several Florida agencies for allegedly adding time to customer phone calls. The company has argued that this was merely the time that its network required to connect the call. But the investigation is becoming serious and ATC's stock is under pressure, so management invites Bernie to make an offer. "I think [some at ATC] were concerned that indictments were possible and felt the best way to make this go away was by selling the company," Charles will recall. "I don't think they would have sold us the company if not for the investigation."

The investigation gives LDDS the leverage to structure a more favorable deal by paying with stock instead of cash. The acquisition of ATC closes in December, 1992. Eventually, new management settles the case and there are no indictments.

The purchase is a defining moment for LDDS. "When we purchased ATC, we leap-frogged the other resellers," Charles will explain. It makes LDDS the nation's fourth-largest long-distance company, behind AT&T, Sprint, and MCI. Bernie is king of the resellers. Three men who will play critical roles in the company's growth—Max Bobbitt and Francesco Galesi who are ATC board members and Scott Sullivan—are about to make their debut with LDDS.

Max is a former Arthur Andersen auditor who is now President and Chief Operating Officer (COO) at Alltel, a prominent Little Rock, Arkansas telecommunications company. The rumor is that he's in line for the CEO spot.

Francesco is a New York businessman who is Chairman and CEO of the Galesi Group—a distribution, real estate, telecommunications, and manufacturing conglomerate. In 1990, *Forbes* ranked him the 205th wealthiest American, with a net worth estimated at $435 million. Francesco first struck gold in real estate, buying unused warehouses near Albany, New York, and converting them into industrial parks. He scored again after investing in telecommunications in the 1980s.

Francesco and Max, will join the LDDS board, with Max becoming the chairman of the Audit Committee, and Francesco a member. The Audit Committee will oversee Internal Audit, the group I will one day manage.

Scott Sullivan, graduated from the State University of New York in Oswego with a degree in business administration and accounting. He started his career with KPMG, one of the Big Eight accounting firms, in Albany, New York. Highly regarded, he was given lead roles on prominent clients like General Electric. Scott moved up quickly, making audit manager in four years instead of the usual five or six. After performing some accounting work for one of Francesco Galesi's real estate ventures, Francesco recruited him to become CFO at Telus Communications, a long-distance reseller Francesco owned in Florida. Scott agreed and moved to Boca Raton, Florida, but it wasn't long before ATC snapped up Telus. Scott accepted a lesser position as assistant treasurer at ATC, still good enough for a six-figure salary by the end of 1992.

Scott will join LDDS as assistant treasurer reporting to Charles Cannada, the CFO. Charles, who has had to advise on acquisitions, oversee accounting, and manage treasury functions, is looking forward to the help. He'll have a good working relationship with his new employee. When they meet, Charles discovers they already have a connection.

"You know my dad," Scott tells him.

"I do?" Charles is surprised. Scott's family is from upstate New York.

"He's in accounting with MidSouth Rail," Scott says.

Charles immediately recalls Scott's father. MidSouth Rail—a Jackson, Mississippi–based start-up that bought several lines from Illinois Central Railroad—was one of Charles' clients at Arthur Andersen. Scott's father was a career railroad accountant who accepted a position in Jackson to bide time until his retirement kicked in. In a strange turn of events, Scott and his dad are now both in Jackson.

LDDS closes out 1992 with revenues of $948 million, but analysts are criticizing Bernie—the company's gotten too big to have so many employees reporting to him directly. Bernie agrees to give up some control and consolidate his organizational hierarchy.

Every Team Needs a Cheerleader

It's January, 1993. Other than Prudential, the only stock analysts covering LDDS are regional Southeast firms like Robinson Humphrey, Morgan Keegan, and J. C. Bradford. For the past few years, Bernie and Charles Cannada have made a point of visiting Wall Street analysts when they're in New York to drum up interest in LDDS.

Sharing their vision for the company is finally paying off. With Bernie making larger acquisitions, prominent Wall Street firms are beginning to take notice. Jack Grubman, the PaineWebber analyst Bernie met several years ago, has just issued his first LDDS research report, recommending the stock as a "strong buy." Jack is one of the Wall Street stock analysts whose job it is to independently research companies and issue recommendations on their stocks. Because investors rely on these opinions to make their investment choices, company executives lobby prestigious analysts to rate the stock positively.

Jack is one of the first Wall Street analysts to believe that telecom resellers have a big future in the wake of AT&T's break-up. There are now three major long-distance players—AT&T, MCI, and Sprint—and hundreds of companies like LDDS that resell their service. Jack thinks resellers will consolidate to a few major players, and LDDS will be one of the winners. Jack's own aggressive personality fits well with the Wild West mentality of the reseller industry. "Jack liked the cowboy style of the reseller business," Charles will recall. "Resellers were much less stable than the Bell companies. Even MCI and Sprint were becoming fairly stable."

Jack also likes Bernie's confidence. He moves quickly in the market and he speaks with his checkbook. After all, Bernie and his top lieutenants were buying the LDDS stock that MidAmerican's parent company wanted to unload several years back. Both Jack and Bernie are risk-takers and instantly develop a rapport, in part, perhaps, because both are self-made men from modest means.

Jack was an only child whose mother worked in a clothing store. His father was an engineer for the highway department. When he wasn't working, Jack's father boxed and was a 1935 Golden Gloves champion with the unusual talent of ripping phone books in half. "I am a blue-collar guy at heart because I grew up in a blue-collar neighborhood," Jack will explain. "There were mailmen, policemen, truck drivers. Probably the most sophisticated people were teachers. You can't change who you are. I am still quite uncomfortable in some frou-frou setting."

When Jack visits Mississippi, he and Bernie sometimes hang out at the Cherokee Inn, a local restaurant with a pool table. "We both come from the wrong side of the tracks vis-à-vis the financial community," Jack will say. "I can relate to [Bernie] far better than most people I deal with. Bernie and I would have a strategic session in Jackson, and it usually was while shooting pool and drinking beer."

Jack started his career at AT&T in 1977, after obtaining an undergraduate degree in mathematics from Boston University and a graduate degree in probability theory from Columbia University. His first job was crunching numbers to predict long-distance usage. But, unlike some analysts, content to sit behind desks buried by numbers, Jack realized early on that cultivating relationships was critical to success. He took time to socialize and build a network that would serve him throughout his career.

Jack was assertive from the start. Once, he confronted superiors at AT&T about a problem with an economic model. "Jack basically said the emperor has no clothes," a former colleague will explain. "For a guy to raise his hand and say this doesn't work was really gutsy."

The break-up of AT&T resulted in more publicly traded telecom companies than ever before. There were 11 significant U.S. players—GTE and the seven Baby Bells selling local; and AT&T, MCI, and Sprint selling long distance—and all the start-ups re-selling long distance. Wall Street went searching for people who understood the new industry. Paine Webber came knocking on Jack's door in 1985. After eight years with AT&T, he decided to leave for Wall Street.

The Richest Man In America

Bernie is on his way to meet John Kluge, who was listed by *Forbes* as the wealthiest man in America in 1989. Several months after the ATC deal, Jack Phillips, the CEO of Resurgens, an Atlanta-based reseller, approached Bernie with a proposal. His company was being sold to Metromedia Communications, a privately-held telecom consolidator controlled by Kluge and a partner. He suggested that Bernie swoop in and buy his and Kluge's company in a three-way deal.

Bernie was intrigued. Knocking out another large consolidator would cement LDDS's position as the Number Four long-distance carrier behind AT&T, MCI, and Sprint. Phillips brokered a meeting with Kluge, and Bernie and Charles are flying on the corporate jet to Kluge's personal hangar at the Teterboro, New Jersey airport. The billionaire's turboprop helicopter waits to whisk them away to a heliport on the East River, where a limousine will ferry them to Kluge's Manhattan penthouse on the Upper East Side.

"His apartment was unbelievable," Charles will say. "After Bernie and I stood for some time in a large waiting room with a fireplace, these two enormous doors that looked like something guarding a vault suddenly opened on these motorized levers. We looked at each other like, What in the world is this?"

Born in Chemnitz, Germany, Kluge immigrated to the United States in 1922 and made his fortune identifying growth industries, investing early to build companies from the ground floor, and then cashing out for billions. If Bernie's strategy is now to build and hold, Kluge's is to build and sell.

Kluge invested millions constructing cellular networks when wireless was unheard-of, then sold them for $4 billion. He acquired independent television stations when many believed they couldn't compete with major networks, then sold them to Rupert Murdoch's News Corp. for $2 billion. Now Kluge is about to unload his long-distance company.

After Kluge and his partner come in, the men discuss the three-way deal and commit to continuing the talks. Bernie and Charles realize they're not the only ones who know how to maneuver. In promising the meeting, "[Jack Phillips, the Resurgens CEO] had acted as if he and Kluge were close friends," Charles will recall. "It was Kluge this and Kluge that. Then, when we finally arrived, Kluge looked at him, shook his hand and said, 'It's good to finally meet you.' Bernie and I just laughed."

In September, 1993, the three-way deal closes, Kluge coming out with over 30 million LDDS shares. He and his business partner, who ended up with the same amount, control over 30% of LDDS's outstanding stock. Meanwhile, Bernie's ownership of outstanding stock drops to less than 5%. While Bernie will continue to hold his stock, Kluge and his partner will eventually sell theirs for a substantial profit. The acquisition is a success for LDDS, which will close out the year with $1.4 billion in revenues.

A Non-Believer

It's October, 1993. While Bernie has sold Jack Grubman on his company's future, skeptics remain, chief among them Dan Reingold, the top Merrill Lynch telecom analyst.

Dan and Jack have been adversaries for years; the press will later refer to them as the "Siskel and Ebert of Telecom Investing." Like Jack, Dan began his career at a long-distance company—MCI. The bad blood began after Jack, already at PaineWebber, wrote a report about MCI that Dan thought was inaccurate and unfair to his then-employer.

The two are opposites in demeanor as well. Dan is quietly methodical, deriving his reports from hundreds of hours of research. Jack is more flamboyant, just as ready to rely on intuition and the close relationships he's built with industry executives. "There are precious few analysts who can look eyeball-to-eyeball with the CEO and take away an intangible feel for the company," Jack will brag to a reporter.

It's been ten months since Jack recommended LDDS as a buy. His ratings, along with LDDS's successful acquisition strategy, are attracting attention from both investors and other analysts. Since Jack recommended the stock, it has vaulted an incredible 63% in value.

A researcher on Dan's staff has been hearing the market buzz about LDDS and has convinced Dan to fly with him to Jackson. Dan is not too keen on flying way down South to check out what he considers to be just another of many resellers, but he promises his researcher he'll go. Besides, "indirectly, there was the hope that they'd also do some of their [investment] banking with Merrill, which might reflect well on me," Dan will write in his memoir, *Confessions of a Wall Street Analyst*. After having to connect in Atlanta—onto a run-down propeller plane—because there are no direct flights from New York to Jackson, Dan's feeling like this trip is way too much trouble for some small Mississippi company. "Singapore Airlines it ain't," he thinks to himself as he boards the plane.

After outgrowing its leased office space, LDDS has just purchased, gutted, and completely renovated the former four-story Southern Farm Insurance building in downtown Jackson. Many LDDS executives couldn't understand why Bernie would invest in such a large building, but with the purchase of ATC, they ran out of space almost immediately after they moved in.

The new headquarters is gleaming by Jackson standards and a significant improvement over LDDS's previous accommodations, but Dan is unimpressed. He thinks the new digs are "forlorn"—a "dingy headquarters." "It looked more like a two-bit actuary's office than a national telecom company," he'll write. His hotel, a "seedy, sorry-looking Holiday Inn" down the street from LDDS, is no more to his liking.

Despite Bernie's attempt to impress the Merrill analysts, the visit is continuing downhill. While Jack Grubman loves Southern food and playing pool with Bernie at his favorite dive, Dan isn't quite so eager. Bernie and Charles decide to take him for lunch downtown, at The Capital Club, one of the city's most exclusive restaurants, with a view of the city and state Capitol building. But Dan decides to go light on the Southern fried food which doesn't sit well with his stomach. And the view isn't up to par. "It was probably the best view in Jackson but it wasn't the Rainbow Room," he'll write, referring to the famous restaurant on the 65th floor of the GE Building in New York.

Dan isn't sure what to make of Bernie, with his cowboy boots and casual dress. "He was so different from the other telecom execs," he'll write, "who to a man were buttoned up corporate straight men with long careers in the industry." At one point, Bernie invites Dan to his office, where just about the only thing on his desk is a notebook filled with acquisition prospects. "The book was full of those green accountants' spreadsheets, and the figures and notations were all handwritten. Geez, I thought. It was 1993, 14 years after I had first learned to model financial forecasts on a desktop computer, and this company's CEO wasn't even working with Excel spreadsheets?"

" 'For each potential acquisition,' Bernie said, according to Dan, 'I have a single sheet. Each sheet lists the synergies [cost savings] we think we can get in each of the first three years after we buy it. Each sheet also lists the impact on the first year's earnings. If the impact is positive, we can do the deal anytime. If the impact lowers our earnings per share, we won't do it.' " Dan is struck both by the simplicity of the strategy and by Bernie's intimate involvement in acquisitions.

Perhaps Dan sees it this way because he mainly deals with established telecom players. But the reseller industry is wild, fast, and loose. Many executives in the sector are entrepreneurs with little or no telecom experience who started their companies because they had an idea and enough cash to hang a shingle. LDDS has been Bernie's baby from the beginning, and many believe it's his personal involvement with acquisitions that has been most responsible for moving the company from just a "country boy's dream" to over $1.5 billion in revenue.

Dan will initiate coverage on the stock, but his recommendation is unenthusiastic. Because he's busy with other things and doesn't believe that LDDS will be a significant player, he delegates the task of covering the company to his associate, who initially rates LDDS "accumulate," a step below "buy," and assigns the stock Merrill's riskiest classification— "speculative." Within months, LDDS's stock price exceeds Merrill's $26.50 target—10.4 percent higher than the $24 price when the opinion was issued. Dan's associate downgrades to "neutral," believing the stock has reached its peak. The tepid reception, quick downgrade, and lack of interest from Dan will make for a tense relationship between Dan and Bernie.

CHAPTER 9

The Hottest Company in Town

It's October, 1993. Lance and I are on the way to Natchez, Mississippi, to stay at one of the city's many antebellum homes for our honeymoon. We were just married at my parents' home in Clinton, with a small gathering of friends and family in attendance. I finally found my soulmate, and to think, he was sitting behind me in ninth grade Algebra.

Lance has been a tremendous blessing. The two of us share a strong bond, having grown up together. We've known each other for 15 years now. After he proposed, he also presented Stephanie with a small ring. She was the flower girl and stood beside me during the ceremony in her white lace dress clutching a basket of flowers.

Soon, there is an exciting professional opportunity as well. Less than two years after I left LDDS, Mike Morgan, the manager of the company's Internal Audit group, calls me. "I'm going to take another position in the company helping with acquisitions," he says. "I wanted to see if you'd be interested in interviewing for the Internal Audit manager position."

I'm definitely interested. Around Mississippi, LDDS is becoming the place to work. The position would allow me to start an Internal Audit department from the ground floor just as Terri has done at SkyTel. While Mike has two entry-level auditors, the group has spent most of its time on acquisitions.

Mike says LDDS is trying to recruit someone who can take this department to the next level, and Charles, the CFO, wants me to consider the position. Charles thinks I have the right skill set and likes that I've seen all sides of the fence now—both external and internal audit, and industry accounting experience with a fast-growth company. Since leaving LDDS, I've continued to build my resume by becoming both a Certified Fraud Examiner and a Certified Information Systems Auditor, and I'm about to sit for the Certified Internal Auditor exam.

I'm disappointed that the position will not report administratively to Charles. Mike Cipicchio, a recent hire through an acquisition and one of Charles' direct reports, will oversee the group. Mike seems affable during our interview, but I get the feeling he had a hard time matching my current compensation. I worry that Mike is also directly in charge of managing departments—Payroll, Accounts Payable, and Commissions—that Internal Audit will have to examine, compromising the independence of the reporting structure.

I'd like to have a line administratively to the CFO and functionally to the Audit Committee. Under such a structure, the CFO would handle administrative functions for Internal Audit, such as approving raises and promotions, while the Audit Committee would provide Internal Audit with some independence from company management by being in charge of approving our budget and annual audit plan. Also, I'd counted on at least a Director position. At SkyTel, Terri is a Vice President—a rung above Director and two above Manager—reporting functionally to the Audit Committee and administratively to the CFO, giving her Internal Audit group clout and greater independence. At many companies, Chief Audit Executives are at least Directors. And the heads of many other departments at LDDS are Vice Presidents.

I was also hoping for funds to hire more auditors and a higher salary, but I will start as a manager with the two entry-level audit staff who had worked under Mike Morgan. I'm concerned that the title, reporting structure, and minimal resources send the wrong message about the department's priority within the company. Internal Audit often delivers its work to the high-level executives who oversee the audited departments. It's difficult for a manager to make recommendations to senior vice presidents and be taken seriously, and I'll be able to complete few audits each year with just two staff who have minimal audit experience.

I relate my concerns to Mike. He runs them up the flagpole, but it's a "no" on all counts, though he assures me an impressive performance during my first year will get me to the Director level and should change management's mind about adding staff and elevating the reporting structure.

In the end, I decide to accept. The opportunity to build my own department at the hot company across town is just too good to pass up. No job is without its challenges and many internal audit groups have had to fight these same battles. I'm confident that I can prove the value of this group and resolve my concerns over time.

I share the news with Terri, my boss at SkyTel, who passes it on to David Garrison, the President. David asks me to meet with him before I make up my mind. SkyTel is looking for a director of customer service to manage its large customer call center, he tells me. He hopes I'll consider the job. I do, and even fly out to Colorado to meet with corporate psychologists, whom the company frequently uses to determine good executive fit.

Perhaps unsurprisingly, the psychologists conclude that it would take too long to re-train me for customer service. I could have told them that. People who manage marketing, sales, or customer service are generally outgoing and gregarious. I'm circumspect and reserved. Sometimes, I don't even want to answer my phone at home! Perhaps handling hundreds of customer calls isn't the right job for me. I recall the hardware store my grandfather once owned. He liked managing the store, but it aggravated him how the customers kept coming in to buy something.

Should We Sell Or Should We Buy?

> This company can go one of two directions. It can be built up through acquisitions. Or we can sell out. Whichever way will make shareholders rich is the course we will choose.
>
> —Bernie Ebbers

It's January, 1994—my first week back at LDDS. I'm glad to see the company has moved to a new building, and I won't have to sit in the middle of the aisle again. This time I'm in an office.

I feel like I have a massive challenge ahead. This executive team is focused on acquisitions and doesn't place much of a premium on internal audit. It will be critical for me to show them why they ought to feel differently.

SkyTel had a "best-practice" Internal Audit department, and I'll use much of the way we operated there as a template, focusing heavily on operational audits. But soon enough, I realize that I may be asking for too much from my auditors, each of whom I've assigned an audit. Because they have little audit experience, I constantly have to step in—to manage, perform staff-level auditing, write the reports. We're working day and night, but it feels as if we're hardly making progress.

The pressure is self-induced. It's not as if executive management is coming by asking, Where are those audit reports we've all been waiting on? They're trying to keep their heads above water with the latest acquisition. But I want to make a good first impression.

While I'm engrossed in my first audits, Bernie continues to hunt for new acquisition targets. I'm about to see first-hand what this management team does best.

It's April 12, 1994. Bernie is speaking at an investor conference in Atlanta sponsored by Robinson Humphrey, the regional investment bank. LDDS has already completed more than 30 acquisitions. "We don't intend to slow down," Bernie tells the attendees. "We can make several hundred million dollars worth of acquisitions a year. Our balance sheet is terribly underleveraged"—that is, the company's financials are solid enough to borrow much more in order to acquire—"and hopefully, we will be able to do a substantial deal and load up on debt. . . . We always do acquisitions on the basis that they contribute to earnings. We would probably never do a dilutive [that is, reducing earnings-per-share] acquisition."

There's great speculation in the market that LDDS will be bought out. People are asking if the hunter will become the hunted. News reports say the company is "prime for buyout" and an "enticing takeover target." Bernie is constantly asked if he'll sell. "We have never had an offer," he publicly tells a shareholder. "The phone's ready. I'll certainly answer it." He quips to an Atlanta reporter, "If it will help them call, you can publish my phone number," adding that he'd like to be fishing in a few years. But for all of Bernie's comments about selling, he seems to be having fun buying, and the strategy is certainly working. And he's only 52—he won't retire for years.

Through acquisition, Bernie has cobbled together a national customer base, but unlike AT&T, Sprint, and MCI, the three largest telecom companies, LDDS owns only a small piece of its telecommunications network. Without these "highways," which transport customer phone calls, LDDS has to lease from its own competitors. Even AT&T, Sprint, and MCI lease from one another to some extent because none of the telecom companies have full interconnectivity. But leasing is becoming more costly for LDDS and cutting into profits, not to mention the diceyness of relying so heavily on a competitor for bandwidth, the fiber-optic capacity to carry data and voice traffic. Bernie believes LDDS must acquire its own network to remain competitive and be a long-term player. There would be a symbolic value as well—without its own network, LDDS is really just a "marketer" of other companies' long distance as far as Wall Street is concerned.

LDDS could build its own network—digging up the streets, obtaining rights-of-way, laying fiber—but that would take valuable time and require an engineering talent pool the company doesn't currently have. There's one other option—buy a network. But other than AT&T, MCI, and Sprint—each much too expensive for LDDS to acquire—there's only one company with a substantial nationwide network—WilTel. Based in Tulsa, Oklahoma, it's a subsidiary of Williams Companies, a public oil and gas company. In a brilliant move, the pipeline executives had 11,000 miles of fiber pulled through abandoned pipelines and started a long-distance telephone company. Not having to negotiate rights-of-way or excavate has given WilTel a cost advantage over competitors and makes it a tempting acquisition target.

Bernie approaches Williams' management, but things quickly turn hostile. "There was a lot of conflict within Williams between the pipeline and telecom guys," Charles will say. "The telecom executives wanted to sell so they could get out from under the thumb of their oil and gas parent. But the oil and gas guys basically told us, 'No. We're not interested. Go away.'" While oil is profitable, revenues aren't growing nearly as quickly as telecom. As Keith Bailey, the Williams CEO, explains to the *Wall Street Journal*, "WilTel is the only asset we have with potential for sustained growth well in excess of the economy over a sustained period of time."

His sights already pointed at WilTel, Bernie isn't giving up so easily. He has an idea. If he finds a way to publicly reveal that LDDS and Williams are in discussions, Williams shareholders can force management to sell. Bernie, always attuned to shareholder value, feels that Williams shareholders aren't receiving maximum value for the telecom assets. "Wall Street's pipeline analysts didn't understand telecom and discounted its value," Charles will explain. "And telecom analysts didn't want to fool with evaluating and recommending a telecom company buried in an oil and gas business."

But there's a roadblock to public disclosure—LDDS signed a confidentiality agreement before starting talks stating that the negotiations couldn't be revealed *unless required by law*. "We thought—how can we make revealing these discussions *required by law*?" Charles will say. "The answer was to make a formal offer to the Williams executives. Once a formal offer is made, the law requires that the public be notified. Some of their executives said, 'Please don't make us an offer.' We did it anyway. Bernie forced the issue, which was his style."

Bernie's formal offer is for $2 billion—all cash. As he hoped, Williams' shareholders react by successfully pressuring management to return to the negotiating table.

Another Company Steps Over the Line

Though Bernie's bid for WilTel is by far his company's largest deal ever, this doesn't stop him from plunging into another venture. In the midst of the WilTel negotiations, Bernie makes an offer for IDB, a start-up satellite company. Since Charles is consumed with the WilTel negotiations, he assigns his new lieutenant, Scott Sullivan, to handle IDB. With each man and an investment banker by his side, Bernie jokes internally that Charles is the "A Team" and Scott is the "B Team."

Based in California, IDB is an industry pioneer known for its transmissions of Gulf War footage to television networks worldwide. Jeffrey Sudikoff, the CEO, was recently named an Entrepreneur of the Year by Ernst and Young, Merrill Lynch and *Inc.* Starting with an initial $15,000 automobile loan, Sudikoff has built the fastest-growing company in satellite transmissions, along with a personal net worth of more than $200 million. IDB holds the Number Four spot for international long-distance and its 1993 revenues exceeded $300 million. Historically, IDB's stock, like LDDS's, has traded at a premium—that is, at a greater price-to-earnings ratio than other companies in its industry—because it's considered a fast-growth company. IDB has used its stock to acquire companies.

But in May, 1994, IDB runs aground. Deloitte & Touche, its external auditor, has resigned, refusing to sign off on the company's financial statements for the first quarter. It seems that this is another case of a fast-growth company whose executives, under pressure to meet Wall Street earnings expectations, made inappropriate accounting entries. Deloitte, which doubted as much as a third of IDB's pre-tax first-quarter earnings, demanded that IDB's management correct the financial statements. But IDB refused and released results in line with Wall Street expectations, announcing "record revenue and earnings." Deloitte had no choice but to drop the engagement.

On June 1, after the controversy becomes public, IDB's stock drops 51% on trading volume of 33 million shares—the fourth heaviest volume ever traded in one day for a NASDAQ listed stock. The SEC initiates an informal inquiry, and a shareholder suit is filed alleging that executives sold $37 million worth of shares before the "improper financial practices" were exposed.

With the financial community in a panic, IDB quickly schedules an investor conference call to spin the situation. The IDB executives adamantly defend their results. Although Dan Reingold, Merrill Lynch's telecom analyst, isn't keen on LDDS, he's been hot on IDB and has a "buy" rating on the stock. Shocked, he dials into the call and peppers management with questions. "Jeffrey Sudikoff and [the company President] had the gall to rant about how unprofessional Deloitte was, insisting that IDB had done nothing wrong," Dan will later write. Sudikoff claims that Deloitte's departure was partially due to poor communication. Getting no good answers, Dan quickly downgrades the stock.

As with ATC, IDB's problems provide Bernie with negotiating leverage and an unexpected opportunity to acquire a company that has a solid customer base, market niche, and strong assets. But because of IDB's problems, LDDS performs extra due diligence, waiting on an Arthur Andersen review of IDB's revenues before making an offer.

In August, with IDB's stock tanking, Bernie seizes the opportunity and offers $936 million in stock. "If both deals [WilTel and IDB] went through," comments a portfolio manager in the *New York Times*, "LDDS could quickly become a full-fledged telephone network on a par with AT&T and MCI Communications." Even though Sudikoff is aggressively defending his company in investor calls and media interviews, IDB shareholders accept Bernie's offer. The deal provides LDDS with licenses to provide telephone service in more than 40 countries.

Some commentators temper their enthusiasm with a note of caution. "They [LDDS] have to keep . . . that earnings stream going," the CNBC analyst David Faber says. "If, one year, they don't make an acquisition, their earnings may suffer as a result, because they have to build from within, which costs a lot more money than acquiring from without."

David adds that one prominent analyst thinks "Ebbers is intent on building the company to a critical mass and then selling out." He also mentions that EDS is rumored to be interested in purchasing LDDS. LDDS stock jumps 11 percent on the news. "We don't comment on rumors," Bernie tells the press.

Adding Some Sweetener

While Scott Sullivan is working on IDB, Charles Cannada is holed up in a Tulsa conference room, on the 50th floor of the Williams building, poring over WilTel's financial records in preparation for the acquisition. The Williams executives aren't exactly happy to see him. "Things were tense," Charles will recall. Williams management continues to look for ways to undermine the sale. "How can you negotiate with people who are willing to just get up and leave the table every time you say something they don't like?" he'll say. He will have an uphill struggle until the end—since LDDS management has heard that the attorney negotiating the contract on behalf of WilTel is adept at inserting "trick" clauses favorable to his client, Charles has to scrutinize every line of a "two-foot-thick" document.

Meanwhile, Bernie's formal offer of $2 billion proves insufficient to persuade shareholders to sell, so Bernie decides to sweeten the offer to $2.5 billion cash. This one's too good to refuse. Williams shareholders vote to sell. Some analysts think Bernie overpaid, but most believe it's a coup, critical to LDDS' future survival.

Unlike AT&T, MCI, and Sprint, which garner substantial revenues from residential customers, both WilTel and LDDS concentrate on more profitable business customers, and they complement each other because there's little overlap between their services. WilTel focuses on more lucrative data products, such as bandwidth for computer data centers, while LDDS focuses on voice calls. WilTel sells primarily to wholesale and larger businesses while LDDS targets smaller businesses. Having its own network will allow LDDS to move up-market and sell to the larger businesses who don't want to deal with a carrier unless it has its own network, not to mention the tremendous cost savings of having to rely far less on leasing network fiber.

And then there are the anticipated benefits of Bernie's spending philosophy. Bringing WilTel's profit margin—currently 17–18 percent—into line with LDDS's 24 percent will add millions in earnings. WilTel's executive suite, where the company makes presentations, has a 72-inch television screen, hardwood tables, plush leather chairs, and large electronic maps displaying the fiber network. In an instant, liquid-crystal windows can be turned from clear to opaque. This place has never seen the likes of Bernie Ebbers.

First Impressions

In May, I attend my first Audit Committee meeting. I alert the committee that I'm down to one auditor, with less than two years' experience, after helping the other move to another position in the company for which he was more suited. I also mention some of our preliminary findings. It seems there's a problem with timely billing and posting of customer payments, which has resulted in unwarranted late-payment fees for customers and billing disputes.

Paul Ogden, an Arthur Andersen partner who works out of its Jackson office, sits in on Audit Committee meetings along with Mark Schoppet, an Andersen partner out of Little Rock who was recently appointed engagement partner, meaning he has overall responsibility for the audit. My team and I have the most interaction with Paul. Mark visits Jackson on occasion, but Paul is in the trenches, managing the details of the audit, and works on-site much of the year. I met Paul when I worked at SkyTel, where he also served as an external-audit partner. He's what one might expect of someone in that position—professional, conservative, and detail-oriented. He's also supportive of my group and gives feedback on our annual audit plan.

Soon, we issue our first reports, audits of billing, customer service, commissions, and credit and collections. We find that as a natural result of acquiring so many companies—all of which are entrepreneurial fast-growth enterprises—LDDS is too decentralized, full of redundant operations and systems around the country, short on standards, and weak on internal controls. Our list of audit findings is long.

For example, sales employees sometimes calculate commissions themselves, and do so manually on spreadsheets, which increases the possibility of fraud and error. Too many company employees have the ability to change billing rates and issue credits. Millions of dollars in disputed bills are sent to a problem file but never resolved.

In addition to 11 separate customer-service centers and three payment-processing departments, there are 20 inbound customer call centers. Some of these have extremely long hold times; a high number of unanswered customer calls; inadequate staffing; a lack of call-center objectives and metrics to monitor performance, and, as a result of the redundancies, too many systems for service representatives to search to address customer queries.

We make scores of recommendations to improve internal controls and the effectiveness and efficiency of operations, and propose dramatic changes in organizational structure: Automate commission calculations, and form a central department in Finance to independently calculate commissions; separate the management of sales and operations at a high level to allow increased focus; restrict system access; consolidate the number of systems, customer service centers, and call centers; and develop standard policies and procedures.

In the company's existence, neither the Audit Committee nor management have seen an Internal Audit report of comparable detail for LDDS. I worry how they will react. Will they take our recommendations seriously and be grateful for the feedback, or unhappy that we're pointing out so many areas for improvement? It's all a big question mark.

One day, I glance up from my desk and am completely startled to see Bernie standing in front of me. I've never been introduced, but I've seen him around the building and remember him well from that accounting staff meeting two years ago.

His frame takes up my entire doorway. Bernie walks around the office in blue jeans, alligator-skin cowboy boots, and turquoise jewelry, an unlit cigar clenched between his teeth. People say he's a huge Willie Nelson fan, and you can see it in his outfits. With sandy brown hair approaching shoulder length, a beard showing the first signs of gray, and piercing, steel-blue eyes, Bernie looks like he belongs on a horse, or a tractor. In fact, I'm told that's exactly where you can find him when he's back at his Brookhaven property, an hour's drive south of LDDS headquarters. "Who invented a tie and why?" he'll ask a reporter in an interview. "Why is it that certain things are expected out of certain types of jobs?"

Bernie's clearly not your typical suit-and-tie CEO, and this, coupled with his casual confidence and easy charisma, has won him a devoted following among employees.

Back in my office, Bernie's giving me a curious stare, studying me intently over his unlit cigar. It would be comical, like something from *The Good, The Bad, and The Ugly*, if his gaze wasn't so intense. He stands looking at me for several seconds in silence.

"How are you?" he says, finally, with the slightest hint of a smile.

"Fine, thanks. How are you?"

"Fine."

More silence. He did come to *my* office, didn't he? He must have some reason for darkening my doorway. What am I supposed to say, Can I help you with something? I'm starting to feel awkward, though there isn't a trace of discomfort in Bernie's face. This, I will learn, is the famous Bernie poker face—perfect for keeping people off-balance, especially if you're negotiating an acquisition.

"I just wanted to see who you were," he adds at last, and disappears down the hall before I've had a chance to reply.

What was *that* about? I wonder.

The next time I run into Charles, he explains. "Bernie wanted to know who was sending him those Internal Audit reports," he says. "He's never gotten anything like that before. I think he liked them."

WilTel Heartburn

It's September, 1994. If I can't hire many auditors, I want to hire at least well-qualified ones, but I'm struggling to find experienced telecom auditors willing to move to Mississippi for the salary I can pay.

After six months of searching, I finally find a strong candidate. Jon Mabry has audit experience with two prominent telecom companies—GTE and Alltel—and is from Mississippi. He has a degree in information systems management from the University of Maryland and a strong background in information technology auditing. Jon held a top secret SCI (Special Confidential Information) Security Clearance when he worked at the Pentagon on the President's "red telephone system"—a tremendous benefit in light of all the systems LDDS has inherited and needs to secure. He's also a former Marine—maybe bringing in the Marines will help. The snag is that he's still with Alltel in Little Rock, where Max Bobbitt, my audit committee chairman, is Chief Operating Officer. Fortunately, Max believes in the free-market concept and doesn't object to my hiring one of Alltel's top auditors.

I have to do some serious convincing to get Jon to accept—he's unsure of moving to such a small, unestablished audit group. But I convince him of the exciting opportunity to help build the department from scratch. Our first mission is to visit WilTel's headquarters in Tulsa. The deal hasn't closed, but I want to get a head start meeting executives and understanding the business.

A few days before we leave, Bernie's administrative assistant informs managers and above at headquarters that Bernie wants to meet to discuss the acquisition. I'm told it's rare for Bernie to call a meeting like this, but, then again, it's a large acquisition. For some, this acquisition may be one of an endless succession, but it's the first since I started, and it's a heady experience to be part of history in the making.

Bernie's in a great mood at the meeting. "Let's go around the room and each of you can give the group an update about what you're working on," he says. When my turn comes, I tell the group about our audit work and the people we plan to meet in Tulsa. Bernie says nothing, and his reaction is hard to read. "We're going to start having a lot more of these meetings," he promises in closing.

Soon after the meeting, Charles stops me in the hall. "Bernie is about to have a heart attack about you and Jon going to WilTel before the deal closes. You're giving him serious heartburn." Apparently my new auditor and I will be the first LDDS representatives to make the rounds at WilTel.

"Well, we can postpone our trip," I say.

"No, you don't need to postpone. Just keep it very casual when you go."

To calm Bernie's heartburn, I call the WilTel employee coordinating our trip and ask her to keep our visit informal. When Jon and I arrive, however, we find our visit to be anything but casual. We're scheduled for back-to-back meetings with WilTel's most senior executives, including their CEO. Everywhere we go, the red carpet comes out. Executives eagerly explain his or her department's role with PowerPoint presentations. Some hand me their resumes, asking if I will pass along a good word. Some groups video-conference employees from around the country.

"What's going on?" Jon asks me, dumbfounded as to why all the top brass is putting on such a dog-and-pony show for two auditors.

"I don't know! This is crazy. So much for a casual visit."

We get our answer when we return to Mississippi. Apparently, Bernie led the WilTel folks to believe that we were some kind of reconnaissance team, sent at his behest. He must have gotten over his heartburn.

Splitting duties has enabled Charles and Scott to close the IDB and WilTel purchases mere days apart—the IDB deal the last week in December, 1994, and WilTel the first week of January, 1995. Though his legal troubles continue, IDB's Jeffrey Sudikoff expresses excitement at becoming a LDDS shareholder.

But within three years, he and the company's president will be indicted on 19 counts of IDB-related securities fraud, insider trading, and failing to disclose stock trades to the SEC. The indictment will allege that the two executives falsely inflated IDB's revenue; altered documents to make it appear that a potential sale to British Telecom had already occurred; and dumped their stock for millions in profits while having knowledge of the company's woes. Government prosecutors will eventually drop some of the fraud charges and opt to settle the insider-trading case. Sudikoff will plead guilty to the count of not disclosing stock trades to the SEC and to two counts of insider trading. He will receive a sentence of one year in a minimum-security prison, three years' supervised release, and a fine of $3 million. The president will plead guilty to one count of securities fraud and receive three years' probation, a fine of $250,000, and be required to perform 500 hours of community service.

CHAPTER 10

Nowhere to Go But Up

Bernie and his management team are acting on many of the recommendations in our first audit reports. The company is forming a group in Finance to independently calculate commissions and consolidating from 11 to 2 customer-service centers for greater efficiency, economies of scale, and standardization of procedures. He's even going with the two locations we recommended—Tulsa and San Antonio. Two Senior Vice-Presidents—Diana Day and Steve Dobel—have been managing sales and customer service together, splitting the country between them. Now, Steve will oversee sales, and Diana the company's customer centers. They'll both continue to report directly to Bernie. (LDDS still doesn't have a COO.) One recommendation that management did not heed was the formation of a company-wide integration team to help absorb new acquisitions. Bernie will continue requiring executives to integrate the departments within their chains of command. I'm disappointed, but also excited that most of our advice is being so well received.

Based on our Internal Audit recommendations, Bernie's decided to bring in a consulting firm to help standardize procedures and consolidate the centers. He's asked me to give my opinion to Diana and Steve on which firm to select. I'm encouraged—I've been with the company for less than a year and the CEO is personally asking me to work on a high-profile project. I'm flying on the corporate jet for the first time, accompanying Diana and Steve to evaluate consultants and visit some of the recently acquired WilTel customer service centers.

The meetings have gone well, and I like working with Diana and Steve, but I sense an underlying tension between them. Every company has its politics. At LDDS, I hear that Diana has a great deal of influence with Bernie. One of the first employees hired by Bernie, she's the only female executive reporting directly to him. "Be careful with Diana," Steve whispers on the plane ride home. "You don't want to get on her bad side. She has Bernie's ear." I note the comment, but I like Diana. She has complimented audit's work, and we get along. "Bernie respects the hell out of you," she once told me. "He thinks you're smart."

Steve is complimentary, too. "You just need to watch and pick your spot in the Company," he tells me, meaning that I could translate success at Internal Audit into a more prominent position at the company. But I like the flexibility and relative independence of my department.

Steve will encourage me throughout my career, and like Charles Cannada, provide me with a glimpse into the workings of Bernie's inner circle. A New Yorker raised in the Bronx, Steve never imagined he would one day come to call Mississippi home. He'd worked only six months for ATC when LDDS purchased it. Before the acquisition even closed, Bernie invited Steve to fly with him on the corporate jet from Florida, where ATC was headquartered, to Jackson, so they could get to know each other.

This was an important meeting. Bernie was considering Steve for a top sales and marketing position. Having never met Bernie, Steve put on his finest Brooks Brothers pinstriped suit, selected the perfect red-and-white tie to contrast, and sported his best pair of tasseled shoes. "I was shocked when I arrived at the Florida airport to find Bernie wearing jeans and boots. I thought—This guy with a beard and boots actually runs the company?" Steve had previously worked at Sprint, where he reported to the President and liaised between Corporate and the sales and marketing groups. "I was used to working with the Sprint executives who dressed formally, ate at fine restaurants and took limos wherever they went."

"It looked like we had landed in the middle of nowhere," Steve will recall of their flight into a small county airport in Madison, Mississippi. "I could see the heat rising from the concrete. There were fields and bales of hay everywhere. I was wondering where in the world we were, and then Bernie said, 'We're very close to corporate headquarters.' I thought, What kind of operation is he running here? I looked around and didn't see any drivers, so I asked Bernie where the limo was. 'There are no drivers. Just throw your luggage in the back of my truck,' Bernie told me, pointing to an old pick-up." Steve followed the instructions, threw his brand-new Hartmann luggage in the open truck bed and stepped into the cab. "We drove down the street listening to Willie Nelson. This was so far out of my realm of experience." That evening, Bernie took Steve to dinner at Ticos Steak House, a favorite among locals, where they talked until midnight. "My opinion of Bernie began to change. I realized that this man knew what he was talking about" Steve bought a pair of jeans and moved his family to Mississippi.

Diana, Steve, and I agree on the consulting firm we like best, a company from the Northeast that will facilitate by bringing LDDS employees—who know their own department's issues better than anyone—on-site to help steer toward solutions. We've visited the consultant for a pilot session, and come away impressed. Diana and Steve have asked me to collaborate on a presentation to recommend engaging this firm to Bernie. "Steve and I will each present a part, but we want you to present three of the five parts," Diana says, "Bernie will listen to you." I'm flattered; this is a great opportunity.

But gradually I develop doubts about whether this is the best consulting firm for this project. In each of our sessions, the facilitators repeatedly ask LDDS staff to help design new computer screen lay-outs—for customer service, order entry, credit and collections. I start to wonder if we aren't about to be pulled into a many-phased systems-development project—in other words, a money pit. Privately, I ask one of the firm's partners what percent of the staff are in computer programming. Almost the entire staff, he tells me. I'm beginning to think we should consider other options—perhaps the consulting division of one of the "Big Eight" firms would be better able to help streamline controls, processes, and procedures.

The problem is that Diana is fired up about this company. This is a management decision, but I want to make my best recommendation. I decide to call Steve for advice. After hearing me out, he agrees that we need to look for another firm. "I'll talk to Diana," he says.

Steve is going to be out for several days, for back surgery. But he calls me the next day, just minutes before being wheeled into the operating room. "I'm sorry, Cynthia," he says. "Diana doesn't agree with us."

"I understand. Just focus on getting well. I'll call and talk to her."

Diana doesn't seem happy to hear my opinion, but she's cordial. She invites me to sit in on the presentation, regardless. I'm disappointed not to have the opportunity to present to Bernie, but I feel obligated to stick to my honest opinion. Bernie, WilTel's CEO Roy Wilkens, and I listen to the presentation. I wait for Bernie to ask what I think, but he never does. Ultimately, LDDS hires the consultants.

I've benchmarked our internal audit practices against other companies as well as guidance and industry data provided by the Institute of Internal Audit. Jon and I have worked hard to develop policies and procedures, an internal audit charter signed by the Audit Committee, and an annual risk-based audit plan. The Audit Committee approves the plan and any changes to it, and key audit issues and recommendations are presented at Audit Committee Meetings to the Committee and partners from Arthur Andersen, the public accounting firm that audits LDDS's financial statements.

I have to convince executive management and the audit committee to allow me to hire more internal auditors. Of course, this will cost more, but the benefits will outweigh the expense. I've recommended to the Audit Committee that we hire at least five more auditors. The company needs to standardize policies and procedures, and confront problems with internal controls, organizational structure, and systems. Max agrees to bring it up with Bernie.

I also revisit my earlier concern about an independent reporting structure, since my boss, Mike Cipicchio, oversees departments my group audits. Max and Charles eventually agree—from now on, Internal Audit will report administratively to Charles, elevating its role in the company. Hopefully, I haven't ruffled too many feathers. It did feel a bit awkward forcing the issue, but I have no doubt this is best for the company.

Max's other news isn't so great—no more auditors, Bernie says. I'm surprised, considering how positive Bernie's feedback has been. For now, I guess I'll encourage my team to put in extra hours, just until we prove our value to management. If we can issue a few more strong audit reports, I'm sure Bernie will change his mind.

At least we're not the only ones in the office at night. It's not just my group that has trouble getting approval to hire more staff. LDDS is known as having one of the lowest overheads in the industry, and employees often react with disbelief at the staff size in acquired companies: "Can you believe they have such a large number of people doing the job it takes only a few of us to do here?" is a typical watercooler comment. Less staff means longer hours—60-hour weeks are common. With all the acquisitions, many employees are burning the candle at both ends just to keep up.

It's early 1995. Charles and Scott Sullivan, the assistant treasurer who also reports to Charles, drop by my office. Charles rarely stops by, and Scott has never been in, even though his office is next door. "I want to focus on acquisitions and spend more time with my family," Charles says, "so Scott's going to take over as CFO." The constant acquisitions on top of regular CFO duties has become more than he wants to manage. The incredible stress of the hostile WilTel takeover was the final straw. Scott is silent. I'm shocked.

I don't know Scott well. He's very dedicated and focused on his career, often working late into the night. I speak to him occasionally in passing. He's always polite but very serious, too busy for small talk. Like many accountants, he seems introspective, something to get used to after Charles' off-the-scales sociability. Within the company, Scott is highly regarded for his financial skills. People say he's the fair-haired boy, an up-and-coming star in Bernie's good graces.

"You'll keep reporting to me," Charles says. "Nobody wanted to take you, so I guess I'm stuck with you." I know he's joking, but I also know there's truth in jest. Well, I'd rather keep reporting to Charles anyway. We have a good rapport, and I've always felt that he tries to look out for Internal Audit.

Shortly after Scott's promotion, Charles summons me to his office for my own evaluation. I'm looking forward to the meeting. Charles knows that I'm working to move to the Director level so that I can continue to grow the department, hire more experienced auditors, and promote my staff, so I sit across from him with great anticipation.

"You're not going to get promoted," he says, forthright as usual. "You've fallen out of favor with Bernie. You were up here and now you're down here." Charles raises his hand high and then brings it low. At first I think he's joking, but I see he's serious. I'm so stunned that I can't hide my disappointment. "Cynthia, I'm sorry," Charles says sympathetically.

"Why have I fallen out of favor?" I ask, trying to regain my composure.

"Diana's mad at you because you disagreed with her decision about which consultant should be hired. She said something to Bernie. And Max told Bernie you came to the Audit Committee asking to hire more staff. Bernie thinks you went behind his back."

"I didn't go behind Bernie's back to the Audit Committee. I also told you I thought we needed to hire more staff. And Bernie asked for my opinion on the consultants. Should I talk to him?" I ask.

"No, you just need to lay low and let some time pass," Charles advises.

I've worked so hard over the past year. And what if Jon, my audit supervisor, who was counting on a promotion to Manager when I moved to Director, quits? How can Bernie go from singing our praises and accepting our recommendations to exiling us just for giving honest advice? Perhaps my views were misrepresented to him?

Sometimes, people don't want an opposing view. Once, at PriceWaterhouse I gave my opinion on an issue being discussed by the audit team. At the end of the day, the senior auditor on the engagement asked me to walk out to the parking lot with him.

"You don't know your place," he said. "You need to learn your place."

"But I was just giving you my opinion," I said.

"If I ask for your opinion, then you can give it, but otherwise you need to learn your place."

Finally, I pull myself together and walk out of Charles' office. I decide to take his advice—he's been at this company far longer than I and has my interest at heart. I guess I'll let the dust settle and press forward.

I run into Steve Dobel—the Senior Vice President who I worked with to find a consultant—shortly afterward. "I told you to be careful with Diana," he reminds me. "Bernie thinks you're not a team player. He says he needs team players."

While my team has fallen out of favor, the men running LDDS have their minds on other things, like deals and meeting heads of state. Charles, Bernie, Scott and five board members are flying to Cuba to meet Fidel Castro and celebrate the opening of telecommunications with the country. LDDS will be one of the few companies servicing the island.

Each of the eight executives is driven to a separate house in an upscale neighborhood, equipped with a kitchen and staff. "It was a place that seemed to be frozen in time," Charles will say. "The cars, houses, appliances, all looked like what my parents had in the 1950s."

In the evening, the LDDS representatives attend a celebration. "At midnight, Castro shows up," Charles continues. The LDDS executives are invited to a small room where they sit in a circle alongside Fidel Castro and several in his entourage, talk, have drinks, and smoke the finest

Cuban cigars. Most of the men sit and listen as billionaire Jon Kluge and Castro discuss building hotels and expanding tourism.

It's been a long night. The men have spent hours traveling earlier in the day, and by 2:00 a.m. everyone is fading. The room is getting hot and smoky. The small air-conditioning window unit keeps freezing up and has to be re-started. Finally, one of the board members stands, mumbles something indiscernible, and passes out cold, hitting the floor at Castro's feet. The men jump in alarm and quickly move him to a couch. Doctors rush into the room to help. Within minutes he comes to. "When he opened his eyes, Fidel Castro was only a few inches from his face peering down at him," Charles will recall. The man's fine, but the evening comes to a close.

It's May, 1995. With its own network, an international presence, and an expanded product line, LDDS has come a long way from its humble origins. The name itself—Long Distance Discount Services—no longer seems to fit, and, in any case, management wants to lose the down-market discount-reseller image. Roy Wilkens, the former CEO of WilTel, recommends a consultant to help select a new name, but, just like that brainstorm at a Hattiesburg diner 12 years before, the initial ideas aren't very good.

"The consultant threw out the most lame names," Charles will say. "His best idea was to use the name Zeus. He wanted to use a picture of an old man with a long beard." But the consultant does mention that LDDS owns the rights to WorldCom, a name IDB occasionally used for its international operations, but remote enough to avoid association with IDB's pre-LDDS scandals.

That's the name that management eventually selects. Later in the year, the company unveils a marquee spokesperson. Bernie goes back to his old-time passion for basketball when he signs on one of the hottest sports figures in the world—Michael Jordan. Bernie's never been a big believer in spending money on advertising and entices the NBA star with the same currency he's used on telecom execs all across America: WorldCom stock. "Michael Jordan came and asked to be a part of our company," Bernie says. "(We told him) 'We can't afford you, but if you want to be paid on the basis of how the company performs, we'll be glad to have you.'"

Michael is an instant believer: "As someone who knows what it takes to win and understands the merits of teamwork, I'm convinced that LDDS WorldCom has the people and resources to be a leader in the telecommunications industry," he says in a press release. Ads featuring Michael using WorldCom phone service everywhere he goes—car, office, locker room—and even cold-calling to sign up new customers, air during the 1996 NBA playoffs. They're viewed by an estimated 50 million households.

Jon, my internal audit supervisor, is growing increasingly frustrated that we can't hire more staff, and that his promotion is being held up by mine. After months of searching, we finally hired an information technology auditor, but within a few months she returned to her old employer. She had come from an 8-to-5 job and a slower-paced work environment with an insurance company. The heavy workload, long hours, and frenetic pace of WorldCom proved unappealing. All I got out of that deal was an ugly letter from her boss telling me that I had taken away his only systems auditor, and that if I kept this up, my reputation would be ruined in the Jackson audit community. (The free-market concept doesn't always win if the market is in a relatively small city like Jackson.)

Soon after, our only other staff-level auditor also decides to leave. He encourages Jon, my sole remaining colleague, to follow: "Cynthia's not going to be able to hire more staff, and they'll never promote her," he tells him, according to Jon, who's now wondering if he should have stayed at his previous company. It's hard to blame them. I myself lie awake at night wondering if I should have stayed at SkyTel.

But at some point, perseverance wins out. I don't want to just quit. I've worked too hard, and I still feel confident that if I can just get a little support, I can build a team of well-qualified auditors who can add value to this company.

I decide to promote Jon to Manager regardless of my position. He deserves it and it's unfair to penalize him. Jon's grateful. "We're two managers with no staff to manage," he says, laughing ruefully. With some pushing from Charles, I finally get approval to increase my staff size to three. With the salary I'm able to pay, it's tough to find senior-level auditors, so we'll hire someone smart whom we can train. Eventually we do find two strong candidates.

But now my staff and I are facing a new challenge: Though Bernie initially seemed to appreciate the value of internal controls, it looks like we have to convey their importance all over again. This executive team consists of insatiable entrepreneurs, always focused on the next acquisition, the stock price, and whether or not they'll meet Wall Street's expectations. Internal controls and my department aren't exactly high on their priority list. They're all about the deal. Each time we issue a report, Jon says the same thing: "I think this one will do it. With all the internal control issues in this report, it's going to change their minds." But eventually, we realize we're being naive.

Charles is in favor of promoting me and growing the department, but he can only influence Bernie's opinion so much, and Bernie's about to get even more irritated with me than before. In a presentation I recently gave to Charles and Scott, I mentioned all the internal control problems my department has identified—certainly a typical internal audit topic. Since Bernie hadn't attended, I dropped a copy in his inbox.

Soon, I get a call from Charles. "Bernie wants to see you in the conference room right now," he says.

For some reason, Scott has been called to the meeting as well, and the three of us wait for Bernie. I'm nervous. This isn't going to be good. When Bernie arrives, he sits at the head of the table. "What are these comments you've put in here about internal controls?!" he says, agitated. His face is blood-red. I've never seen him so upset.

"I'm sorry, I'm not trying to make you mad," I respond. "This just talks about internal control weaknesses we've seen based on our audit work." Bernie thinks my wording is harsh. He seems to be taking our issues and recommendations personally.

"What if this ends up on the street?" he says, brandishing the papers in the air. I try to explain that these are routine internal presentations. All companies have areas in which operational processes and controls need to be strengthened. I don't know if he's having a bad day, or he's just showing me his moody side. Maybe this has to do with my falling out of favor over that consulting decision, or he doesn't like someone pointing out problems with the company he's built. It's a guess, though one thing's for certain: Bernie doesn't understand what Internal Audit does. But it's equally obvious that now is not the time to educate him. Charles and Scott aren't saying anything. Bernie calms down by the time he walks out, but I'm bending my pen clip back and forth until it finally snaps.

"Have you ever seen him get like that before?" I ask Charles.

"That's just Bernie," Charles says.

"Yeah, that's Bernie," Scott reiterates.

Several days later, I see Charles in the hall. "Bernie doesn't want you to use the words "internal controls" in any more of your audit reports," he says. "It aggravates him."

"What do you mean it aggravates him? We have to use the words 'internal controls.' Reviewing internal controls is part of what we do."

"Well, he doesn't understand what 'internal controls' mean. You'll have to find another word that gets the same point across."

Asking internal auditors not to use the words "internal controls" is like asking a physician not to use the word "prescription." Though work increases with each acquisition, I can't hire the auditors I need, and now I'm not supposed to refer to a central aspect of my job. I learned from Terri Hudson, my boss at SkyTel, that tension with management sometimes was inevitable for an internal auditor, but WorldCom and its CEO are proving to be more of a challenge than I ever anticipated.

Usually, I develop a rapport with people quickly, but Bernie is inscrutable. Apparently circumspect and private, he seems uncomfortable making small talk. But when he's not silent, he's shooting at your feet to make you dance. As a reporter who interviewed Bernie will write, "It can be hard to know sometimes whether Mr. Ebbers is extremely confident, a touch myopic or just self-conscious." Maybe he doesn't want to be fully known. Maybe he depends on the mystique when he's negotiating.

Even some of Bernie's closest friends find him perplexing. "Bernie was a paradox," David Singleton, one of LDDS's founders, will recall. "He wore the clothes of a good old boy. And he kind of wanted to be one of the good old boys. But . . . he was always somewhat confrontational, and in-your-face, compared to most of us in the Deep South . . . and that created some problems for him sometimes. Conversely, he could be extremely compassionate. I've seen him in church, not infrequently, just weep. And he is very caring of anyone he would perceive to be an underdog, while on the other hand, if he . . . smelled competition, he became another person. He could be rude. In competition, he is fierce and, in a business sense, he'll cut your heart out. I know of times in merger situations where it would come down to the eleventh hour of negotiation and he'd close the book, get up and walk out of the room. And leave the other party just sitting there. He usually won in those cases."

For now, Charles, part of Bernie's inner circle, is my guide to the do's and dont's of interacting with Bernie. "Don't ever go in to meet with him on a Monday morning. He's a bear on Monday mornings," Charles counsels. "Make sure you keep your meetings brief, no more than 10 minutes. He's impatient and has a short attention span." I've learned that Bernie's legendary over-involvement in the minutiae of office life can quickly shift to impatience. As one executive will remark after seeing Bernie become fidgety during a meeting, "you just want to know what time it is, and we're telling you how to build a watch." "The closer you are to Bernie," Charles says ominously, "the greater your chances of falling out of favor. Be glad you have me as a buffer."

People ask Deborah, Bernie's administrative assistant, what kind of mood he's in before deciding whether to pay him a visit. But when Bernie summons you, usually without warning, you don't have a choice.

Two weathered floor-to-ceiling wooden doors with black wrought-iron locks—from an old Mexican church, I'm told—guard the entrance to Bernie's office. Whenever I approach, it feels as though I'm going to see the great Oz, my heart beating faster and faster. Lighten up, I told myself once. He's not going to jump across the desk at you. Now and again, I've even seen him fighting back a smile through his poker face. While Bernie supposedly keeps his pulse on the business, his desk is always immaculate. His office feels somewhat cold and sterile. It's an invitation to leave without lingering, and I take it up eagerly—I'd rather be at the dentist than called to Bernie's office.

But underneath Bernie's tough exterior is a man who can also be very generous and caring. He's often the first to help an employee in need, has paid college tuition for students struggling financially, and has given large amounts to charity without fanfare. He opens every shareholder meeting with a prayer and teaches Sunday school at First Baptist Church in Brookhaven. Some of his top executives even complain that Bernie doesn't have the heart to lay off lower-level employees who live paycheck to paycheck, often delaying staff cuts after an acquisition.

"Somebody who worked for us . . . wound up in trouble with the law," David Singleton, one of the early LDDS investors, will remember. "It was a white collar crime of some kind . . . [Bernie] led us as a board to continue to pay that salary and provide for that family because I think the guy was in for 18 months or something. It was not an extremely long sentence. But we fed that family. And that's very Bernie. Very Bernie. On the other hand, if somebody didn't perform, he would escort them out of the building."

Unlike some companies that allow only higher-level executives to participate in the stock option programs, Bernie makes sure all employees down to the entry level are able to own stock. While salaries are low compared with other companies in the industry, he wants everyone to be a shareholder.

"Bernie was smart to make everyone in the company from the secretary to the President a stockholder," Steve Dobel, head of Commercial Sales and Marketing, will say. "People wanted to work harder because they had ownership in the business." For the first five years of my employment, a period during which the company more than doubles in size, Bernie will approve end-of-year cash bonuses for every employee.

I've been following Charles' instructions to lay low with Bernie, but the strategy isn't working. So I decide to go the opposite route and call a meeting of senior executives, including Bernie, to explain internal controls. Maybe it's presumptuous of me to do so, but the only thing Bernie can do is fire me. If that happens, I'll just go back to my cold-call list. At this point, I have nowhere to go but up.

I need Charles' ok, but worry that he won't want to bother Bernie. I decide to be casual. "I'm calling a meeting with you, Scott, and Bernie to give you an update outlining what we're working on," I tell him one day in the hall.

"Okay," he says with a mischievous smile, as if he knows I'm up to something. "I'll come, and Scott may come, but you'll never get Bernie to come."

"I'll get him to come," I insist, smiling back, though I'm worried. My team coordinates with each executive's administrative assistant, setting the meeting for 8:00 a.m. one day next week. We set to practicing the presentation. Jon knows a director in the company who's developed a WorldCom-themed presentation video. "It'll liven up the presentation," Jon says. "They'll all three be impressed with it."

Bernie, Charles, and Scott think they're coming for an update, but my actual task is much bolder: To convince Bernie that internal audit departments play a critical role, and to explain internal controls. I've always preferred to let my work speak for itself. But Jon has been trying to convince me that I must change my communication style with my male superiors.

While women often view modesty as a virtue, I've observed that men are more inclined to let people know about their accomplishments. I notice that every time Jon runs into Charles in the hall, he mentions what we're working on, emphasizing why it's critical to the company. "I'm selling," he explains to me.

I wish he wouldn't brag, I think to myself sometimes. My pastor tells a story of men standing in a circle: I fell this weekend and broke my leg, one says. Oh, that's nothing, another replies: I fell from a roof once and broke both legs. Oh, that's nothing, the third chimes in: I was once in a full body cast for an entire year. And so on.

This is one of my early epiphanies about how differently men and women communicate in the workplace, and how tweaking communication style can make a difference in career success for women. In a professional setting where there are few senior positions, the greater ease with which men tend to assert themselves can negatively impact women's chances for advancement unless women learn to push beyond their natural comfort levels. "Cynthia, you've got to sell yourself and the group to these guys every chance you get," Jon often tells me. "Put on your sales hat." I take a bit of convincing, but finally agree. Selling the value of my department to the Audit Committee and executive management isn't bragging. It's the only way to make sure these executives take our work seriously.

How do I convert a subject that seems to matter little to management into something they care about, I wonder to myself. I know these executives like to think in terms of dollars and cents; I'll show them how ineffective controls can cost the company and its shareholders money and reputation.

Scott and Charles arrive on time, looking polished in their tailored suits. They must have a meeting outside the company today. I step out to call Deborah, Bernie's administrative assistant. "He hasn't made it in yet," Deborah says. "I'll send him down as soon as he gets here." I go back and try to occupy Charles and Scott, but I see they're growing antsy. I call Deborah again. "He's here, but he's on the phone," she says. I'm not sure how much longer I can hold Scott and Charles hostage. When I walk back in, everyone looks completely bored.

"You're going to have to go ahead and give the presentation without Bernie," Charles says impatiently, pointing to his watch. Although Charles may not realize it, Bernie is the primary audience. Charles and Scott both have external audit backgrounds; they know what an internal control is. Bernie's the one who needs the tutorial.

I motion Jon into the hall. "Try to keep them occupied for a few more minutes," I say. "Just go in there and talk to them. You're a talker, You'll think of something." Jon gives me a look, but then nods. He's very extroverted, and I know that if anyone can keep them going, he can. I dash upstairs to Bernie's office. For a third time, I tell Deborah what she already knows. But Bernie is still unavailable.

I return to the conference room. We've been waiting now for close to an hour. There's no choice but to go ahead without Bernie. I've gone through a part of the presentation when he finally appears, in a white jogging suit, his toes peering through his sandals, a cigar in his mouth. Word around the office is that Bernie is in a good mood when he's chomping on a cigar. We're about to put that theory to the test. All eyes are fixed on him, but he only glares around the room, quite obviously annoyed at being summoned. He slouches into a chair in the front row and gives me an unfriendly scowl.

"We'll start again," I say. Charles rolls his eyes. I feel like a preacher repeating my sermon. Lisa Smith, the new staff auditor, plays our music video, the one Jon was sure would impress. "WorldCom! VOICE! DATA! VIDEO!" blares from the speakers as company images fly back and forth across the screen. Bernie stares, unimpressed. The room feels awkward. Then, out of nervousness, Lisa accidentally hits the button again, a moment she won't live down for a while. It's "VOICE! DATA! VIDEO!" all over again, sounding even louder this time.

Lisa gives me a horrified look. The expression on Bernie's face has changed from aggravation to total disgust. "What in the hell is the purpose of this meeting?" he barks under his breath.

"I'll get to that," I say calmly. Fortunately, our first PowerPoint slide reads "Purpose." "The purpose of the meeting is to give you an update on what we're working on and what we have planned for the rest of the year." After only a few minutes, I can see Charles in the back of the room rolling his hands over each other and pointing to his watch, trying to speed me up.

Charles is trying to save me from Bernie, but I don't want to be saved. Charles treats me a bit like his kid sister. He's always the first to come to my defense. It's great to know I have his support, but sometimes I don't want to be the kid sister. I'd rather just sink or swim on my own. I smile at

Charles but go on speaking as if he weren't there. He'll have to come up with a giant hook and sound the gong if he wants me to stop. I haven't yet come to one of my main points, defining for Bernie what an internal control is and why it's important.

Internal controls are critical to a company's well-being, but I can see how non-auditors might find the details a bit dry. I try to explain as simply as I can that internal controls help the company and management meet its objectives, and even provide some simple examples. For instance, authorization rules can prevent abuse by requiring higher levels of management approval for larger expenditures. Segregation of duties is another example—the person who deposits cash for the company shouldn't be the one reconciling the bank statement.

There are two ways to audit internal controls. We can merely identify the problem, or, for missing or weak key controls, we can also try to quantify the financial impact, so executives can easily envision the potential loss to the company.

Jon and I have chosen the latter approach. One example relates to customer billing. We're under-billing customers. There are inadequate controls to ensure the WorldCom network "highways" that transport customer phone calls are properly flagged to bill customers. We believe that the company is missing out on millions of dollars. ($8 million annually, in fact, as our final testing concludes.)

Jon uses a simple analogy to help Bernie understand. "Think of the telecom switches [equipment that captures information about customer phone calls for billing] as cash registers. If you don't have strong controls, people can walk into the store and steal money from the registers." As I continue, Bernie's mood seems to be softening. He's sitting more upright, the scowl is gone, and he's asking questions about our testing. He seems intrigued.

Finally, I finish. We survived. "I need to get back to work," Charles says, standing. Scott follows. But, to everyone's surprise, Bernie remains seated. "You can leave if you want to, but I'm staying," he says, cocking his head toward them. Charles and Scott walk out, and Bernie starts sharing stories about the old days, when he worked in the garment industry in the small town of Brookhaven, Mississippi, and the process improvements he put in place.

Maybe we've finally been able to translate internal controls and internal audit into something Bernie can understand. Maybe he just saw three young people trying hard. But whatever the reason, something clicks. The day feels like a turning point, and, in fact, many of the controls we recommended will be put in place.

Feeling like I've opened a line of communication, I invite Bernie to the next Audit Committee meeting, whose meetings he never attends. If Bernie really has the impression that I go to the Audit Committee behind his back, I want him to come and hear me firsthand. I don't want other people speaking to Bernie for me anymore. Something has obviously been misrepresented. I want to speak for myself.

"I invited Bernie to the meeting," I tell Charles and Scott, as we sit waiting for the Audit Committee meeting to get started. They both chuckle. "He's not going to come to an Audit Committee meeting," Charles says just before Bernie strolls through the door. He listens and even makes a few comments, though it will be the first and last Audit Committee meeting he attends.

CHAPTER II

A New Era

Anyone in this industry who dismisses Bernie Ebbers will find him eating their lunch.

—Jack Grubman

The Telecom Act is the legislative equivalent of Lindbergh's crossing the Atlantic.

—Charles Lee, GTE Chairman and CEO

We only have 5 percent of the market, so we're kind of like a gnat on an elephant's back. A gnat on steroids.

—Bernie Ebbers

It's January, 1996. Congress is on a deregulation roll. Electricity has already been deregulated and banking is soon to come, but now it's the telecommunication industry's turn to open markets for competition.

Since AT&T's break up in 1984, it has been illegal for long-distance companies to sell local phone service and vice versa. But Congress is considering a revolutionary telecom act to open the markets for greater competition. If the new bill passes, everything will be up for grabs. Long-distance companies will be able to sell local service, and, after meeting certain requirements, local phone companies will be able to offer long distance service.

Bills to deregulate the telecom industry have been put forward before, and died in committee, but this time is different. The explosive possibilities of the Internet are changing everything. Vice President Al Gore is throwing his weight behind the bill, touting something called an "information superhighway." If companies can converge local, long distance, data, and Internet networks together in an end-to-end seamless fiber-optic highway, the sky will be the limit in terms of new technology, products, and services. One-stop shopping is quickly becoming the new buzz phrase conveying the vision of customers one day buying local, long distance, wireless, data, and Internet from a single company.

Local and long-distance companies are battling it out in Washington, lobbying Congress for more favorable wordings of the bill. Because the local Bell companies have near-monopolies in each of their markets and own the "last mile"—the on- and off-ramps that originate and terminate phone calls into the customer's home or business—the long-distance companies fear they will be the long-term losers of this bill. The argument is that since the Bells "control" the last mile, they "control" the customer, and would have a much easier time selling customers "bundled" local and long-distance service. Meanwhile, it would be tremendously expensive for long-distance companies to build their own last miles, running fiber into endless homes and businesses. But the local companies insist it will be just as hard for them to break into the long-distance market.

Bernie, who serves as president of CompTel, a telecom association, is camped out in Washington, pulling late nights and ordering pizza as he and others in the group compose legislative language favoring long distance for Congress to consider. Just before the bill goes to the floor for a vote, AT&T even sends groups of employees to Washington to protest the bill in its current form. It's all to no avail. Long-distance players will get some changes, but, in the end, the bill passes with language many believe favors the Baby Bells.

On February 8, President Bill Clinton signs the Telecom Act of 1996 into law, transforming a once-stodgy industry into the hottest game in town. The land grab is about to begin. I got a taste of the capital market mania of the 1980s—leveraged buyouts (LBOs)—when, as a young auditor, I worked on the RJR Nabisco engagement. But the 1980s will have nothing on the 1990s capital-market mania I'm about to witness.

The next few years will be marked by record-breaking mega-mergers, initial public offerings with stock prices soaring to astronomical levels often on the first day of trading, and debt offerings on an unprecedented scale. Telecom start-ups with hastily composed business plans will spend billions to go toe to toe with established players. And my company will be center-stage.

In executive halls across the country, planners are trying to determine their companies' next plays and anticipate competitor strategy. Many executives believe the telecom wars could end with only a few winners sharing the entire market, so they're antsy to make their moves. But so little is clear about how all this will play out that they don't know which way to turn out of the gate. One wrong move and they could be out of the game altogether.

While analysts agree that only a few large players will be left standing, there's disagreement on which—the new start-ups, the established long-distance companies, the seven Baby Bells, the cable companies? Should long-distance companies try to break into the local market on their own, or form partnerships, or merge? And if so, then with a Baby Bell, a cable company, a European telecom, or one of the few U.S. start-ups selling local service?

True to form, the two most prominent telecom stock analysts—Dan Reingold of Merrill Lynch and Jack Grubman, now at Salomon Brothers—have completely different views. Dan believes the Baby Bells will be the winners, and that within seven years, they'll command 25% of the $70 billion long-distance market. But Jack refers to analysts who recommend the Baby Bells as "starry-eyed," "bull-headed," and "nuts." He recommends that investors buy stock in WorldCom and hot-shot telecom start-ups that are building out state-of-the-art networks to compete with the established players. While Dan says the Baby Bells will be quick studies in long distance, Jack thinks otherwise. Who is an investor to believe? The telecom debate digresses into a personality war. "I bet you that in college, Dan was prepared for every test, while I was cramming at the last minute," Jack tells a reporter. "Before making conclusions, I try to do the work," Dan retorts.

While others are still mulling over the implications of the new law, Bernie charges into action and shocks the market by announcing, on the same day that the Act is signed, landmark partnerships with GTE and Ameritech, two of the country's largest local telephone companies, who will now resell WorldCom long distance just as WorldCom once did. How did Bernie beat the Big Three for the business, everyone wants to know?! WorldCom may be the fourth-largest long-distance carrier in the country, but it's still a small fish compared to AT&T, MCI, and Sprint.

Head of the Class

> [WorldCom] now sits alone at the head of a class of hundreds of long-distance concerns created since the breakup of AT&T.
>
> —*Wall Street Journal*

It's February 29, 1996. Three weeks after the Telecom Act is signed, the *Wall Street Journal* reports that out of a thousand tracked companies WorldCom delivered the highest average return to shareholders over the past decade. The *Journal* notes Bernie's "dumb-as-a-fox approach." But "don't let the toothpick and aw-shucks fool you," Jack Grubman tells the paper about the pickup-driving exec.

Bernie is concerned that the (Jackson, Mississippi) *Clarion-Ledger* is not equally upbeat. He believes the hometown paper stints on news favorable to WorldCom. John Palmer, the chairman of SkyTel, has complained about the same thing in a letter to the editor, and Bernie seconds him:

> I strongly concur with John Palmer's comments in the March 4 [1996] "Readers' Views" section pointing out the *Clarion-Ledger*'s policy of downplaying or totally ignoring positive business news in deference to negative reporting or conflict-oriented coverage. An example of this policy was evidenced as recently as last week when the *Clarion-Ledger* failed to cover a prominent national news item about: WorldCom, Inc. On Feb. 29, the *Wall Street Journal* ran a profile of WorldCom, Inc., in its "Shareholder Scoreboard" section, naming the Jackson-based company as the "Best 10-Year Performer" based on rate of return on investment. Until Thursday [March 7], the *Clarion-Ledger* had not covered

this story about one of Jackson's largest and most successful companies. Ironically, though, the Tulsa *World* included coverage of the *Wall Street Journal* ranking on the front page of its March 2 business section. It is indeed unfortunate and implausible that our local newspaper would fail to support a successful, home-grown company's attempts to keep its corporate headquarters in Jackson. I urge the *Clarion-Ledger* to immediately review its policy relating to local business news and do all it can journalistically to make Jackson and Mississippi good places to do business. We all benefit when that occurs!

—Bernard J. Ebbers

Investors like Bernie's focus on shareholder returns. "Our goal is not to capture market share or be global," Bernie says, "Our goal is to be the No. 1 stock on Wall Street." He's creating a new generation of millionaires. According to a presentation Bernie will deliver in July, a $100 investment in 1989 in AT&T would now be worth $140; in MCI—$131; in Sprint—$142; and in WorldCom—$2,473.

In March, WorldCom becomes part of the S&P 500. In May, Bernie is No. 54 on a *Forbes* list of 800 of "Corporate America's Most Powerful People." And it's WorldCom that's just been asked to step in at the last minute and solve an urgent telecommunications problem at a resort on Egypt's Red Sea coast where President Bill Clinton and 30 world leaders are meeting in a "Summit of the Peacemakers." WorldCom, through its new subsidiary IDB, is supplying two "flyaway" satellite earth stations that will be used for telephone, fax, and computer connections. IDB has installed flyaway stations after catastrophic events such as the Oklahoma City bombing, the San Francisco earthquake, and Hurricane Andrew. Within 72 hours, WorldCom packs eight tons of equipment and works through the logistical roadblocks to ship it from Dallas, where IDB is located, through New York and the United Kingdom to Cairo. The round-the-clock work pays off and the problem is solved.

There are rumors that Bernie will run for Governor of Mississippi. "I don't rule anything out," he tells the local paper. But the article questioned whether Bernie, who seems shy in the spotlight and doesn't like his picture taken, will make a good political candidate.

Speculation about a buyout continues as well. "Let's be honest about it," Bernie tells the *Clarion-Ledger* when asked if he would stick around after an acquisition. "People who have been at the apex of a business are not going to want to be number two."

Though he's squarely in the limelight, Bernie is as unpredictable as ever, tossing out the offbeat comments for which he's notorious. "We have never had an approach," he tells the *Clarion-Ledger*. "It would be fun to have one. To some degree we are a victim of our own success."

But savvy readers know better. WorldCom hasn't moved to the head of the class without a plan. There's a smart strategy, and it's very much set and driven by Bernie himself. First, Bernie reduced cost per phone call by rolling up resellers in the same geographic region. Then, he expanded from the South across the country by buying up companies with operations in contiguous states. He focused on small business customers, a niche mostly ignored by large competitors, and avoided residential customers, who frequently switch carriers and are less profitable due to heavy marketing costs and unrelenting price wars between AT&T, Sprint, and MCI. In the early years, he employed a very decentralized management style, allowing for a more personal customer experience. He's kept sales, general and administrative costs the lowest in the industry by running a no-frills operation, offering lower salaries supplemented by stock options, and minimizing advertising. Once he assembled a national customer base, he reduced costs further by buying WilTel's state-of-the-art fiber network. And he's expanded products sold to include not just voice phone calls but more profitable data transmission and international. Bernie may be employing a back-of-the-envelope strategy, again avoiding an expense by doing without a team of planners and analysts, but it certainly is a strategy. And no one can argue its success so far.

Acquisition, a key part of his strategy, has grown WorldCom much faster than internal evolution would have. So far, Bernie's purchased only those companies that deliver immediately, adding to earnings per share in the first year. Bernie "realized long ago," Jack Grubman tells the *Wall Street Journal*, "that acquisition was not a dirty word."

Bernie is the first to admit he doesn't have technical telecom or financial training—"people that have problems admitting what they don't know are people who get in a world of trouble," he says—and has surrounded himself with lieutenants he believes have the skills he lacks. ("You don't have to be very smart to be smarter than Bernie Ebbers," he'll tell an interviewer.) "I'm the coach," he will explain to the *New York Times*. "I'm not the point guard who shoots the ball."

When the *Times* reporter asks Bernie a marketing question, Bernie throws the ball to WorldCom's marketing officer. When asked for financial details, Bernie calls Scott. "Almost instantly, Scott D. Sullivan, WorldCom's Chief Financial Officer, appeared through the galley door to provide a detailed answer."

Bernie is the savvy dealmaker and Scott is the numbers guy. Because they often give presentations together, Wall Street will dub them "The Scott and Bernie Show." In March, 1996, the 34-year-old Scott, whose prominence has been rising since Charles decided to take a lesser role, is appointed to WorldCom's Board of Directors, a bone of contention for Charles, who will never be appointed to the board. Wall Street will come to see Scott as a financial wizard and a straight shooter. He has prodigious recall when it comes to WorldCom statistics. "He is one of the brightest CFOs I have ever met," telecom analyst Tony Ferrugia will tell *CFO* magazine. "He just gets it."

Bernie has transformed WorldCom into a high-profile company with the highest ten-year returns using the Breckenridge Group, the small regional investment bank out of Atlanta. What Bernie lacks is a strong bond to the Wall Street investment banks. But that is about to change, thanks to Jack Grubman.

Jack is fast becoming one of the most respected telecom analysts on Wall Street—soon to be #1 in *Institutional Investor*'s coveted rankings. But his activities range far beyond stock analysis. Executives across the industry consult him on their strategies of attack as telecom deregulates and reporters call him for quotes. He has assembled a far-reaching network of contacts.

Jack recently moved from PaineWebber to Salomon Brothers, another Wall Street investment bank. When Salomon Brothers wanted to recruit Jack to become a stock analyst, he was approached not by the head of research, who independently manages the analysts, but by Eduardo Mestre, the head of investment banking. Investment banks compete fiercely to win business from companies undergoing IPOs, mergers, and acquisitions, and analyst research reports are playing increasing roles in winning deals, threatening the firewall that must exist between analysts and investment bankers to protect investor interest. If a public company's management believes an investment bank's analyst will be a cheerleader for its stock, it may be more likely to hire the investment-banking side of the company for deals, an arrangement that would provide the bank with millions in fees.

Meeting Jack at the prestigious Yale Club in midtown Manhattan, Eduardo offers him the lead telecom analyst position and a multimillion dollar salary, with the opportunity for more if he delivers on investment banking.

Jack scales the firewall and never looks back. Soon after joining Salomon, Jack starts courting Bernie for investment-banking business, but so far, Bernie is resisting out of a sense of loyalty to the Breckenridge Group. Breckenridge was there from the beginning, when the big Wall Street firms wouldn't give WorldCom the time of day.

Jack isn't about to give up on Bernie. He's an investment banker's dream—a perpetual acquirer who regularly doles out millions in investment banking fees in an industry about to go through an astounding number of record-breaking mega-mergers.

The Crown Jewel

Behind the scenes, Jack is brokering a meeting between Bernie and another executive with whom he's worked closely, Jim Crowe, the CEO of Metropolitan Fiber Systems (MFS), an Omaha, Nebraska–based company that is the Baby Bells' leading competitor selling local service. WorldCom and MFS are two of Jack's favorite stock picks, and now he's advising Bernie to leap ahead of the competition by purchasing MFS. If the deal goes through, Jack will be credited with making millions in banking fees for Salomon.

WorldCom owns the "highways" that carry phone calls across the country, but not the "last mile," which is owned by the local phone companies. MFS—born after Jim Crowe, who was previously with an Omaha construction company, talked management into laying fiber-optic cable—has built these "ramps" in cities across the States and Europe.

Bernie and Scott meet with Jim on Bernie's yacht. Initially, Bernie is unimpressed. After many years in the business, MFS is still unprofitable, largely because of its massive initial investment to lay cable. "These guys don't know how to run a company," Bernie grumbles, as Steve Dobel, then the head of commercial sales, will remember.

But the allure of not having to build a local network of his own is too great for Bernie. Building will take too much valuable time, and local is not WorldCom's area of expertise. If Bernie buys, the company gets the networks and the people who understand the business overnight. Jack and the bankers convince Bernie to break his long-held rule of only buying companies that add to first-year earnings. In August, 1996, six months after the Telecom Act is signed, while most other telecom companies are still easing into the new telecom game, Bernie switches boots and jeans for suit and tie and heads to New York to announce that WorldCom will purchase MFS for a staggering $14.4 billion in stock, well above market value.

What Bernie doesn't yet realize is that the real crown jewel of the purchase is UUNET—a Fairfax, Virginia start-up that operates the country's largest Internet backbone and was purchased by MFS just six months ago. Jim Crowe, the MFS CEO, was one of the industry's earliest visionaries for how Internet and telephony would converge. While the Internet craze is just around the corner, even industry analysts don't yet fully understand the possibilities. Merrill Lynch's Dan Reingold doesn't until he visits Jim Crowe to learn more about WorldCom's acquisition of MFS. "I was mystified," Dan will later write. "Although telecommunications and the Internet would later become as linked as Siamese twins, I didn't quite see the connection between the two."

When the MFS purchase closes, WorldCom becomes the first company to offer long-distance, local, Internet, data, and international service; and the first since AT&T's break-up to own both local and long-distance networks. Overnight, WorldCom has become the largest Internet Service Provider in the world and has local networks in 41 cities.

It's a big leap. It was relatively easy to integrate when WorldCom was essentially buying up reseller customer bases. But now we're forging into unfamiliar businesses with complicated networks, systems, and products.

Because MFS won't immediately add to WorldCom's earnings, the stock price is cut in half, but the drop will be temporary. Bernie believes buying MFS is in WorldCom's best long-term interest. "I swallowed deep, ducked my head, and did the deal," he explains when asked about buying an unprofitable company.

Bernie, Scott, and Jack have formed a partnership that will propel them and WorldCom to the big leagues. It's the perfect marriage—Jack Grubman, the Wall Street power broker; Scott Sullivan, the astute numbers guy; and Bernie Ebbers, the aggressive deal maker. It's the perfect time—Internet mania; a bull market firing on all cylinders and sending stock prices sky-high; deregulation providing new opportunities; low interest rates and a high WorldCom stock price to provide cheap capital for expansion and more acquisitions. The wind is at their backs.

After the deal, Jack continues to sing Bernie's and the company's praises. "He's organically smart," Jack tells a reporter. "He does not believe in management by committee. He trusts his instincts and then has the guts to act on them." WorldCom jumps from 498th to 341st on the 1996 Fortune 500. Nineteen of the 24 analysts covering the company have a "buy" or better rating, with none, even Dan Reingold, the perennial WorldCom skeptic, recommending "sell." Dan will concede that the acquisition "made tremendous strategic sense," but sticks with "neutral" because he thinks WorldCom overpaid and that MFS' unprofitability will put pressure on WorldCom's earnings per share.

Since WorldCom and MFS are Jack's two favorite companies, and both are Salomon clients, it doesn't take the industry long to figure out that Jack orchestrated this deal. He's being looked to as a hero, as someone who understands the industry better than anyone else. Jack is telling investors to buy start-ups, whose aggressive style naturally appeals to his own. He will have a tremendous say in how this sector continues to create itself. When telecom start-ups receive a separate category in the *Institutional Investor* ratings, Jack will win the top analyst spot.

In 1996, he helps to win $60 million in investment banking fees for Salomon Brothers, $7.5 million from WorldCom for the MFS purchase alone. The days when top analysts made a few hundred thousand dollars to churn out research reports are long gone. Jack's salary for the year is $3.5 million.

Clinton's Cinderella Story

It's September, 1996. After only a few years in our new headquarters, we've already outgrown the facility. It's a zoo around here. Employees are practically sitting on top of each other. Hundreds of boxes of work files line the halls because we're out of storage space. Earlier in the year, Bernie announced a plan to triple the size of our headquarters by constructing a 12-story, 250,000-square-foot building next to our current space. Jackson city planners were skeptical: The new building, at Spengler's Corner, a historical area that includes late–nineteenth- and early–twentieth-century buildings, would tower above them by more than a hundred feet.

So, in typical fashion, Bernie scraps the plan and announces that the company will instead build a new, 420,000-square-foot campus-style headquarters in Clinton, the small town where I grew up and home to Mississippi College, Bernie's alma mater. WorldCom is purchasing the land—84 acres—from the college. The plan calls for three interconnected four-story chrome and glass buildings, a lake with walking trails, a cafeteria, and a gym.

Clinton is about to become one of the smallest American towns to host a Fortune 500 company. It's "the coup of the century for the city," Howell Todd, the Mississippi College president, says. It's a coup for the college as well. There's a special announcement waiting for the thousands of fans who've poured into the stadium for the homecoming football game. After the college band plays, blue and gold balloons—the college colors—are released into the sky, and Bernie takes the stage. He waits for the crowd of 5,000 to quiet so he can make the announcement.

"Today, we begin a new phase in Mississippi College history," he booms to the crowd. "I am pleased to officially kick off a capital campaign designed to take Mississippi College into the 21st century. The goal—$80 million!" President Todd follows: "It gives me great pleasure to announce that an anonymous donor has made a challenge gift of $25 million." The crowd roars in approval, quite sure the "anonymous donor" is the man who was just on the stage. They're right.

Bernie has also taken an interest in the town. Hundreds of community volunteers, including my father, spent days building Kid's Town Playground at a local park just down the street from my parents' home. It had slides, swings, turrets, bridges, and a roofed fort in the middle. To help raise money for the project, my parents bought a brick, to be placed in the park's walkway, with my daughter's name engraved on it. Upon completion, there was a big celebration. At the ribbon cutting, one of Clinton's small bakeries brought a cake sculpture designed to look like Kid's Town. It was so large that several people carried it on two pieces of plywood. But several months after the playground was finished, a fire accidentally started by three boys burned the wooden structure to the ground.

Bernie is the first in line with a personal check for $50,000 to help rebuild the park. He also shows compassion for the boys who were responsible for the fire. When the press makes negative comments, Bernie calls Clinton's Mayor Rosemary Aultman. " 'I've been where those kids are, not in this same type of situation, but I can tell you this is not helping them,' " he says, according to the Mayor. " 'I gave the money to get the community focused on the positive side. We don't need to focus on the negative side.' "

The Dinner Speech Heard Round the World

It's December 5, 1996. Alan Greenspan, the highly respected Chairman of the Federal Reserve Board is delivering a dinner speech in Washington, D.C. The talk, titled "The Challenge of Central Banking in a Democratic Society," is long and dry, and some attendees fade out as he goes on.

And so, few notice that in the midst of his assessment of the history of economic policy, Greenspan wonders if the current market is exhibiting "irrational exuberance." But the next morning, the words reverberate around the world. Speculation about Greenspan's intent is rampant. Was he hinting that the Fed would try to cool an overheating stock market by raising interest rates, or was he just making a casual comment?

As it turns out, the comment was premeditated. "It was not a shot-from-the-hip," Alan Greenspan will later explain to a Senate panel. "We thought long and in detail that any such statement could very well have immediate market effects." At a meeting of the Federal Reserve Board on September 24, 1996, with the bull market running full-speed, Lawrence (Larry) Lindsey, a Fed Board member who would become George W. Bush's chief economic adviser, had raised concerns about a bubble. "What worries me . . . is that our luck is about to run out in the financial markets because of what I would consider a gambler's curse: 'We have won this long, let us keep the money on the table,'" he said. "I can attest that everyone enjoys an economic party, but the long term cost of a bubble to the economy and society are potentially great. . . . As in the United States in the late 1920s and Japan in the late 1980s, the case for a central bank ultimately to burst that bubble becomes overwhelming. I think it is far better that we do so while the bubble still resembles surface froth and before the bubble carries the economy to stratospheric heights. Whenever we do it, it is going to be painful, however."

"I recognize that there is a stock market bubble problem at this point," Greenspan responded, "and I agree with Governor Lindsey that this is a problem that we should keep an eye on." The Fed could raise interest rates or increase margin requirements—that is, reduce the amount investors can borrow relative to the value of their investments. "I guarantee that if you want to get rid of the bubble, whatever it is, [raising margin requirements] will do it," Greenspan said. "My concern is that I am not sure what else it will do."

So Greenspan decides to deliver his "irrational exuberance" speech. The global stock market takes an immediate nosedive, and he comes under political fire for his comments.

"You know I've always been a little nervous about the Fed, quite frankly," Senate Majority Leader Trent Lott tells *Fox News Sunday*. "I try not to be a Fed-basher, but I sometimes think they focus too much on one side of the equation, rather than the broader basket of things. And I'm a little nervous about the degree of [their] independence. And I think probably the Chairman would say, 'I wish I had chosen some other words.'" Lott adds: "Interest rates should be lower, even than what they are, certainly." Greenspan backs off the rhetoric. The Fed does not increase margin requirements, and, except for a minor rate increase in 1997, the Fed will continue to lower interest rates until June, 1999.

The last half of the decade will bring tremendous speculation in the stock market, record investing on margin, and massive borrowing by telecom and dot.com companies taking advantage of the low interest rates. "The Fed, in short, was feeding cheap money into the bubble," the financial journalist Peter Hartcher will write in his book *Bubbleman*.

"People said, 'How dare you take our bubble away!'" Larry Lindsey will recall. "The political reaction [to a proposed increase of interest rates during the early bubble years] was extremely hostile. Greenspan decided that he didn't have a mandate. The lesson from the irrational exuberance speech was that you have a democratic society in which the vast majority of people benefit enormously from something that may be hazardous in the long run."

CHAPTER 12

The Glass Sieve

Bernie picked well when he decided to partner with GTE to resell WorldCom long distance. While Ameritech sales increase slowly, the GTE partnership is an immediate success, and our billing scales rapidly. Then, just as suddenly, the honeymoon is over. GTE executives say WorldCom isn't billing them in accordance with the contract; they're refusing to pay their WorldCom bills, disputing practically every invoice. GTE executives waste no time escalating their concerns to the man at the very top of WorldCom. "I want you to do an audit and figure out what the problem is," Bernie tells me. "If the issue's on our side, I want to know about it."

It looks like Internal Audit has turned the corner with Bernie. GTE is holding millions of dollars owed to WorldCom, and he has turned to us to get to the bottom of things. The company's reputation is on the line. A soured relationship certainly won't help future sales.

Since Charles, my boss administratively, negotiated the contract, it's a little awkward for audit to interrogate its terms—a situation not unlike when I audited areas of the company that were overseen by Mike Cipicchio, who was also the Internal Audit supervisor—but we pin our hopes on diplomacy and move on.

Polish Your Shoes, Boys

Bernie's called an emergency meeting in Tulsa, Oklahoma with the executives responsible for servicing the GTE account, most of whom are from WilTel, the company Bernie snared from the Williams oil and gas company. He's asked me to join him in Tulsa. Charles and Jon Mabry, my Internal Audit manager, are also coming along.

Jon once worked in Internal Audit for GTE and realizes that he knows the GTE employee disputing the WorldCom billing. He's a former internal auditor. "He's one of the best auditors I've worked with," Jon says. "If he says there's a problem, there probably is one."

And Jon has a more colorful tip. "As a side note, you may want to know that the GTE liaison [to the WilTel executives in Tulsa] is a woman. The word is she thinks some of the men she deals with in Tulsa are chauvinistic, and that WorldCom is nothing but a good ol' boy network. She says they don't even polish their shoes out there." I chuckle; so much of business comes back to relationships—certainly not something I would have identified auditing contract compliance.

When I board the plane, I remember Charles' advice: "Bernie usually likes to sit by himself and not be bothered." After waiting to see Bernie take a seat in the back, Jon, Charles, and I choose spots up front. But midway through the flight, I hear: "Cooper." I walk to the back and take a seat across the aisle from Bernie. "Give me an update on what you've found in your audit so far," he says.

I share the results of our testing. Many of GTE's complaints appear to be legitimate. In the rush to market, it seems that WorldCom launched the product before it was properly tested. We've agreed to terms and conditions our billing system can't yet support. Effectively, GTE is serving as a kind of guinea pig, performing the quality assurance for us and finding kinks that are typically worked out before a service is sold.

For good measure, I throw in what Jon told me about the shoes. Bernie listens intently, but, as always, his face is unreadable. On the other hand, it's always clear when a meeting with Bernie is over. I make my way back to the front, leaving him chewing on his cigar.

A driver meets us at the hangar and delivers us to WilTel's former headquarters. As we walk into the conference room, I can't help noticing that, with the exception of one female mid-level manager, the assembled executives are all male. I refrain from looking at their shoes.

Bernie is the last one to come in. Though he's got a cigar in his mouth, usually a favorable sign, his look is all-business. With everyone else seated, he stands at the head of the table staring down the line of executives. "Let me make it very clear that WorldCom wants to keep the GTE business and the company's service to this customer is a top priority," he says. "We are going to do whatever it takes to fix these problems. I've asked Cynthia and her team to conduct an audit, and I'll be monitoring the situation and what they find closely." Suddenly, my department has moved from being hammered to being the hammer itself. The coach continues chewing out the team for another ten minutes.

In conclusion, Bernie glances my way and adds: "One more thing: You may be used to running a good ol' boy network out here in Tulsa at WilTel, but that's not how we operate in this company. We have women executives." I can't believe my ears. But he isn't done yet. "And by the way," he adds, slowly taking the cigar from his mouth, "it wouldn't hurt you boys to polish your shoes every once in awhile." As he walks out, several executives stare at their shoes in bewilderment.

That's Bernie's sense of humor. His quick-witted one-liners catch the recipient completely off-guard. Often, he's long gone before I even think of a good reply to his jest. Shareholders look forward to Bernie's antics, which are always good for a laugh or two at the annual meeting. On a previous visit to Oklahoma, just after the company had purchased WilTel, a young employee with long hair raised his hand during a meeting with Bernie. "Yes, young lady, what is your question?" Bernie asked, before proceeding to tell the young man to get a haircut. Word traveled quickly about the new CEO and his colorful comments. Employees weren't quite sure what to make of their new boss. "That's just the fun part of me, I don't do it to be rude or anything," Bernie will explain to a reporter. "It's just fun."

Sometimes, I think Bernie says things just for the shock value. Though he runs a technology company, he rarely uses e-mail and peppers public presentations with comments like "I'm not a technology dude." When two-way wireless pagers became all the rage, he refused to carry one and chastised executives who did, saying they were a waste of time.

"In this business, we tend to talk a lot about technology and strategy," Bernie will say in a speech. "All that makes me sick. The only statistic that matters—because everything else is derived from this one statistic—is how much new revenue your sales rep sells every month." "I wish Bernie would stick to the script," Beverly Buckley, his speechwriter, once lamented to me. "It's when he gets away from it that he gets in trouble." But Bernie won't be scripted.

As Charles and I head back to the airport, he's still laughing at the sight of the WilTel men staring at their shoes. "Maybe now is a good time for me to ask Bernie for your promotion," he says, changing the subject. "Why?" I ask. "I just think it is," Charles says.

It's November, 1996. Bernie has been invited to be the luncheon speaker at an analyst conference in New York, so the Audit Committee and Board of Directors have decided to have its meetings there as well. I'm flying with Bernie, Charles, and Scott on the corporate jet to attend the Audit Committee meeting.

"What are you going to do while we're at the conference?" Charles asks me.

"I don't know—I guess go to my hotel room."

"Scott," he calls to the back of the plane. "Do you care if Cynthia goes with us to the conference?"

"No, I guess that's fine," Scott says, though he sounds aggravated.

When we reach the enormous ballroom where the conference is taking place, I see firsthand just what a rock star Bernie has become. Analysts and investors crowd him from all sides. I sit at an elaborately set lunch table beside Jim Crowe, the MFS CEO, but he seems uninterested in conversation. In fact, he doesn't seem very happy to be here at all. I wonder if he will be another of those former CEOs who will leave soon after the deal has gone through. Bernie often has a tense relationship with the top executives who join the company after an acquisition. There's a revolving door of senior execs, briefly in and quickly out.

Francesco Galesi, the New York businessman who received a board seat when we acquired ATC in 1992, invited us to have the Audit Committee meeting at his penthouse on East 52nd Street, which occupies the building's top two floors and overlooks the East River. When we arrive, an attendant lets us in the building and escorts us to the elevator.

"Henry Kissinger lives in this building," Charles says.

"Really?" I look around as though he's going to appear just because we said his name.

Always down-to-earth and gracious, Francesco greets us at the door and gives us a tour of his home, a showplace of artwork and antiques, some still with original fabric, tattered and worn. Why doesn't he reupholster these pieces, I wonder naively.

Bernie jokes that Francesco is an "international playboy." At age 70, he looks like he's in his 50s. I once heard that *Vanity Fair* listed him as one of the country's most available bachelors.

The room where we will meet is outfitted with floor-to-ceiling views of the East River. As we sit around a long dining table, a team of waiters bustles around us serving breakfast. This opulent lifestyle is far from my life in Mississippi. It's interesting to visit, but I don't think I'd feel comfortable living this way.

After the meeting, some in the group say they're going to take a tour of Francesco's home.

"What are they talking about?" I ask Charles. "I thought this was his home."

"No, he also has a place in the Hamptons," the retreat of the affluent on Long Island, he says. "It's built like a real castle."

I skip the tour, but maybe I shouldn't have. On the beach in South Hampton, Francesco's home covers 55,000 square feet and has 60 bedrooms. Built by Henry F. du Pont in 1929, it was, at one time, the largest house in the Hamptons. After du Pont sold it, the new owner transformed the stately property, to the horror of neighbors, into a Gothic castle complete with an in-door saltwater aquarium, spires, and gargoyles. In the 1990s, after the owner went bankrupt, Francesco purchased the mansion, restoring it closer to its original dimensions, and changing its name from Dragon's Head to Elysium. Elysium can mean the abode of the blessed after death, or a state of perfect contentment. Either way, it's an improvement over Dragon's Head.

Our Own Boys' Club

I have no illusions about the fact that I'm a young woman in the midst of a boys' club. I'm not sure what's been the bigger obstacle to promotion, trying to prove the value of a start-up Internal Audit group or being a female. While women have made tremendous strides, we're still only the second generation of women whose professional choices range beyond teaching, nursing, or working as a secretary. Even in public accounting, where women have been particularly successful, only a small percent of the partners are female. "There's no such thing as a glass ceiling," as a female executive will tell me. "There's now a glass sieve—a few of us get through."

"Until there are more companies with female CFOs, there won't be many female audit partners," one of the partners at Arthur Andersen, WorldCom's external audit firm, once told me when I asked how many female partners his firm had. "CFOs who are men want audit partners who are men so they can hang out with them and do guy things."

Is there truth to what the partner is saying? Was his comment an honest acknowledgement of something known though unspoken? "I was eating dinner recently with a bunch of the guys," Charles tells me one day. "They say you're too impatient about getting promoted. I told them, 'Look guys, you wouldn't be saying she's too impatient if she were a man.'" I recall the adage I heard as a young woman—"If you want to succeed in the corporate world, look like a woman, act like a man, and work like a dog." But is it not enough if a woman excels in the workplace? Are there also unwritten "guy things," some rites of exclusively male bonding, covered neither in college nor on the CPA exam, that have to be mastered to move to the highest levels?

Golf, typically a male pastime, has been the catalyst for many a corporate deal. If golf is part of that secret rulebook, I certainly didn't help my cause the one time I went out on the course with Scott Sullivan and several Arthur Andersen partners at a Jackson country club.

After a lunch and audit planning session, the Andersen partners invited everyone onto the course. It was a beautiful day, and the proposition certainly beat returning to the office for the afternoon grind. Only one problem: I'd never played golf.

I've never excelled at sports. In elementary school, I was inevitably one of the last ones chosen for the playground teams, and with good reason. In 8th grade, I was kept off the honor roll one semester for having a C on my report card. "How in the world does someone make a C in Phys Ed?" my mother wanted to know.

In college, a friend who played on the university tennis team determined to teach me the game. "There's never been anyone I couldn't teach," he said confidently. For weeks, we went to the courts, but the harder I tried, the worse I got. "Maybe tennis just isn't for you," my friend finally conceded. "Maybe not," I agreed, relieved.

Given my history with sports and the fact that my husband finally hung a string with a ball on the end from the ceiling of our garage so I would know when to stop the car, there was no way I was going to accept the invitation to embarrass myself on the golf course that day. But after some prodding, I agreed to go along and ride in one of the two golf carts. I wouldn't play, but riding in the golf carts seemed harmless enough.

The guys had just finished a hole when one of them decided to walk to the next tee box, and the other two jumped into the cart ahead of me.

"Cynthia, can you drive the other cart down?" one asked.

"Sure," I said, climbing into the driver's seat. As everyone took off for the next hole, I canvassed every part of the dash, trying to find the key, but I couldn't. I knew I was about to be embarrassed.

"Come on!" I heard.

"I can't find the key," I called back, my voice breaking the calm of the course.

"Just push the pedal!" someone yelled as everyone erupted in laughter.

I might never learn golf, but I can now maneuver a cart quite well. And I picked up a valuable lesson that day: If you can't play golf, stay off the course. While I'm comfortable in the board room, I felt like a fish out of water on the course that afternoon, to no fault of the partners. I was just in unfamiliar territory.

But there were uncomfortable moments that had nothing to do with my golf skills. When I finally arrived at the next hole, Scott was struggling to make a putt. "You're going to have to turn around now, Cynthia," he said. "I may have to take out my special tool." I let the comment pass.

There have been other awkward occasions at social gatherings outside the workplace. At a lunch with an all-male group of WorldCom executives one afternoon, a director at the other end of the table—a rather large man regularly shrouded with gold chains and diamonds—motioned to me.

"Hey, Cynthia, why don't you come down here and sit on Papa's lap," he said, patting his leg. The men sitting next to him, including one of my employees, burst into laughter. I was caught off guard and embarrassed because it was a joke to the guys at my expense. "That's completely inappropriate," I said to him and everyone at the table. I stayed through the lunch, but did not feel at ease for the rest of the meal.

CHAPTER 13

The Tide Comes In

Charles's conjecture that it was a good time to ask Bernie for a promotion on my behalf has come to nothing. Charles wants to help me, but it's not up to him. When I accepted my position, I was told by my first boss that I would be promoted within a year if the department did well. It's been three. And when we've acquired a company with its own head of Internal Audit, my position has been re-evaluated to see which of us should serve as Chief Audit Executive.

Jon, the audit manager, is leaving to work for another WorldCom department in Dallas, liaising between WorldCom and GTE. When I hired Jon, I promised we would build this department together, but as hard as I've tried, I haven't been able to keep my promise. In the past three years, we've made hundreds of recommendations to improve the effectiveness and efficiency of operations and strengthen internal controls. We've quantified millions of dollars in resulting losses, with the company managing to recover well over $10 million, enough to pay for my tiny group for years. But somehow, it hasn't been enough.

Jon has worked unbelievably hard, and it's unfair for someone so talented to stay stuck. After the GTE contract audit we did for Bernie, I worked with the WorldCom vice-president covering the GTE account to help Jon get the opportunity. Jon will help resolve many of the problems we identified in our internal audit of WorldCom's compliance with the GTE contract. He will be a driving force in repairing the relationship with GTE, which will become WorldCom's largest customer. Jon will quickly move up the ranks from Manager to Director to Senior Director.

I can complain about not being promoted to the Audit Committee, but it would likely prove futile—Max would just go to Bernie, as he did on staffing. "A career is like a tide," Steve Dobel, the head of commercial sales, says to cheer me up. "It may go out for long periods, but then when you least expect, it comes in."

I know perseverance is a virtue, but at some point, maybe it's better to change the track you're on altogether. It's been one step forward, two steps back the whole way. What if you run as fast as you can and find you're in the wrong race? What if the tide simply never comes in?

Charles would tell me later: "Bernie suddenly hated Internal Audit after the fall-out about the consultants. It was the lowliest department and you were the lowest common denominator. He thought it was a complete waste of time. I was proud of the fact that you stood up for what you thought [with the consultants], but, quite frankly, I was surprised you stuck it out and didn't leave."

I decide to give things a push. A director position in operations has opened up in Tulsa, and I'll interview for it. If I don't get more support here, I'll move on. The position would report through Diana Day, the executive who supposedly disliked my change of mind about the con-sulting firms, but the dust seems to have settled. She's liked some of our recent audit work and asked me to consider working in her group.

After interviewing in Tulsa, I drive around to check out different neighborhoods. Suddenly, a dust storm begins, tumbleweeds rolling across the highway and blotting out my vision. The desolate look of the dust and dried vegetation leaves me feeling anxious to get back home.

Several days later, Charles tells me that Bernie wants to see me. "Diana is telling him she's going to hire you," Charles says. "He wants to know if you're going to accept her offer."

"I need to know what you want to do," Bernie says when I stop by his office. That's Bernie: right to the point.

"Well, I would prefer to grow Internal Audit and move to the director level," I say, "but not without more support. I love my job and the people I work with, and my family lives here. I don't want to move. But it seems like this department isn't valued."

Bernie stares at me attentively, but, as usual, his face is a mystery, and he gives no clue as to what, if anything, he intends to do about the situation. He just listens and thanks me for coming.

It's done. My cards are on the table. One way or another, I'll be moving on.

It's January, 1997, Bernie is hosting a retreat for WorldCom, MFS, and UUNET executives at the Ocean Reef Club in Florida, a world-class country club with golf courses, croquet lawns, yachting, and a private executive airstrip. Fine dining requires a jacket, and don't consider stepping foot on the croquet lawns unless you're clad entirely in traditional white. Bernie has certainly come a long way from counting guests' towels at his motels.

In such a sprawling company, this is a rare opportunity to meet so many colleagues. As we mingle on Bernie's new 132-foot yacht, aptly christened the "Aquasition," it feels like there's an underlying anxiety. One of the post-acquisition rituals is the layoff of redundant positions, and everyone's jockeying for place, anxious to find out who Bernie will anoint at the retreat's business meeting. After every acquisition, there's an us-versus-them mentality separating WorldCom staff and new employees from the acquired company, until Bernie's assignments create a new "us" and the next acquisition brings in a new "them."

From what I can tell, I'm the only person at the retreat who isn't at least a Director, and the MFS Chief Audit Executive isn't here. I guess that means Bernie has decided I will continue to manage audit. I sympathize with the MFS executive, knowing too well how it feels, but I'm also relieved.

Jim Crowe, the MFS CEO, is also nowhere in sight. I will soon learn that my hunch about him at the analyst conference in New York was right. He's leaving the company, taking many of MFS's highest-level executives with him to start a rival telecommunications company called Level 3 Communications. It seems odd that Jim wasn't required to sign a non-compete. But apparently he experienced friction with senior WorldCom executives from the start. "He didn't like us, and we didn't like him," Charles will say.

"Bernie was just glad to see him go," Steve Dobel will add. Jack Grubman, who helped broker the sale of MFS to WorldCom, will now recommend Jim's new venture, while Jack's employer, Salomon Brothers will provide investment banking services worth tens of millions of dollars.

However, John Sidgmore, the CEO of UUNET—the Internet company WorldCom inherited with the MFS purchase—is sticking around. John is a pioneer, having led UUNET to one of 1995's most successful IPOs. The company's revenues are exploding. "No one has ever seen this kind of growth," John says in a speech. "In fact, my network engineers tell me, 'John, if you're not scared, you don't understand.' This is mind-boggling, explosive growth."

Like Scott Sullivan, John is not an Ivy Leaguer. "I went to the State University of New York at Oneonta," he'll tell a reporter. "It's funny talking to all these Harvard and Stanford guys that go, 'Oh, that's good, a state college in New York.'" John is frenetically active. "I drink 20 cups of caffeine a day—12 to 14 cups of coffee and five or six Diet Cokes."

John has convinced Bernie to keep UUNET in a cocoon and refrain from integrating it with the rest of the company. He's afraid of losing momentum and wants to maintain UUNET's techie culture, with odd work hours and flip-flops as standard attire.

The next morning, it's finally time to kick off the business meeting. Bernie flashes one organization chart after another on the overhead, announcing who will lead departments and offering comic relief along the way. "The devil you don't know may be worse than the devil you know," he says in jest, explaining why he decided to leave Charles, my boss, in his position. Of course, Charles' position was never in jeopardy.

He continues through the rest of Charles' organization. I wait in anticipation. I have a strange feeling my promotion is about to come, but I've had that feeling several times before. My instinct says that it would be just like Bernie to tell no one, announcing my promotion in a forum like this. And that's exactly what he does.

"Cynthia Cooper will be the Director of Internal Audit," he says and flashes forward to the next slide. Several of my peers catch the change in title and turn around, smiling.

Charles quickly finds me after the meeting.

"Congratulations," he says, hugging me. "It's well-deserved."

"Did you know he was going to promote me?" I ask.

"No, I had no idea," he says. I'm not surprised. You would think Charles, a Senior Vice-President who reports directly to the CEO of a Fortune 500 company, would at least know in advance that an employee he oversees was being promoted, if not actually promote me himself, but that's just not the way Bernie operates.

The celebration over my promotion ends quickly. At 93, my beloved Nannie Ferrell, has become very ill with pneumonia.

Nannie and I are very close, but my brother Sam, who is now in college, is the undisputed king of her affection. All stopped for Nannie when Sam, named after her husband—our grandfather—walked into the room. "I have three granddaughters but only one grandson," she would explain, smiling. My mom calls Sam at school and asks him to come home. "And pack a suit," she says.

By the time Sam makes it back from school, Nannie is calling for him. We pray and hope, but her condition suddenly deteriorates. The last time I visit her, she doesn't even recognize me. After three days, she finally goes home to Granddaddy Ferrell.

When Brother Bill, Nannie's pastor, concludes his tribute at the service, Sam walks down the aisle to the piano and plays a piece he had composed as a gift for Nannie's 90th birthday. At family gatherings, she would roll her wheelchair beside the piano in my parents' living room and say, "Sam, play my song for me." She would stare intently at him, eyes shining, as he did. Without fail, she would announce, as if we did not know, "He wrote that for me."

Shortly after Nannie passes away, Sam marries his college sweetheart Rachel. "Nannie must have arranged this marriage from heaven," a relative will say, as Nannie's own parents were also named Sam and Rachel.

Nannie had a tremendous influence on my life. "She has the peace that passeth all understanding," people in our family would say, and, as my mother wrote in the church bulletin in honor of Nannie, "grace in accepting the inevitability of change and beauty in an all-encompassing love for others." Each person who came into contact with her felt noticed, loved. Nannie greeted everyone as if they were the very person she hoped to see at that moment. Even in her final days in the nursing home, she helped those around her. "It's better to give than to receive," she would say until the end.

Her faith was not just saved for church on Sunday. Each day, Nannie stopped the busy world to be still with God. I think it's what helped her run the race well, live by her values, and stay true to her purpose. "Remember: God first, others second, yourself third," she would say. "God should be at the center of your life." More than anyone I've known, she lived what she spoke, and more than anyone I've known, she seemed truly happy.

CHAPTER 14

The Minnow Swallows
the Whale

Every time there is . . . another merger, I ask myself, "How can you top this?" And every time, there has been something new to come along to offer that challenge that makes this life so interesting.

—Scott Sullivan

It's June, 1997. The world's largest telecom companies are beginning to consolidate through record-breaking mergers. But Bernie, ever the iconoclast, says he now wants to sit tight—good news for WorldCom employees already overwhelmed with the MFS and UUNET acquisitions. "We will not be forming international alliances and consortiums with the likes of Deutsche Telekom and France Telecom like Sprint did, or merge like BT [British Telecom] and MCI [plan to]," Bernie tells a reporter. "We intend to go it alone, build our own facilities, sell our own products and collect the revenues that we produce ourselves. We do not see a need for more acquisitions because we are participating in all markets with the infrastructure that we're building. But I won't rule out acquisitions that would increase our shareholder value."

The problem with Bernie's plan is that the company is in thrall to Wall Street's praise of it as a "fast-growth" company—a rate of growth usually achievable only by external acquisition, not organic internal evolution.

If WorldCom ever stops acquiring, growth will most likely slow, which will negatively impact analysts' ratings and WorldCom's stock price.

As always, investors wonder if Bernie will sell WorldCom. He won't rule out a sale if "the price is right," *BusinessWeek* reports in July. But WorldCom is now far too expensive for most other telecom companies. Because it's growing so rapidly, investors are paying a premium for the stock, driving the company's price-to-earnings ratio to higher levels than many competitors.

Jack Grubman is promoting the potential mega-merger between BT and MCI, the second-largest U.S. long distance company. Last November, BT offered $21 billion to buy MCI, 40 percent more than MCI's stock was worth at the time. If the deal closes, it will be the largest foreign acquisition of a U.S. company in history.

With each day, Jack Grubman acts more like a strategist and investment banker than an analyst. Recently, he even helped Qwest Communications, a Denver-based start-up broadband company, recruit a new CEO. "I bet I could get you Joe Nacchio," he told billionaire Qwest founder Philip Anschutz, referring to the head of AT&T's consumer business unit. Within months, Nacchio was working at Qwest. On occasion, Jack even attends strategy and board meetings for telecom companies he follows.

The *Wall Street Journal* recently profiled Jack as the "Big Telecom Rainmaker," a "swashbuckling deal broker who can sometimes make or break a telecom merger or stock offering." Within Salomon, Jack wields so much power that a Salomon banker says "Jack has veto power over what the firm can do or can't do in telecommunications." The *Journal* calls him "a Jack of all trades" who represents "a new breed of Wall Street analyst. Analysts increasingly play a central role in snaring investment banking business." What differentiates "Grubman from the rest of the analyst pack is how skillfully he manages to walk the divide between banking and research, with his credibility intact."

The Securities and Exchange Commission does little to discourage the conflict of interest. "There are no hard and fast federal laws that say you can do this and you can't do this," enforcement chief William McLucas tells the *Journal*. "It really is a question of navigating the problem case by case." Some on Wall Street believe that the comment signals that the SEC plans to do nothing about research and banking conflicts.

A week before announcing its second-quarter earnings, MCI quickly arranges an analyst conference call. With analysts and investors on the edge of their seats, MCI's CFO delivers bad news that could put a damper on its planned merger with BT—MCI is lowering next year's expected earnings by a whopping 40 percent.

Part of the reduction has to do with the extra costs MCI has incurred attempting to break into the local telephone market. It entered the deregulated local phone market alone, incurring massive expense to build local networks from scratch. But roughly a third of the revision comes from declining long-distance revenue. Customers are switching to cell phones, and MCI's rates are being driven down by relentless consumer price wars with AT&T and Sprint. MCI's losses in the second half of 1997 will be $800 million, nearly twice what was anticipated. Merrill Lynch's Dan Reingold—who's been hot on MCI—has dialed into the call from his vacation in Italy and is stunned by the size of the revision. "With one exception," he will later write, "this . . . was by far the largest cut I had seen in my 14 years in the telecom industry."

Jack Grubman remains upbeat, insisting to the Street that BT won't back out or renegotiate. Dan, however, says that there must be a new deal to reflect MCI's lower earning potential. BT—which already has a joint venture with MCI called Concert, and holds three seats on MCI's board and 20 percent of MCI's stock—is scrambling to decide what to do. Its executives turn to Dan for advice. He tells them the revised figures mean BT/MCI will face a whole host of new competitive challenges in the U.S. market. As a result, BT reduces its offer to $19 billion.

By September, the deal looks like it's on the verge of collapsing altogether. Jack is in a precarious position: Based on his assurances about the deal, Salomon's arbitrageurs—traders who make bets on the likely impact of mergers and acquisitions on the stocks of the companies involved—have invested enormous amounts of company money to wager that BT will successfully purchase MCI. Because the acquiring company's stock usually declines after an acquisition while the acquired company's stock rises, the traders purchased MCI stock, and, as a hedge, sold BT. But with the acquisition in question, the market is working in the opposite direction.

Scott and Bernie have just met with investment bankers from Goldman Sachs, who invited them to New York with a proposition: Would WorldCom consider acquiring AT&T? Bernie and Scott are skeptical that WorldCom, the Number Four long-distance carrier, can purchase the nation's top long-distance company. But the bankers also have another idea: AT&T is looking for a new CEO. "The Goldman bankers said, 'Get AT&T to buy you, and Bernie can be installed as the CEO,'" Charles will recall. "I was initially excited about the idea. How sweet is that deal? Our shareholders get the premium of being bought out, and WorldCom management gets control of the company." But the idea fizzles when a member of AT&T's executive search committee responds to Goldman's inquiry with: "Bernie who?"

On the way to the airport, Scott catches up with Eduardo Mestre, head of investment banking at Salomon, which is overseeing WorldCom's $2.4 billion acquisition of Brooks Fiber, another local carrier that competes with the Bell companies. After talking about issues with the Brooks purchase, Eduardo complains about Salomon's arbitrage losses in the BT/MCI deal. Scott's mind begins racing. Would it be possible for WorldCom to buy MCI? "We might be able to help out," he tells Eduardo on a whim.

On the plane, Scott crunches the numbers. MCI is more than three times the size of WorldCom. Its 1996 revenue was $18.5 billion, to WorldCom's $5.6 billion. Is it possible for a minnow to swallow a whale? The more Scott calculates, the more he's convinced WorldCom can pull it off. The high premium of WorldCom's stock—trading at some 90 times earnings—compared to MCI's will provide enough leverage to offer a higher price than BT. Scott mentions the idea to Bernie. Forget AT&T. Buy MCI instead. Scott thinks MCI is worth a lot more than BT is willing to pay, and that WorldCom can afford to outbid BT because an MCI/WorldCom combination would provide greater cost reductions for WorldCom than an MCI/BT merger would for BT.

Bernie is receptive, quickly dismissing his prior comments about no big mergers, and Salomon—which could have as much as $100 million in arbitrage losses according to Wall Street rumors—begins aggressively lobbying WorldCom to take BT's spot. "We were exuberant," Scott will say. "This was putting a stamp on communications history."

> WorldCom's bold takeover of MCI, a company four times its size, was the event that signified the arrival of telecom to the center of the world stage.
>
> —Dan Reingold

It's October 1, 1997. Bernie, the "Man from Mississippi," makes his way back to the Big Apple to make corporate history. Early in the morning, just over a month after BT reduced its offer, Bernie calls Bert Roberts, MCI's CEO, from his New York hotel. But Bert hasn't made it into the office yet.

Finally, at around 8:30 a.m., Bernie's phone rings. Bernie tells Bert that WorldCom will make an unsolicited $30 billion stock offer for MCI. If the deal closes, it will be the largest acquisition in corporate history.

After speaking with Bert, Bernie heads to the Pierre Hotel for a press conference announcing the MCI offer. Jaws drop—the media and the market are shocked. What truly astounds Wall Street is that WorldCom is working three major deals at once. Bernie announces an offer for Brooks Fiber on the same day; the company is also shepherding a complicated three-way deal with AOL and CompuServe.

Bernie is in high spirits and full form, exchanging friendly banter with reporters and lobbing zingers that leave reporters wondering whether he's serious or joking. AT&T was our "other choice," he says, but when we called one of the AT&T directors, he "didn't know who we were." He adds, "after we get our deal done with MCI, we may acquire BT." He even razzes Bert Roberts for not being in the office when he called. If Bert comes to work at WorldCom, he'll have to get to work "a little bit earlier," Bernie adds.

Not everyone believes WorldCom is serious about buying MCI. "I'm putting the likelihood at 1 in 10 of WorldCom pulling off the merger," says Tom Aust, a telecom analyst with Citicorp Securities. "I think it is a big PR grab—a move to say we are a player." Soon, it looks like his prediction might come true. In mid-October, GTE—a major WorldCom customer—throws a wrench into Bernie's plans by making a $28 billion all-cash offer for MCI. Although less than Bernie's offer, MCI shareholders may prefer the cold cash instead of WorldCom stock. A major bidding war erupts.

Scott returns to the drawing board. He's practically working 24/7 to manage the three deals. "I worked with Scott at ATC," Steve Dobel will say. "Even then, he always worked unbelievably long hours. It was nothing for him to still be in the office at midnight." He lives, breathes, and sleeps WorldCom.

Analysts and reporters speculate as to which company will win the battle for MCI. The *New York Times* writes: "Some investors and analysts sense that British Telecom would be able to work more easily with the buttoned-down [GTE Chairman Charles] Lee than with the cowboy boot–wearing Mr. Ebbers." But for the right price, the BT and MCI executives just may be willing to put on a pair of cowboy boots after all.

At one point, Scott runs into my former colleague Jon Mabry, now WorldCom's GTE liaison, on the elevator. "I told him 'You're making my customer [that is, GTE] mad,'" Jon will recall saying. "Scott said, 'I'm about to make an offer GTE can't match. I've talked to Salomon and it's over.'"

On November 10, WorldCom bumps its offer up to $36.5 billion, this time in combined cash and stock. Scott was right; the offer is too rich for GTE. BT happily runs for the hills. While other MCI shareholders are receiving WorldCom stock, according to the deal, WorldCom must pay BT $7 billion in cash for its 20% stake in MCI.

In the end, Bernie won the deal in part by throwing down his trump card—the position of Chairman. "Executives close to the negotiations said that the offer by Mr. Ebbers to make Mr. [Bert] Roberts chairman of the combined company and to secure senior management positions for Mr. Roberts' team helped sway MCI toward WorldCom." Upon announcing the deal, Bernie makes no jokes about what time Bert will have to come to work. Instead he refers to his new chairman as "boss man."

On March 11, 1998, WorldCom shareholders approve the deal, and WorldCom and MCI officially merge on September 14. Bernie and Scott have outdone themselves. The financial and telecom industries are in awe and have been praising them in lavish hyperbole since the deal was announced:

> Mr. Ebbers will release many trillions of dollars in wealth in Internet commerce and communications. He is a hero of the dimensions of Rockefeller and Milken.
>
> —technology analyst George Gilder, in the *Wall Street Journal*

> I think the world changed today.
>
> —portfolio manager Bruce Behrens,
> referring to WorldCom's new ability to
> offer one-stop shopping for all voice communications

> [Bernie] was an outsider, a nobody, in telecom. Today, he is considered one of the industry's most powerful people.
>
> —*Network World*

> He's the Ted Turner of the telecommunications industry, and Jackson, Mississippi, is the hot bed of the communications industry. . . .
>
> —Peter Bernstein, editor of *The Journal of Portfolio Management*

[Bernie] has proven to be unpredictable, ruthlessly practical, at times difficult and above all aggressive—whether in a drive to the basket or to the top of the Nasdaq.

—Reed Branson, Memphis *Commercial Appeal*

Ten years ago, WorldCom was a mouse among elephants. Now it is literally bringing the elephants down.

—Daniel F. Akerson, former MCI president

That's what makes [Bernie] so good—he does things out of the box.

—TIAA-CREF telecom analyst William Newbury, in *Business Week*

The MCI deal . . . has become the stuff of legend.

—Joseph McCafferty, CFO *Magazine*

WorldCom is here to stay.

—*Time* "1998 Top 50 Cyber Elite"

Scott is being celebrated as one of the country's outstanding CFOs. It's his fifth year with WorldCom and third as CFO. For his entire time with the company, he's been commuting between his primary residence in Boca Raton, Florida, where his wife lives, and a small waterfront condominium in Ridgeland, Mississippi, just northeast of Clinton. The long-distance lifestyle is taxing, but the sacrifice and hard work are beginning to reap enormous financial rewards for the man who will be referred to as "Master of the Mega Merger." In 1997, Scott's total compensation is worth more than $19 million—the nation's highest-paid CFO, according to *CFO* magazine. Much of the compensation comes from stock options and bonuses. He tells *CFO* that he'd rather have the opportunity to earn large bonuses, based on the company's success, than make a higher salary: "I'm willing to lay it all on the line in terms of performance."

Scott receives the 1998 CFO Excellence Award for mergers and acquisitions from *CFO* magazine. He was selected by a panel that included some of the most prominent CEOs and board chairs. The magazine's citation refers to him as a "37-year-old whiz kid." Its editor will later tell *USA Today* that, at the time, Wall Street believed Scott "walked on water." Bernie credits Scott as the driving force behind the MCI acquisition. "He has no peer in his ability to earn the trust and confidence of the investment community," he says. Even Dan Reingold will come to respect Scott's expertise. "Scott's intimate knowledge of every cost item was impressive," he will write, referring to an analyst call about the MCI offer. "He sure seemed to have a handle on the details."

Thanks to Bernie and Scott, Jack Grubman has maneuvered out of a very tight corner, and works to burnish his dented reputation. Meanwhile, Salomon has minimized the losses of its arbitrage department, which is soon shut down to prevent another fiasco.

A Good Marriage?

Only a few large telecom players will survive, so "get big or get lost" seems to be the industry sentiment these days. The purchase of MCI certainly counts for big. It increases WorldCom's long-distance market share from 5.5% to 25%, the second-largest in the United States behind AT&T. It also gives WorldCom the prestigious MCI brand, tremendous marketing talent famous for its innovative "Friends and Family" campaign, and the ability to save millions by combining networks and cutting MCI's relatively high rate of spending on expenses like travel and entertainment. It also means one less competitor. And there's little overlap between MCI and WorldCom business customer bases. WorldCom sells to middle-market businesses, billing from $2,500 to $75,000 a month. MCI targets the high end, billing $100,000 and above.

To accommodate its new size, WorldCom starts constructing a massive complex across 535 acres in a remote part of northern Virginia. "We put in a lot of the amenities that are required to get people excited about life in the hinterlands," John Sidgmore, the head of UUNet, who urged Bernie to build the campus, tells a reporter. It includes a 2.5-mile walking trail, a cleaners, and a bank.

But is WorldCom–MCI a good marriage? MCI deals in the residential market WorldCom has so far avoided because it suffers from shrinking margins. Also, three-fourths of MCI's 1997 revenue of $20 billion came from less profitable voice service carried over an older telecom network, whereas WorldCom's revenue streams are more balanced between voice and more lucrative data and Internet transmission. Start-ups like Qwest and Jim Crowe's Level 3 are turning the screws by building state-of-the-art fiber-optic networks using newer technology to drive down voice rates to as little as 7.5 cents per minute, compared to MCI's 12.5. Just matching that rate would decrease MCI's voice revenue from $15 to $9 billion. And no one knows where the price pressure on long distance voice will end.

In keeping with Bernie's philosophy of avoiding residential sales, some believe his original intent was to eventually sell MCI's consumer division and keep its higher-margin components—long-distance and Internet sales to business customers. But when John Sidgmore mentioned the plan in a statement to the press, before the acquisition was complete, regulators were not pleased. "When John Sidgmore . . . told Wall Street that high-flyer WorldCom planned to jettison MCI's 20 million LOLITAs (telecom-speak for Little Old Ladies In Tennis Apparel) a firestorm erupted in Washington," John Wohlstetter, a senior fellow with the Discovery Institute, will write. Bernie was furious with John. But "within 24 hours Ebbers pledged to keep Grandma. He thus sealed WorldCom's fate: His New Economy business was now fatally entwined with Old Economy voice." To close the deal, regulators forced WorldCom to sell MCI's Internet network instead, which the government believed would have given WorldCom control over too much of the Internet backbone.

With each acquisition, there are cultural differences and the same old "us" and "them" mentality I've seen so many times now; but the clash between WorldCom and MCI is particularly pronounced. As Bernie would explain, "WorldCom starting the way it started and acquiring mom-and-pop kind of small operations, was always regarded in the industry as the Wal-Mart of telecommunications, and MCI was kind of like the Goldman Sachs of telecommunications."

The MCI executives do seem more polished. One of its sales and marketing execs, I hear, even has a personal speech coach. As a former WorldCom director put it: "[MCI executives] appear on stage like politicians running for Congress. They have a fancy slide presentation for every occasion, hold so many meetings I wonder when they have time to get things done, and show up with an entourage of unnecessary people at each meeting." WorldCom executives, on the other hand, are more informal: Roll up your sleeves and focus on the work.

It quickly becomes clear that some of MCI's executives, many of whom work out of Washington, resent having been bought by a much smaller company in Mississippi with a CEO who is all too eager to cut costs. MCI executives have much higher salaries, cushier spending budgets, and more perks. Some top executives have personal limos and drivers.

Though MCI executives are big spenders and the company is three times larger than WorldCom, it has a smaller Internal Audit group: While my staff has grown to ten, MCI has only six auditors. I soon learn that its audit group has also struggled for executive management's support and approval for additional hires. The MCI audit team also focuses on operational and systems auditing. Because most of the companies World-Com purchased had no internal audit function, this will be the first time I've added staff through an acquisition.

"These limos will be the first thing to go," Bernie promises soon after the acquisition, according to Steve Dobel, who visited MCI with him. MCI is receiving the old WorldCom welcome—in lieu of exquisite hotels and fine dining, a ham sandwich and a good night's sleep at the Hampton Inn.

MCI executives have a private dining room with chefs who prepare three-course meals. Bernie soon closes this, too. At WorldCom, the executives head to the company cafeteria, wait in line to pay for their food, and eat lunch alongside their employees.

Then there's the MCI fleet of planes, with stewardesses who serve meals selected prior to the flight. "We ran our two WorldCom planes around thirty hours a month," Charles will recall. "[The MCI execs] averaged a thousand hours a month on their five jets. We had a meeting . . . soon after the merger. When we arrived, three of the MCI planes were lined up side by side in the hangar. Each executive had flown in a separate plane. 'Can you believe this?' we said." Bernie sells several of the aircraft, does away with stewardesses, and instructs MCI's Atlanta-based executives to drive to Jackson instead of flying. As for the few planes that remain, executives now pick up their own sandwiches—stocked by the pilots— and fix their own drinks.

The business press loves Bernie's fierce cost-cutting. "Unloading the planes won't have much of an impact on the balance sheet of the $30 billion company," Fortune writes. "But analysts and money managers consider it strong evidence that Ebbers is delivering the kind of savings and synergies he promised when WorldCom outmaneuvered British Telecom and GTE to take over MCI."

Bernie clearly enjoys the image. "I always take a cab," he says, referring to the penchant for limos among the telecom elite. And "I look at every single line item on the budget. . . . I think the MCI people are amazed about the level of detail I get into."

As if to demonstrate the point, Bernie removes the bottled water from the MCI offices. Let them drink tap. What does stay is MCI's decades-old sponsorship of the Heritage Classic golf tournament. Maybe Bernie decided that too many deals get struck on the golf course.

CHAPTER 15

Finding Balance

I love my job and the people I work with, but I'm still struggling to balance between work and home, between being a wife, mother, and career woman. At work, new acquisitions are announced often before the previous one has closed. It's an adrenaline rush to see a new company come into the fold to heaps of praise from Wall Street, but the pace is grueling, and it's easy to allow the workload to consume nights and weekends. Things at work will slow down, I used to tell myself. But the corporate train doesn't offer many chances to jump off. Its whole point is to keep going forward, faster and faster. There was a time when I bought into the idea that you could have it all—super-wife, super-mom, super-career. Now I know better. There are only 24 hours in a day. "You don't get a trial run at life," my father told me when I was young. "You have to make the most of every day." But this simple wisdom is much easier to believe than find a way to act upon.

Miss Oseola McCarty

> Do not wait for extraordinary circumstances to do good; try to use ordinary situations.
>
> —German writer, Jean Paul Richter

As the frustrations of being spread too thin take up my mind, my mother again reminds me of what matters most. She's written a tribute to

163

Miss Oseola McCarty, an 87-year-old African-American woman from Hattiesburg. At age 12, Ms. McCarty had to drop out of school to help her family as a laundress. For 75 years, she worked from sun-up to sun-down, six days a week, meticulously washing, starching, and ironing garments. All along, she saved and saved. In that time, she accumulated $250,000, of which she has given $150,000 to the University of Southern Mississippi (USM), to be placed in a scholarship fund for students in need.

Her generosity has inspired people across the nation. President Clinton invited her to Washington to receive an award. Moved by Miss McCarty's story, my mother wrote:

> When we despair at the wrong in this world, a light comes shining, lifting our spirits to a higher level by the sheer eloquence in depth of character that transcends the language. Your generous gift from a hard-earned financial security, guaranteeing others the opportunity for an education you did not have, touches the heart of our nation in a manner unparalleled by any endowment from a major corporation and reaches beyond the enlightenment of young minds. Your gift to each of us is the sterling example of assurance that one person can make a difference, and your unselfish motivation beckons to that which is best in all of us. As a state, Mississippi is graced with honor by your presence. As a people, our lives are enriched to have known such a lady as Miss Oseola McCarty.

My mom mailed the tribute to Mississippi Governor Kirk Fordice, asking if he would consider formally commending Ms. McCarty. He graciously agreed, and used my mother's tribute in his formal commendation. My parents attended a ceremony at USM where the Governor presented the commendation to Miss McCarty.

My mother asked me to attend, but I couldn't, busy at work with something that seemed important at the time, though what I now can't recall. Instead, a photograph of Miss McCarty, my mother, Governor Fordice, and Horris Flemming, the USM president, sits on my desk at work. After the commendation, my mother gave Miss McCarty a silver-heart jewelry box with brooches that had belonged to Nannie Ferrell. "They go as they should, from one special lady to another," a note in the box read.

My mother saw Miss McCarty only one other time, at a graduation ceremony where she was granted USM's first honorary doctorate. John Grisham delivered the commencement address, and a picture of him with my mother joins the other on my desk.

Miss McCarty's example will continue to guide, proof that neither bright spotlights nor prestigious titles are prerequisites for a life of significance. Countless moments of greatness occur—quietly, in ordinary circumstances—because someone chose to give the best within them.

Stay-At-Home Dad

It's November 1998. Lance and I have wanted a baby since we married, but we decided to wait so our blended family could grow into itself and I could achieve my career goals. But I'm almost 35. At the same time, if we have a child, we'd like one of us to have more time at home.

The problem is that we can't afford for me to resign—I have the higher compensation, and, in any case, I've always been more career-oriented. But maybe Lance could find a less demanding job? He's not happy at his current position in computer programming, and has thought about going on his own, maybe in real estate, or refurbishing old homes.

"You could be a stay-at-home dad," I say half-seriously.

But Lance is receptive. We've saved over the years, refraining from trading up on our house or cars. With our savings and my salary, Lance thinks we can do it. But we're both apprehensive; not everyone agrees it's a good idea, and we even get some disapproving comments from older members of our family who question the idea of the husband staying home.

But my dad has more practical advice. "If Lance is going to quit, you should at least diversify your investments by selling some of your WorldCom stock," he encourages us one evening. "It's just not smart to keep all of your eggs in one basket. I'm concerned about WorldCom being able to service this huge debt load they've taken on with the MCI purchase."

There goes Dad, the worst-case scenario specialist. No one else I know seems to be worried about WorldCom's debt load. Besides, it's well-rumored that Bernie, who regards shareholding by employees a loyalty issue, rarely sells his stock and doesn't like it when employees do. He even receives a list of who sells and how much, and sometimes has something to say about it to the employee, though usually good-naturedly.

But Lance agrees with my father. We sell some of our WorldCom stock and put the gains against our mortgage instead of back into the stock market. Of course, WorldCom's stock price has a phenomenal run-up soon after we sell. As expected, Bernie gives me a hard time: "Cooper, why did you sell your stock at such a low price?!" he razzes.

For the first few weeks after turning in his resignation, Lance has buyer's remorse. But soon enough, we realize how much the change has benefited all of us. It seems like life has slowed down. Suddenly, it's no longer a mad rush to get the errands done, take our daughter to the doctor or school, help with homework, clean, cook, grocery-shop. Stephanie can join more extracurricular activities and doesn't have to stay at an after-school care program. Because Lance picks up more of the home activities, I'm not as tired, and we have more family time together.

"What exactly does he do during the day?" a woman acquaintance once asked me in a sarcastic tone. The gender bias, it turns out, runs in both directions. Of course, she wouldn't have asked the question about a stay-at-home mom. Lance is our anchor—steady, devoted, dependable. I'm results-oriented, but Lance knows how to enjoy the journey, how to keep perspective. I help us move to the next task, but he helps us live in the moment.

CHAPTER 16

Top of the Mountain

It's June, 1999. After last December's performance reviews, I received the news that I was being promoted to Vice-President. Considering how much of a struggle the move to Director had been, I'm grateful that I didn't even have to ask for this one. This time, Charles made the decision and obtained Bernie's approval without my knowing.

My company is also on top of the world. The excitement—of working for the industry pacesetter, helping to build the "information superhighway"—is electric. WorldCom's stock has just reached an all-time high of $64. It is now the country's fifth most-widely-held stock, with a market capitalization of $115 billion. In July, the company moves from 71st to 14th in market value in the world in *BusinessWeek*'s Global 1000 list.

WorldCom is Mississippi's Cinderella story. Our CEO is a local folk hero. Mississippians like his dressed-down style and that he doesn't take on airs—it wouldn't be unusual to bump into him at the all-you-can-eat catfish buffet. Bernie has built a Fortune 500 company in the unlikeliest place while donating millions to local colleges and creating the higher-paying professional jobs that many young Mississippians used to leave the state to seek. It seems everyone wants to work here. When people find out you do, their tone gains a measure of respect. Some slip you the resume of a friend or relative trying to get on with the company.

Shareholders are happy, too—WorldCom has one of the longest bull runs in stock market history at its back. Many employees, from entry-level staff to top executives, sell stock for a new car or home down payment. Several small businesses—a music store, a photography shop—open in Clinton, thanks in part to WorldCom stock. Late one afternoon, as I walk through the parking lot with my colleague Steve Dobel, we marvel at how many old, run-down clunkers have been replaced by shiny new BMWs, Lexuses, and Mercedes-Benzes.

Debates about the ideal time to sell stock make for typical watercooler conversation. Some employees have even placed runners on their computer screens to monitor the stock price. While some have taken care to diversify their investments, many don't, some even borrowing against their stock. Even though the wealth of most investors is purely theoretical until they decide to unload their stock, the "wealth effect" is quite visible. People "feel" richer, overleveraging to borrow for new homes and new investments.

Many in the younger generation, which haven't lived through a bear market, seem to believe stocks will go up indefinitely. Quitting your job to become a day trader is the latest incarnation of Jack's magic beans. Everyone seems to know someone who knows someone supposedly making a mint day-trading. Many technology start-up employees are instant millionaires thanks to their stock ownership. In the last six months of 1999, stock in ten IPOs will jump by over a thousand percent on the first day of trading.

Several factors encourage the mania—open competition unleashed by the 1996 Telecom Act; the belief that the first companies to build information superhighways and expand their networks will grab the most market share and remain the only ones standing; productivity gains due to technology development; cheap capital, thanks to the Fed's consistent reduction of rates; and the view that we have entered a "new economy" of phenomenal, limitless growth spurred by the Internet.

Venture capitalists are throwing money at anything that moves. A lot of capital chasing a limited number of investments has created tremendous pressure on venture firms to snap up opportunities quickly, which means hasty due diligence—if a venture-capital firm scrutinizes a business plan too closely, another one may steal the investment. As long as the plan features certain key buzzwords and the requisite talent, let's give it a shot.

Besides, traditional ways of valuing a company, like earnings and positive cash flow, are being discarded as old-hat. Internet start-ups with no earnings are being judged according to new metrics like "page views," "eyeballs," and "engaged shoppers." Guessing quickly, investors spread their bets across many start-ups, and wait to see how the market shakes out.

Companies, WorldCom included, use marketing campaigns to transform their images from "old-economy brick-and-mortar" to "agile new-world." Some in the dot.com industry adopt the razor scooter as a symbol of the new zip-zip digital generation. Young WorldCom employees have been sited riding them through the office. Wasting no time, our marketing department creates an ad featuring several young riders.

Suddenly, everyone is a voracious consumer of business news. There's a glut of new publications devoted to the dismal science—*Business 2.0*, *eCompany Now*, *Fast Company*, *Wired*. Amazingly, CNBC viewership has climbed above CNN's.

Wall Street analysts—Jack Grubman, Henry Blodget at Merrill Lynch, Abby Joseph Cohen at Goldman Sachs, Mary Meeker at Morgan Stanley Dean Witter—and CEOs are the public's new knights. In 1990, CEO compensation was, on average, 85 times greater than that of regular employees. By 1999, that factor has increased to 531.

Build It and They Will Come

> Like the attic of a house gets filled, no matter how much bandwidth is available, it will get used.
>
> —Jack Grubman

There are now over 3,000 telecommunications companies in the United States. The dot.com and telecom upstarts turn to more established companies like WorldCom to lease bandwidth. WorldCom competitors—Qwest, Level 3, Global Crossing—are also leasing bandwidth until they complete construction of their own networks. Even Enron is leasing fiber from WorldCom as part of a plan to trade telecom capacity, just as it has done with energy.

Because WorldCom, through its purchase of UUNET, owns the country's largest Internet backbone, it's the go-to bandwidth supplier for market entrants. But even so it can't keep up with demand. World-Com is digging up city streets the world over to lay fiber. It's also working construction sites in major U.S. cities around the clock to build "web hosting" centers. From 1998 to 2000, the telecom sector will issue $323 billion in new debt, much of which goes toward expanding networks and purchasing telecom equipment. In the late 1990s and early 2000s, over $1.2 trillion in capital will be invested in the telecom sector.

Telecom equipment and fiber-optic companies like Cisco, Lucent, and Corning can't fill orders fast enough and see explosive revenue growth. Because there isn't enough equipment to go around, the telecom carriers that use the equipment to provide services to resellers, start-ups, and customers pay premiums and over-stock to avoid delays in construction. Since the long-distance carriers have a tremendous backlog, their customers often place orders with more than one. When one delivers, they cancel the orders with the others. WorldCom employees rush to deliver service only to see orders canceled at the last minute.

The Internet has been experiencing exponential growth. Scientists, government officials, and telecom execs are mouthing the mantra that Internet traffic is doubling every three months. A report by the U.S. Department of Commerce restates the claim and predicts that by 2002, Internet commerce is going to be a $300 billion industry. "To a man, WorldCom engineers told us that as soon as they finished the current network expansion they would have to start expanding it all over again because the network was already oversold," an Internal Audit director will recall. Jack Grubman seems to believe demand is infinite. "We've always been bandwidth junkies," Jack will tell a reporter. "You build a fatter pipe, and trust me, people will figure out how to fill it."

Some industry experts believe that we have entered the age of a "new economy." Until now, the economy has worked in alternating expansions and contractions. In 1869, the Transcontinental Railroad, which spanned the United States, allowed the West to be settled. Soon, investors were scrambling to back additional railroads. Four new east-to-west routes were laid. The result was too much rail capacity. In 1873, the railroad bubble burst, leaving 89 failed companies and a mass of unpaid debt. The bust was followed by four years of depression. But now, some experts say, the "new economy" of seemingly unlimited growth has made this model obsolete. "Conventional economics is dead. Deal with it!" proclaims Mark McElroy, a principal in IBM's Global Knowledge Management Practice, in the *Wall Street Journal*.

The skeptics are few and lonely. Warren Buffett is not investing in the dot.coms because he says he doesn't understand them. In general, he believes that investors are not examining the numbers. "The Tinker Bell approach—clap if you believe—just won't cut it," he insists. Maybe, some wonder, he's too old-school and just doesn't understand? After all, it's Jeff Bezos, the founder of Amazon.com and the man who coined the term "dot.com," whom *Time* Magazine names Person of the Year in 1999.

For many telecom execs, whether this is a new economy or just an old-fashioned bubble is an afterthought. For telecom suppliers to slow production and for WorldCom and other behemoths to stop expanding networks is to leave opportunity on the table.

Meanwhile, the acquisition rate has hardly slowed down. Bernie is about to acquire my old employer SkyTel, the two-way wireless paging company, for $1.8 billion in stock. Initially, according to Charles, Bernie says my department can keep only two of SkyTel's five internal auditors, but Charles advises me to lay low and perhaps Bernie will forget about the other three. And that's exactly what happens. My department adds critical expertise, but, as always, building Internal Audit is an uphill battle.

A Hole in WorldCom's Strategy

There's only one thing preventing WorldCom from establishing a "one-stop shopping" powerhouse. An AT&T executive had pegged it back in

1997: "They're beginning to put together some of the pieces, but there are big holes.... They're missing a key ingredient called wireless." Residential customers are continuing to migrate to cellular, but WorldCom doesn't have its own wireless network. It only resells wireless service.

John Sidgmore, the head of UUNET, urges Bernie to buy Nextel, one of the few wireless companies with its own nationwide network available for purchase. But Scott Sullivan doesn't like Nextel and adamantly opposes the idea. Within an eight-day period, Bernie will manage to enrage both, with Scott threatening to quit, and find himself backed into a corner.

Bernie and several of his lieutenants test the Nextel phones to see how well they work. The service is good, but Nextel has a unique technology only supported by Motorola. "If Motorola suddenly decided not to support it, we'd be screwed," Charles Cannada will recall, "and Scott didn't like Nextel's heavy debt load. John was pounding the table for the deal. Scott was pounding the table against it. Bernie asked me, 'What do we do?' I said, 'It's a coin toss as far as I'm concerned.'"

Bernie finally decides to make an offer to Nextel. "He called me in to his office and said, 'Congratulations, they accepted the offer,'" Charles will say. "They had a gentleman's agreement. I went in to tell Scott and he said, 'Dammit. I'm quitting. I can't believe we're buying this [expletive] company.'" Steve Dobel, head of Commercial Sales and Marketing, will recall: "Scott was so angry he exercised a huge amount of his stock options."

Not wanting to lose his CFO, Bernie decides to back out of the deal. But now John Sidgmore is livid, and eventually resigns as the President of UUNET, retaining only a strategic advisory role. Within days, however, there's an exciting new opportunity: Sprint CEO William Esrey calls Bernie from his ranch in Wyoming. "'You don't need to buy Nextel,'" he tells Bernie, according to Charles. "'You need to buy us.'"

This time, Bernie and Scott agree, but now Charles is in dissent. He thinks buying Sprint would be a disaster. "Sprint had wireless spectrum throughout the country and great technology, but it was going to be horribly expensive to buy them," he says. And wireless is only part of Sprint's business; it also owns an older telecom network—largely redundant for WorldCom—that, like MCI, has a substantial residential component.

Charles pushes for a different strategy. "I believed the only way we could be a final survivor was to buy one of the Baby Bell companies" that own the last mile, Charles will say. "Bernie said, 'You're probably right, but it will take us three years to get it done.' The Bells were regulated monopolies. There were too many regulatory hurdles." Charles repeatedly urges Bernie not to buy Sprint and reminds him that Washington regulators specifically told him [Bernie] after the MCI deal that they wouldn't approve another acquisition of a large long-distance company. "Bernie wouldn't listen. He said, 'We're doing this deal. The Sprint lawyers tell me we can get this done.' "

In October, Bernie offers $127 billion for Sprint, dwarfing the MCI purchase and astounding Wall Street. If he manages to make this happen, it will, once again, be the largest acquisition in corporate history. In addition to the FCC, the deal must be approved by the Department of Justice and the European Union because both companies operate in Europe. "When we made the offer for Sprint, Bernie told me, 'This will make us bigger than AT&T,' " Charles will recall. "I think there was a lot of ego involved in us buying Sprint."

CHAPTER 17

A Double-Edged Sword

The thing that has helped me personally is that I don't understand a lot of what goes on in this industry.

—Bernie Ebbers

It's January, 2000. After more than a decade at WorldCom, my boss Charles is calling it quits. He's had enough. After years of long hours and one acquisition after another, he's burned out. But it's more than that. Bernie is becoming increasingly difficult.

"I love the guy," Charles will tell me, "but it's like the old saying—you can love somebody but that doesn't mean you can live with them." The camaraderie that once existed in the executive suite has faded. Bernie's personality and management style, coupled with the constant drive to acquire, has put a strain on relationships with some of his top executives.

Bernie can be petulant, imperious. "On Monday, he was always in a terrible mood," Charles will say. "If you said black, he said white. Tuesday was a little better. Wednesday and Thursday were as good as it was going to get. By Friday, he was so euphoric and excited that you couldn't get anything done or get his attention. So my objective became to get as much as I could done with him on Wednesday and Thursday." And Bernie sometimes avoids difficult decisions. "He would always put off making any tough decisions" when it came to the internal workings of the company, Steve Dobel will say. "He would allow redundant functions to run, creating in-fighting."

Without Bernie, WorldCom would have likely died a quick death almost as soon as the original investors set up shop. It's where it is today thanks in no small part to him. But his skill carries with it a bigger-than-life personality with plenty of good and bad, strengths and weaknesses. And the limelight has done nothing to temper Bernie's unpredictable style. He's still kind, witty, and the first to help one moment and cantankerous, overbearing, and curmudgeonly the next.

My interactions with Bernie are sporadic. I don't report directly to him, and my office is in a different building. It's Charles who constantly faces the heat. "Early on, you could have a good fight with Bernie and he'd get over it," Charles will say. "Later, nobody could tell him he was wrong. He wouldn't tolerate it."

"Bernie only focused on what he liked and understood," Charles will go on. "He loved sales. He could understand that. And he understood things like how much we were spending on coffee and travel. He once went off complaining about people leaving computers on all night. He would focus on someone spending $900 instead of $600 on a plane ticket. But I could never get him to look at a capital budget for billions of dollars. He didn't want to understand the details of building networks or capital plans because it was too complex. He'd complain about someone who was $500 over budget on some line item but ignore $200 million in capital being spent. I had difficulty getting him to formally approve a budget. He'd say, 'We'll just start with this and see how things go ...'"

In meetings, Bernie is regularly bored, whereas in the company's early days he was always engaged. Perhaps the business was easier for Bernie to understand when it was a modest underdog with manageable assets. Maybe this is why he now continues to focus on the more tangible details. In some ways, Bernie is still focused on slicing tomatoes "this thin" like he did at his hotel restaurant more than 20 years ago.

But even when focused on the less significant details of the business, his management seems inconsistent and impulsive. Bernie's top executives never know when he might randomly undercut their authority. Steve Dobel once purchased personally engraved organizers for his top sales representatives. Minutes before presenting them onstage at a group meeting, his cell phone rang. Somehow, Bernie had gotten wind of the gifts. " 'You weren't authorized to buy those and you will not give those out,' " Steve will recall Bernie telling him. "I said, 'Bernie, we've already paid for them. They already have names on them.' It didn't matter. I wasn't allowed to hand them out."

Charles once tried to plan a meeting in Dallas. "Bernie told me, 'You can't do that. It's a waste of money,' " Charles will recall. "Even though I had the budget, I wasn't even able to hold the meeting. It was ridiculous. I used to tell Bernie after the company grew—Bernie, your problem is you want to give people responsibility but never any authority. You can't continue to run this company like a mom-and-pop business."

I think Bernie tries to give people the impression that he's watching their every move. If he sees or hears about something that aggravates him—spending he thinks is frivolous, employees taking too much time outside smoking or on the outdoor walking trail—he'll chastise. But it all seems unpredictable, on a whim, the emotion of the moment—his idea of the paternalistic, eyes-everywhere coach.

Soon after I began working at WorldCom, Bernie arrived to find *Wall Street Journal*s lining the receptionist's desk. My department's copy was in my name. Soon, every employee receiving the paper, top execs included, received a curt e-mail: If we weren't personally paying for the newspaper, we'd better cancel our subscription immediately.

In his personal life, too, Bernie doesn't always seem to monitor or grasp the big picture. "When Bernie began building his home [a multi-million dollar Colorado-style lodge] in Brookhaven, I thought—this will be a disaster," Charles will say. "Bernie will focus on how much a shingle costs and ignore the overall cost of the project. That's exactly what happened. There were huge cost over-runs." One contributing factor: A roof designed, in accordance with Colorado standards, to withstand substantial snowfall—not a likely scenario in Mississippi.

I Don't Need This

Charles has already told Bernie he's resigning. "When I told Bernie I wanted to leave the company, he said, 'I don't know why you're leaving now,'" Charles will recall. "'Within a three year window we're going to sell [the company].' I told him, 'Bernie, you've been saying that since the beginning. You're never going to sell.' Those of us who had been around since the beginning were tired. We would have been happy to sell the company long ago, but Bernie would hear nothing of it. I told Bernie: 'I don't need this anymore.'"

Though Charles is the top acquisitions executive, Bernie has been turning to Scott for acquisitions work, perhaps because Charles opposed the Sprint deal and Scott received the credit for being the brains behind the MCI purchase. "Bernie isn't even keeping me in the loop on the Sprint deal," Charles says in frustration.

Disappointed about Charles leaving, I tell a few office friends, unknowingly creating a fiasco for Charles. Before the day is out, the grapevine reaches all the way back to Bernie's desk. Bernie's beyond furious. Apparently, he wasn't ready for Charles' departure to be announced. "I've been trying to get Bernie to work out a plan so that I could leave for weeks and couldn't get him to respond," Charles tells me. Maybe Bernie thinks Charles let out the news as some sort of power play. Maybe he's just unhappy that one of his top lieutenants is leaving after so many years, or maybe he's angry at Charles for making his own decisions. "[Bernie's] a monarch and wants courtiers and vassals," a former senior executive will tell a reporter. Whatever the reason, Charles is feeling his wrath—no hellos in the morning, no invitations to lunch.

Charles' last day with the company is approaching. I don't have lunch with Charles often, but I want to visit with him before he leaves. I've invited him to sit with me in the WorldCom cafeteria. I can see Bernie, Scott, and several other top executives sitting at their regular lunch table. Usually Charles sits with them, but Bernie's still not speaking to him. It's like junior high school again.

"You're going to report to Scott, but I don't know whether he'll have you report directly to him or to someone who works for him," Charles says.

"Why would he push me down to someone reporting to him?" I ask.

"I don't know. He may not. I don't think Scott likes you," Charles tells me with his usual forthrightness.

"Are you serious? Why? Did he say he doesn't like me?"

"No. I just get the feeling," he says.

I'm taken aback. As far as I know, Scott and I have a decent rapport. Granted, we don't make much small talk, but Scott seems all-business with everyone. He's been aggravated once or twice with the Internal Audit reports, but he seemed to get over it. If you're doing your job as an auditor, usually someone won't want to hear what you're saying.

Still, I'm concerned. I've finally been able to get more support for my department and hire more auditors. My total headcount is now 35. I have five directors reporting to me with teams in Clinton, Washington, and London. In the last year, they have completed more than 45 audit projects in the States, Europe, Asia-Pacific, and Latin America. The team is small for a $37 billion company, especially one that has grown so rapidly through acquisitions. Still, we've come a long way from the days when the department consisted only of Jon Mabry and myself. But now, am I about to get a boss who may not like me and may demote my department in the reporting structure?

Charles typically doesn't talk to me about how he's feeling, but today is different. "I've given all these years of my life to this company, and I feel like I'm being run out on a rail," he says sadly, glancing over at the table where Bernie and Scott are sitting. The man who has been a mentor to me will leave with no public or private expression of appreciation from Bernie. "I didn't need a going-away party," Charles says, "but it did hurt my feelings when Bernie sent out a press release on something else that simply mentioned my departure as an afterthought."

Charles says Scott is having strained interactions with Bernie as well. Maybe Bernie lowered the microphone before Scott spoke one too many times at the shareholder meetings. And, one executive will later say, Scott privately refers to Bernie as "the milkman" and a "red-necked hillbilly."

But for the public, Bernie and Scott continue to put on a happy face, and they continue to sit together, as they always have, at the same lunch table in the cafeteria. "Bernie and Scott were like a couple that seemed to get along great at social events and you're surprised that they got a divorce," Scott Hamilton, WorldCom's Vice President of Investor Relations, will later tell the *Wall Street Journal*, "Suddenly, you find out that they didn't get along privately at all."

A Symbol of 21st Century America

Though there is tension in the executive suite, WorldCom is still being hailed as an industry revolutionary. Bernie has now led the company through more than 65 acquisitions; has successfully completed the MCI purchase, then the largest in corporate history; and, if approved, will soon pay nearly $130 billion for Sprint, setting another record for the largest acquisition.

But there's noise in the system about the Sprint deal being a tough sell to regulators because of anti-trust issues. "We have mega-merger-mania and it must be stopped," says Consumers Union Co-Director Gene Kimmelman before the Senate's Commerce Committee. When the WorldCom/MCI merger was approved, FCC Chairman William Kennard warned that large long-distance players were "just a merger away from undue concentration." On a later occasion, responding to a question about a potential merger between WorldCom and Sprint, Kennard warned: "American consumers are enjoying the lowest long-distance rates in history.... That's a function of one thing: competition. We cannot allow any merger to happen in this industry that turns back the clock of competition."

On January 12, Bernie gives a luncheon speech at the National Press Club titled "Strong Enough to Fight Back," implying that the acquisition of Sprint would allow WorldCom to compete effectively with large international players and the phone companies that dominate local. He insists the merger will provide consumers with more choice, not less. "The opportunity—in fact, the imperative—created by the Telecom Act [is] to become a full-service provider for the communications needs of customers. If you are not all-distance in this business, you won't go the distance. That means providing local, long distance, international, data, Internet, wireline, and wireless. All services—all distances."

To allay concerns that the combined company would so dominate the long-distance market that it could raise customer rates, Bernie reminds the assembled that increasing prices will not be possible for two reasons—there's "too much competition and too much capacity." More than 600 domestic companies sell long distance, with 19 making the Fortune 500 list. The rush of new entrants into the market following the Telecom Act of 1996 has resulted in a "flood" of fiber capacity. Since WorldCom announced its merger with MCI in 1997, capacity within cities has more than doubled. Within the last five years, Bernie adds, the share of long-distance route miles owned by companies other than the Big Three—AT&T, MCI, and Sprint—has grown from 5% to well over 50%.

On March 1, 2000, WorldCom unveils its new facility in Ashburn, Virginia. President Bill Clinton attends the opening ceremony. "Mr. President, we're very pleased to welcome you to ground zero of the communications explosion," Bernie says. "We're in 65 different countries right now, and we're expanding as fast as we can." Bernie's certainly right about that. When I started six years ago, annual revenues were around $1.5 billion. Now, they're tracking toward $40 billion.

President Clinton delivers a speech to WorldCom employees. "We live in a time when...doing the morally right thing happens to be good economics," he says. "I came here today because you [WorldCom] are a symbol of 21st century America. You are an embodiment of what I want for the future."

Retirement Planning—Gunslinger Style

Meanwhile, Bernie, the acquisition king, has been applying his workplace strategy to his personal life. Approaching 60, Bernie's been thinking about retirement. A few years ago, he told several board members he wanted to be out by this year, and he's been purchasing assets to manage when he leaves. As with WorldCom, his purchases have gotten larger over time. Within just a few years, Bernie has acquired over $700 million dollars' worth of retirement projects: a rice farm ($13.8 million), a yacht-building company ($14 million), the largest working ranch in North America ($65 million), and, the pièce de résistence, 548,000 acres of timberland ($658 million).

In the early years, Bernie held fast to his conservative roots, living in a modest house and driving an old beat-up Ford truck. Many Mississippians still see him in that regard. But things have changed for Bernie. In June, 1999, when WorldCom's stock hit an all-time high of $64, his net worth was more than $1.3 billion. He also made big changes in his private life. In 1997, Bernie divorced Linda, his wife of over 30 years. Two years later, he married Kristie Webb, a former WorldCom sales representative more than 20 years his junior. At their wedding ceremony, at Provine Chapel on the Mississippi College campus, Bernie wore his usual cowboy boots and jeans with a tuxedo jacket.

It seems as though impulse has guided Bernie in some of his personal purchases. Initially, Bernie, a yachting enthusiast, hired a yacht-building company to build several yachts for resale. Relaxing one day on the deck of his own Aquasition with one of the shipyard executives off the coast of Hilton Head, South Carolina, he thought: Why not just buy the entire shipyard? Bank of America loaned him the money.

Then, Bernie purchased the Angelina Plantation—a 21,000-acre rice and soybean farm in Monterey, Louisiana, 75 miles west of his Brookhaven home. Bank of America again came through with the loan.

But only three months later, Bernie was back at the doorstep. This time, he wanted to buy a ranch—Douglas Lake Ranch in British Columbia, the largest working ranch in North America, with 500,000 acres, 20,000 head of cattle, ranch hands, a fly-fishing retreat, and a grocery store. The property was so exclusive that Queen Elizabeth and Prince Phillip had spent time there. This time, Bank of America refused the loan. So Bernie turned to Toronto Dominion Bank, which proved more willing.

Last summer, Bernie even bought a stake in the minor-league Chesapeake (Maryland) Ice Breakers, bringing professional hockey to central Mississippi for the first time in history. Mississippians poured into the coliseum to catch a game and perhaps a glimpse of Bernie, who was often sitting just off the ice. Thousands sent suggestions for a contest to name the team. Bernie and the other owners finally settled on "Bandits," a reference to the legendary 19th-century outlaws who robbed people as they traveled the old Natchez Trace, the 500-mile trail from Natchez, Mississippi to Nashville, Tennessee used by traders and settlers. Many never made it home, overcome by bandits who replaced the gold in their trousers with rocks and sank their captives in the Mississippi River.

Then, Dick Molpus, Mississippi's former Secretary of State, who owns one of the most successful timberland management companies in the country, convinced Bernie that timber was a good investment. He'd lined up a buyer for 460,000 acres of timberland in Mississippi, Alabama, and Tennessee, but, at the last minute, the buyer walked. Bernie stepped into the gap. He figured trees, a renewable resource, were a good investment. Citibank loaned the money.

Bernie could have sold some of his more than 18 million shares of WorldCom stock and paid cash for the assets. But he's a die-hard believer in holding the stock, so he opted to borrow on margin from the banks instead, using his stock as collateral—a risky investment strategy. No one at the company knows that Bernie's private funds are leveraged to the hilt.

It's March 2000. The U.S. economy has just set a record for the longest economic expansion in history. In the last month alone, the stock price for 27 IPOs doubled on the initial day of trading, and the NASDAQ has doubled from a year ago. With the low interest rates, many people are borrowing. In fact, "margin debt"—borrowed investment funds secured by the underlying stock purchased—will soon hit a record high of $278 billion.

Bernie could have used the assets he was buying as collateral. But stock is much easier to value and saves the time needed to perform due diligence on the asset before approving a loan, allowing Bernie to move more quickly with his purchases. The banks also prefer the stock because it gives them a liquid asset more easily sold than a rice farm or a yacht-building company. The fact that Bernie has purchased relatively illiquid assets, unlikely to be sold quickly if he needs to raise cash in an emergency, makes his investment strategy all the more daring.

Citibank and Bank of America have given Bernie most of his loans; both had an incentive to do so. They want more WorldCom business and, for all practical purposes, Bernie is the decision-maker when it comes to which companies receive WorldCom's investment banking. Bank of America, which provided lead financing for WorldCom's acquisition of WilTel in 1994, administers WorldCom's multibillion dollar credit facility. And Salomon Smith Barney—the Citigroup subsidiary that employs Jack Grubman—has pocketed some $100 million over the years for advising WorldCom. While Jack Grubman recommends World-Com's stock, another division of Citigroup is loaning money to World-Com's CEO backed by WorldCom stock.

As long as WorldCom stock stays high, Bernie's OK. But if it falls below a certain level, he could be in serious trouble. With margin loans, banks require the collateral to remain at a certain percent of the loan. If Bernie's pledged stock drops below this threshold, the lender will issue a margin call, requiring Bernie to come up with the cash to pay down enough of the loan to bring the percentage back in line. Otherwise, the bank will force a sale of his WorldCom stock. A large stock dump like this could cause panicked selling by investors, driving the stock price down further, leading to even more margin calls for Bernie, and more forced sales.

But Bernie is a believer in WorldCom, aggressively so. "He almost played with reckless abandonment—he was full force," a college basket-ball teammate of Bernie's once recalled. It seems Bernie has a similar approach to investing. But will his bets continue to pay off?

CHAPTER 18

A Titan Stumbles

It's only when the tide goes out that you learn who's been swimming naked.

—Warren Buffett

Analysts on the Hot Seat

It's May, 2000. The NASDAQ has been on an ominous downhill slide since hitting its all-time high in March. The rise of dot.com stocks turned out to be another tulip mania, and now the bubble has burst. With investor losses piling up, Wall Street analysts are coming under increasing scrutiny for continuing to recommend stocks at prices beyond what their fundamentals support. Investors want to know: What role did analysts play in building the stock market bubble?

Within the telecom industry, Jack Grubman, the Salomon analyst, has played a critical role in hyping stocks and pushing companies to spend billions expanding networks and merging. Now his objectivity and independence are being questioned. "Would he ever trash WorldCom?" an executive will ask *BusinessWeek*, "or is he just too close to Bernie?" Jack is receiving the most stinging criticism for his upgrade of World-Com's biggest competitor—AT&T. Last November, after having been negative about AT&T for years, even making derogatory comments in presentations, Jack suddenly upgraded the stock to a buy, causing it to be the most actively traded that day on the NYSE. One week later, AT&T announced it was spinning off its wireless unit in the country's largest equity offering ever, and Jack's employer, Salomon, won a portion of the business, earning more than $60 million in fees. Some question whether the upgrade was made purely to win the investment banking deal.

I've never met Jack Grubman. But it's no secret that he's tight with Bernie and Scott, and WorldCom's biggest fan on Wall Street. Any company would like to have such an ally. Internal Audit is not required to listen to a company's quarterly analyst calls, but over the years my staff and I have sometimes dialed in: Jack Grubman is typically the first analyst allowed to ask management a question. Like a faithful ally, he's sure to make glowing comments about the company followed by questions that seem scripted as if management was already well-prepared to answer them.

Jack is unapologetic about the role analysts play in investment banking. "The *Wall Street Journal* tried to make a big deal out of the [AT&T] upgrade," Jack tells *New York* magazine, "but the reality of the world is that analysts are becoming increasingly important in the banking practice of firms, not just for underwriting but also for mergers and acquisitions. It just is what it is; it's part of the business." Although the dot.com bubble has burst, Jack is still preaching "that this is a brave new world and that telecom's going to be a big part of that in terms of demand for bandwidth, data, and Internet services . . ."

On May 15, 2000, *BusinessWeek* profiles Jack and questions whether he is providing objective analysis. Some say Jack is "turning the roles of the stock analyst inside out" and that his actions are "scandalous." Again, Jack doesn't deny that his work has an impact on winning investment banking business—the world has changed. "What used to be a conflict is now a synergy," Jack says. "Someone like me who is banking-intensive would have been looked at disdainfully by the buy side 15 years ago. Now they know that I'm in the flow of what's going on. That helps me help them think about the industry." He also defends his close relationships with management of companies he follows. "Objective? The other word for it is uninformed."

Despite the dot.com implosion, Jack is confident that over the next several years the telecom industry will double to $2 trillion; and he believes that in order to win in this new environment, companies must get bigger by investing more in their telecom networks. "He has had a thesis for creating value in the telecom sector that's been dead right: Build it and they will come," says Eduardo Mestre, co-head of Salomon investment banking. The industry is taking heed. The *New York Times* will report that within a two-year period, companies will spend $35 billion to lay 100 million miles of fiber, "more than enough to reach the sun." Telecom companies are still building like crazy, but will Jack's theory—the attic always gets filled no matter how large—hold?

Industry executives praise Jack's knowledge and clout in the telecom industry. "He can move billions of dollars into or out of a stock with just one research report," *BusinessWeek* writes. Jack agrees. "I'm sculpting the industry," he says. "I get feedback from institutions and CEOs. It feeds on itself. It's a virtuous circle."

On May 17, 2000, just after AT&T disappoints the Street with earnings, and only three weeks after the wireless spin-off is complete, Jack comes down hard on AT&T in a research report due to what he says are "deficiencies in its data strategy." Only a few months later, in October, he drops his AT&T rating down two levels to a "neutral." The public is left to wonder what was behind Jack's AT&T recommendations.

The 92nd Street Y

It will later be reported that Jack's negativity on AT&T had become awkward for Sandy Weill, the CEO of Citigroup—Salomon's parent company. Sandy served on AT&T's board, and Michael Armstrong, AT&T's CEO, served on Citigroup's board. It was Sandy who asked Jack to take a "fresh look" at AT&T.

Documentation later released by Eliot Spitzer, New York's Attorney General, will reveal that the reasons Jack upgraded AT&T may have been multifaceted. Jack had been working hard to enroll his two children in one of New York's most elite preschools—the 92nd Street Y—where annual tuition runs around $15,000 a year. Having no luck, he decided to ask for Sandy Weill's help. On November 5, 1999, Jack sent Sandy a memo titled "AT&T and the 92nd Street Y." In it, he discussed the progress he was making on his "fresh look" at AT&T. Then, he turned to the problem he was having with preschool. "On another matter, as I alluded to you the other day, we are going through the ridiculous but necessary process of pre-school applications in Manhattan. For someone who grew up in a household with a father making $8,000 a year and for someone who attended public schools, I do find this process a bit strange, but there are no bounds for what you do for your children. . . . Given that it's statistically easier to get into the Harvard Freshman Class than it is to get into pre-school at the 92nd Street Y. . . , it comes down to 'who you know.' Attached is the list of the Board of Directors from the 92nd Street Y. . . . If you feel comfortable and know some of these board members well enough, I would greatly appreciate it if you could ask them to use any influence they feel comfortable in using to help us as well. . . . Anyway, anything you could do Sandy would be greatly appreciated. As I mentioned, I will keep you posted on the progress with AT&T which I think is going well."

Citigroup pledged to donate $1 million to the 92nd Street Y to be paid over five years from 2000 to 2004. On November 29, 1999, Jack upgraded AT&T. "You know everyone thinks I upgraded [AT&T] to get lead for [AT&T's wireless spin-off]," Jack will soon write in an e-mail to his friend Carol Cutler, an analyst with the Government of Singapore Investment Fund. "Nope. I used Sandy to get my kids in 92nd Street Y pre-school (which is harder than Harvard) and Sandy needed [the AT&T CEO's] vote on our board to nuke Reed [another Citibank board member] in [a] show-down. Once [the] coast was clear for both of us [Sandy won his board battle and kids were confirmed in school] I went back to my normal negative self on [AT&T]. [AT&T's CEO] never knew that we both (Sandy and I) played him like a fiddle." Jack adds in subsequent e-mails: "The biggest thing that [angered me] is that

[AT&T] did exactly as I knew they would for precisely the reasons I thought . . . collapse because the core business would fall apart. . . . I always viewed [AT&T] as a business deal between me and Sandy."

In his memoir, The Real Deal: My Life in Business and Philanthropy, Sandy Weill will strongly refute the allegations in Jack Grubman's e-mail. "[His]claims were outrageous; one could see by reading the e-mails that Grubman had invented the stories to impress [Carol Cutler]." He'll add, "The notions that I used our analyst to prevail over Reed and that I had helped Grubman's kids get accepted into nursery school as a quid pro quo for his change of heart on AT&T were bizarre and ridiculous." Weill will also point out that the pledge to the 92nd Street Y was made some time after Jack's children were accepted into the preschool, and that the school is "an important cultural institution in New York which was deserving of corporate philanthropic support." The Y hosts various events for the performing arts as well as lecture series. Additionally, the gift amounted to only one percent of Citigroup's annual budget for philanthropy.

"In asking Grubman to take a fresh look at AT&T, I only thought the advice would lead him to see the same value which had led me to make purchases of over $3 million of the stock for my own account," Sandy will write. "It was clear that I never pressured our analyst's change of rating; and finally, Grubman repeatedly disavowed under oath the controversial contents of his e-mails relating to the Y and my board fight with Reed." The Attorney General will conclude that there is insufficient evidence to continue pursuing Sandy Weill.

While many individual investors had believed research reports issued by analysts were independent, in fact there were significant conflicts of interest. The "Chinese Wall" that once existed between analysts and investment banking had been torn down. The compensation of Jack Grubman and many other Wall Street analysts was tied to how much investment banking business they were credited with, causing analysts to feel beholden to the bankers.

Eliot Spitzer will eventually release e-mails that show example after example of analysts feeling pressured by investment bankers or recommending stocks against their personal beliefs. After reiterating a buy on Focal Communications, one of Salomon's investment banking clients, Jack will hear Focal's management isn't happy with his research note. "I hear [Focal] complained about our note," he will write a Salomon investment banker, "I did too. I screamed at [the analyst] for saying "reiterate buy." If I so much as hear one more [expletive] peep out of [Focal] we will put the proper rating . . . on this stock. . . .We lose credibility . . . because we support pigs like Focal."

"If anything the record shows we support our banking clients too well and for too long," Jack will write to one of his staff as he continues to come under pressure. "If [a senior investment banker] starts up I will lace into him," he will write to another colleague. " . . . most of our banking clients are going to zero and you know I wanted to downgrade them months ago but got huge pushback from banking."

The head of Salomon Smith Barney's Global Equity Research Management will also write in an internal memo that there is "legitimate concern about the objectivity of our analysts which we must allay in 2001." His internal presentation states that out of 1,179 stocks rated by the firm, none were rated "sell" and only one "under-perform."

One Too Many Acquisitions

> We're not trying to be an MCI or a Sprint. Never will. We really don't want to be . . . If we stay committed and don't get off line with what we can handle, we should be able to survive the industry.
>
> —Bernie Ebbers speaking to the *Jackson Journal of Business* in 1988

It's June, 2000. Just last month WorldCom raised capital by selling $5 billion in bonds. But the company's seemingly unstoppable ascent comes to a rude halt. The regulators finally have a decision on the Sprint merger. It turns out my former boss Charles was right—the Department of Justice and the European Union both reject the deal. "This merger threatens to undermine the competitive gains achieved since the Department challenged AT&T's monopoly of the telecommunications industry 25 years ago," explains Attorney General Janet Reno. "It is critical to our economy that we preserve competition for services that so many of us rely upon in our everyday lives."

This is the first time a WorldCom acquisition has ever been denied and with the market turmoil, it couldn't come at a worse time. Jack reassures investors: "Likely collapse of the [Sprint] deal is unfortunate," he writes, "but, we believe [it] doesn't disrupt co's ability to grow at a double-digit rate for top & bottom line growth. . . . we cannot strongly emphasize enough how compelling we believe [WorldCom] is at these levels. . . . The reality is that [WorldCom] remains the company that every major global telecom company wants to look like in terms of assets." But WorldCom is running out of companies to purchase. When a company is small, it's easier to double revenues by acquiring other companies. But, the larger a company's revenue base, the more difficult it becomes to maintain high growth rates.

From an internal audit perspective, buying another enormous company would have made our jobs all the more difficult. My team and I continue to issue hundreds of recommendations to improve operations and strengthen controls. We've seen plenty of success, and many of our recommendations have been implemented. But this is a tough audit environment, and we continue to face a multitude of challenges. We audit in a company and an industry on steroids. Both have been recreating themselves since the break-up of AT&T, and everything about the environment is complex, fast, and demanding. The internal auditors must be quick studies as they are constantly thrust into new areas where the risks and challenges change often. Because of the difficulty of auditing in this environment, I've hired auditors who are seasoned professionals with a multitude of professional certifications, graduate degrees, and years of audit experience.

We are still a small staff compared to many companies our size, and some of our resources are being diverted to make recommendations and help compile a report for the executive team that shows where customer orders are being delayed in the activation process. It has been approved by the Audit Committee, and while we don't mind helping, I've asked to hire additional staff, but Bernie and Scott won't budge.

WorldCom is a patchwork of companies piled one on top of another. The result is an environment that is never stable and a quagmire of duplicate systems and processes. WorldCom has not one but 11 accounts receivable systems, some 60 billing systems, and overlapping telecommunications networks. As each company acquired comes into the fold, there is a clash of cultures, political jockeying, management turnover, and reorganization. And key executives are scattered: Boca Raton, Florida (head of human resources); Washington, DC (chief legal counsel); Dallas, Texas (Chief Operating Officer); Clinton, Mississippi (head of commercial sales).

We have a CEO whose passion and focus is on acquiring as opposed to integrating and managing the operations. The audit universe has grown increasingly complex as WorldCom has moved from long distance into a multitude of other services and expanded to Europe and Asia. Since each of the companies acquired was entrepreneurial, and many of them relatively young and growing rapidly, they were loosely controlled compared to companies in a more stable and established industry. Sometimes the infrastructure simply hadn't caught up with the expansion. Time and again, we must educate and sell new executive teams on the importance of internal audit and internal controls.

And WorldCom has always been better at acquiring than integrating. Eliminating redundant systems takes years and must be done cautiously to prevent customers moved from one system to another from being negatively impacted. Often, there is little time for employees to even focus on integration as it's all they can do to keep up with servicing customers and the next acquisition. And, since there is always another acquisition on the horizon, integration is sometimes delayed in anticipation that the next company might have superior systems. But running so many overlapping systems is inefficient, costly, and requires that internal controls be implemented across each system.

Acquisitions have allowed my team to benchmark many different companies. While some had efficient operations and strong controls, others did not. WilTel seemed to be the most well controlled of the companies purchased. Perhaps it was because the parent was a long-established pipeline company, and conservative engineers dominated the executive ranks. But even though WorldCom is less efficient or controlled than other companies in stable environments, it employs some 100,000 people and successfully connects phone calls, makes Internet connections, and transports data for hundreds of thousands of customers each month, billing over $38 billion in annual revenue.

My team regularly deals with navigating the corporate cultures under the WorldCom umbrella. They manifest themselves in many ways, right down to how people dress. "In Washington, we have the pinstripe boys," Bernie says, referring to MCI executives. "The UUNET environment has the cutting-edge type of people. You don't wear pinstripes there." UUNet does foster an informal environment. "You have to wear something, and no anatomically correct Spandex," Michael O'Dell, UUNET's chief scientist, once told a reporter. "You can't show underarm hair," John Sidgmore, head of UUNet, added.

Since Bernie has kept UUNET in a cocoon of sorts—not integrating it for fear that it would lose its techie feel, where people work unusual hours and wander the halls in shorts and sandals—it has maintained its culture. "WorldCom was smart enough not to break the new toy," said Michael O'Dell. "It's a matter of pride to [the employees] that they're part of an Internet company," John Sidgmore added. "I said from the beginning that as long as I'm here, we're not going to integrate it." But allowing such autonomy also has its share of complications. UUNet and WorldCom sales representatives end up competing against each other, often contacting the same customer and undercutting each other's price.

Bernie's Hand Gets Called

From January to July, WorldCom's stock price has dropped some $13, reducing Bernie's net worth by almost half. Even so, he continues to borrow and buy, purchasing KLLM, a Mississippi trucking company facing a hostile takeover. "He was trying to do his best to help these local companies out and keep local people on the payroll," David Kaufman, an attorney representing Bernie, will tell the *Wall Street Journal*.

It's September 6, 2000. The NASDAQ has continued to slide since the dot.com bubble burst in March. Many investors who dumped dot.com stocks transferred their money into the telecom sector. But by September, telecom stock prices are getting pounded as well. Some say there is a second market bubble that is finally bursting. Others believe it is a temporary downturn. Either way, it's bad news for Bernie. With World-Com's stock price less than half its all-time high of $64, Bernie receives a margin call from Bank of America. He must come up with cash or the bank will sell some of his stock. The Compensation Committee of the board is meeting today. Before the meeting, Bernie discusses his predicament with Stiles Kellett, Chairman of the Committee.

The Committee decides to loan Bernie $50 million. They believe the loan will be short term, just until the stock price turns around; and they reason it's better for shareholders if Bernie doesn't dump a large block of stock. Many board members are also substantial owners of WorldCom stock. Stiles Kellett holds WorldCom once valued at worth approximately $100 million.

The loan is a real sign of faith in Bernie, as it will later be revealed that the funds were given quickly, without the Committee researching Bernie's financial situation, obtaining collateral, agreeing on a maturity date, or even setting an interest rate. Stiles and fellow Compensation Committee member Max Bobbit figure this is a simple issue of liquidity, not insolvency; Bernie's WorldCom stock should be more than enough to cover any loan from the company. What the Committee members won't learn for some time is that Bernie's stock is already pledged to the banks. The Compensation Committee members decide not to mention the loan at the next day's full board meeting. Stiles Kellett will later say he didn't think the loan required approval by the board.

As September draws to a close, Bernie receives additional margin calls. But this time, instead of borrowing from WorldCom, he enters into a $70 million forward sale with 3 million shares of his WorldCom stock to cover the call. When word of the sale hits the street, WorldCom's stock takes an immediate dip.

Line of Fire

On a brisk day in October, Bernie comes by Steve Dobel's office to grab him for lunch. It's a routine the two have followed many times. As Bernie, Scott, and Steve head downstairs to the company cafeteria, they make small talk. Nothing seems out of the ordinary.

Last month, Steve told Bernie that he wanted to transition to another role that would allow him to work less overtime without constant travel, so he can spend more time with his family. Since Steve still feels a loyalty to the company and his employees, he has agreed to stay on as head of Commercial Sales until he and Bernie can work out a smooth transition plan to move him into a less demanding role. Steve's recommended replacements for his position and is waiting for Bernie to come back with a final proposal.

Returning to his office after lunch, Steve sits down to check his e-mail. Hitting the refresh button to make sure his messages are current leaves Steve with a shock. Just as he and Bernie were enjoying lunch, an e-mail on Bernie's behalf was sent to top company executives stating that last month Steve had expressed his desire to resign and that today would be his last day of employment. Steve is stunned because he's been working with Bernie on a transition plan and all seemed well. He soon realizes that Bernie has already spoken with some of his direct reports, as the memo indicates several of Steve's employees will now assume his responsibilities. Steve has worked at WorldCom for eight years and helped build the company from just $900 million to over $38 billion in revenue. He's in charge of 7,000 sales reps, $7 billion of the company's revenue base, and one of the top performing sales divisions.

As with Charles, Bernie's message includes no expression of appreciation for Steve's eight years with the Company. Steve hasn't even had an opportunity to personally inform the employees who work with him.

He spends the next few hours packing his personal items into boxes. But there's another nasty surprise waiting for him when he calls Salomon Smith Barney to exercise his vested stock options, that is, those whose attached stock he can now sell. While Steve had previously obtained written authorization from Bernie to exercise his options, for some reason they've been frozen. Furious, he storms over to the executive offices. The two enormous doors leading into Bernie's office, usually open, are closed and Bernie's assistant says he's not available.

"I'm not leaving until I've spoken to Bernie," Steve says adamantly.

When Steve is finally able to get in, he finds that Bernie is nonchalant, boots propped up on his desk as if Steve is paying a social visit. "He asked me, 'What seems to be the problem?' as if nothing unusual had happened since lunch," Steve will later recall. "I said, 'my options are frozen, that's what the problem is. You can't just go and freeze all of my options. I want them unfrozen right now.' He stared at me and said, 'That's a matter for the board to decide.' I said don't give me that [expletive], Bernie. You are the board!"

Bernie's e-mail regarding Steve's departure does close with an expression of appreciation and encouragement, not to Steve but others. "As we struggle to overcome the challenges we currently face as a company I am thankful to all of you for putting your hands to the plow. I personally believe the rainbow is just over the hill."

"Steve's in his office packing his things," a colleague tells me. I'm both surprised and sad. Steve has been a good friend, and he's highly respected in the company. From my perspective, Bernie is no more or less difficult than usual to get along with, but his reaction to Steve seems just as irrational as when Charles left. Maybe the pressure of the Sprint denial and the stock market turmoil is getting to him.

More Margin Calls

It is October 20, 2000. Bernie's received more margin calls from Bank of America and Citibank. The Compensation Committee is engrossed in helping him resolve his financial situation. Max Bobbitt and Lawrence

Tucker, two Committee members, go with Bernie to meet the President of Bank of America. The three try to convince him to defer margin calls and take Bernie's non-stock assets as collateral. Bank of America doesn't bite, but it does agree to take a guaranty from WorldCom on Bernie's behalf.

Bernie also makes a plea to Citibank (the commercial banking arm of Citigroup) for relief by turning to their sister company Salomon Smith Barney, where Jack Grubman works as an analyst. Citibank wants to force a sale of some of Bernie's WorldCom stock to cover their margin call. To prevent Citibank from selling, Salomon Smith Barney strikes an unusual deal, agreeing to guarantee Citibank's loan, accepting all future loan risk. Salomon Smith Barney executives also convince the banking arm to change the threshold for future margin calls so that it is more favorable to Bernie.

Bernie's association with WorldCom clearly makes a difference with Citibank. "[Bernie] is associated with the number one fee-generating client [i.e. WorldCom] of [Salomon Smith Barney] . . . ," a high-ranking Citibank executive who helped arrange the refinancing wrote in an e-mail. With Bernie's stock backing Citibank loans, Salomon now has added incentive—beyond the hope for more investment banking fees—to pump WorldCom's stock price.

On October 26, 2000, WorldCom announces third-quarter earnings in line with analyst expectations. Still, the stock price drops $3.50 to $21.75 on news that WorldCom will soon announce a restructuring plan. Jack Grubman again issues a "buy" rating on WorldCom, saying shares are "dirt cheap." On October 27, the Compensation Committee loans Bernie another $25 million to cover more margin calls. WorldCom has now loaned Bernie $75 million directly, and could be forced to pay the bank another $75 million under the guaranty. But on October 31st, when the full board meets, the Compensation Committee members make no mention of the loans.

It's November 1, 2000. Speaking in Manhattan before a large group of stock analysts, Bernie announces that WorldCom is lowering the earnings estimates for the fourth quarter and 2001. The new guidance is far

below analysts' expectations. "I've let you as investors down," Bernie
tells them. "I've let myself down." He adds: "I'm sure with the recent
performance of the stock people have a legitimate right to ask if I'm the
right person to lead this company."

That same day, WorldCom announces that it's splitting its stock into
two tracking stocks, WCOM and MCIT. All of the company's faster-
growth revenue streams—Internet, web hosting, data, wireless and
international—are consolidated under the WCOM tracker, while "high
cash flow" low- or no-growth areas like residential long distance, fall to
the MCIT stock. "The new structure is designed to create greater shareholder value by providing shareholders with two distinct, clear, and
compelling investment opportunities, while ensuring a seamless transition for WorldCom customers and employees," Bernie says.

Regardless, the stock takes a beating, dropping 20% in one day.
Within a week, the price drops down to less than $19, below the recently
renegotiated margin call threshold with Citibank. Salomon Smith
Barney, which has accepted the risk on the loan, still thinks the business
relationship is worth the trouble. "On the strength of the corporate
finance relationship between [Salomon Smith Barney] and [WorldCom],
[Salomon Smith Barney] effectively guaranteed the Private Bank's
exposure, and has elected not to enforce the margin call provisions, . . . "
writes a Citibank executive in an internal e-mail.

On November 16, over two months after the first loan was made to
Bernie, Stiles and Max—the Compensation Committee members—
inform the full board of the loans and guaranty at the regularly scheduled
board meeting. As is the custom, Bernie opens the board meeting with a
prayer. After Stiles explains the rationale for the loans, Bernie says the
idea originated with the Compensation Committee and adds that
although he agrees the loans are in the best interest of the company
and shareholders, he's not convinced they are necessarily in his best
interest. Max confirms that the loans were in fact the Committee's idea.
The board unanimously approves the loans. Board members will later
give a variety of reasons—the belief that the loans were short-term, that
WorldCom's stock price would recover, and that Bernie had the ability to

repay the debt; reliance on the opinion of the Compensation Committee; and the feeling that there wasn't much they could do since the loans had already been made.

My team and I learn of the loans along with the rest of the world, when they are finally publicly reported. While many think it sounds like a bad business decision, the board has reviewed and approved the loans; they are legal and have been publicly reported in the company's public filing with the SEC as required, and Andersen has reviewed them.

The fourth quarter of 2000 continues to be brutal for telecom companies. While some experts question whether the industry has overbuilt network capacity, Jack Grubman sees no problems. "Is there a bandwidth glut?" he writes in early 2001. "As we have written many times: No." But others predict a rough year for telecom companies. "Analysts said gloomy outlooks were priced into AT&T, WorldCom, and Sprint shares," wrote CNETNews.com. "WorldCom . . . will be hit hard by the evaporation of long-distance revenue."

Though Bernie remains on *Forbes'* list of wealthiest Americans in 2000, he falls from the 174th position to 368th. But he's still being lauded. In March, 2001, he is the only person named by *Network World* as one of "the 15 most important people, inventions and events that shaped our networked world," a list that also includes the personal computer, the Internet, and fiber-optic networks. "Ebbers has demonstrated how an entrepreneur with an idea could change the structure of an industry," Dave Neil of the research firm Gartner Group comments.

For me, everything at work moves far from my mind in July, 2001. Lance and I have just had a beautiful baby girl named Anna Katherine. Though there are initially complications and she has to stay in the intensive care unit, we are finally able to bring her home. I'm excited about taking a few months off to be home with her. This time, I don't have to rush back to work as I did with Stephanie.

But before this blessing, there was a tragedy in my family. In April, my father called. "I'm on my way to the hospital with your mother," he said, "She's slurring her words. I think she may have had a stroke." The doctors soon confirmed his hunch. She lost her ability to swallow and couldn't eat anything, but the doctors were hopeful it would come back.

One day, as I sat outside my mother's hospital room, my father rushed out of the room. "We need some help," he yelled. "Help! Somebody help!" I yelled as I ran down the hall. What appeared to be every medical professional on the floor came zooming past me toward my mother's room. I could hear her gasping loudly to breathe. I thought she was dying.

Finally, there was quiet in the room. My father came out and told me she was okay. It turned out she had tried to drink some water, against her doctor's orders. After several minutes, she was finally able to breathe freely again. Even in her state, my mother was as willful as ever. Later, tired of the IVs in her arm, she simply jerked them out while no one was looking.

Fortunately, things turned out well. My mother regained her ability to swallow and was able to come home.

Penny Wise and Pound Foolish

Throughout 2001, the telecom industry continues to sink. "The U.S.'s number two long distance carrier took a battering in the third quarter with both of its trading stocks—WorldCom Inc. and MCI—recording substantially less net earnings than a year ago," writes the press in October, 2001. The fourth quarter 2001 is no better. Privately, Verizon offers to buy the company at its current stock price of $13, but Bernie declines.

Telecom executives throughout the industry are dumping shares of their company's stock. Philip Anschutz, founder of Qwest, sells almost $2 billion; Joseph Nacchio, the CEO of Qwest will sell some $248 million prior to being forced out in June, 2002; Gary Winnick, founder of Global Crossing, will sell $734 million prior to the company going into bankruptcy in January, 2002; and John Sidgmore, former head of

UUNET, will sell $87 million. "Hundreds of telecom executives, almost uniformly bullish, sold at least some portion of their stock and made hundreds of millions of dollars, while many investors took huge, unprecedented losses," the *Wall Street Journal* will later write.

By the end of 2001, the telecom market has still not turned around. Executives cling to the hope that the industry will soon recover. But the telecom party—driven by the Telecom Act of 1996, low interest rates, and the belief that the Internet would continue to grow at a phenomenal rate—is over. Bernie and the top executives I once saw laughing at their cafeteria lunch table are now often sitting quietly, saying nothing as I pass, the stress and worry apparent on their faces.

Bernie holds a meeting with some of his top executives and gives instructions on how they can cut costs: Stop making color copies, turn out the lights before leaving, and use less air conditioning. He even mentions the possibility of replacing all of the plants in the buildings with plastic plants. The execs think Bernie's ideas are over the edge. Some jokingly refer to the new rules as Bernie's "seven points of light," but they spread the message through their departments. "Bernie is running a $40 billion company as if it were still his own mom-and-pop business," a WorldCom executive who was at the meeting will later say. "He doesn't know how to grow the company, just shave pennies."

Bernie takes away the free coffee after someone tells him coffee expense has become excessive and someone may be stealing. "Cynthia, don't make any more color copies," Scott Sullivan tells me, "Bernie thinks it's a waste of money. He thinks that if people are careful about spending small amounts, they will be careful about spending large amounts."

While there appears to be an immense sea change going on in the telecom industry, Bernie is preoccupied with color copies and coffee.

Conflicts of Interest

The probe into analyst conflicts of interest continues to gain momentum. The House Subcommittee on Capital Markets has recently held public hearings to discuss the issue. "A goal of this hearing is to begin speaking openly about what has apparently been unspoken in the past," said Chairman Richard Baker. Congressman Michael Oxley expresses concern: "I am distressed by the statistics that as the markets were crashing last year, less than two percent of analysts' recommendations were on the sell side. It is no wonder there is public outcry about analysts' independence when the statistics are so stark."

These hearings are only the beginning of multiple investigations into analyst conflicts. Within Salomon, the conflicts of interest are highlighted by the disparity between how investment bankers and stock brokers view Jack Grubman's research. Each year, they rank the firm's analysts and provide written comments. In 2000, Salomon's bankers, who profited from Jack's recommendations, ranked Jack first among Salomon analysts, giving him the highest score possible. In 2001 they also gave him a high ranking. But the brokers, who used his research reports to sell stock to their clients—many of them individual investors—and received angry complaints when their recommendations tanked, ranked him dead last of some 100 analysts for both 2000 and 2001. New York Attorney General Eliot Spitzer will later release many of the comments brokers included on Jack's internal report cards.

"Mr. Grubman should decide what he wants to be—analyst or banker."

"Jack Grubman has lost all credibility. . . . The conflict with banking is unbelievable."

"His cheerleading and lack of objective analysis has been a disaster for my clients and myself."

"I realize that Jack makes the firm a lot of money but he is death to the retail broker. . . . "

"Not all four letter words are bad ones. Perhaps . . . Grubman, should consider this one: SELL."

"In my 16 years in the retail brokerage business, NEVER have I received such misguided, horrific recommendations from an analyst."

One chagrined broker does come to Jack's defense: "Please do not fire Jack. He is my No. 1 indicator—I just do exactly what he says not to."

CHAPTER 19

The Rule of Ten

It's January, 2002. Since coming back from maternity leave four months ago, the Internal Audit department has been a whirlwind of activity. Bernie has called on my team to investigate an alleged commission fraud scheme. According to the employee who gave him the tip, sales representatives are somehow manipulating commissions to receive large payments on sales they didn't make. Bernie seems determined to get to the bottom of the accusation and is disturbed that some sales employees may be stealing from the company.

If word of our audit leaks or we make a wrong step, it could compromise the entire investigation. We work surreptitiously. We've been at it countless hours, mostly coming up empty—Bernie has no names and no idea how the scheme might be perpetrated. We test commission records and large payments, and trace suspicious transactions. Sales representatives appear to be collecting commissions on accounts sold by others and old accounts that have already been commissioned, but we can't quite figure out how—WorldCom has a byzantine tangle of billing and commission systems.

With assistance from the legal department, we begin narrowing in on e-mails describing the mechanics of the scheme between employees who appear to be involved. The list of suspects includes both top performers and high-level executives. Slowly, we begin to connect the dots. To effect the scheme, employees in different departments—sales, billing, commissions—each play a role. Some involved are being manipulated by sales employees and don't even seem to be aware that their actions are facilitating the overpayments.

The fraud is considerable—sales reps have collected more than $10 million they haven't earned. They've done so in part by shifting customers back and forth between various WorldCom billing systems so that they would appear as new sales and re-generate commissions, and by re-tagging accounts sold by sales representatives in other divisions to themselves. In addition, because sales divisions have separate commissions systems, two sales reps from different parts of the company are being paid on the same account without detection.

"These sales reps in the field have absolutely no ethics," Scott says when I deliver our findings. But when I mention that internal control weaknesses in the Commissions department—which reports to Scott—are part of the problem, he becomes irritated.

"Your team should treat the people in Commissions the way you would want to be treated if it were you," he says tersely. Scott seems to think we're being unfair. But we've made no personal judgments and are simply presenting the facts.

After hundreds of hours of research by my team, Dean Taggart, an Internal Audit director, flies to Washington along with a member of in-house legal to interview some of the employees who may be involved. Some sales representatives admit complicity, others don't.

"I've got support for all of those commission payments in my office," one sales manager tells Dean.

"Okay, let's go take a look," Dean says, following the man to his office. Dean sits in the guest chair for 30 minutes looking on as the employee tears through his office, scouring every drawer, until the top of his desk is completely covered.

"You don't have it, do you?" Dean asks.

"No," the manager finally admits.

Security escorts the man off the premises as Dean calls the next sales representative in for an interview.

Several employees are soon terminated, and word of our audit leaks to the press. To his surprise, Dean opens the *Wall Street Journal* one day in February to see his name and details of our investigation. The SEC will later open an inquiry—into Bernie Ebbers' loans and several WorldCom accounting issues—that was jump-started by SEC staff who didn't like what they saw in the *Journal*'s expose of the commissions audit.

With the sales force now on notice about the intensity of Internal Audit's investigation, many of the implicated employees rush in their resignations. The company freezes commission payouts to the implicated individuals while the investigation continues and recovers millions. My department has unraveled an ugly fraud scheme, but it will pale in comparison to the crisis that looms.

The Wireless Train Wreck

It's a week before the March Audit Committee meeting in Washington. As usual, I prepare a brief on Internal Audit work to mail in advance to the committee and forward it to Scott for feedback. Usually, he has only minor comments, if any, but today is different.

"I want to take these sentences out," he says when he calls, referring to problems Internal Audit has identified in the Wireless resale business unit. Scott is straining to sound nonchalant, but I detect a hint of nervousness in his voice.

Wireless sales have exploded, but the infrastructure—billing systems, customer service, internal controls—is inadequate and can't handle the customer volume. Since WorldCom still doesn't have its own wireless network, the company simply resells another carrier's wireless, just as we did in the early days with long distance. But while the unit takes in around a billion dollars in annual revenue, it's not making a profit.

Our audit work indicates that customer subscription fraud—sales to customers who never intend to pay—is prevalent, as there are insufficient up-front internal controls. Customer billing had been months behind as the billing system buckled under the load. Now customers are sending hundreds of complaint letters and refusing to pay. Two of my own relatives—my father-in-law and a cousin—have even called me about their terrible experiences. But Scott thinks we're making too much of the problem.

I'm surprised by Scott's directive. My mind starts racing—how can I diplomatically decline my boss's request? I think the wording in our Wireless report is a fair reflection and view these issues as serious.

"Scott, I don't feel comfortable taking the comments out," I say finally. "I feel an obligation to report this to the Audit Committee."

"You feel an ob-li-ga-tion, you feel an ob-li-ga-tion," he says sarcastically, throwing his voice into a higher pitch and drawing out the words as if talking to a small child.

I try to ignore his tone, and to convince him that the problems are significant. Why don't we just phase out the Wireless resale channel or at least stop taking new customer orders since it's losing so much money and having such difficulty implementing controls?

"John Stupka [the head of Wireless] is working to get the controls in place," Scott says, still agitated. The conversation is over.

I hang up the phone, shaken. Scott is livid. I talk to Lisa Smith, the Internal Audit director who is managing the Wireless audit. She's just as taken aback as I am by Scott's behavior. I feel strongly that the Audit Committee needs to know about the issues, so I leave the information in. I'll just have to let the chips fall where they may. I tell myself not to be intimidated—the worst Scott can do is fire me.

After work, I meet my husband at the park where he's pushing Anna Katherine around the walking trail in her stroller. As I walk beside him still in my suit and heels, I explain the situation at work. Lance understands the role of Internal Audit—to maintain an independent frame of mind even if it means serving as the cop on the beat. It's not always comfortable, but it's part of the job, and this is only one of many times my team has been forced to stand up for something. Years ago, I saw Terri, my boss at SkyTel, fight more than a few battles—it comes with the territory.

"I'm mailing the package as it is," I say.

"You should," he encourages.

After updating Bernie on the commissions fraud investigation, I decide to mention Scott's request. Because of Scott's abrasiveness, I want to make sure he hasn't misrepresented our conversation to Bernie. I tell him that I've already mailed the package and included the information Scott believed too harsh. "Tell the Audit Committee what you need to tell them," Bernie responds with his usual brusqueness.

It's the early morning of March 6, 2002. The Audit Committee meeting is this afternoon in Washington. Several of us are flying on one of the corporate jets. After one of the pilots takes my bag, I walk up the steps to board, wondering if Scott is on the plane. He's not, and I'm somewhat relieved.

On the flight to D.C., I take an empty seat next to Kenny Avery, one of the Arthur Andersen audit partners. Kenny began working on the WorldCom audit several years ago, taking the place of Paul Ogden, the partner my team and I had coordinated with for five years. In 2000, after being promoted to partner, Kenny began attending Audit Committee meetings. He's moved up quickly within Andersen, and has worked on some of its most prominent clients, like Federal Express. I want to get his perspective on the Wireless issues. Kenny says that Andersen knows about the Wireless billing, service, and collection problems. He's been reviewing them closely. I'm relieved to hear it.

I brace myself for what I feel certain will be an unfriendly encounter with Scott. After we arrive in Washington, he approaches our group. He shakes everyone's hand but mine. He doesn't even acknowledge me with a glance—an ominous sign, I think, of the tone he'll take with me in the meeting. But when the Audit Committee gathers, he's cordial and even seems to support much of what I say about Wireless. Now I'm really bewildered about his intent.

But as I give a staffing update, Scott makes an announcement that stuns me.

"Bernie proposed a 50% reduction in Internal Audit compensation expense," he interjects. "I convinced him to limit it to a 10% reduction." There's a plan to cut my staff essentially in half?! And this is how I find out? After all these years, my department is still fighting the same battles.

When the Andersen partners step out to allow management and the WorldCom Audit Committee members to have a private discussion, Judy

Areen—one of the committee members and the Dean of Georgetown Law School—expresses concern about continuing to engage Andersen, as it's been sullied by its role as external auditor for Enron. Many of Andersen's clients are engaging other firms, but Scott forcefully opposes Judy's suggestion. It will take new auditors too long to get up to speed, he argues. The committee closes by deciding to continue evaluating the situation.

As usual, Bernie doesn't attend the Audit Committee meeting, but he's here in Washington for the full board meeting. As everyone leaves for the day, I ride down on the elevator with him, Scott, and several others. "Cooper, how did the Audit Committee meeting go?" Bernie asks.

"Pretty well," I say, smiling.

"Good," he replies, smiling back.

In the back of my mind, I wonder if Bernie really made the comment about staffing. He may well have, but now is not the time to ask. In the elevator, Scott seems tense and says nothing. He's loaded down with a large briefcase bulging with documents. "Why don't you get a rolling bag?" I ask, trying to break the ice.

"No. I'll never roll a bag," he replies. "Charles Cannada used to pull his briefcase. I asked him, 'How many dresses can you get in that bag?'" Some in the elevator chuckle at his implication: Real men don't roll. At least Scott is speaking now.

It's late March, 2002. John Stupka, the President of the Wireless resale unit, has come to me with concerns about the allowance to cover non-paying customers. John is Scott Sullivan's peer in the corporate hierarchy—both report to Bernie. The business unit John manages continues to have serious issues with customers not paying their World-Com invoices. "This unit is a train wreck waiting to happen," he tells me. To account for the problem, accountants in Wireless set aside amounts to cover non-paying customers, but John says Scott Sullivan's Corporate accountants keep reversing their entries—leaving John with nothing to offset the shortfall.

"Scott assures me the shortfall is being made up in other areas of the company," John says, "but I'm still not comfortable. Maybe you could take a look."

Because Internal Audit is heavily focused on auditing company operations, we haven't tested the allowance, which is the external auditor's domain. Arthur Andersen tests it each year as standard procedure. I speak to Kenny, the Andersen partner, but he says he's not worried about the reversals—if the allowance is low in Wireless, it's high elsewhere. "From a total company perspective, the allowance is adequate," he says. Maybe, but I don't understand why the company wouldn't just leave the proper amount at the Wireless business unit level in the first place. Why rely on overages in other areas of the company? The effect is to make Wireless seem to be losing less money than it really is because it's setting aside less allowance, as if it has fewer bad-debt customers.

The next afternoon, I leave work early to make a scheduled hair appointment. With an eight-month-old at home and the demands at work, time for me is in short supply. I'm looking forward to enjoying an afternoon of being pampered, reading the latest *People*, and maybe even having a manicure. I'm happy to turn my thoughts away from solving problems, if only for a few hours. It's a beautiful day for a drive across town. We've made the turn out of winter, and the temperatures are already in the high 70s. Bradford pears scattered about the WorldCom property are beginning to bloom. Soon the azaleas lining the side of our home will blossom bright-pink, just in time for Easter, when my family snaps our traditional picture in front of the flowers. This year our family photo will include an addition—it's Anna Katherine's first Easter.

My salon time starts out well enough. Todd, the stylist, and I chat about what each of us has been up to since my last visit. I carefully carry out my assignment—handing Todd three-inch squares of tinfoil as he covers my hair with bleach. As I'm handing tinfoil over my shoulder, a woman calls my name over the intercom: Call for Cynthia Cooper. I excuse myself, half my head in tinfoil antennas. It's my husband Lance. Scott's assistant called. He needs to speak to me urgently. Must be—Scott has never tried to reach me outside the office.

Blow dryers are going full force, water is running, and ladies all around are giving instructions on how they want their hair cut and styled. My face is almost hidden under a mass of shining silver. Having a serious conversation while looking like some sort of a Star Wars character will be a challenge. But I have no choice; I dial Scott. Half of my hair is already processing with bleach; if I stay on too long, the two sides of my head will end up different shades.

I hold the phone to one ear and cover the other to muffle the noise. After I'm transferred to Scott, he puts me on hold. "David, are you there?" he asks, clicking back in. He has conferenced in David Myers, the Controller, who runs WorldCom's Accounting department.

"Yes, I'm here," David answers.

"Okay, just a minute," he says, putting me on hold again. Is he conferencing in someone else? When Scott comes back on the line, I'm on speaker phone, though he hasn't announced anyone else on the call.

"I understand you had a meeting with Kenny Avery yesterday," Scott says curtly. "I want to know what you discussed."

I review my conversation with Kenny. When I mention the allowance, Scott bristles. It's clear this is the reason for his call, and he's been waiting to ambush me.

"If you have questions about the allowance, you should be going to David, not Arthur Andersen," he says condescendingly. Kenny seems to have spoken to Scott about our talk. What did he say to make Scott so hostile?

"David doesn't audit the allowance," I reply. "Internal Audit hasn't tested it, so I went to the external partner, who does. What are you telling me, guys? That I can't talk to the external auditors?"

"No, but you should have gone to David. I've talked to John Stupka [the head of Wireless]. He says it's not him who's driving these issues with Wireless and the allowance. It's you." Scott chuckles oddly. He sounds like he's performing for someone, and I wonder again if someone else besides David is in on the call. And David's saying nothing, seemingly brought in only to observe Scott put me in my place. So now, the top executives are on the same page and I'm out on a limb by myself. "That's all I have to say," Scott says. The phone goes dead.

As I return to the stylist's chair, I mull over the call. Why is Scott acting like this? If you're an auditor, and someone is acting hostile and out of character, you want to find out why. If there's nothing wrong, why does he care if I talk to the external auditor? This kind of consultation is certainly standard procedure. Does he have something to hide?

The next day, I decide to call Scott. I want to clear the air and clarify my position. But Scott is still on the warpath. He says John Stupka was standing in his office door when he called me at the salon and is angry that I'm looking into the allowance and suggesting that management consider phasing out his unit.

"John says you're probably a decent auditor, but you don't have the business expertise, and you're trying to tell him how to run his business while he has over 27 years' experience. It's you who's driving this!" Scott shouts.

Each conversation with Scott is worse than the one before. This time, I can't stop the tears. My voice is shaking, but I keep talking. I tell Scott not to patronize me and try to move the conversation back to the issues.

"Why are you all so intent on continuing to run this sales channel?" I say. I still don't understand why the company doesn't phase out the Wireless resale unit or at least stop taking new orders. Even under a best-case scenario—that is, with customer activation, billing, and collections running smoothly—the unit would have almost no net profit margin. To be significantly profitable in wireless, WorldCom would have to own its own wireless network instead of reselling other companies' wireless. I'm beginning to wonder if executive management doesn't want to give up the revenue even though, after costs, the unit is losing money. Wall Street analysts closely monitor company revenue; if it begins to grow too slowly, they may decide to stop recommending the stock. Wireless sales increase WorldCom revenue by a billion dollars annually even though much of it has to be written off as a bad-debt expense down the road when customers refuse to pay.

Scott reiterates that management is working to get the controls in place. His tone has softened, but he has to hang up for another call. I wish I hadn't started crying, but his increasing hostility and the stress are starting to weigh heavy.

In the workplace, people are expected to be stoic. But men and women often express stress differently. Whereas women are more inclined to cry, men are more apt to become angry. They're just different ways of expressing frustration.

Later in the morning, Scott leaves me a voice-mail. It's as baffling as his demeanor the last several days. Since we spoke less than an hour ago, Bernie and Scott have suddenly had an epiphany. Scott says they agree that the Wireless resale channel should be phased out: "Um, it's time to bite the bullet on the thing. And, um, so, um, I'll get with John [Stupka] and see exactly how quick, you know, it can happen and all that stuff. But, um, Bernie has finally given up on it, so, uh, and, uh, again, the one last thing I'll emphasize is he has always gone [at] it from a legitimate perspective—that we could put the controls in place and be successful in this thing."

The nervousness of the message is odd: Usually Scott is very articulate. He later calls again to second Kenny on the adequacy of the total-company allowance. When I run into David Myers working out in the company gym during his lunch break, he also volunteers that he believes there are no problems with the allowance.

That night, as I lie in bed, I keep trying to figure out how to explain what's happening and replay conversations in my mind. I think about my recent interactions with my boss and the Andersen partner. In a recent Audit Committee meeting, one of the committee members expressed concern that the Andersen partners weren't able to answer some questions about their audit testing. Earlier in the year, one of the Andersen partners told me that his boss was concerned because Internal Audit was bringing so many control weaknesses to the attention of the Audit Committee while Andersen wasn't bringing any. In fact, Andersen hasn't issued a management letter citing any internal control weaknesses for several years. And now, Andersen has been indicted for destroying documents related to its work on Enron.

Between my recent encounters with Scott and the growing concern about Andersen, I wonder if my team should start performing financial-statement audit work even if it means duplicating Andersen's efforts. Is Andersen's testing of the allowance adequate? Why has the company been lowering the Wireless allowance? Something in the pit of my stomach tells me to take another look.

The next day, Lisa Smith and I ask an employee in the Wireless unit where its allowance would be without the Corporate reversals. We also request additional detail for the accounting entries being reversed. We scour the spreadsheets and don't like what we see—a pattern of large amounts being reversed multiple times by Scott's accountants. While Lisa continues to study the numbers, I ask Gene Morse, a member of Internal Audit who has strong computer skills, to trace the reversed accounting entries through the system. Gene tries, but he soon comes back to tell us that his system access is allowing him to trace only a portion of the activity.

Recently, Buddy Yates, an accounting director, called to tell me that Information Technology (IT) was consolidating system-access levels. "Your internal auditors will still be able to view everything they have in the past, but only after the books and records are closed for the month," he said. My team agreed that this was fine as long as we could have access after the books closed. And if we needed it earlier, we would just ask. But now I wonder if he was straightforward with me.

I'm about to call to request full access when Gene tells me that he has an acquaintance in IT who has developed a new tool to trace accounting entries and is struggling to find someone willing to "beta-test" it. "Let me volunteer to test it and see what happens," he offers. If Gene can pull it off, we'll be able to trace the accounting entries without making a big stir. And, indeed, he succeeds in using the program to provide a backdoor into the accounting system.

I know word could get back to Scott that I'm still pursuing this issue, setting off another series of confrontations. Several of my auditors believe it's a matter of time before I lose my job. "You're on Scott's to-do list for continuing to push this," one of the Internal Audit directors warns. "He just hasn't gotten to you yet."

"Cynthia, Scott cornered me in the cafeteria," Lisa says one day. He said, 'Hey Lisa, so what are you working on?' It's rare that he's ever spoken to me. I just gave him a generic answer."

Several afternoons I ask my father, who lives only minutes from the office, to pick me up for lunch. I feel like I need to get out of this place for a while. He's a reassuring sounding board, and I've shared with him the level of pressure I've been under at work and that I fear my job could be in jeopardy.

"I'm going to start taking my personal things out of my office in case I get fired," I tell him. I don't want to be forced to pack my belongings in a cardboard box in a hurry as a security guard waits to escort me out.

"That sounds like a good idea," he says. "Do you want me to help you?"

"No. I'll take a little home each day. I don't want to upset my staff." I decide to leave the pictures on the walls, hoping they won't notice that my office décor is becoming increasingly sparse.

The quickest way to resolve the allowance issue, I think, might be to look over the external auditor's testing of the allowance. I hope it'll show that I'm over-reacting and we can close the issue. But Kenny, the Andersen partner, isn't eager to share Andersen's workpapers. "You guys are being difficult about letting us look at your allowance workpapers," I tell him. His response is surprising.

"I report to Scott and David [the Controller]," he says to me and members of my team. "These workpapers belong to them." Maybe he's being flippant? External auditors own their workpapers, and certainly don't report to their client's executives.

"Well, I'm also a client," I say, "and I'd like to look at the workpapers."

The partner tells me that I'll have to get permission from David or Scott, so I call David. I'm upfront with him. David is agreeable and has no problem with my request. I finally persuade Kenny to turn them over, and pull in several members of my team to review them with me. Since most of us have prior external audit experience, we know what we're looking for.

After sifting through the testing, we come to a disappointing conclusion. The answer is not what I'd hoped or been led to believe.

We see no excess amounts in other areas of the business to make up for the Wireless shortfall, which appears to be as much as $300 million or more. In fact, the total company allowance looks substantially short.

I call David Myers and ask if he has some time to meet with us. Within minutes, he walks through the conference room door. He seems sincerely concerned and surprised when I show him our findings, but it's hard to dispute the numbers.

"I think it's time for us to have a serious heart-to-heart conversation with Scott about this," he says, adding that management has been planning to increase the Wireless allowance by $40 million this quarter to sustain the unit until it's phased out. Soon after David walks out, Kenny shows up and asks for the workpapers. The timing is strange. I wonder if David has given him instructions to retrieve them? He seems irritated. Clearly, I'm exceeding some kind of boundary.

I'm not looking forward to talking to Scott about this, but finally, I leave him a message to call me. Several days pass before he calls back: "Cynthia, we've taken a good look at the allowance, and we're going to increase it by $40 million a quarter," he says with what is becoming his customary condescension. "Based on the rule of ten, the allowance will be fine by the end of the year." Before I can ask him what he means, he has to run and hangs up. Once again, it sounded like Scott was performing for someone else in the room. And what in the world is the rule of ten? In accounting, if a company determines that there's a shortage in the allowance, it can't be increased incrementally over time. It must be booked immediately. There is no rule of ten. It's an absurd comment. If there were such a thing, my college professors certainly forgot to mention it.

"He wouldn't have talked to you that way if you hadn't been female," a colleague says later. Maybe. Scott has made jesting comments about women before. I remember a conversation between Scott and a telecom consultant during which Scott mentioned a woman who was trying to advise him on stocks despite knowing little about investing. "I told her,

'Why don't you go buy some more high heels?' " Scott said. Neither the consultant nor I laughed, and, several minutes later, Scott turned to me: "Cynthia, I didn't mean anything by the high-heel comment. I was just kidding." Perhaps Scott's recent comments to me have nothing to do with gender. Maybe this is just someone backed into a corner being defensive. I can't say and don't give it much thought, refocusing my effort on the objective at hand.

Finally, management increases the Wireless allowance by some $300 million, having realized from audit's findings that $40 million wouldn't be nearly enough to cover losses. But my unease about Andersen persists. What if there are other company allowance accounts that have problems like Wireless? I mention to Scott that Internal Audit will start doing financial-statement auditing to double-check Andersen's work. "Sure, that sounds like a good idea," he says. I ask my team to incorporate financial-statement auditing and ask to review Arthur Andersen's work-papers for each of the internal audits going forward.

But when Scott learns that we've started performing financial-statement auditing and are alerting the Audit Committee about this, it's as if he's hearing it for the first time. "It's my decision whether or not you incorporate financial-statement auditing," he barks. "My decision! Not the Audit Committee's. And if you do any, it will be low-level work that Andersen doesn't want to do." He slams the phone down without saying goodbye. I close my door and take a few minutes to myself. I later consult with Max Bobbitt, the Audit Committee Chairman. Max is supportive and says he's comfortable with us shifting to more financial auditing.

This is not what I expected on coming back from maternity leave. I'm drained. Still, there have been positive accomplishments. I've been able to present important, if uncomfortable, news to management and the Audit Committee without being fired. The sales reps who were involved in commission fraud have resigned or been terminated, and the Commissions department is instituting necessary internal controls. Management has agreed with the idea of discontinuing Wireless resale, and has substantially increased the allowance. Max is backing us. Scott has been difficult to deal with, but perhaps that's temporary. Perhaps the rough stretch is over.

It's Easter. It's a beautiful Sunday in the South. Stephanie is 12. Anna Katherine is eight months old and starting to show so much personality. As I stand beside Lance with our girls for our Easter picture in front of the azaleas, I'm reminded how blessed I am.

CHAPTER 20

What is Prepaid Capacity?

It's late April, 2002. There is startling news when I arrive to work one morning. Bernie is no longer with the company.

"He's gone," Dee Dalton, one of the internal auditors says. One of the mailroom employees told her that he saw Bernie pull a U-Haul into the small executive parking area over the weekend. He spent an entire day loading up his personal items, including his desk and chairs.

I can't believe it. "It's true," Dee repeats. "He's gone. Go to the executive floor and look at the glass cases that held all his awards. There's nothing left." I walk up to the executive suite, and see that Dee's right. Bernie, who has spent 17 years at the helm of WorldCom, is gone, as unceremoniously as the senior employees he turned away without fanfare.

As I will soon learn, Bernie did not volunteer to leave. While the board had given Bernie loans to cover his personal margin calls until the market revived and he could repay the company, the market did not turn around. Bernie, once one of the wealthiest men in America, began moving closer and closer to personal bankruptcy, clinging to his WorldCom stock all the way. As the dot.com and telecom bubbles burst, driving down World-Com's stock price, Bernie began receiving one margin call after another. By April, the Board of Directors had approved and loaned him over $400 million, including interest, over the previous 18 months. As the *Wall Street Journal* would later report, Bernie had borrowed over $900 million from seven separate banks to finance his personal investing. While some of the loans had been used to pay off existing loans, he was the owner of more than $750 million in assets, including control of over a million acres of land.

When WorldCom paid off hundreds of millions of Bernie's margin debt, the banks released more than nine million shares of his WorldCom stock, which Bernie pledged as collateral to WorldCom. But the stock was inadequate to cover the company's loans to Bernie. Max Bobbitt and Stiles Kellett on the Compensation Committee had been asking Bernie to sell some of his non-stock assets like the ranch in Canada, but Bernie kept rejecting the offers he received for his properties as too low. Max and Stiles were also pushing to perfect the company's security interest in Bernie's WorldCom stock and non-WorldCom assets, which meant the company would be first to be repaid if Bernie sold assets.

At a difficult time for the company, Bernie's loans were consuming the Compensation Committee's attention—it had met to discuss the loans 26 times in the last year and a half. Finally, Stiles and Max decided to draw the line. On April 26, just over a week after successfully perfecting WorldCom's interest in some of Bernie's non-stock assets, Stiles called a board meeting in Washington with outside directors to discuss ousting Bernie.

The board was angry that Bernie had taken so long to put up his non-stock assets as collateral, concerned that Wall Street had lost confidence in Bernie and WorldCom, and fearful that Bernie didn't have a strategy following the failed Sprint merger. The vote for resignation was unanimous.

On April 29, Bernie signed a separation agreement, which entitled him to a $1.5 million annual compensation for life, the right to continue working out of WorldCom's downtown Jackson office, and the support of an administrative assistant.

As it had started to seem likely that Bernie was going to lose his job, some board members began angling for the top slot. The board, roughly divided between those members who had been with the company the longest and those who had joined after UUNET and MCI were acquired, became a cauldron of maneuvering, intrigue, and dissention. The press would later report that Max Bobbitt, the Audit Committee Chairman, worked behind the scenes to force Bernie's resignation and install himself as interim CEO. Some board members would tell *BusinessWeek* that Max was offering several executives, including Scott Sullivan, annual retention bonuses of $1 million for life if they supported his bid. (Max later insisted to me that there was no truth to the allegation.) There was an anti-Max faction supporting its own candidate for CEO, John Sidgmore, the former head of UUNET who was now Vice Chairman of the Board. In the end, John, not Max, emerged as the victor, if there was such a thing in this case.

Speaking to a local television station just after announcing his departure, Bernie is visibly shaken but evinces his usual optimism. "I feel like crying," he says. "I am one thousand percent convinced in my heart that [the company's trouble] is a temporary thing." Today, April 30th, would have marked his 17th anniversary with WorldCom. "I have had an incredible opportunity," he says. "John will be a great leader of the company. I'm going to continue to be at his disposal, I'm going to do everything I can to help WorldCom turn its act around. . . . Now rest assured, I would much rather have taken this action when the stock was at 60 dollars. But you have to look at yourself honestly in the mirror and I can do that with peace in my heart and say I've done absolutely the best I can."

Bernie claims he doesn't feel betrayed by the board: "You wonder sometimes why people you counted on, you can't count on anymore. But in the bigger picture, I really think this is a good decision for the company."

He says his plans are to repay the money he owes and make more time for his beloved pastimes. "I'm just going back to Lincoln County. I'll spend a little more time on the farm there with my brother. I've got a lot of grass to cut and I love that. I'm going to spend more time involved in the Lord's work. . . ."

In one of his first acts as interim CEO, John promotes Scott Sullivan to Executive Vice President and the two hold analyst calls to calm Wall

Street's anxieties about the changing of the guard. As my staff and I listen to them speak, we become more optimistic about the company's future. Times have been tough for WorldCom, and morale has been flagging. Maybe this can be a fresh start. John is an outstanding communicator. He says the new management team will take aggressive steps to move WorldCom forward.

Soon, the company announces two plans to strengthen WorldCom's cash position and simplify the corporate structure: Discontinue the Wireless resale business as planned and do away with the MCI tracking stock, which represents WorldCom's lower-value businesses. This should result in annual cost savings of nearly $300 million because the tracker pays dividends to shareholders, and even more savings with the phase-out of Wireless resale. Over the past year, WorldCom's stock price has dropped substantially. Many people think it's now a great buy. I decide to buy some more shares, as do my parents. One of my staff says he plans to buy some for the brokerage account he manages for one of his parents. Charles Cannada, my old boss, buys a substantial amount as well.

Scott and Ron Beaumont, the COO, hold a rally in Clinton to reassure employees. Ron says that the company will go after Bernie's cats and dogs if it has to in order to get its loans repaid. And, he adds, the free coffee's coming back. The crowd roars with excitement.

It's May, 2002. Glyn Smith, a senior manager in Internal Audit, saunters into my office with his typical calm demeanor, holding several sheets of paper. "Mark Abide in the Property Accounting department sent me this article. He says this may be worth looking into from an audit perspective."

The article, called "Accounting for Anguish," appeared in the *Fort Worth* (Texas) *Weekly* on May 16, 2002. It describes the ordeal of Kim Emigh, a former WorldCom financial analyst who was laid off on March 2, 2001. Kim—who joined the company on the MCI side of the house before WorldCom purchased it—said he had complained over the years about potential abuses related to capital spending. "They used to say MCI was spending like a bunch of drunken sailors," he said. While he said policies tightened up after WorldCom bought the company, he was still concerned by some relationships with vendors. His complaints included vendors billing WorldCom extravagant amounts for minor services, charging for new equipment while sending second-hand products, and contractors charging for people who didn't appear to be working on WorldCom jobs. But his bosses didn't want to hear his complaints. Because of pressure from his superiors, Kim changed company divisions, but his old boss was none too happy about this either. "The last words he said to me were 'I'll have your [expletive] job,'" Kim told the reporter.

In one instance, he received a directive to mis-allocate hours worked on capital projects because his division was over-budget on capital spending. The action would have entailed tax fraud, as it would have made the company appear less profitable, though the main objective of the perpetrators was simply to avoid being called on the carpet for going over-budget. Kim refused and ran some of his concerns up the chain of command. Although during his work at MCI/WorldCom he had been promoted five times and received positive performance evaluations, ten weeks later he was laid off. "[My supervisor] said, 'Prepare for the worst,'" Kim recalled, "I said 'Oh, am I going to get fired?' He just nodded."

Kim went 14 months without employment. In the article, he claimed that his WorldCom bosses either didn't return calls from Kim's prospective new employers or gave poor references even though his performance reviews indicated otherwise. With his wife pregnant with their third child, they spent their children's college savings, nearly lost their house, and had to depend on family for help. "Your kids have been through what you've been through," the article quoted his wife Janet saying. "You can never go back and be the person you were prior to it happening." I'm taken aback by what I read, but I have no idea just how painfully relevant her words will be.

An audit of capital expenditures—amounts spent to purchase physical assets, like equipment or property—is on Internal Audit's schedule for later in the year, but Glyn says he can have a look now. "I've finished my audit and am almost ready to start something new," he says. "I could go ahead and kick off the capital expenditure audit and test these allegations as part of it."

"Okay, that sounds good," I say, staring at the papers he's handed me, then go back to the many projects I'm juggling.

Over the past 35 years, lives connected by the small town of Clinton unknowingly passed one another many times before coming together at WorldCom. My parents and their home drew me back to Clinton from Atlanta. Glyn also spent much of his childhood here. Our parents still live only blocks apart. Though I had never met Glyn before he joined WorldCom—after it acquired SkyTel in 1999, where he was an internal auditor at the time—his mother taught me accounting at Clinton High School 20 years ago. She was an excellent teacher, and—fortunately for many of her students, who would rather talk about their weekend plans than accounting theory—very patient. Though I didn't know it then, her teaching would go a long way toward persuading me to major in accounting in college.

And if I could have peered into the future from my desk that year as I listened to her explain that debits are on the left and credits on the right, I'd have seen that she would have an even more profound impact on my life. At home, she was raising a 13-year-old son who would come to stand beside me during the most difficult trials of my life. I have heard it said that adversity introduces a man to himself. I would add that it also introduces a man to others.

Like me, Glyn took his mother's class and decided to get an accounting degree. He also started his career in external audit. On his way to internal audit, he's acquired an alphabet soup of professional certifications— Certified Public Accountant, Certified Internal Auditor, Certified Control Self-Assessment—and is highly regarded by peers. For years, he has taught courses on internal controls and auditing for the Institute of

Internal Auditors. Glyn is methodical and prompt, preferring to stick to a schedule, and always puts family first, typically leaving the office at a reasonable hour to spend time with his wife Marla, their 7-year old daughter and a new baby boy.

At 35, Glyn's a dead ringer for a young Billy Bob Thornton, with the more than laid-back personality to match. I admire Glyn's composure. He's always the same calm Glyn with a quiet, self-assured presence, a dry wit, and a great sense of humor. He even gestures and speaks slowly, his Southern drawl as smooth as molasses.

His life is full of hobbies and he's famous around the office for his sideline business—candid photography. Glyn teaches a young couples' Sunday School class at the First Baptist Church in Clinton, the same church Bernie sometimes attended during college. Glyn and Marla met his freshman year at Mississippi State University in Starkville, where he played the drums and Marla sang in a Christian band called The Fishermen. "I was enamored by her beauty and finally got up the nerve to ask her out," he once told me.

It's Wednesday, May 29, 2002. Glyn has kicked off the capital-expenditure audit. Tonia Buchanan will be the senior auditor on the engagement, reporting to Glyn. Having received an undergraduate accounting degree from William Carey College and a Masters of Accounting from the University of Southern Mississippi, Tonia started her career with KPMG in Jackson. She's a highly skilled auditor. Internal Audit Directors often request her to work on their projects as she is professional, hard-working, and always warm and congenial. Recently married, Tonia and her husband Jimmy, a successful insurance agent, are avid sports fans and often attend Bandits hockey games. But her true passion is volunteering; Tonia helps feed people in need, assists with building houses for the homeless and works with battered women's shelters.

Several of us are meeting in the conference room just outside my office with Sanjeev Sethi, one of the Finance directors, who has provided several capital-spending schedules for the audit. Two of the schedules differ in amount. When asked to explain, Sanjeev easily gives descriptions of several items but then mentions that a portion of the difference relates to something called "prepaid capacity." We've done several operational audits of capital expenditures before, but none of us has ever heard the term "prepaid capacity."

"What's prepaid capacity?" one of the auditors asks.

"I don't know," Sanjeev answers, with a hint of discomfort in his voice. "If you want to know more, you'll have to ask David Myers." It seems strange that Sanjeev doesn't know what the item represents since he provided the schedules and the department reporting to him approves requests for capital spending. I try to probe, but Sanjeev is adamant: He has no clue what "prepaid capacity" represents. He says that David Myers provides him with the amounts for his schedule. We have a number of "techie" auditors on our team who've honed their computer skills. I turn to Glyn and ask him to see if any of them are available. Perhaps they can look through the computerized accounting system to see if they can find any entries labeled "prepaid capacity."

Glyn soon comes back with Gene Morse, the auditor who helped pull system reports for the Wireless allowance. While Gene isn't scheduled on this audit, he's about to be drafted to work with Tonia and will become an integral part of the team.

Gene is gregarious, energetic, and fast-moving. Like Glyn, he's a devoted family man. His wife, Lynda, teaches children. When I met Gene in 1997, they had no children. Just several years later, he's already the father of three! With dark hair and glasses, he looks the part of a studious Wall Street analyst. Extraordinarily bright, he is a Chartered Financial Analyst and a Certified Internal Auditor, and is now a senior auditor in line for promotion to manager.

Gene also received his undergraduate degree from Mississippi College. Now in his early 40s, Gene worked a number of jobs—bartender, waiter, art director, stock broker, medical sales representative—until the mid-1990s, when he decided to take his career in a new direction and apply to graduate school. After receiving his MBA from Tulane in 1997, Gene joined WorldCom through a program that rotated MBA graduates through various finance departments. Following his rotation, Gene decided to become an internal auditor.

I explain to Gene what Sanjeev has told us about prepaid capacity. "Can you look in the system and see if you can find anything with that description?" I ask.

"Well, I need to know where to look first," Gene says. "What's prepaid capacity?"

"I don't know," Sanjeev reiterates, sounding aggravated at having to repeat himself, adding that he has no idea where to find the amounts.

The meeting concludes, and Sanjeev leaves, but he's piqued my interest. What's prepaid capacity? I could walk over and ask David but I prefer to just take a look for myself after the recent reactions I've had from him and Scott on Wireless and Commissions.

Gene doesn't even know where to begin scouring for clues, so I ask him to sit in on our next meeting, with Mark Abide, who forwarded the "Accounting for Anguish" article to Glyn. Since he's the head of Property Accounting, maybe he'll know what prepaid capacity is.

But Mark's reaction is just as odd as Sanjeev's. "I make some of the accounting entries for prepaid capacity, but I'm not sure what it is," he says. "Talk to David Myers."

"Can you give us the accounts you book the entries to?" I ask.

"Yeah, just a minute," he says, looking for the information. "I record the entries in 'transmission equipment,' 'communications equipment,' and 'furniture, fixture, and other,'" he says. He adds that Betty Vinson in General Accounting tells him what amounts to book. Unlike Sanjeev, Mark actually manually keys in some of the accounting entries, but even he says he doesn't know what prepaid capacity is.

The three accounts Mark has given us contain thousands of accounting entries. Finding an entry for prepaid capacity will be like searching for the proverbial needle in the haystack. But the next day Gene manages to find our needle.

"I found an amount in one of the accounts described as prepaid capacity," he tells me excitedly.

"What does the system say it is?"

"I don't know. It just says prepaid capacity. I can't tell where the amounts are coming from."

"Can you trace it through the system?"

"I'll give it a try," he says. As with the Wireless audit, Gene's access shows only one side of the accounting entry because Internal Audit's system access has been limited. But we still have the system tool he's "beta-testing."

After only a day, Gene succeeds. "I was able to trace it through," he announces, laying a sheaf of papers on my desk. The initial amount led Gene to additional accounting entries, though he hasn't had time to sort through the jumble of paper. Grabbing various documents, he attempts to line them up in some semblance of order. The entries are a maze.

"Let's go to the conference room," I say.

I grab a cup of coffee and gather several other staff in our conference room. It's a dreary place without windows, but large enough for us to spread out, and has a white marker board that covers an entire wall. But even with several CPAs with strong finance backgrounds in attendance, we have a hard time following the amounts moving between various accounts.

"Let's go back to T accounts," I say, seeing that everyone's getting a bit frustrated. T accounts are the accountant's most basic tool—debits on the left, credits on the right. Gene grabs a marker and starts filling up the board, shuffling through the stack of printouts, scrutinizing some pages, tossing others aside, reminding me of an intense college professor. As we work through the entries, we discover some of them are out of proper sequence. When all the entries and amounts are written in proper sequential order starting with their origin and ending in what we presume is their final resting place, one thing is clear—prepaid-capacity amounts are jumping all over the place, from account to account. From my experience, amounts typically don't shift this much between accounts.

After digging around in the "furniture and fixtures" account where Mark told us he booked prepaid-capacity entries, Gene came across a $500 million increase to computer equipment with the all-cap description "PREPAID CAPACITY." It was made in March 2002. Using our new system tool and this single thread, Gene wound his way back through a garble of entries to try to determine its origin.

It looks like the amount was moved from an asset account called "intercompany asset transfer clearing." But the trail gets fuzzier from there. Gene thinks the amount in "intercompany" is coming from an account called "transmission equipment," which represents amounts spent to build out WorldCom's telecom network. But the amount in "transmission equipment" traces back to three separate line-cost expense accounts—payments to other telecom carriers to originate and terminate phone calls or lease fiber.

I stare at the marker board. Why run these amounts in and out of so many different accounts? The transfers seem nonsensical. But if you disregard the intermediate transfers, you're left with a large round dollar amount moving from the income statement to the balance sheet. Moving amounts to the balance sheet will increase the company's profit.

It's not unusual to see large amounts on the balance sheet—WorldCom and other big telecom companies have been spending billions in capital expanding networks since the 1996 Telecom Act. And this is now a company with $38 billion in revenue that takes in and spends billions. However, this entry is for a large round dollar amount.

As we try to sort through the entries, several auditors propose explanations for what they could represent. "It's probably some type of telecommunications equipment for our network," one auditor says. "It's probably capitalized labor and capital leases," ventures another. It could be. Sometimes, it's perfectly appropriate to move expenses to the balance sheet.

"Okay, so what?" seems to be the feeling of many in the room. Most think the entries don't amount to anything and that we're wasting time discussing them. Others aren't so sure. No one expresses a sense of alarm. I'd like to take a second look at these entries and make sure we haven't missed something in trying to trace them through the system. I'd also like to see another one of these prepaid-capacity entries in the system—does it move through accounts in a similar way? I ask Gene to look.

On Monday, June 3rd, Gene takes a scheduled vacation day, then spends the rest of the week pulling data. But, for days, he finds nothing.

CHAPTER 21

Growing Suspicions

It's June 4, 2002, four days after Internal Audit gathered in the conference room to study the prepaid-capacity entries. At 6:17 pm, an e-mail from David Myers arrives in my inbox. David wants to know why we're auditing capital expenditures: "What is there to do in Capex since we are spending nothing in relative terms?" His comment seems strange. We may be spending less compared to prior years, but the company is still spending billions. He continues by complaining that we're drawing Finance employees like Sanjeev—who is taking time to pull together documents for Internal Audit—away from the work they owe Scott. The company is close to negotiating additional bank financing to sustain WorldCom until the telecom industry turns around, and David claims he needs his people to ready the necessary paperwork. "Not trumping you, but we have to get this credit facility work finished," he writes. "I have our boss breathing down my neck. I am sure you have never had that happen, right?"

I ignore David's claim that we're wasting time on capital expenditures and respond only to the rest of his message, agreeing that Sanjeev can hold off on helping Internal Audit until he's finished with his work for Scott. Is David really concerned about Sanjeev's priorities or does he not like that we're looking at capital expenditures?

I have my answer soon enough. The next morning, David fires off a second e-mail glossing over Sanjeev and reiterating that Internal Audit's time is better spent on areas other than capital expenditure. "My point

is . . . Seems we can spend time on areas where there are ways to save
$ in operating cost. It is critical that you, me and every single person figure
how to drive cost down faster than we see revenue fall. Please excuse me if
I am on my soapbox. It is because I have spent every waking hour over the
last month with banks, bankers, and E&Y [Ernst & Young] as Financial
Advisors to the banks." While the first e-mail was signed, simply, "D,"
the second is signed "David F. Myers."

Glyn and I both feel like David sounds on edge in his e-mail. What did
Sanjeev tell him? The e-mail makes me uneasy and even more curious
about prepaid capacity. I decide not to reply.

What I won't learn until two years from now is that David's first e-mail
sounds strange because it's completely untrue. Sanjeev is not working on
any urgent projects for Scott. In fact, Scott instructed David to send the
e-mail to stall our audit.

The next day, I have a meeting with Farrell Malone, the external-audit
partner with KPMG, which was only recently retained after Arthur
Andersen's collapse because of the Enron debacle. KPMG has purchased
Arthur Andersen's Jackson, Mississippi practice and the Andersen auditors are still working on the WorldCom engagement for continuity, but
Farrell is from KPMG not Andersen, and is new to the WorldCom
account. He's a seasoned auditor who's well-respected within KPMG.
He seems down to earth, and I can tell he's a straight-shooter. After
introducing him to several ongoing audit issues, I decide to show him the
prepaid-capacity entries. As Glyn and I walk him through the pages,
we explain how the amount moves between accounts. Farrell doesn't see
anything inappropriate on the face of the entries. He is, however,
concerned about the allowance issues. Even though the Wireless allowance has been increased, Internal Audit has discovered a long list of
allowance accounts in other areas of the company with balances going in
the wrong direction.

Then I hand Farrell a copy of the e-mail from David Myers. "Will you
read this and tell me what you think?" I ask.

"He's probably just having a bad day," he says after scanning the
e-mail.

"Maybe so," I say. But maybe Farrell hasn't been here long enough to realize that the tone is unusual for David.

"Have you told the Audit Committee about these accounting entries yet?" he asks, referring to prepaid capacity.

"No—we don't know if they are something or nothing."

"My advice is not to go running to the Audit Committee every time you find a potential issue," he says. "Make sure you separate emotion from business." I appreciate his words, but I know well enough not to cry wolf. Do that and you lose credibility and respect quickly. If Farrell doesn't see any cause for concern on the face of these entries, there may well be a sound explanation, and this doesn't appear to be an area of particular concern to the SEC, as capital spending is not part of its inquiry.

But I still want to take a closer look. What if this turns out to be something aggressive like the Wireless allowance? I'm wondering whether I should approach Scott, David, or one of the staff accountants directly about the entries. I could ask Kenny Avery. But last time I asked him about the Wireless allowance, I got a call from Scott Sullivan. I'm none too eager to antagonize Scott again, so Glyn suggests I keep things casual and send him to ask David. I decide to wait until Gene finds a second entry. It could change our opinion, and I don't want to be an alarmist unnecessarily.

Gene is pushing the accounting system to its limit. He's downloading enormous amounts of data—searching accounts that have more than 300,000 transactions each month spread across a hundred legal entities. He's sifting through one of the accounts that the last entry was funneled through, gambling that another prepaid capacity entry may have moved through there. But it's a dead end.

After querying Essbase—a database-management system that combines the data from the various financial systems WorldCom has accumulated through acquisitions—Gene dumps data into an Access database that allows him to further sort and mine the data on his own computer. He also uses the tool we're beta-testing, a program originally created to help the accounting staff more easily mine data in Essbase. We're the first to try it out. Though someone has cut our system access—so that we can only see the balance-sheet half of any accounting entry and not the income-statement side—the tool allows us to see both sides and trace entries through the system.

But Gene is pulling so much data that he's regularly crashing the accounting servers and slowing other people's work. His own computer struggles to handle the load and crashes regularly.

Such a sudden spike in queries hasn't gone unnoticed. "[The IT system administrator] is asking me what in the heck is going on," Gene tells me. "He had to go into the system and kill my queries because they were keeping other people in Accounting from running reports." In fact, temporarily, no other users could get onto the system.

I know that if someone in IT tells Scott or David that my group is pulling millions of detailed accounting transactions and shutting users out, someone is bound to show up at my office door. And the IT administrator sits right in the middle of the accounting department.

"Can you run the reports at night?" I ask. Few people would even be using the system then, allowing us to fly under the radar screen. Everyone agrees to put in the extra hours.

My team and I begin working at night. Since Gene's cubicle is out in the open, I ask him to clear the prepaid-capacity research from his desk and relocate to the audit library, our de-facto junk room. It's at the end of a hall, tiny, windowless, and crammed full of boxes. Almost no one ever goes in there. Gene moves his things, carves out a spot amid the boxes, and locks himself in. Night after night, he downloads data. Day after day, he ferrets through the hundreds of thousands of transactions.

As far as I know, neither Scott nor David are aware that Gene is scouring the accounting system. But I've prepared him just in case. "I don't expect Scott or David to ask what you're working on," I tell him, "but if someone has leaked information back to them, you can tell them you're on the international capital expenditure audit since that's the audit you're assigned to, and you're still working on it. But, if they ask you directly about the data we've pulled, you should go ahead and tell them we pulled the entries."

One afternoon, Gene rushes into my office. "I saw Scott in the cafeteria at lunch," he says, his face flushed. "He walked straight up to me and said, 'So Gene, what are you working on these days?'"

"Do you think he was just making conversation?" I ask.

"Cynthia, he's probably spoken to me two times since I started working here."

"What did you say?"

"I told him what you told me to say. I just kind of stared down at my shoes and mumbled something about the international audit," he says. "It was very uncomfortable. I got out of there as fast as I could."

"Just stay in the audit library and keep digging," I tell him. Scott confronted Lisa Smith in the cafeteria several months ago, and now he's asking Gene what he's up to.

I ask a few of my staff what they think about these entries. Most believe there will be a sound explanation. "I think you may be chasing your tail on this one," one says. But as auditors, we have to stay with leads and keep reviewing the issues. At times, it is a slow, plodding process of checking and re-checking facts, developing theories, trying to find connections, and thinking through the issues until you get it right.

Periodically, I check in with Glyn, Tonia, and Gene to discuss progress. Glyn and Tonia are compiling and analyzing capital-spending schedules. I want to continue to question and re-evaluate the data. Do we have all the facts? Have we made any errors? In the audit library, Gene continues to dig through the accounting system, but for days, he finds nothing. Some of the accounts are dead ends. Various staffers check the data to see if it will provide any new leads or theories. Over a week has passed since Gene found the first prepaid-capacity thread. "Nothing yet" is the refrain.

But on Monday, June 10th, Gene finally finds several entries labeled "prepaid capacity." They appear to be moving large amounts from the income statement to the balance sheet—$743 million in the third quarter of 2001, $941 million in the fourth quarter of 2001, and $100 million in the first quarter of 2002. Now, as with the first find, we have to trace the amounts from account to account through the system to see where they land.

The following morning, there's a message on my voice-mail from Scott: He asks me to give him a call "right away" and says that he'd like to meet in ten minutes to discuss the status of audit projects and several promotions I had forwarded him for approval. He'd like to spend an hour and go through things "pretty extensively." I should bring copies of audit reports and organizational charts showing my group's reporting structure.

This is out of character. Scott never wants to go over things "extensively." And the urgency is hard to explain. Regardless, I ask several Internal Audit directors to quickly gather copies of recent reports and current audit projects. They're still running after me, sliding documents into my manila folder, as I rush out of the office, trying to make Scott's deadline. The prepaid capacity entries we identified are not in my package, but I do have a copy of "Accounting for Anguish."

Scott's office is located in an executive suite across a skywalk that connects our buildings. Since Bernie's departure, only one other executive works there—John Stupka, the head of Wireless. I pass through the double glass doors leading to the suite and wait until Scott becomes available. Unlike some of our recent encounters, he's warm and cordial, inviting me to sit at the small conference table parallel to his desk. But as soon as we sit down, he stops the meeting.

"I need to make a phone call to Mike Salsbury," he says. Mike is WorldCom's general counsel. Based in Washington, he joined the company after the MCI acquisition and worked with me on the commission fraud audit. He was no-nonsense and decisive—I came to respect him a great deal.

I listen to Scott's side of the conversation as he and Mike discuss Max Bobbitt, the chairman of the Audit Committee.

"So Max will be leaving the Audit Committee," Scott says. "Max will no longer be on the Audit Committee," he repeats, as if to confirm. His tone appears to be for my benefit. As the head of Internal Audit, I report functionally to the Audit Committee and administratively to Scott. While Scott determines my compensation and promotion, the Audit Committee approves our audit and special-project plans. Less tangibly, the Audit

Committee also provides Internal Audit with independence from management. Scott's call, in hindsight, will come to feel like a veiled admonition that Max may not be there to support me.

I've known Max since I started working at WorldCom over eight years ago. He has a friendly personality, and everyone in my department who has met him likes him. We especially get a kick out of the way his slight Arkansas twang transforms my name into Cynthierrr. I don't mind. I find it endearing. Max always saves me a seat at the Audit Committee meetings: "Sit here by me, Cynthierr." Since retiring from a successful career at Alltel several years ago, Max has been playing a lot of Florida golf, as evidenced by his perpetual tan.

When Scott hangs up, our meeting continues as strangely as before. First, he mentions all the infighting on the board, which has continued even after John Sidgmore became CEO. "Some members on the board can't keep their mouths shut," Scott says, referring to leaks to the press. "You may not know this, but Max tried unsuccessfully to take over the company following Bernie's departure, which has created tension." He says I should be careful about what I say to the board. Scott usually holds things close to his vest. Sharing insider gossip like this is not his style.

"I want to start spending a lot more time with you on Internal Audit work," he goes on. I don't remember him being so interested in Internal Audit in the past. "I've looked at these promotions you forwarded," he says. "I'm going to hold them for a while until I get to know more about the people and the projects they're working on."

Scott hasn't held promotions for my staff in the past, but I'll fight that battle later. He wants us to walk him through our recently completed audits, I ask the auditors who worked on them to come by Scott's office one at a time.

As Glyn Smith describes his recent audit of inventory, Scott is closely engaged, asking questions every step of the way and complimenting Glyn on his work. But I'm only half-listening. My mind is racing. Scott is negotiating billions of dollars in new bank financing. Why is he devoting so much time to Internal Audit, especially when he never bothered in the past? Does he want me to think he's keeping a close eye on me? Or is he trying to make things less adversarial? Why is he alerting me that Max is off the Audit Committee and advising me to be careful with the board? Why is he holding promotions?

As Glyn stands up to leave after his presentation, I decide to chance a gamble. "Glyn, why don't we talk to Scott about the capital-expenditure audit while you're here?" I say, motioning him to sit back down. Glyn is caught off-guard, but he masks it well.

I give Scott a copy of the *Fort Worth Weekly* article and mention that it jump-started our audit. Scott says he's never seen the story, so I fill him in on the allegations and how we will test them. Then I mention our findings on another subject.

"In our audit, we've identified something called prepaid capacity," I say. "Can you tell us what it represents?" I watch Scott's face closely. His voice is calm and confident and he doesn't seem surprised in the slightest.

"Prepaid capacity represents costs associated with no or low-utilized Sonet Rings and lines which are being capitalized," he explains nonchalantly. "While revenues have declined, the costs related to certain leases are fixed, creating a matching problem."

Though it's hardly clear at the time, what Scott means is that the amounts represent costs related to the company's leased fiber lines that have little or no customer usage due to the implosion of telecom. The company continues to pay to lease them, but they bring in little, if any, revenue. However, instead of expensing the lease costs as they are incurred, the company is reclassifying the amounts as capital assets, which means it can expense them over longer periods of time, as is the case with other capital assets like buildings and equipment. This allows the company to stretch out this deduction to company earnings, buying time for revenue to catch up.

"I know there are some issues with capital," Scott goes on after I ask for more information. "All of the capital-expenditure issues will be cleared up in the second quarter of 2002." At that time, he expects to take a restructuring charge related to prepaid capacity, effectively writing off the bulk of the amounts that have been capitalized. From that point on, he says, the company will no longer capitalize line costs as prepaid capacity, instead allocating these costs between a restructuring charge and an expense.

"I'd like for you to postpone this audit until third quarter so that you can look at second-quarter numbers," he says. As we continue to talk, Scott repeats the request several times. Each time he asks, he looks to me for an answer. Each time I dodge the question by asking one of my own or by pointing out that the audit has already begun, making it awkward to stop in mid-stride. I am simultaneously trying to understand what Scott is telling us; think about what else I should ask, given this rare occasion to; and how many different ways I can diplomatically say no if he keeps asking me to delay the audit. I did not plan on interrogating my boss today. So I turn to Glyn.

"Glyn, do you have any more questions?"

"No, I don't think so," Glyn says.

"I have to make a phone call but we can get back together this afternoon," Scott says. He still seems unperturbed, and we say goodbye as if we were discussing something entirely ordinary. I'm glad for the break. Scott was rattling off his explanation as if I should understand exactly what he was talking about. But there are thousands of pages of accounting rules that are revised and added to every year. If Glyn didn't have any questions, maybe he understands Scott's explanation.

As Glyn and I walk back to our building, we discuss Scott's responses. But Glyn is just as unclear as I am. When you cut through the accounting lingo, what's the bottom line of Scott's commentary? I will later find myself wishing I had asked even more questions about the types of leases and how amounts were determined. But with Scott continuing to ask us to delay the audit, the whole scene was beginning to feel uncomfortable.

Scott is the accounting guru. Few have his level of expertise or respect. There are instances when it's appropriate to capitalize leases, and he gave the explanation confidently.

Still, we can't help feeling that it all sounded strange.

That night, I'm awake again in the dark hours of the early morning. Some aspects of accounting depend on judgment. Maybe the prepaid capacity stuff is aggressive, but perfectly legal, accounting. Still, something feels off. I think about Farrell's advice to keep emotion in check. Am I jumping the gun? No, I tell myself. You've taken a step back and thought it through clearly. The meeting with Scott has made me even more suspicious.

I decide to consult Max. Even if he's coming off the Audit Committee, he's still on as of now. I ask Glyn to sit in. But my office, which is in the middle of my department, with employees going past all the time, is not an ideal place for this kind of conversation.

"What about the back corner office?" Glyn suggests. "It's empty." Glyn gets the office key from our administrative assistant.

We dial Max at his home. When Max picks up, I decide to get straight to the point. "Max, this is Cynthia. I have Glyn Smith here with me. We've identified several accounting entries made in the third and fourth quarter of 2001 and the first quarter of 2002 totaling $2.5 billion that we have some concerns about."

After Glyn and I explain, Max doesn't show any panic either. "Cynthia, get with Farrell [the KPMG partner] and discuss these issues. We'll discuss this in the executive session of the Audit Committee meeting on Friday, [June 14]. Don't have any further discussions with David Myers or Scott Sullivan until we can reach a consensus on how to proceed at the meeting."

I agree to hold off until then.

We're all still working at night and behind closed doors. I ask Glyn and Tonia not to leave any documents relating to the audit on their desks, and to intensify the search. Time could be running out for us.

I also want to make sure we don't lose any of the data. Scott now knows we're looking at prepaid capacity. I think it's unlikely, but I want to be prepared in case someone tries to erase the information. Gene uses his own money to buy a CD burner and makes a copy of the data. "I'm taking it home with me at night," he says. Wherever he is, Gene doesn't let his briefcase stray from sight.

The next afternoon, Max arrives in town for the following day's Audit Committee meeting. The annual shareholder meeting is also tomorrow; the Board of Directors is meeting as well.

We speak in the early afternoon. "Hey, Cynthia. I'm over at the Hampton Inn," Max says. "Why don't we meet around 5:00 and discuss what we're going to do tomorrow."

"Okay. I'm bringing Glyn."

"Why don't you just come by yourself, Cynthia? Farrell is coming as well."

I gather three copies of a two-page document summarizing the prepaid-capacity entries and head out the door. We've now found 28 entries over four quarters, going back to the second quarter of 2001.

The Hampton Inn is a small, no-frills, three-story hotel down the street from WorldCom's office complex. Most out-of-town employees and board members stay here. When I walk into the hotel, I see two visiting board members in a conference room with floor-to-ceiling glass windows. I smile and wave, hoping they won't come out to speak or mention to Scott that they saw me here. Farrell, Max, and I meet in a small conference room across from the check-in desk. Each of us pulls up a chair and we sit in a small circle. I unfold the spreadsheets and explain what we've found.

In one of the schedules, we did a calculation to show what the income statement would have looked like without these entries. Line-cost expense as a percent of revenue moves from around 42% to as high as 53%; and net income takes a dive, moving from a profit of $130 million in the first quarter of 2002 to a net loss of $395 million. I add that Tonia, one of the senior auditors working on the capital expenditure audit, didn't receive Max's request not to ask Finance for more documents for the audit because she was off the previous day. When she asked Sanjeev Sethi, a finance director, for some schedules, he told her that David Myers directed him not to provide them. David also told Sanjeev that the audit was being postponed. As I will later learn, David had also instructed Sanjeev to do what he could to stall our investigation.

"I told you not to talk to anyone else until after we met to discuss the entries!" Max reprimands, his voice rising. His face is turning crimson, and I can feel mine getting flushed. I'm embarrassed in front of Farrell. I've never seen Max like this before.

"You have no idea what I'm having to deal with on the board," he says. Max's life seems stressful these days. He's under increasing pressure for serving on the Compensation Committee that approved Bernie's loans, and there's still conflict between the two factions on the board. With all the upheaval, Max feels there's going to be controversy at tomorrow's board meeting. He's concerned that he may even get ousted, and based on Scott's conversation with general counsel, that looks like a reasonable concern.

"Tonia was out of the office and simply didn't get the word that you had asked us to wait." It was an honest mistake. Max is talking over me and I have to ask him to stop and listen. Finally, he calms down.

While Max said we would discuss the issue in executive session tomorrow, he's changed his mind. He now thinks it's premature to discuss prepaid capacity with the full Audit Committee.

"We should at least inform the other members about the issue," I say, but I'm outnumbered. Farrell agrees with Max.

Max says he wants an opportunity to personally discuss the entries with Scott before I do anything else. He's flying back to Florida with Scott tomorrow; he'll ask him then. "I'll talk to you when I get home this weekend and tell you what he says and how to proceed."

Early the next morning, prior to the Audit Committee meeting, Max calls to ask if I'll make copies of several documents. Elaine Saxton, an Internal Audit director, walks in the room and hands me a sealed envelope containing the copies. David Myers, the Controller, is sitting across from me. While the contents have nothing to do with the prepaid-capacity entries, I can feel David's eyes following me as I hand the large envelope to Max.

After the Audit Committee meeting, I ask Elaine to take a sealed envelope to Max. This time, it does contain schedules related to prepaid capacity. "Go straight to Max and put these directly in his hands." Elaine is one of the first auditors I hired years ago. I know I can trust her to take care of it.

After the Audit Committee meeting, Glyn and I walk down to the shareholder meeting in the employee cafeteria. As I enter the room, John Sidgmore, the new CEO, and Scott pass by. Both go out of their way to say hello, and John shakes my hand. As they make their way to the front of the room, Glyn and I stand in the back. Betty Vinson—one of the Accounting employees who, according to our research, physically entered some of the suspect entries—is a few rows in front of us.

The place is packed with shareholders. Because WorldCom is the only Fortune 500 company headquartered in my state, many Mississippians have significant amounts of savings tied up in the stock. Many employees, including myself, have a lot of retirement funds in WorldCom stock. As I stand listening to John talk to the crowd, I wonder—if our discoveries turn out to be a real problem, what will that mean for the shareholders and the company?

After Friday's meetings are over, Max and Scott fly to Florida on the corporate jet. I call Max on Saturday. He says he and Scott addressed the issue at a "high level" and that he told Scott that "there seemed to be some tension between [Scott's] group and audit related to obtaining documentation."

Scott will remember it differently. According to him, the two discussed the capital-expenditure audit, but not prepaid capacity specifically because Max appeared to be consumed by other issues that day.

"I don't want you to ask for support for the entries yet," Max instructs. "Scott is going to call you on Monday, and I believe he'll have a good explanation for these accounting entries."

This has nothing to do with tension between our groups, I tell Max. And I feel like I've already heard Scott's explanation. But I'll wait for his call.

CHAPTER 22

A Surprise Visit

It's Monday, June 17. When I arrive at work, my voice-mail light is on. Scott left a message on Saturday: "Hey Cynthia . . . Max mentioned tension between your group and David Myers' group . . . so I want to find out what that is all about and, uh, put that one to rest."

I play the message again. What is he talking about? This has nothing to do with tension, and I still don't understand why Max presented it that way to Scott. Should I stay with Max's instructions to wait to talk with Scott again or go ahead and ask the Accounting department for support. I think about this all morning and pray, God please give me strength in making the right decisions.

Finally, I decide not to wait any longer. I've already heard Scott's explanation. I'm going to ask for support. If nothing's out of the ordinary and Scott and David have a good explanation, why would anyone care if I do? I'm not comfortable going against the Audit Committee Chairman, but I'm not comfortable with the instructions he's given either. Max didn't sit across from Scott as I did last week.

Having to go against both Max and Scott is not something I take lightly. I respect both of them, and there are likely to be repercussions. But as I've done throughout my career, I'm going with my intuition. Usually, it serves me well. Everything inside me, my instinct as well as years of audit and fraud training, says to go to Accounting. If I've made a mistake, I'll apologize later.

I ask Glyn to come along. I want to start our interviews with Betty Vinson, the accounting director who entered some of the amounts into the system, and work up the chain of command, going from office to office until we determine if there's support. I suggest we go unannounced. If we just show up, people may be more inclined to give honest answers.

Before we go to Accounting, I ask to meet with Kenny Avery, the Andersen partner who preceded Farrell. Kenny has joined KPMG and is continuing to work on the WorldCom account. I want to see if Andersen ever looked into this issue. I ask Farrell to also sit in. We meet in the conference room outside my office at 2:30. As we talk, it becomes clear that Andersen conducted very limited testing of capital expenditures. Kenny says Andersen tested only ten capital additions from January, 2001 to August, 2001, and none during the second half of the year, instead relying on internal financial controls.

"Are you familiar with something called prepaid capacity?" I ask.

"No," Kenny says.

"Did Arthur Andersen's testing of capital expenditures identify any capitalization of line cost?"

"No."

"Are you aware of any accounting standards that would allow for capitalization of line cost?"

"No," he repeats. I can tell Kenny finds it odd that I'm peppering him with so many questions while Farrell and Glyn are listening so intently.

I also ask Kenny for Arthur Andersen's workpapers on its capital-expenditure testing, but Kenny says Arthur Andersen won't release them to KPMG because WorldCom hasn't yet paid its final outstanding invoice for the work.

Sitting alone later, Glyn and I discuss the conversation with Kenny. We both have the same take. It appears that Arthur Andersen's audit testing didn't pick up on these entries. Kenny seemed to be completely unaware of them. We decide to head to Accounting, two buildings over, to begin our door-to-door interviews.

As we get close, I pause to compose myself. "Let's stop for just a minute," I say. I'm nervous. As I hold up my hand, my fingers are shaking. My heart is thumping wildly. "Are you nervous?" I ask Glyn.

"No," Glyn replies, laughing at my trembling hands.

"You never get nervous." I'm impressed that Glyn can be calm. I wish I felt calm. I'm still hoping that the accountants will give me solid support, that I made a mountain out of nothing. But there's a lump in my throat and an anxiety that won't go away.

"Okay, let's go," I say after a minute of breathing slowly, inhaling and exhaling. Our first stop will be Betty Vinson's office.

It's 3:20 p.m. Glyn and I walk into Betty's office and sit down as I ask her for a few minutes of her time without giving her an opportunity to dismiss us. She smiles and agrees. In her mid-40s, Betty is soft-spoken and quiet, with a reputation for diligence and devotion to her job. At the moment, she's looking up from the scores of accounting papers covering her desk.

"We identified some accounting entries with a description of prepaid capacity," Glyn says. "We wanted to see if you could tell us what it represents and give us some support for the entries."

"I guess you saw my name on some of the entries," Betty says.

"Yes," I say.

Betty gives a half-smile. "I made the entries, but I don't know what they're for, and I don't have the support for them," she says, looking at me.

"So you made some of the entries, but you don't know what they're for?" I repeat. I find it difficult to believe that an Accounting director could make an entry for hundreds of millions of dollars without understanding its merit or seeing support. "Who gives you the amounts for the journal entries?" I ask.

"David or Buddy," she answers with some hesitation, referring to her two bosses, the Controller and the Director of General Accounting. "They should have any support."

"Is the entry going to be booked this quarter as well?" Glyn asks.

"I don't think so," she says.

Glyn and I thank Betty for her time and walk out of her office. I'm anxious to speak with Buddy. Without stopping to discuss our conversation with Betty, we walk two doors down to see her boss.

I can see Buddy approaching us down the hall. He peers at us quizzically, but doesn't say anything as he heads into his office. We walk in right behind him. While I sometimes run into Buddy in the community and at church, I've never shown up at his door unannounced, and he looks surprised to see us. We take the guest chairs across from his desk.

Glyn mentions our discoveries. "Are you familiar with these entries?" he asks. I'm watching Buddy intently.

Buddy leans further back in his chair, clasping his hands behind his head. Tilting his head back, he stares down at us in silence, moving his eyes between Glyn and me for several seconds.

"I don't believe I know what you're talking about," he finally proclaims, furrowing his brow.

I'm not buying it. "Have you ever heard of prepaid capacity?" I repeat.

Silently, Buddy shakes his head back and forth and purses his lips.

"Betty said either you or David would have given her the amounts for any prepaid capacity entries that she books and that either you or David would have any support."

Buddy shrugs his shoulders and tells us we'll have to see David.

"Can a person reporting to you book a billion-dollar journal entry without your knowledge?" I ask, incredulous.

"David calls people who report to me all the time and asks them to book entries. Besides, most of the accounting is done in the field and not in my group."

"Okay, thanks," I reply in disbelief. Glyn and I walk out, the room tense behind us.

We walk the 150 feet down the hall to David Myers' office. David will be the sixth Finance employee whom I've asked about prepaid capacity, and still no support. As we approach his office, time begins to slow down for me. David is the last person who can explain these entries and show us support. If we run into another roadblock, I could find myself being sent full-circle back to Scott. My heart is racing and my palms are damp with sweat. As we walk up, we can hear him talking on the phone. A second line keeps ringing over and over, but he doesn't answer it. His administrative assistant, who sits just outside his office, is nowhere in sight.

"We'll wait," I tell Glyn as we stand outside his door.

Again, his second line rings, and again, and again. Someone is desperately trying to get through to David, but he's engrossed in his phone conversation and ignores the non-stop ringing. "It's Buddy calling to warn David we're coming," I say. I keep glancing down the hall half-expecting Buddy to come tearing around the corner on his way to David's office.

"What would he do if I picked up the phone?" Glyn says, looking down at David's assistant's phone, which has access to David's line. I smile, glad for the moment of relief.

Finally, after 10 very long-seeming minutes, we hear David hang up. His office goes silent. We walk in right away, not giving him a chance to tell us he's too busy to meet. I close the door behind me.

Like Buddy, David looks surprised to see us. I can't remember a previous time when I've just barged in like this, without making an appointment. David has a very tight schedule, and he often has to cancel and reschedule meetings.

But before we can begin, the phone rings. Turning his back to us as we sit down, David answers it, listening intently.

"You're too late, they're already here," he says.

He hangs up and turns around, acknowledging Buddy was the caller, though he says nothing else about their conversation.

David is cordial, as he usually is. He starts making conversation, perhaps thinking that he can divert us from the point of our visit if he talks long enough. Maybe I don't really want the small talk to end either. We talk about baseball, working out at the gym. As the conversation dies, an awkward silence descends. Glyn is the first to break it. For the third time in the last half-hour, he describes the prepaid capacity findings. I tell David that Buddy said he didn't know what they represented.

"He does know," David says. "I don't know why he told you that. Cynthia, I thought you already had a conversation with Scott about this," he goes on, looking carefully at me. "What did he tell you?"

"Scott says it is for zero- and low-utilized leased lines," I say, choosing to offer only a brief explanation.

David begins to talk about the company's cost structure. It's gotten too high and if that doesn't change, "we might as well shut the doors."

"Do you have the support for these entries?" I ask.

"No. I could go back and construct support, but I'm not going to do that," David says calmly. What does he mean there's no support? He's saying it as if that's perfectly normal.

"How were the amounts for the entries derived?" Glyn asks.

"They were booked based on what we thought the margins should be," he answers matter-of-factly.

"Are there any accounting standards supporting the entries?" I ask.

"No, there are no specific accounting standards supporting them," David says. He pauses. "We probably shouldn't have capitalized the line cost." He pauses again. "But once it was done the first time, it was difficult to stop. I've felt uncomfortable with these entries since the first time they were booked."

This is hard to believe. After being stonewalled by so many people, David is deluging me with information—there's no support, no accounting standards supporting the entries, the amounts were booked based on what margins should be, and they probably shouldn't have made them. But if what he says is true, how can he be so calm? Why doesn't he seem more upset? But I don't think he's making up the story as he goes. It seems as if David feels relieved, as if a burden has been lifted.

"How would you explain this to the Securities and Exchange Commission?" Glyn asks, recognizing that David's composure suggests that he thinks he hasn't committed a serious offense.

"I had hoped it wouldn't have to be explained."

My heart sinks. All of the anxieties that have been building over the previous weeks culminate in these few dreaded moments. I know that something is terribly wrong.

"Are you aware of other companies in the telecommunications industry who are using this same accounting treatment?" Glyn continues, wondering if this is some sort of common aggressive accounting technique.

"No, but other companies have to be doing the same thing," he says. "I don't see how they could keep their cost structure so low otherwise."

"Are there any other entries you feel uncomfortable with?" I ask.

"None other than these," he says, shaking his head.

I thank David for his time and tell him I'll get back with him tomorrow.

"Where will this go from here?" he asks me with an emotionless expression.

"Well, the audit will continue," I say, almost at a loss for words.

"I wouldn't expect you to do anything less," he says.

Glyn and I don't say a word until we're out of Accounting. It's 4:00 p.m., only 40 minutes after we spoke to Betty. We walk into my office and shut the door. I need a few minutes to compose myself. Gene joins us.

"They have no support," I tell Gene. We're all shocked, dumbfounded, and silent. This is incomprehensible.

"I want to go ahead and call Max," I tell Glyn after I've had time to collect my thoughts. I dread making the call. When Max answers, I fill him in on our conversations. He seems aggravated that I asked for support.

"Did Scott call you?" he asks.

"He left me a voice message but I never spoke to him."

"Why didn't you wait for Scott to call you? I told you to wait for Scott," he says, sounding frustrated.

"Scott left me a message saying something about tension between Internal Audit and Accounting, but this is not about tension, Max," I respond firmly.

"Update Farrell and call me back in the morning," he snaps.

"Will the next step be to call a full Audit Committee meeting?"

Max says he's not sure and definitely not before we talk to Farrell. I don't understand why Max doesn't seem more alarmed. I think he's still missing the seriousness of this issue. It's not easy to wrap your mind around billions of dollars in potentially fraudulent accounting entries. The whole thing seems completely surreal. How much time should I give him to inform the other Audit Committee members? What if he doesn't call a meeting?

It's 7:00 in the evening. I call Farrell—who's still working on-site in the Clinton office just one building over—and ask him to come by. When he arrives, Glyn, Farrell, and I make our way down the hall to the small room where Tonia has been compiling work papers and Gene has spent countless hours excavating data from the bowels of the accounting system.

There's so much stuff scattered around the room that it's hard to maneuver. We each pull up a chair. In a low voice, Glyn and I recount our conversations with Betty, Buddy, and David. Farrell seems shocked.

"Are you sure that's what David said?"

"Yes."

"Maybe he's playing some sort of joke," he says with a confused look on his face.

I can understand why Farrell is skeptical. I don't know what's more improbable—that Scott, David, and David's team would manipulate the financials by moving billions of dollars to the balance sheet or that David would just own up to it. I encourage Farrell to talk to him.

Suddenly, there's a knock at the door. We start, staring at each other in silence. If we say nothing, maybe the person will just go away. But there's another knock. Glyn stands and slowly moves next to the door.

"What's the password?" he says jokingly, breaking the tension. There's no password—we haven't gone that far.

"Financially fraudulent transactions," Gene blurts.

Farrell, the elder statesmen, and a reserved one at that, is horrified.

"You have to tell Gene he can't say things like that, even in jest," he cautions.

"I'll talk to him," I whisper.

I crack the door. Gene hands me several schedules related to the accounting entries. After a few more minutes, the rest of us leave the library.

"I'll call Max and go see David in the morning," Farrell says.

The next morning, I call David and tell him I've spoken to both Max and Farrell, and that Farrell will probably come talk with him later in the day. For several seconds, there's silence on the other end. "Okay," he finally says, softly, before hanging up. In a meeting with Farrell, David confirms what he told me. Late in the day, Max asks me to fly to Washington to meet with him and Farrell first thing the following morning. Will he finally call an Audit Committee meeting?

CHAPTER 23

The Confrontation

It's late afternoon, Tuesday, June 18, 2002. I'm still scrambling to book a flight out of Jackson when Scott's assistant calls. Scott is in Washington, working with bankers to obtain additional loans to sustain WorldCom. "Scott wants David and you to fly to Washington tonight and meet with him," she says. She doesn't say why. I explain that Glyn and I are already on our way there to meet with Max.

Soon, there's a follow-up voice-mail: "Cynthia . . . Scott said that it was not necessary for Glyn to come, especially tonight." After thinking about it, I decide I won't meet alone with Scott at this point. I'll still take Glyn, but I'm not asking anyone's permission this time. There are too many unknowns and too many strange things happening. A few of my staff are concerned about my physical safety and warn me to be cautious. Glyn has been involved in the audit since the beginning and should be there.

My administrative assistant hurriedly books Glyn and me on a flight to Washington, but has to switch the reservations when we learn David's taking the same flight. This has become much too serious for banter at the airport. I call Lance at home. "I have to go to Washington tonight. Do you mind packing a suitcase for me?"

"Don't worry about anything here," Lance says. "I'll take care of the kids. You just do what you need to do."

I barely have time to pull in the driveway and grab the suitcase. After I say goodbye to my two daughters, Lance puts my luggage in the car and hugs me. "Remember I love you," he says.

Glyn goes home to pack and tell his wife and kids goodbye. He calls his mother and tells her he's headed to Washington.

"Is there anything I can do?" she asks.

"I can't tell you specifics, but this could be really bad," Glyn replies. "Please pray for everyone involved."

As I race to the airport, I'm wondering what will happen in Washington. Glyn hopes Scott will miraculously pull a rabbit out of his hat at the last minute. I'm no longer hopeful. It's late at night when Glyn and I finally arrive and rent a car. We soon find ourselves completely lost in Washington. Everywhere we look are burglar bars securing the doors and windows of the buildings we pass.

"I have no clue where we are," Glyn says, pulling over to ask directions. Finally, after midnight, we find our way to the hotel.

The next morning, I'm scheduled to meet Max and Farrell at 8:00 a.m. in the dining room of the Monarch Hotel, where they—and Scott—are staying. After last night's ordeal, Glyn and I take a cab. We arrive early and take a walk near the hotel to pass the time.

"What's Max going to think about me just showing up here in Washington with you?" Glyn asks.

"I guess we'll find out."

At 8:00, we enter the hotel. I'm hoping not to run into Scott. Thankfully, he's nowhere in sight. Farrell is already waiting. Max arrives minutes later. The waitress seats us at a small corner table, providing some privacy. If Max minds that I brought an uninvited guest, he doesn't show it.

Everyone is grim. The mood is tense. We all order, and soon Glyn, Farrell, and I receive our meals.

"Go ahead and eat," Max says.

"Pour Max some coffee," Farrell motions to me, pointing toward the pot that's just been delivered to our table. I fill Max's cup as he begins to pull schedules out of his briefcase.

As we talk, Max glances at waiters as they hurry by our table serving others. "Where's my meal?" he finally asks, frustrated that we're almost through with our breakfasts while he hasn't even received his.

"You ordered the buffet," Glyn gently reminds him.

"Oh, that's right," Max says, rising to serve himself.

When he returns, I reiterate my discomfort with the fact that only one Audit Committee member knows about the entries while three remain in the dark.

"If this turns out to be nothing and it leaks out to the public, that could be very damaging," Max says. "We have to make sure we know what's going on with this before we call a meeting. There's a lot on the line here." He also tells me that because this deals with accounting, it is an external not an internal audit issue, and KPMG will take it from here. Max told us the same thing just before I met with him at the Hampton Inn—back away and External Audit will handle it.

"I don't care whose issue it is as long as it's addressed appropriately," I say. There's an edge to the conversation now.

Finally, we agree that Farrell will meet with Scott later in the day to give him an opportunity to explain his rationale. Then Farrell will update me. We end the meeting on good terms. Glyn and I leave with an entire day to do nothing but wait. We each go back to our hotel rooms to work. I call Lance and try to rest. Glyn touches base with Tonia and Gene back in the office. We eat. We talk. We wait. The day passes excruciatingly slowly.

That evening, Glyn and I sit in a Washington restaurant finishing dinner. We're anxious to hear from Farrell, but there's nothing. We keep looking at the clock. It's 10:00 p.m., and still no phone call. I dial the Monarch and ask to be connected to Farrell's room.

Farrell tells me that he met with Scott and David for some three hours that afternoon. "Nothing changed," he says. "Scott provided a rationale that may make sense from a business perspective, but not an accounting perspective." Scott is now trying to find amounts inappropriately recorded in the opposite direction—that is, expensed instead of capitalized—to offset the prepaid-capacity entries and attempt to avoid restating company earnings.

There's a frantic flurry of activity in the accounting department.

At 8:03 p.m., Buddy Yates had sent an e-mail to Mark Abide, the head of Property Accounting, and two others in International Finance.

"Urgent project," the subject line read. "Guys, we need to look at all expenses to see if there is any undercapitalization or any overstated liability on the books. . . . We need to be very aggressive and very fast as we look at this and nothing is more important."

Minutes later, Buddy sent a follow-up to Mark: "Mark, you know what the issue is. We need to look at everything in the world to see about an increase in Capex [Capital Expenditures]. We will talk as soon as I get in." But the search yields little, and, in any case, off-set entries would not have made the original entries appropriate.

It's Thursday, June 20. So far, we've found a total of just over $3 billion being moved over four quarters—the last three of 2001 and the first in 2002. Eight days have passed since I first called Max about these entries, but the Audit Committee still hasn't been summoned.

"Is Max going to call an Audit Committee meeting today?" I ask Farrell.

"I don't know."

"I still don't feel comfortable with the other committee members not knowing about this. Please tell Max if he doesn't call a meeting today, I'm going to get on the phone and call one myself," I say.

"You can't do that!" Farrell exclaims.

"I can and I will," I respond.

"Well, just hold tight and let me talk to Max," he says. "Max is talking to some attorneys today, and he has told [Audit Committee member] Judy Areen about the issue."

"So now we have two Audit Committee members who know and two who don't," I say.

"I understand what you mean," Farrell agrees, "I'll talk to Max."

Later in the morning, Max calls. "We've scheduled an Audit Committee meeting at 4:00 this afternoon at KPMG's office. You and Glyn can come if you want to," he says gruffly. I'm guessing he's so abrupt because Farrell relayed my message.

"You seem aggravated," I remark.

"Do you have any idea what I'm about to have to do?" he says. "I'm about to blow up this company!" The gravity of the issue is weighing heavy on Max. "And I don't need any confrontation between you and Scott at this meeting," he goes on.

"What do you mean 'confrontation'? There won't be any confrontation."

"Scott told me you wouldn't even ride up here on the plane with David Myers."

"That's true, but only because Glyn and I didn't feel comfortable."

"Okay. You and Glyn just come to the meeting at 4:00," he says in a more conciliatory tone.

I relay the conversation to Glyn. "Maybe you should call him back and tell him we'll make sure we don't come in smacking gum during the meeting," he says. He's irritated that we're being treated patronizingly. I double over laughing. It feels good to have a light-hearted moment.

Glyn and I grab a cab and head for the meeting at KPMG's office. Farrell and Max are already waiting in a large conference room. Farrell introduces me to a KPMG partner who he has invited to sit in on the meeting. Soon, Judy and Francesco Galesi, two of the remaining Audit Committee members, arrive. James Allen, the fourth member, joins by telephone. We sit quietly and wait for Scott. The mood is somber.

Scott arrives almost an hour late, trailed by a large entourage: David Myers; John Sidgmore; Ron Beaumont, the COO; Mike Salsbury, the general counsel; and a team of high-powered attorneys from Simpson, Thacher, & Bartlett, a prestigious New York firm with an office in Washington.

A few people awkwardly shake hands. Passing behind me, Scott briefly rests his hand on my shoulder, but doesn't say anything and keeps walking. I have no idea whether he means it as a friendly gesture. I've had no interaction with him for six days.

Farrell takes a seat at the head of the conference table, facing an attorney representing WorldCom, while the rest of us line the sides. Around 5:00 pm, Max opens the meeting, handing out several of the charts Internal Audit has put together summarizing the accounting entries. Calmly and fluently, he presents the findings.

"Internal Audit has discovered some questionable transfers from line-cost expense accounts to asset accounts beginning in the second quarter

2001 and continuing through the first quarter 2002," he says. "The cumulative total of the transfers is $2.24 billion in 2001 and $818 million in 2002." Max adds that the impact to WorldCom's financial statements is to increase reported earnings each quarter by the amount transferred. He then turns to Scott, asking him to explain his rationale for the entries.

"I would like to get KPMG's comments on this issue first," interjects one of the outside attorneys.

Farrell is calm but firm. He explains that he's not aware of any provision in generally accepted accounting principles that would support these entries.

Scott adamantly defends the transfers. He first gives the business rationale for the journal entries. He explains that starting in 1999, WorldCom invested heavily in assets to expand the telecom network, anticipating enormous future demands in customer traffic. WorldCom not only purchased equipment and fiber, but also signed a significant number of long-term fiber leases with third parties to carry the expected telecom traffic. But when the telecom industry imploded, starting in 2000 and continuing through 2002, the customer usage anticipated never materialized. Now, large pieces of both owned and leased portions of the telecom network either have no or very little customer traffic. Scott has provided his business reason for the entries, but he hasn't provided an accounting rationale for why he moved these lease amounts from an expense on the income statement to an asset on the balance sheet.

Next, Scott launches into accounting shop talk—usually the point at which non-accountants' eyes begin to glaze over, but not today. Today every person is hanging on his every word, aware that the company's future hinges on the validity of what he says. Scott deflects the discussion to the "matching principle"—an age-old accounting convention that delays expensing costs so that they are more aligned with the future benefit an asset will generate. But the "matching principle" only holds if the original journal entries to account for the leases were correct.

Scott again deflects by throwing out a second accounting issue— "impairment" of the company's asset base. He argues that based on the economic downturn in telecom, and the decline in WorldCom's first quarter revenue, it is now apparent the company's capital assets, including the telecom network and amounts he transferred from line cost expense to assets, are of less value than the amounts currently on the books. Therefore, he wants to take an "impairment charge" in the second quarter 2002, effectively writing off the line cost amounts booked as capital assets. Scott has again moved the discussion away from whether the original journal entries were proper, to whether an impairment charge should be taken, presuming the original entries were correct.

Scott continues to sidestep the real issue, insisting the entries weren't made to meet earnings; that accounting for "line costs" requires judgment; and that the transfers were made using estimates. He also says he didn't see the need to consult anyone from Arthur Andersen on these matters.

Scott adds that David can provide support. I'm wondering if he knows David has already told me there is none. David is listening blankly from the end of the table. Scott asks the Audit Committee if they will give him some time to provide support for his claims.

Max decides to take the meeting into an executive session. Ron, Scott, David, Glyn and I are asked to leave. The CEO, general counsel, outside counsel and external audit partners stay.

Those of us who leave the room go to a small conference room to wait. I stand by the door and listen as everyone begins to make friendly conversation. Glyn is trying to be cordial. The severity of the situation doesn't seem to be sinking in with Scott. He's showing Glyn all the cool stuff his latest BlackBerry can do and discussing plans to move to Clinton so he can be closer to the office. Does Glyn know of any good apartments in the area, he asks? Earlier today, Scott even made a courtesy visit to a WorldCom customer.

It feels too awkward to stand here listening to everyone make small talk. I walk out after only a few minutes, standing alone in the foyer area just outside the executive session. Mike Salsbury comes out briefly to make a phone call. He's clearly upset. I call out to him but get no response. Soon after, David Myers walks by. Seeing I'm distressed, he puts his hand on my shoulder. "I know you were just doing your job," he says. David seems as calm today as he did when we met with him in his office five days ago. Again, I have a strong sense that he's somehow relieved.

After what seems to be an hour or more, Max finally comes out. KPMG hasn't made a final decision on the accounting. Scott is given the weekend to support his position with evidence from accounting literature. The Committee will meet again on Monday to listen to his argument. Max tells Scott and David that they can leave. I watch as they walk out the door.

"Cynthia, now I want you and Glyn to go on back home," Max says in a fatherly tone, huddling us both together, his hands on our shoulders. "You've done your job and you need to go home now. You can continue working on your capital expenditure audit, but I don't want you working on this prepaid capacity anymore. This is an issue between KPMG and management. KPMG will handle it from here."

"Okay," I say, deciding not to press him for details. It's been a long day. We're all wrung out.

"If I have to listen to one more patronizing comment . . ." Glyn shakes his head as we make our way down the hall. "I don't like it either," I tell him, "but unfortunately, it sometimes comes with the territory. You have to choose your battles."

For the first time in what seems an eternity, I feel relief—the issue is finally being looked into by the Audit Committee. But my mind eventually goes back to Scott's arguments in the meeting. Was it all just one big smokescreen? I don't believe Scott can support the entries, and my relief quickly fades when I think about the likely consequences—for employees, shareholders, the company.

Exhausted, Glyn and I head to the airport to board a plane.

Scott is in the office this weekend, working feverishly with one of his staff to compose a white paper defending his position. Like his arguments at the Audit Committee meeting, it will rely heavily on the "matching principle."

Since the Audit Committee meeting, we've fished out even more suspicious entries. I now have a full view of 49 prepaid capacity accounting entries, totaling $3.8 billion, recorded over all four quarters in 2001 and the first quarter of 2002.

The more I stare at the entries, the more sinister they seem. They're different from each other, the pattern of movement between accounts changing from one quarter to the next. Still, the entries all have the same end result. While some are described as prepaid capacity, others are labeled, simply, "SS entry." Mark Abide will later testify that he keyed in Scott's initials because he was told by another accounting director that the entries were coming from David and Scott.

It's a spider-web of amounts moving as many as three times and finally spread in smaller dollar increments across a multitude of assets, mostly telecom fiber and equipment. If the amounts are funneled through enough accounts and then spread out, someone seems to have thought, they'd come out on the other end less detectable by the external auditors.

The entries are "on-top" (made at the Corporate level) and "post-close" (made after the books are closed). As management will later admit, it compared company results to the earnings guidance that had been given to Wall Street and then made adjustments to make up the difference. Because this was done at the Corporate level, employees within the business units whose numbers were being manipulated didn't have access to the entries.

Based on the user IDs we see in the system, employees in two different accounting groups—General Accounting and Property Accounting—physically made the entries. Sometimes mid-level managers—Mark Abide and Betty Vinson—made the entries. Sometimes lower-level staff reporting to them keyed in the figures, perhaps without understanding their significance.

It's Mark Abide and one of his staff who divided amounts in smaller increments. In one quarter, Mark made 10 entries, each for $54.4 million and all to the same "fiber optic cable" account. In another quarter, Mark instructed one of his employees to make 12 entries, this time to different accounts, and in descending round dollar amounts—$52 million, $51 million, $50 million, and so on.

While Mark sent us the article "Accounting for Anguish," the allegations in it would not have led to the prepaid capacity entries. If we hadn't already had a capital expenditure audit on our plan, we likely would have just tested the article's allegations, but the wider net we cast uncovered much more.

Though KPMG and the Audit Committee haven't made a final decision, Max has asked David to prepare revised financial statements. Over the weekend, Max asks me to take David and Buddy a spreadsheet detailing our findings to help with the restatement. I agree, but I'm uncomfortable. If they made these "on-top" entries, it seems like they should already know how to unwind them.

Gene and I come in to drop off the spreadsheets. Buddy Yates is sitting with his back to the door, intensely studying his computer screen. One of his managers is leaning over his shoulder. "Buddy, these are several spreadsheets Max asked me to bring you," I say, sitting a copy on his desk. He glances back at me with an unhappy expression and quickly turns back to his computer saying nothing.

When we meet with David, he doesn't seem nearly as relaxed as the last few times we've met. Maybe it's sobering to see each of the 49 entries, with the amounts detailed into their individual, appreciable increments, as opposed to the more abstract massive figures that we initially mentioned. This is probably the first time David is seeing the transferred amounts laid out before him in such detail.

As will later be revealed, it was David who had intentionally reduced my team's access to the accounting system to prevent us from finding the entries. "What access do the internal audit people have?" he wrote in an e-mail to an IT staffer in the fall of 2001. "Do they have access to corporate cost centers? If so, remove it immediately."

"I guess you somehow got access to the actual journal entries," David says, staring down at the schedules. I can tell he's stunned at the level of detail in our document and is wondering how we got to the actual transactions. I don't respond to David's question. Neither does Gene. David moves on without prying.

It's Monday, June 24. Glyn and I are meeting with Troy Normand, a mid-level accounting director, who's providing some information for the capital-expenditure audit. As we sit with him, he becomes visibly upset. He tells us that he's known about the prepaid-capacity entries since the first time they were made. And there's something else. Troy mentions another type of accounting entry that he believes is "aggressive." For the last two quarters in 2000, management made the company appear more profitable when it drew down "rainy day" line-cost reserves, thereby reducing expenses.

Troy says that in the second half of 2000, he relayed his concerns to Scott. "Scott explained the business reasons behind the entries and assured me that everything would be okay," Troy says. "I didn't know enough to refute his explanation." Troy says he expressed concern again in 2001, also to no avail. After he saw the future earnings guidance Scott recently provided Wall Street—impossible to meet without further manipulation—Troy says he considered resigning. He says he never told Internal or External Audit about any of the entries because he was concerned for his job and had a family to support. "In hindsight, I wish I had," he tells us.

Later as Glyn and I sit in my office, we are disheartened, not only by Troy's revelation, but also by the situation in which he found himself. "Troy seems to be the nicest person," I say. "Yeah, like the guy who lives next door," Glyn says. We have to document our meeting with Troy, and know that what we write might have grave implications for him. We sit silently in Glyn's office until he finally turns toward his computer. We begin to recount the conversation, but after a few minutes, Glyn becomes upset.

"I'm sorry, I have to go outside and walk around for a few minutes," he says, getting up and moving toward the door. This is the first time I've seen Glyn so distraught.

"I know. I feel the same way. Just take your time."

I think Glyn identifies most closely with Troy and the pressure he must have felt. They are around the same age and level in the company. Like Troy, Glyn is his family's provider and has young children at home.

After some 20 minutes, Glyn comes back and we finish our memo. But are the entries Troy told us about aggressive or worse?

Unbeknownst to us, Glyn and I aren't the only ones to whom Troy is telling his story. I will later learn that he, Betty, and Buddy have a secret meeting with FBI agents and officials from the Securities and Exchange Commission and the Department of Justice at a Courtyard Marriott in Jackson today. After Glyn and I confronted them last week, they decided to retain an attorney. Buddy had visited a lawyer earlier in the year but decided, in the end, not to engage him. Now he's changed his mind. The three have asked their attorney, who's located in Jackson, to schedule a meeting with officials from the Mississippi U.S. Attorney's office. If they volunteer the truth now, it could affect whether federal prosecutors choose to indict them. While there are no guarantees, their attorney has received signals from the Mississippi U.S. Attorney's office that they will have a good chance of avoiding indictment if they talk now.

As Betty, Buddy, and Troy quietly meet with law enforcement, Scott and David are flying to Washington so that Scott can present his white paper to the Audit Committee. The flight is tense. They sit far apart from each other and speak little. Scott makes himself eat a chocolate doughnut, the only food he's been able to tolerate for days.

At this second Audit Committee meeting, Andersen representatives say Andersen's prior clean opinion on WorldCom's 2001 financial statements is no longer valid. They add that Andersen wasn't aware of the entries but decline to give insight into why the transfers weren't detected through their audit testing.

I will later learn WorldCom management took steps to keep Andersen from finding the entries. They worked to control the audit by requiring Andersen to funnel requests through a single person. In addition, Andersen did not have real-time access to WorldCom's accounting system. In April 1999, David sent an e-mail to another WorldCom employee, "I was concerned that [Andersen] in general had [accounting system] access, which we cannot do . . . we fought [Andersen] during the past two years as they wanted access as part of the audit and we would not let them do it. . . . " While Andersen auditors asked management whether there were any "on-top" entries, they didn't obtain access to search the system themselves.

In August 2001, an Andersen partner sent WorldCom accounting management an e-mail outlining some of their proposed testing procedures, losing the element of surprise and unintentionally giving the people committing fraud time to cover their tracks. David asked Mark Abide and Troy Normand if they were "comfortable" with Andersen's procedures. "[Mark and I] discussed this yesterday," Troy wrote in an e-mail to David, "You know what my only concern is. We may want to discuss how that can be avoided." Troy told David they were worried Andersen would find the entries since some prepaid capacity amounts were sitting in an account listed as one of Andersen's first test procedures. At David's direction, Mark quickly moved the amounts out of the account Andersen was testing.

Scott presents his white paper employing the same reasoning he used the week before. The Audit Committee and KPMG conclude that Scott's argument doesn't pass muster. His actions did not constitute a suitable example of the "matching principle." The lease amounts he capitalized are operating, not capital. The amounts were transferred with no analysis of leases, apparently to meet Wall Street's earnings expectations. Taking an "impairment charge" in the current quarter is not an appropriate solution. The prior period financial statements must be corrected.

Before David leaves, one of WorldCom's attorneys advises him to retain private counsel. Until now, David has believed that his position as Controller was secure, especially because one of the board members assured him that he probably wouldn't lose it. But now he understands that this is going to be worse than he thought. The fact that he was simply following orders may not save his job.

In fact, the company asks for both his and Scott's resignation that very evening. David's WorldCom-appointed attorney phones him at his hotel. He tells David that it would be tough to make the case that Scott was the sole architect of the fraud. David calls his wife and finally tells her everything. He cries, worrying what people who know him will think. She cries, too, and tells him that he's "a good man and nothing would change that. . . . " David would hold on to these words in the weeks that followed.

CHAPTER 24

A Desperate Search
For Counsel

It's June 25, 2002. "I don't want to hear that you report to some freakin' board member! You fax it to me, and you fax it to me now!" the voice on the other end of the line screams over the speakerphone before the receiver comes crashing down. I stare at Glyn across the table, stunned. "Do you think he's mad?" Glyn deadpans.

Mike Salsbury, WorldCom's general counsel, has always been cordial. I certainly didn't expect him to begin shouting at me when I returned his message from earlier in the day. "I need you to fax me a copy of the memo where you documented your first meeting with Max Bobbitt," he demands, referring to the first time we alerted the Audit Committee chairman to the unusual accounting entries.

"Okay," I tell Mike. "But let me call Max first just to make sure he's okay with it." I'm trying to be tactful but firm.

"No, I need you to fax it to me now," he says, raising his voice.

"Well, I feel like I need to touch base with Max since I report to him," I reiterate. That's when he starts yelling. He sounds as if he wants to reach through the phone and strangle me. I'm happy there's a thousand miles between us—Mike is in Washington.

I know Mike is under pressure, but when someone is this aggressive, it makes me stop dead, take two steps back. He might as well have flipped a switch. The chilly reception I got from him at the Audit Committee meeting and his hostility makes me uncomfortable. I'm not clear on protocol. I don't know how many people knew about these entries. I don't know who to trust. One board member has even cautioned me to be careful about sharing information with another board member who is particularly close to Scott.

I begin working the phones, wanting to get back to Mike quickly. After unsuccessfully trying to reach Max, I go down the list of Audit Committee members, next calling Judy Areen, Dean of Georgetown Law School. I feel like she'll know how to advise me. Judy's advice is to fax Mike the memo. I do, but I'm still uncomfortable.

David has resigned but Scott refused, so the board has just fired him. He will later say he chose to be terminated rather than resign so that he could keep his retention bonus. Like David, Scott initially doesn't have a clear picture of the grave consequences of his actions. It's during his exit interview with John Sidgmore and Mike Salsbury, when Mike mentions prison time, that Scott's perspective finally changes.

At 3:30 p.m., WorldCom's management meets with SEC officials and informs them that the company has to restate its financials by $3.8 billion. Soon after, the company issues a terse press release: "As a result of an internal audit of the company's capital expenditure accounting, it was determined that certain transfers ... were not made in accordance with generally accepted accounting principles." The announcement also says WorldCom will lay off 17,000 people, over 20% of the company's employees.

WorldCom quickly becomes the lead story and front page news. The fraud is the largest in corporate history. "I'm concerned about the economic impact of the fact that there are some corporate leaders who have not upheld their responsibilities," President Bush says while at an economic summit of eight nations. He promises reform and a full investigation.

The Securities and Exchange Commission quickly files a civil lawsuit against WorldCom. "What happened at WorldCom...is an outrage.... I'm mad as hell and I'm not going to take it anymore," Harvey Pitt, Chairman of the SEC says, quoting a line from the movie *Network*.

The news causes an immediate frenzy. WorldCom employees begin to brace themselves—"Will I be one of the 20%?" they wonder. Many of my staff who are primary supporters of their families are worried that they will lose their jobs.

The stock market goes crazy, investors rushing to unload shares of WorldCom. The NASDAQ stops trading the company's stock, the price hitting a low of $0.09 before the halt. What will untimately happen to shareholder stock? Will the company be forced into bankruptcy?

Many Mississipians will remember where they were when they heard the news. Phones ring off the hook in the company's offices; employees are simply stunned. Shareholders are panicking. The company has announced a restatement, but will the amount of impropriety continue to grow? Will the entries Troy told us about turn out to be bad as well?

When I finally reach home, it's all I can do to sit on the couch in a daze, tears falling silently. The past several weeks have been traumatic, but little do I know that my nightmare is only beginning.

An Urgent Message

The next day, as I'm talking to another auditor in the hall, Stephanie Scott, the Vice President of Financial Reporting, is rapidly walking toward me, one arm extended straight forward in front of her waving a piece of paper. She has a frantic look. She quickly hands me the note and strides away as rapidly as she came, telling me the message as she disappears down the hall: "Mike Salsbury is trying to get in touch with you. It's urgent. He says you have to be in New York first thing in the morning."

"Okay, I'll call him," I say, puzzled, talking to her back. I grab Glyn, and we hurry to the conference room to return the call.

Mike starts by apologizing for his comments the previous day. Then he says that I need to be in New York by 10:00 a.m. the next morning to meet with the Justice Department. He explains that after Internal Audit's commissions fraud investigation, he was asked by the Southern District of New York in Manhattan, which prosecutes federal criminal cases related to southern New York state, to give them an update on our audit results. Since then, he says he's committed to keep the prosecutors informed about the company. He needs me to come up to New York tonight to walk through everything with the prosecutors first thing tomorrow.

I still feel guarded after my discussion with Mike yesterday. I begin asking questions.

"How does this work? Is it a sworn testimony or some kind of informal interview?"

"I believe it's informal." He adds that there could be a struggle over jurisdiction within the Justice Department, but New York believes they will handle the case. He says either he, another member of in-house Legal, or Simpson Thacher attorneys—the counsel that accompanied Mike and the management team at the Audit Committee Meeting—would go with us to the interview.

Mike has been cordial so far, but when I ask him what happens if we can't get a flight out today and aren't there by ten in the morning, his tone changes.

"What's your administrative assistant's name?" he asks, telling me to transfer him so he can book the tickets himself. "If you don't come by tomorrow morning," he warns ominously, "the United States Marshals will come and pick you up. Do you hear me, Cynthia? Are you listening to me?"

The abruptness and urgency seems odd, so I continue to ask for more details.

"Do you have a subpoena?"

"Uh, yes, we do."

"Is it just for me, or both Glyn and me?"

"I think it's for Glyn and you."

"Well, since I'm not an attorney, how does it work? Are the subpoenas in the company's name, or do they have my name and Glyn's name on them?"

"I believe they have your name and Glyn's name on them," he says, uncertain. "Are you listening to me, Cynthia? Do you hear me? Who books your plane reservations? Transfer me to them now."

"Can you read the subpoena to me?"

"It's in the other room, in my briefcase," another WorldCom attorney with Mike says.

"Well, can you go in the other room and get it?" I ask.

In a few minutes, the attorney comes back. "I can't get into the other room. It's locked."

My antennas are up. Why are the subpoenas locked in another room? I thought subpoenas are supposed to be hand-delivered by someone. They can't even tell me for sure in whose names the subpoenas have been issued. It's already late in the day—why the urgency to meet first thing tomorrow morning? Do I really want to go to New York and sit down with someone who's being hostile and patronizing? If I don't, will the U.S. Marshals come to my house tonight and take me into custody? I've received no clear answers. My gut instinct is to slow down and sort through the situation. I have no idea what's truly going on, but I refuse to take any chances.

"Well, when you get into the other room, just fax the subpoenas to us, and we can call you back and talk about it," I say. Not the answer they're looking for. Mike keeps demanding we book our flights, but I don't want to be badgered any more and close the call.

"Something isn't right," I tell Glyn. "Let's grab our stuff and get out of here." It's odd that while they initially said it was going to be an informal interview, suddenly they have subpoenas. Subpoenas don't sound very informal to me. On our way out the door, Glyn asks Gene Morse if he'll keep an eye on the fax machine in case the subpoenas arrive. We have to move quickly. I call my parents, who live 10 minutes from the office.

"I can't explain now, but Glyn and I are coming over."

"Okay, come on," my dad says without prying further.

As Glyn drives, we begin to discuss whether or not we need to find an attorney.

"Do you know any attorneys who handle this kind of thing?" I ask, looking over at Glyn.

"No, do you?" he says, glancing back at me as he drives.

I don't. I suppose a general business attorney who handles wills and real estate closings won't do. We need someone experienced in dealing with the federal justice system. Not knowing any attorneys of the sort, once Glyn and I arrive at my parents' house, we go for the Yellow Pages, paying special attention to the half- and full-page ads, and pictures—maybe not the soundest of strategies, but we're feeling desperate. Frantically tearing through the phone book we write down names and begin making calls.

My dad suggests we try James Tucker—a former Assistant United States Attorney and an old friend from high school—who is now with the same law firm as the brother of my former boss, Charles Cannada.

"Hi James, this is Cynthia Cooper with WorldCom. I need your help," I say when I reach him.

"Yeah, right," he says, laughing.

"No, I'm serious, I need your help."

"Are you kidding me?" WorldCom's troubles are front-page news, and James apparently thinks someone's pulling a prank.

Eventually, James believes me, but, after investigating, he calls back to say he won't be able to represent us because of a potential conflict of interest. Though he doesn't specify, I'm guessing it has to do with Charles' brother being a partner at the same firm.

Gene calls. Two subpoenas are sitting in the office fax machine. He says he'll drive halfway to give them to Glyn. I'm getting more and more anxious. It's almost 6 p.m. Glyn checked on flights, and the last one this evening is leaving at 7:10 p.m. There's another at 6:00 a.m. tomorrow morning. The minutes are slipping by and still no attorney. Glyn and I are starting to have visions of being carried away by U. S. Marshals.

"What about this guy?" Glyn says, looking at an advertisement for Joe Hollomon.

"His ad says he's a former Assistant District Attorney and Assistant U.S. attorney," my dad reads.

To my great relief, Joe answers the phone when I call. I recount our story. "I don't even know if we can get a flight out today. Can United States Marshals really come and arrest us if we're not in New York by 10:00 in the morning?" I ask.

"No, that's ridiculous," Joe says. "Come on down to my office. I'll wait for you."

Glyn and I jump in the car, faxed subpoenas in hand, and take off to Joe's office, less than 30 minutes away in downtown Jackson. He's waiting for us at the door when we arrive. Joe dials Mike's cell phone and puts him on speaker phone. Mike is on a train, presumably returning to Washington from his conversation with Justice prosecutors in New York. He sounds agitated to hear that we've retained counsel—he must now engage our attorney on all legal matters instead of contacting us directly. Mike passes the phone to another member of in-house Legal.

Joe reminds the attorney that faxing a subpoena is not proper service. He says that he'll personally talk to the Southern District to arrange a meeting. Suddenly, the tone on the other end of the line is entirely different, and it's no big deal to work out a more reasonable time for the interview.

"We're going to quash that subpoena in the morning," Joe tells the attorney on the other end. Neither Glyn nor I have any idea what quash means, but we like the way it sounds.

The next morning, Joe calls the Assistant U.S. Attorney in the Southern District of New York to arrange a time to meet, but it seems it's far from final which office of the Justice Department will lead the investigation— the Southern District of New York or the Southern District of Mississippi. Both districts want to handle the high-profile case. A huge political battle is heating up. Joe says the issue has been escalated to the highest levels of the Justice Department. I wonder if the urgency to get us to New York had anything to do with politics. Joe later says that he thinks Mike offered us up, so to speak. "I bet he obtained the subpoenas only after you spoke to him," Joe tells me.

The next day, one of WorldCom's attorneys leaves a message for Glyn, saying FBI agents investigating the case are canvassing the buildings and want to talk to him. If he's not available, they may come to his home. If they're looking for Glyn, presumably they'll be knocking on my door as well. We try calling Joe, but he's not around. Are we supposed to just sit down and start talking to the agents? Having no idea, we again decide to leave the premises.

We quickly exit the building keeping an eye out for anyone who looks like law enforcement as we walk to the parking lot. We drive in circles around Clinton as we wait to hear from Joe. We pass by Glyn's house, but see no unusual cars. Just in case, Glyn calls his wife, at home with the baby, to warn her not to answer the door. Joe finally gets back to us. He says to be polite if agents appear, but to decline any conversations at this point. The FBI agents never show.

The following day, Glyn and I are sitting in Joe's conference room when he leans forward with a concerned expression.

"There's something I need to tell you," he begins slowly. "I'm also representing three other WorldCom employees in this case."

"What?"

"Who?" Glyn says, as we both stare at Joe in disbelief.

"Buddy Yates, Betty Vinson, and Troy Normand."

I can't believe what I'm hearing. Apparently, the afternoon that Glyn and I interviewed Betty and Buddy about prepaid capacity, the two left the office along with Troy to retain an attorney—Joe Hollomon. My jaw just about hits the floor. I know Jackson is relatively small, but what are the chances we'd find our way to the same attorney? "Maybe they went to the Yellow Pages," Glyn jokes.

"I wish we'd known about this sooner," I say. Glyn and I have already recounted much of our story to Joe. His conference room is covered with boxes containing copies of our workpapers. I trust him, and am certain he won't share information between clients, but it's just too disconcerting to think that some of the people who may have been involved in the fraud are also coming in and out of this place. But Joe, who's already accompanied Betty, Buddy, and Troy to their meeting with officials from the SEC and

DOJ, thinks there won't be a conflict because he feels he's close to striking a deal that will help them avoid indictment.

For several days, Glyn and I struggle with whether or not to continue with Joe. The decision would be easy if we weren't so comfortable with him. He was there for us when we were under the gun, and we've been impressed with his take-charge, reassuring personality. And we're hearing that our interviews with the DOJ, FBI, and SEC could happen soon. We decide it's just too late to change attorneys and start over. Neither of us has the energy to go in search for another attorney. We're sticking with Joe, at least for now.

The next afternoon, Saturday, June 29th, four days since the fraud was announced, Glyn and I are in Joe's office when he receives a call with news of our initial interview. There was no need for subpoenas, as Glyn and I are simply going in voluntarily for the interview. For now, until top Justice officials make a final decision, the two districts have been instructed to work together. And so, while the first interview will take place in Mississippi, prosecutors and FBI agents from New York will also attend. Joe puts his caller on hold, and leans in to speak to me "Cynthia, I've just been told some officials from the SEC and prosecutors from New York are at the airport right now boarding planes to come to Jackson. They want to interview you and Glyn first thing in the morning."

"On Sunday? Can we do it Monday?" I ask.

"No, we have to do it tomorrow. They're already at the airport."

Glyn and I meet Joe in his office the next morning. I have no idea what to expect. I'm getting flashes of an interrogation under bright lights as people around a table fire questions. What if I forget something, or don't know the answer?

They call Glyn first. I stay at Joe's office as he and Glyn head over to the Southern District of Mississippi. I sit waiting, for hours. It feels like forever. Finally they return. "It wasn't stressful," Glyn reassures me. "They made me feel comfortable. You'll do fine."

When I arrive, the room is packed with 15 to 20 officials, who are seated around the long conference table. One of the New York prosecutors is on a large screen at the front of the room, joining by videoconference. I take my seat next to Joe. Glyn was right—everyone takes pains to make me feel comfortable. Each person introduces himself or herself, and an official from Mississippi explains how the process will work and takes the lead asking questions. I scan the room for a friendly face, landing on Charles Niemeier, Chief Accountant for the SEC's Enforcement Division, who is sitting across from me. Before joining the SEC, Charles was a partner at the law firm Williams & Connolly in Washington, and before that practiced public accounting for ten years. Near him is David Anders, a young New York prosecutor with black curly hair. He's friendly and tries to comfort me about the subpoena issue—I flew down here just to show you that we aren't so bad up there, he says.

As an auditor, usually I'm the one asking questions, but this day, I'm here to answer. My mouth feels dry. I keep drinking water but the feeling won't go away. One person sitting across from me asks most of the questions. Occasionally, various people break in with their own. Everyone is intensely focused working to understand the basic facts of the case. I'm relieved when it's over. The anticipation was much worse than the event. But this will turn out to be only the first of hundreds of hours of interviews, depositions, and witness preparation.

Take Your Vitamins and Hire a Washington Lawyer

As I sit in Joe's conference room one afternoon, my cell phone rings.

"Cynthia, it's Stephen Martin." Stephen is a former federal prosecutor in Washington. He's also a friend and former WorldCom attorney who worked with me to unravel the commissions fraud scheme. He recently left WorldCom to join the law firm of Steptoe & Johnson in Phoenix.

"How are you?" he asks.

"I've been better."

"I hear you've hired an attorney from Mississippi."

"Yeah. He's very good, but are we even going to need an attorney going forward?" I'm hoping he'll say no.

"You absolutely need an attorney. Anyone going through something like this needs an attorney just to help navigate through the legal process. I want you to listen to me. I'm sure your Jackson attorney is good, but this is a very big deal. It looks to me like you may have to testify before Congress. As a friend, I'm telling you, you need to get a Washington attorney, someone who knows their way around the Hill."

"Well, let me think about it," I say softly, not wanting Joe, who's just one room over, to hear what we're discussing. "I wouldn't even know where to start, how to find someone in Washington."

"The firm I'm with has someone who's highly respected and understands how Washington works. His name is Reid Weingarten, but you need to call him today. There are a lot of people looking for attorneys in this case, and I'm afraid he won't be available for long. I don't think he's representing anyone yet, but I wouldn't waste time before calling him."

"I'll talk it over with Glyn and call you tomorrow," I whisper.

Before hanging up, Stephen offers some final advice. "Cynthia, be sure to take your vitamins and drink lots of juice. This is going to be tough." I'm not thinking about vitamins and juice at the moment, but I'm grateful for the kind words.

After talking it over with Glyn, we agree that perhaps it would be best to take Stephen's advice, but he was right when he said I had to move quickly. "It's too late, Bernie Ebbers has retained Reid," Stephen tells me when I call him back the next day.

Several years later, I would run into Stephen at a conference. "I called Reid to tell him I knew you might be looking for legal counsel in D.C. because you were getting called before Congress," Stephen told me as we caught up. "Reid said, "Well, that's great, but we don't want the snitch. We want the bad guys."" That's a rude thing to say, I thought. But I guess it goes with the territory.

The Press is Here

Watching the news one evening, I'm shocked to hear my name being mentioned on various shows by Congressmen and commentators. They are calling me a whistleblower. "Why are they calling me a whistleblower?" I ask my husband. "I was just trying to do my job." I never expected to be labeled a whistleblower. To many, the term has a negative connotation. I even check to see how our dictionary defines it—"one who reveals wrongdoing within an organization to the public or to those in positions of authority."

At work, I soon receive a call from Brad Burns, the Vice President of Public Relations. Tall with dark hair, Brad has a friendly, outgoing personality along with a broadcaster's voice, calm and soothing. Brad and I have not interacted much, but I remember him at Scott Sullivan's baby shower last year saying that he counsels Bernie before his television appearances: "Wear a blue shirt instead of white, so you don't look washed out."

Brad has unsettling news. "Cynthia, the press is calling and they want to speak to you."

I'm completely taken aback. I never contemplated being thrown into the public spotlight and am completely unprepared for it.

"I really don't want to talk to the press," I say firmly. "Can't you speak to them?"

"I can, but they want to talk with you, and I don't think that they're going anywhere fast." Brad tries to reassure me and says he'll do what he can to field press questions. I don't envy his position as the main company liaison to the media. The next year will be extremely difficult for him, and I can already sense his exhaustion when we speak.

Teams of press representatives are camped out under enormous satellite dishes just outside company headquarters in Clinton. As employees leave the building, reporters approach the exiting cars, microphones in hand, hoping someone will stop. Reporters are soon walking my neighborhood and my parents' neighborhood asking if anyone knows anything about me; and calling members of my church, my high school teachers, my former classmates. The phone is ringing off the hook with major networks asking for interviews. I receive a letter from Matt Lauer of the *Today* show. Connie Chung sends a letter with her personal cell phone number. A *Nightline* producer shows up at my front door with three satellite trucks, hoping for an interview. Even DreamWorks, the film company, will get in touch.

I decline any requests for interviews. Our attorney advises Glyn and me to refer the press to WorldCom's public relations department out of respect for the legal process. My parents decline as well, explaining that they don't feel it is their place to be making statements in the press. Shareholders, employees, and many others are suffering in the wake of the terrible news. The last thing I want is to be in the headlines. I'm comfortable living a private life. Just months ago, my life was routine. I went to work each day to help support my family. My weekends were filled with church and family activities. I devoted my free time to my husband and two daughters, who are 12 years old and eleven months.

Sitting alone one afternoon in our conference room, contemplating the disaster all around us, I put my head down on the table. I'm finally starting to struggle under all of the pressure. It feels as if I'm mourning a death. Walking by, Farrell Malone, the KPMG audit partner, sees me and stops in. Farrell has become a friend and someone I respect a great deal. He's a no-nonsense, serious person, but he also has a big heart.

"Cynthia, come here, I want to show you something," he says.

"Hey, Farrell. What is it?" I ask.

"Just come down here for a minute," he says. I follow him out and around the corner to the end of our hall.

"Look at that sunset," he says enthusiastically, gazing out the window. "Isn't it beautiful?"

"It is beautiful," I say.

"And you know what? It's going to set again tomorrow."

I smile. "Thanks, Farrell."

Keep things in perspective, Farrell would often remind me. If you're around Farrell when the sun sets, as I will later learn, he may well stop you to watch the sun as it relinquishes another day, promising a new one tomorrow.

But the heat from the press keeps up. One afternoon my husband calls the office: Neighbors are calling to tell him that reporters from across the country, including the *New York Times*, the *Wall Street Journal*, and the *Washington Post* are going door to door inquiring about me. "I've closed the blinds and I'm not going to answer the door," he says.

But one day, he slips up. "I forgot and answered the door," he says when he calls me at work.

"Oh, well. Who was it?" I ask.

"It was a woman, a reporter."

"What did she want?"

"Well..." he says with a long sigh, and pauses.

"Well, what did she want?"

"She asked if Cynthia Cooper lived here."

"Okay. And what did you tell her?"

"Well..." Another long pause. "I froze," he says. "I said I didn't know."

"You what? You told a reporter you didn't know whether or not your wife lived there?!" I can't keep from laughing.

"We might see a headline tomorrow: 'Husband not sure whether wife lives in house,'" Lance says, laughing, too.

Another morning, a photographer from the *New York Times* is waiting at the foot of the driveway when Lance goes out to get the paper at 6:00 a.m. "There are no pictures of Ms. Cooper and I was wondering if I could come in and take a photograph," she says. "She might as well do it now on her own terms because if I don't do it somebody else will." I must confess that I'm not looking my best at 6:00 a.m., which gives me a good excuse to decline.

For months, my family peeks out from behind the blinds, on the lookout for reporters, before leaving the house. Coming home, we pull our cars into the garage, quickly shutting the door behind us. "Cindy," my mother says in her Southern drawl, still calling me by my childhood name, when she calls one day, "I need to run an errand but there's a car that's been parked in our driveway for hours. The people keep getting out and knocking on the door, but I haven't answered."

On one occasion, after ignoring a knock on the door, my mother watches a reporter walk down the driveway to the house behind hers. She quickly starts calling neighbors to ask them to refer all journalists to Brad

Burns at the company. "You're too late," her friend Bobbie says. "He's sitting right here having a cup of coffee with me. He says that if you can't give him a recent picture of Cynthia, he'll be forced to run her high school yearbook picture. He also has a list of background questions that he wants me to bring you, things like where Cynthia graduated from college. He says the *Wall Street Journal* wants to do a profile on her."

"Well," my mother says, "she doesn't want them to do a profile on her."

"Well, honey," Bobbie replies, "they're going to do it anyway."

My mother calls me at work. "What do you want me to do?" she asks. I try to recall what I looked like in the high school yearbook. I'm pretty sure that was the Farrah Fawcett "big hair" era. And what if they find that picture of me as the pink fairy in "A Midsummer Night's Dream"? I tried out for the school play and was rewarded with a part that had only three lines. I was the pink fairy and my best friend Susan Sheffield was the green fairy. I gave her two of my lines. The audience roared as we flitted out onto the stage in our matching tutus. It was the beginning and end of my acting career. Better to give them a recent photo, I think, and I ask my mom to share one from her collection.

CHAPTER 25

Washington Attorneys Visit
the Deep South

It's July 2, 2002. I'm sitting at my desk, trying to focus on work and help my team maintain some sense of normalcy, though this has proven futile for some time. I'm interrupted by two strangers standing in my doorway, a woman and a man with a gun strapped to his waist. They're saying something about being with the FBI. The woman explains that they need to retrieve some documents and copy my computer's hard drive.

After they introduce themselves, the male agent places some sort of hard-shell case on the floor. Opening it, he starts pulling out strange-looking tools and spreading them across my desk. As I watch, he proceeds to dismantle my computer piece by piece without saying a word. I know he's just doing his job, but I feel invaded all the same. I try to make small talk with him, but to no avail—no smiles, no conversation, strictly business.

Finally, I decide to get out of the way. As I leave, the other agent stops me. "I want you to know how much respect I have for what you and your group have done," she says in a low whisper. I thank her for her kind words. After removing and copying my hard drive, the man with the gun begins rifling through my desk and file cabinets, taking various documents to our copy room. But while the agent has successfully dismantled my computer, he runs into trouble with the copy machine. There's a brief moment of humor as he calls for help and Elaine, one of the Internal Audit directors, has to go to his rescue.

As the FBI agents rummage through my office, I'm waiting for a call from Bob Muse, an attorney with the Washington firm of Stein, Mitchell & Mezines. Bob also teaches Congressional Investigations at Georgetown Law School and has handled high-profile matters before Congress. Stephen Martin, my former WorldCom colleague, suggested I try Bob after I received word that I will definitely be called to testify before Congress and a national television audience in public hearings. I am terrified.

"I don't even like to speak in front of a small group. How can I speak in front of Congress?" I had recently asked Joe, our Mississippi attorney, as Glyn and I sat across from him. "If we go to Washington to testify before Congress and members of the press stick microphones in your face, what will you say?"

"Don't worry about that. I'll just say I'm Bubba from Mississippi, and I've come up to advance my catfish legislation," Joe drawled, laying on a little extra Southern accent for effect.

"That works," I said, laughing.

"And I'll wear my Billy Bob teeth," Glyn added.

"Great. I feel much better now."

I'm a long way from the sophomore-year presentation I gave about my violin in a college speech class. That speech met with an unfortunate end, concluding as soon as it began.

As I held my violin with one hand and the bow with the other, trying to explain the mechanics of the instrument, my heart began to pound as if it was about to run away from me. My palms were sweating. "I can't do it," I said. "Yes, you can," my classmates tried to support me. But it wasn't to be. I left, humiliated, and had to try again another day, successfully this time. But at the time it seemed like the end of the world.

Graduate school helped me become a better speaker—there was no way to get around all the required presentations. But during my first speech there, I made the mistake of trying to take a sip from a cup of water. As I brought the cup to my mouth, my hand began shaking. Glancing up at my classmates, I grabbed it with both hands. My hands were trembling so hard that it was impossible to take a drink, so I simply put it back down. "Great content," my professor, who gave me an A on the project, wrote. "But you seemed a little nervous." He was being generous.

What if I go before Congress and the same thing happens? I've heard polls show that public speaking is one of people's greatest fears, even more than death. Given my battle with stage fright, the idea only adds to the anxiety I'm already feeling.

I'm hoping Bob Muse can navigate the Hill and help prepare me for testimony. In the midst of the chaos going on in my office, the phone rings. I take his call in the next office. "Bob, thanks for calling me back," I say, introducing myself. "There are FBI agents in my office as we speak."

"What? Are you serious? Are they authorized?"

"I think so. They say they are."

"That's highly unusual. What are they doing?"

"They're taking my computer apart and copying documents."

"Can I speak to one of the agents?" Bob has a brief conversation with the female agent.

"You're right, they have a warrant," he says. "Cooperate and be respectful, but don't discuss anything of substance. Monitor what they're taking if you can, just so you'll know what has been removed. As soon as the agents leave, go somewhere off the premises and call me back."

"Okay. My parents live 10 minutes from here. I'll go there." As I drive to their house, the situation feels surreal. Closing myself in my old childhood bedroom, I dial Bob's home number. He puts me on speaker phone.

"Cynthia, I have my colleague Bill Corboy here," Bob says. "He'll be working with me. Start at the beginning and walk us through what's transpired." I've already gone through the facts with one attorney, and now I have to recount the story on the phone to two men I've only just met. I talk rapidly, pacing back and forth, occasionally having to pause to catch my breath.

At one point, I open the bedroom door to find my father mulling just outside. He's concerned and wants to help, but I need privacy. I wave my hand, motioning him to go away. My father's concern for my well-being will become a running joke between Glyn and me. Several times, he would mysteriously appear wherever Glyn and I happened to be. One Saturday afternoon, as we were leaving Joe's office, Glyn squinted his eyes and said, "Hey, is that your Dad walking down the street?"

"It is. What in the world is he doing down here?" I muttered to myself as we approached him.

"Oh, hi. I just came downtown to watch a little of the bicycle race," my father greeted us.

"Yeah right, Dad. Give me a break," I replied as Glyn and I laughed.

There was, in fact, a bicycle race. The streets were blocked off and teams of racers in brightly-colored suits were speeding by, but I don't recall my father ever expressing an interest in cycling.

On occasion, during our visits to Washington or New York, Glyn will break the tension by pointing randomly into the distance saying, "Hey Cynthia, isn't that your father standing over there?" It's always good for a laugh.

As I finish telling Bob and Bill about what I've recently been through, both are reassuring. "We'll keep going through this," Bob says. "I think we should plan a trip to Mississippi." I agree. I retain Bob to work along with Joe. But, I have no idea whether or not the company will pay Bob's legal fees.

A Personal Toll

The control over my life that I used to feel has vanished, replaced by feelings of depression and anxiety. I had done what I believed was right, but there's an emotional and physical price. There's rarely a moment when I don't feel nauseous. I have trouble falling asleep, but once asleep, my body doesn't want to get up. I suppose sleep is my only escape from the grim reality of what's happening around me. I'm tired with a tiredness that won't ease its grip.

Lance is doing everything he can to keep the world stable for our daughters and handle the daily routine so that I can focus on what has to be done at work. My teenage daughter has written notes of encouragement. My youngest daughter is a source of joy and laughter for us all. They are all a blessing.

I decide to take a few days off of work. Maybe that will help me adjust to the chaos and pull out of this depressed state. Lance encourages me to spend a few nights at my parents' home, which may be a quieter place to rest. As I lie down in my old childhood bedroom, I desperately want to disappear. It does feel comforting to be here. Just as it was when I came home as a single parent from Atlanta, this is a place of healing and refuge for me. But I know that tomorrow when I wake, I'll still be in the middle of a nightmare. Unable to sleep, I sit leaning forward, my face in my hands, making no sound, just an unending stream of silent tears. Logic tells me worse things in life come calling, but logic holds little sway at midnight.

My parents comfort me as best they can. I think they're grieving as much as I am. One evening, my father sits at the foot of the bed with the King James Bible. Opening to the 23rd Psalm, he reads,

> The Lord is my shepherd; I shall not want. He maketh me to lie down in green pastures: he leadeth me beside the still waters. He restoreth my soul: he leadeth me in the paths of righteousness for his name's sake. Yea, though I walk through the valley of the shadow of death, I will fear no evil: for thou art with me; thy rod and thy staff they comfort me. . . .

"Will you read it again?" I ask.

"Yes" he says. And he reads it again.

Just as my mother prodded me after my divorce, she gives me a swift kick. "Cindy, you have to go on," she says. Of course, she's right, lying in bed won't solve any problems nor will it quiet the storm. I know I must find the strength to push forward and face whatever lies ahead.

I've been through grief and difficulty before. I've always considered myself a realist, accepting the fact that tragedy is a part of life, but this tragedy is different. There is so much coming at me all at once from different directions and at breathtaking speed.

The telecom industry is in shambles. WorldCom will likely file bankruptcy. Everywhere there are innocent victims. My team and I watch as people we've worked with for years lose their jobs and leave the building carrying their belongings in small cardboard boxes.

Our world has been turned upside down. Everyone must save all documents, voice mails, and e-mails. Men with dollies arrive and carry away all of the shredders in the building. People are afraid to mention the word "shred" after Arthur Andersen's indictment related to shredding Enron documents. We are bombarded with requests for documents and interviews from numerous groups conducting often redundant investigations. People we work with may be facing prison. And they aren't just numbers to us. They are people we have known for a long time, trusted and respected. Many of us know their children, husbands, and wives. We talked with them in the halls and saw them in the cafeteria. I see Buddy Yates at church each week. Our children attend the same school and sing in the church choir.

With Congress calling, the press roaming my neighborhood and FBI agents at the door, I have been thrust into a world completely foreign to me. I feel many emotions. But mostly, I feel heartbroken. And with each day that passes, the place in which I find myself feels darker and lonelier. There seems to be no end in sight. How will I navigate the storm? How can I keep myself and my team focused?

I can't go on in this state. I've decided to visit Dr. Estess, the local Clinton doctor who has taken care of my family and my husband's family for nearly 30 years. While most physicians now work in groups because of the prohibitive costs of working alone, Dr. Estess has managed to hang on as a sole practitioner, the last of a disappearing breed.

I sit on the crisp white paper sheet at the end of the patient bed and wait quietly, staring at the brown panel walls that haven't changed since I was a kid. I think the same thing every time I visit: "I wonder why he doesn't get rid of this old paneling." But now I like the nostalgia of it, the comfort of having something stay the same.

For years after Lance and I were married, Lance's brother's childhood picture still hung alongside many others on a bulletin board at the entrance to Dr. Estess' office. I would chuckle each time I passed it. "I can't believe Christopher is now a grown man and his picture is still hanging in the doctor's office!" I'd say to Susan, the receptionist.

Finally the door opens and Dr. Estess, a huge bear of a man, comes in. He already knows what's going on with WorldCom from press accounts. Immediately, he gives me a hug and offers words of support. Never rushed, he has a kind and gentle bedside manner and is the kind of doctor who makes you feel better just by taking the time to really listen and understand your problems.

"I was hoping you'd come in," he says, smiling.

"We have to come up with a long-term plan to get you through this with your health intact," Dr. Estess says. He encourages me to try and exercise, eat well, and get as much rest as possible, but he's convinced that I need medication to help me sleep and relieve the depression.

"I'd like to give you a prescription for an antidepressant. I want you to think about taking it. This is going to be a long road." He explains how intense stress over a long period of time can be very damaging if it isn't managed. And he encourages that, in time, I will work through this. As much as anything, it is his reassuring words that greatly comfort me.

I'm fine taking something to sleep but feel hesitant about the anti-depressant. I'll get the prescription and hold it. Maybe in a few weeks, I can pull out of this. But as the pressures continue, I decide to try it and see if it makes a difference. Everyone is different, but for me, it was helpful.

I also do things to help keep up my strength. I begin working out every day, listen to encouraging music, and read inspiring books like Rick Warren's, *The Purpose Driven Life* that remind me suffering is part of life and God has a plan and a purpose even though I may not understand it.

We Each Have Our Doors

As my dad told me as a young child, we each have our doors of adversity. This just happens to be mine. If we live long enough, we're sure to face heartbreak—death of a loved one, divorce, illness, loss of job. For me, my faith, family, and friends will be a tremendous source of strength.

The time I feel a real sense of peace is when I am reading my Bible, in prayer, and in church. It is here that I will find the greatest comfort and am reminded of my Nannie Ferrell who each evening, without fail, read from the Bible she kept on her nightstand.

There is much to be thankful for, I tell myself, and everywhere I look, there are small acts of kindness. Friends, professors, members of my church, even people I've never met take the time to offer a kind word of encouragement. My extended family rallies around me. My church pastor calls to encourage me.

My friend Dee Dalton, an auditor at WorldCom, goes shopping for a suit I can wear if I have to go to Washington to testify. "Don't worry," she says, holding my hand. "I'll treat you like you were my own sister."

A neighbor leaves a note with a Bible verse taped to my front door "Do not be anxious about anything, but in everything, by prayer and petition, with thanksgiving, present your request to God."

My directors put in long hours and sacrifice holiday weekends with their family to help prepare material in case I must go before Congress. One morning as I walk in my office, there is a piece of paper folded and stapled on my desk. It reads: "Cynthia—A verse got me thinking this morning. *'For no sooner has the sun risen with a burning heat than it withers the grass; its flower falls, and its beautiful appearance perishes. So the rich man also will fade away in his pursuits.' James 1:11*. It reminded me that I should keep my attention on those things with eternal value: God, family, and friends, and not so much on those temporary things that will 'wither' away. Just wanted to share that with you. Glyn Smith." Going through this process makes me realize how important it is to be there for others during tough times, and that even the simplest of acts can have a powerful impact on people's lives. Again, I think of Nannie Ferrell, the grieving hands she held, always one of the first to arrive when others were in need.

Independence Day

It's July 4th. I've been at my attorney's office most of the day. As I pull in my driveway, the American flag is blowing in front of our house.

We usually watch fireworks at Clinton's annual celebration. Lance urges me to go, but I'm hesitant because the press is still everywhere. When I look out the front door, I see a small brown paper bag with a miniature American flag sticking out. Inside is a note from a reporter saying happy Independence Day and that he is around if I would like to speak.

Four days later the House Committee on Financial Services holds hearings chaired by Congressman Michael Oxley. Thankfully I am not there. I was to sit on a late afternoon panel with John Sidgmore, the CEO and Bert Roberts, the Chairman of the Board. However, days before, the Justice Department asked Congress not to call me. Because I may be a key witness in future criminal litigation, they preferred that I not make public statements.

The hearings are scheduled to start at 1:00 p.m. (EST), and I'm waiting to see how my former boss and CEO will respond to the Congressional Committee. I haven't spoken to Bernie since he left the company or seen Scott since the Audit Committee meeting. Will they answer questions or invoke their Fifth Amendment right? Glyn and I sit with Joe, our attorney, and watch from my living room as Jack Grubman, Bernie Ebbers, Scott Sullivan, and Melvin Dick, an Arthur Andersen partner who worked on the WorldCom audit, are sworn in. Chairman Oxley gives each panel member an opportunity to give an opening statement. Scott declines to give a statement, but Bernie seizes the opportunity: "When all of the activities at WorldCom are fairly aired . . . I believe that no one will conclude that I engaged in any criminal or fraudulent conduct during my tenure at WorldCom."

While Bernie seems relaxed, Scott is tense, his voice cracking. I stare at the television as Bernie and Scott each invoke their Fifth Amendment right, declining to answer the Committee's questions. Scott simply invokes his right. Bernie goes on at length: "Although I would like, more than you know, to answer the questions that you and your colleagues have about WorldCom, I have been instructed by my counsel not to testify based on my Fifth amendment constitutional rights. After careful consideration I have decided to follow my counsel's instructions, even though I do not believe I have anything to hide in these or any other proceedings. I have reached this decision because, one, the investigations appear to be open-ended examinations of a variety of activities at WorldCom, details of which have not been provided to me. Second, I have not been advised of the specific conduct of mine that is being called into question, and, third, I understand that preliminary statements can be taken out of context, as inquiries such as these become focused over time. . . . I do not believe that I should be subject to legal harm as a result of my exercise of a basic constitutional protection found in the Bill of Rights."

Several Congressmen become angry that Bernie made a statement and then chose to take the Fifth. "I don't think it's right to defend yourself in one breath and invoke the Fifth in the next," Congressman Max Sandlin says, adding that he plans to pursue contempt of Congress charges against Bernie.

While Bernie and Scott take the Fifth, Jack and Melvin answer questions for hours. Melvin began serving as WorldCom's engagement partner in 2001, after he took Mark Schoppet's place (SEC rules required Mark to rotate off after seven years). A Congressman notes that Andersen was the external auditor on many failed audits—Enron, Sunbeam, Waste Management, Global Crossing, McKesson, and the Baptist Foundation of Arizona. Melvin describes Andersen's testing procedures, saying they relied heavily on internal controls, but also tested a sample of transactions, performed analytical reviews comparing financial statement ratios, and asked management whether there were any significant on-top journal entries. "On each occasion, management represented to Andersen that there were no such entries," Melvin says. "As with any audit, we planned our audit of WorldCom in general reliance on the honesty and integrity of management of the company. One of the key elements of evidence all auditors rely upon are management's representations." The external auditors also used "sophisticated audit software" to analyze financial statement line items, but it identified no anomalies. Melvin says Andersen auditors saw nothing that led them to believe they should perform additional testing.

Congressman Michael Oxley expresses concern about conflicts of interest between analysts and investment banking. Jack acknowledges his close working relationship with WorldCom management and that he attended three WorldCom board meetings where acquisitions were discussed. But he's adamant that his recommendation of WorldCom stock went along with his long-held thesis that "the newer, more nimbler companies would create value." Congressman Bernie Sanders suggests that one reason for the thesis could have been the hundreds of millions of dollars in investment banking fees these companies generated.

When asked, Jack explains why Wall Street analysts didn't detect the WorldCom fraud. "Based on the financial statements that [WorldCom] filed, their capital expenditures were in line," he says adding that the company's 2001 capital expenditures were significantly lower than in 2000. He also says that the trends on WorldCom's reported EBITDA margins [earnings before interest, taxes, depreciation, and amortization] seemed right compared to "their only real competitor, AT&T."

It will later be revealed that since Scott was aware of what auditors, analysts, and investors would evaluate, the fraud was perpetrated in such a way that financial ratios and line items on the face of the financials appeared proper. Ratios such as line cost as a percent of revenue were comparable to prior quarters; and capital expenditures were typical of amounts being spent in the industry to expand networks.

Fried Green Tomatoes

The next day, Bob Muse, our new Washington attorney, and Bill Corboy arrive in Mississippi. We're scheduled to meet at the office of Joe Hollomon, our Mississippi attorney. Since there are still rumblings that I might be called to testify in future Congressional hearings, their main objective is to prepare me for testimony. Glyn and I are eager to meet Bob and Bill but we're worried about how our two legal teams will get along. We're also mindful of Joe's feelings. We like and respect him. He's been good to us during a very traumatic time.

"Before we park, let's circle the building and make sure there are no reporters," I tell Glyn as we pull up to Joe's office, though I doubt reporters would actually have his office staked out. My family and I have been besieged by the press, but as far as I know, no reporters are aware that Glyn and I have retained counsel. The coast seems clear. The only person on the sidewalk is a young gentleman in mirrored sunglasses looking in the window of an adjacent building.

"Why don't you get out here, and I'll park the car in the lot off to the side," Glyn says as he stops in front of the door to Joe's office. Both arms full of documents for our attorneys, I jump out of the car and go for the door, but before I can open it, I hear a voice calling.

"Excuse me, are you Cynthia Cooper?" someone shouts. Panic. Is there a reporter? Maybe I can make a run for it. No. Joe's warned me: Whatever you do, don't run from reporters. I turn to see the harmless-looking young gentleman who had been peering into the building next door.

"I'm Jared Sandberg with the *Wall Street Journal*," he says, dashing toward me.

"Hi, it's nice to meet you," I reply.

"I was wondering if I might have a few minutes to speak with you."

"Maybe we can talk later," I say. "I'm scheduled to meet with my attorneys," I explain. I take his business card, thank him, and hurry into Joe's office.

The Washington attorneys arrive soon after we do, but they aren't exactly what we were expecting from the capital's elite. Bob Muse arrives carrying some sort of knapsack, his clothes a bit rumpled. "Aren't Washington attorneys supposed to show up with starched shirts and nice leather briefcases instead of knapsacks?" I later joke with Glyn.

I can tell Bob is being careful to avoid tension with Joe, as it's still unclear who will ultimately represent us. But I'm getting the distinct impression that Joe isn't thrilled about these attorneys invading his office.

He calls me into the hall. "Why are these guys even here, anyway?" he whispers. "We don't need them."

"I know. Look—just humor me for a while. They know their way around Washington. If we find out there aren't going to be any more Congressional hearings, I can send them back."

This is the first time Bob and Bill have been to Mississippi. They seem to be experiencing a bit of culture shock. Welcome to life in the South, I think. I hadn't realized fried green tomatoes would be such a culinary oddity. At dinner, Bill would get his first taste, along with sweet tea, and, of course, he couldn't get enough.

As I'd later learn, Bill isn't an attorney, but a former Washington homicide detective whose crime-solving skills are legendary in the area. He certainly looks the part. A tall, dark-haired Irishman, he's a tough-guy Clint Eastwood type who speaks deliberately and slowly by anyone's standards, particularly for a Northerner.

He's the guy you want standing next to you in the alley when things aren't looking good. He would never cut and run. He's the one who takes charge at the crime scene, directing others while sirens blare and lights flash, a no-nonsense leader with a clear purpose who wants to get right down to business. When Glyn and I later visit Washington and Bill comes into the room, that means it's time to get serious. The joking and bantering stops. He asks questions with the same discipline he must have used as an investigator in his earlier career. While not a lawyer, Bill is as good as any at asking the right questions. He's a great listener, connecting the dots and mentally peering ten steps ahead.

Joe runs a one-attorney operation. His office has character, but I imagine it's the opposite of what you might find at a high-powered Washington law firm. It's cramped, with a small office and conference room. Located in a historic district just across the street from the old state Capitol, it's tucked into a long row of narrow buildings. The external brick from the building next door serves as Joe's interior wall.

On Bob and Bill's first visit, the five of us are huddled in Joe's small office when the sandwiches we ordered earlier arrive. It's now long past lunch and we're all starving. Everyone starts for the conference room where the sandwiches are laid out, but before we can get out the door, Joe's assistant announces, "That'll be $6.50 each."

I can see the surprise on the big-city lawyers' faces. I'm sure this isn't the way they would have handled a client luncheon. Nevertheless, everyone, including Joe, begins frantically digging through their pockets.

"I don't have any money with me," I say.

"I'll get yours," Bob says as he scrounges another $6.50 out of his pocket. Bob would later joke that buying my lunch was the best $6.50 he ever spent to win a client's business.

After lunch, Glyn and I settle in the conference room next to Joe's office and begin recounting our story to Bob and Bill. It's apparent that they've done their homework—they already know much of what happened. But we keep stopping, as there's one distraction after another. With only a partial partition separating Joe's office from the conference room, sound carries easily between the rooms, and there's a constant flow of traffic through the place. At one point, an attractive woman with a dark tan and high heels confidently strides through the office. "Who is *that*?" Bob asks, obviously distracted. I'm beginning to wonder if we'll ever be able to finish our work.

Repeatedly throughout the day, I walk to the front of Joe's office, and almost every time I see the mirrored sunglasses look in and then disappear.

"Joe, he keeps walking back and forth," I say. "I can't believe he's still here." I begin to feel guilty that no one has yet spoken with Jared. "How many times is he going to walk up and down the street? It's a hundred degrees outside."

"Don't worry about it," Joe says. "He'll be fine. We have too much work to stop now."

Jared disappears for a while, perhaps to get lunch, so Bob takes Glyn and me on separate walks around the block. He wants to make sure that we're comfortable with the way he's approaching the case. Bob and I walk across the street from Joe's office to the old Mississippi Capitol, now a museum, and sit on a bench to talk. We're in an outdoor sauna called summer in Mississippi—the heat is sweltering, and, in minutes, we're sweating profusely. "It's hot as hell out here," Bob says. "This has got to be the hottest day of my life!"

"You'll never get used to it," I say. "If I've been traveling up north, I always know I'm home when I get off the plane. The humidity hits you in the face and you feel like you can't breathe."

"Let's go back in," he finally says, wiping the sweat from his forehead with the back of his hand.

Mid-afternoon, Joe's assistant comes back to our room and tells us that the *Wall Street Journal* reporter came by to ask to use the restroom, but that she refused. "Shouldn't you at least let him in to use the restroom?" I ask.

"No, he may try to come back to the conference room," she says.

I return my attention to Bob—"On the one hand, you may get called to testify, but on the other hand, you may not"—but I'm also finding myself distracted by everything else going on in the office. Now there's a lady in Joe's office telling him how terribly her boyfriend is treating her.

After repeated interruptions, Bob's at the end of his rope. "This is like Grand Central station! Who is that? What's that noise?" Bob's concerned about who might be listening to us talk. I look outside the office to see a man with tools working on the door that leads to a small back alleyway.

"It appears to be a door repairman," I report back.

"It's probably the reporter," Glyn jokes. "The door repairman may be dead in the alley."

We work until late in the day. Finally, Glyn and I are ready to go home.

"Surely Jared has left by now. Joe, will you check?" I ask.

"He's still sitting there in a red car," Joe says after looking.

"I feel terrible that he's been sitting outside for the entire day."

"You and Glyn go out the back door, and Bob and I will stop and speak to him on our way out," Joe says. Glyn and I slip out into the alley and make our way to the parking lot.

The next day we meet again, but Bob and Bill are late. Forgetting they were no longer in Washington, they were standing in front of their hotel waiting to hail a cab. "There's no taxi around here," a passerby tells them. "You want a taxi, you gotta phone for a taxi." Thirty minutes later, their cab finally arrives. This is only the first of their taxi adventures. On a later visit, their cab driver gives them his business card. "The Jazzman," it reads. His car door doesn't open from the outside, the radio doesn't work, and he has no air conditioning. What he does have is a large boom box, which he asks Bill to hold all the way to the airport as they listen to tunes. "That visit was like a scene right out of a John Grisham novel," Bob later said.

Jared is also back the next morning. He hand-delivers a letter to Joe's office describing his tough time the previous day. Susan Pulliam, Jared's *Wall Street Journal* colleague, calls as well. For the first time, I develop an appreciation for what reporters must endure behind the scenes to get a story. Apparently, the day before had been quite unpleasant for Jared, one of the worst of his career. He alternated between sitting in his car and pacing up and down the street in the unbearable heat and humidity all day. No one on the block would let him use the restroom. Thinking him a loiterer, one of our well-meaning citizens even called the police.

Bob finally invites Jared in, explaining that it isn't a good time for an interview since Glyn and I are likely to serve as key witnesses for the Justice Department. He later calls Susan Pulliam and explains the situation to her as well.

Several years later, I'll have an opportunity to meet Susan. She'll recall other reporters and herself rolling with laughter as Jared periodically reported back about his misadventures that summer day in the Mississippi heat.

CHAPTER 26

Navigating the Storm

You gain strength, courage and confidence by every experience in
which you really stop to look fear in the face. You are able to say
to yourself, "I lived through this horror. I can take the next thing
that comes along" . . . You must do the thing you think you cannot do.

—Eleanor Roosevelt

It's July 21, 2002. WorldCom has just filed the largest bankruptcy in
corporate history, listing $41 billion in debt and $107 billion in assets.
Less than two weeks before, John Sidgmore, the temporary CEO, had
warned the market that the company would run out of cash by September. At the time of the filing, WorldCom still employs some 60,000
people, down from its high of over 100,000, and the layoffs will continue.

Filing bankruptcy means outstanding stock and options are now
worthless. When WorldCom emerges from Chapter 11, stock in the
new company will be offered for sale on the open market. If previous
shareholders want to recover a portion of their losses, they must file civil
lawsuits, which often recover mere pennies on the dollar.

WorldCom employees and shareholders aren't the only victims. Other
telecom companies and their employees suffered as they attempted to
keep up with a company that was cheating. Now some competitors
believe that allowing WorldCom to reorganize under the protection of

bankruptcy laws, which will allow the company to shed much of its heavy debt load, gives it an unfair advantage.

As more financial restatements and frauds occur across corporate America, it will become increasingly clear that internal and external auditors, regulators, boards, and management must make changes to improve the quality of financial reporting, minimize restatements and fraud, and detect frauds more quickly when they take place. The Association of Certified Fraud Examiners—established by author and fraud expert Joseph T. Wells to promote fraud prevention and detection—provides valuable statistics in its 2002 Report to the Nation, Occupational Fraud and Abuse: Financial statement frauds continue, on average, for 25 months before being detected; tips by employees tend to be the primary means of fraud detection, emphasizing the importance of an anonymous fraud hotline (WorldCom had no such hotline); the second-highest percent of frauds are detected "by accident."

The report indicates that frauds were detected by external audits in only a small percent of cases. Industry watchers will give a variety of reasons. For example, in the 1990s, auditors sometimes acted more like client advocates than independent auditors. And external audits were often the loss leader used to win lucrative consulting contracts. (In the cases of WorldCom and Enron, Arthur Andersen made far more in consulting and tax fees than from auditing the financial statements). For some audit engagements this meant reduced testing; fewer auditors, usually with less experience; and heavier reliance on a company's internal controls and analytical reviews in lieu of detailed testing of transactions.

But over-reliance on controls and analytics can be risky. The World-Com fraud, as well as other high-profile frauds, involved collusion by executives at the highest levels. Basic controls provide less protection in such cases—senior executives working together can often bypass them without detection. In the case of WorldCom, Andersen auditors reduced detailed testing because, as they indicated to the Audit Committee, financial reporting controls were operating effectively, but time will show that there were a number of material control weaknesses. And

when Arthur Andersen performed quarterly analytical reviews—
for example comparing line cost as a percent of revenue to prior
quarters—the ratios looked to be proper since the perpetrators made
sure that the fraudulent entries kept the statistics in line with what
Andersen expected.

I've heard rumor that President Bush has asked the Justice Department
to move quickly in the WorldCom case. Investor confidence must be
restored. The Sarbanes-Oxley Act, proposed after the Enron scandal, is
quickly passed by Congress and signed into law. President Bush says it
includes "the most far-reaching reforms of American business practices
since the time of Franklin Delano Roosevelt." The President is also
establishing a Corporate Fraud Task Force, calling for additional funding
for the Securities and Exchange Commission, and saying we must have
longer prison sentences for white-collar crimes.

Typically, jurisdiction over federal cases goes to the state in which a
company resides, but because one of the Mississippi prosecutors owns
WorldCom stock, creating a conflict, the Southern District of New York
wins the battle. The struggle over the case was tense. I will later hear from
an official close to the case that the New York prosecutors were quite
brusque with their Mississippi counterparts. The Southern District of
New York is known for their successful efforts in prosecuting white collar
crime and for employing some of the best and brightest prosecutors in the
country. They are tough. They are aggressive. They wield tremendous
power. "Some less admiring types even refer to them as the Sovereign
District of New York," my attorney jokes.

On August 1, 2002 Scott Sullivan and David Myers are arrested. My
staff and I watch the news as hundreds of cameras flash while they are
taken on "perp walks." Scott is charged with seven fraud-related counts,
and David is named an unindicted co-conspirator. The public is outraged,
and there is little sympathy. Some in the press report that when David

arrives at the car in handcuffs, the doors are left locked for a time, purportedly to allow the press to film and take pictures.

One method some districts within the Justice Department have used successfully in prosecuting white collar crimes is to quickly obtain guilty pleas from lower-level employees who, in exchange for the possibility of a lesser sentence, agree to cooperate in building a case against more senior employees. Just over three months after the WorldCom fraud is announced, David Myers, the Controller, is the first to plead guilty. His plea is quickly followed by three of his employees—Buddy Yates, Betty Vinson, and Troy Normand. The government's action sends a clear message—just because someone was lower in the reporting chain and was following a boss's orders will not necessarily save him or her from prosecution. With four of his staff cooperating with the government, Scott Sullivan is under increasing pressure, but he continues to maintain his innocence.

Betty and Troy both say at their court hearing that their bosses asked them to make adjustments to WorldCom's books. "I came to believe these adjustments being made . . . contravened Generally Accepted Accounting Principles," Betty says. As Betty speaks, her voice is so faint that her attorney adjusts the microphone and U.S. Magistrate Judge Andrew Peck asks her to talk louder.

Several articles on WorldCom will give poignant reminders that when people break the law, their children, relatives, and friends also suffer. Fraud has a ripple effect. Betty will begin to talk to her 12-year-old daughter about the fact that she may be required to serve time in prison. David Myers' young son gave him one of his most prized toys to keep with him when he went to New York to turn himself in to federal officials.

On August 8, 2002, WorldCom announces that an additional $3.3 billion must be restated, increasing the restatement to $7.1 billion. And the amount will continue to grow. The additional entries Troy Normand told us about appear to have been made simply to meet earnings guidance. In some cases, the amounts siphoned were in accounts that had no relationship with the line-cost expenses they were being used to reduce.

Once lavished with praise, Jack Grubman is now under fire for his central role in stoking the telecom market bubble. *Business Week* hammers Jack in a feature article and a camera crew hounds him about WorldCom in front of his home.

On August 15, Jack resigns his position at Salomon, though he doesn't leave empty-handed: The company agrees to cover his future legal fees and sends him off with a severance package in excess of $30 million, including forgiveness of a $15 million loan. From 1999 to 2002, Jack's compensation, including severance, was more than $67 million. During the same period, his employer made $790 million in banking fees from the telecom companies Jack followed. "The relentless series of negative statements about my work, all of which I believe unfairly single me out, has begun to undermine my efforts to analyze telecommunications companies," Jack writes in his resignation letter.

In addition to uncovering conflicts of interest by analysts who rated stocks positively to win investment-banking business, an investigation by the New York Attorney General will expose a practice called "spinning"—the allocating of coveted IPO stocks to executives in a position to award investment banking business. These executives often sold the shares for millions in profits as the prices jumped in the first few days of trading. The Attorney General will file a lawsuit against five current and former CEOs and Board Chairs, including Bernie Ebbers, alleging that they personally profited from hot IPOs awarded by Salomon Smith Barney and that the transactions weren't properly disclosed to the public. The suit will allege that Bernie made $11 million trading hot IPO stocks during roughly the same period in which WorldCom paid Salomon Smith Barney over $100 million on 23 investment banking deals.

"It was simple. It was brazen," Spitzer will say describing the various abuses and conflict's of interest his investigation uncovered, "The evidence was overwhelming." An analyst's compensation was sometimes tied to how much investment banking business the analyst procured. "What we found was that analysts were involved from the very beginning of the investment banking relationship; going out there, soliciting a client, promising. 'If you bring your business to our firm, we will take your company, proclaim to the world that it is the best thing since sliced bread, take your company public, keep a strong buy on your stock . . . and become part of your management team.' There were analysts who routinely were present at board meetings."

Because Spitzer believes Wall Street's "business model" is so broken, that its problems are too pervasive to be solved by punishing any single firm—and because losing one of the major Wall Street firms would harm the economy—he will not opt to criminally indict any individuals or firm. "I believe that there are theoretical criminal cases that could have been brought . . . The judgment call that I have made, obviously, is, in the context of Jack Grubman and others at Citi, to bring . . . civil charges, leading to a civil resolution that bans Grubman from the industry for life, imposes a financial penalty, and imposes on the company a structural reform."

Spitzer, the SEC, and a number of other regulatory groups will soon announce an individual settlement with Jack Grubman and a "global settlement" with ten investment firms. Jack must pay $15 million. The ten firms will pay a combined $1.4 billion and implement reforms. For example, analyst compensation can no longer be tied to investment banking business; investment bankers can't evaluate analysts; and spinning will no longer be permitted.

A New Sheriff

It's October 2002. At work, my department continues to complete audits. Through an accounts payable audit, we've found that Stiles Kellett, a WorldCom board member, has been leasing one of WorldCom's corporate jets for $1 a month, plus hourly usage fees of $400 an hour. (He also serves on the committee that approved Bernie's loans, which will lead some to speculate that Bernie awarded him the favorable leasing deal in exchange for his support of the loans). We've turned the information over to the Audit Committee.

Hundreds of contract employees—including a temporary CFO and COO—descend on Clinton to help restate the company's financials and fill the gap left by terminated executives. Although my reporting structure has been elevated to John Sidgmore, the interim CEO, I haven't heard from him since the fraud was announced. Some of the executives in Washington don't want to speak to me directly. Instead, they send messages through the contract CFO.

"There is a new sheriff in town," the temporary CFO announces. Though I don't report to him, he soon begins issuing directives. "I want you to move your group next to me and the accounting department," he tells me adamantly, as if I have no choice in the matter. It seems pointless to make my entire department pack and move to another building. When I ask why, the only answer I receive is that "it would be a very good idea." I get the distinct impression he's been told to keep an eye on us. Some employees are angry with my team and me for coming forward about the fraud. I decide not to move my team and see if the issue eventually dies.

My department and I find ourselves in extremely awkward situations. The two men I now report to—John Sidgmore, the CEO, and Max Bobbitt, the Audit Committee Chairman—don't like one another, and the Board infighting hasn't ceased. Two board members ask us to investigate allegations of impropriety related to other board members. I don't want my department to be used as a weapon in the Board's battles. How can my team carry out our duties and keep from being pulled into the middle of personal vendettas?

The environment within the boardroom becomes even more toxic as members continue to leak negative information on one another to the press. In October, *BusinessWeek* publishes an article titled, "How Ebbers Kept the Board in His Pocket." The article says four Board members— Stiles Kellett, the Compensation Committee Chair; Carl Aycock, one of the original WorldCom investors; and Max Bobbitt and Francesco Galesi, members of the Audit Committee—were nicknamed by other directors as "Bernie's Boys." The article says these four were "Ebbers loyalists," according to "current and former WorldCom directors and executives," who elected to hold most of their WorldCom stock until the bitter end and lost hundreds of millions of dollars. Though approved by the full board, the article says Bernie's loans were "spearheaded" by the four; and that Max, who once had $300 million in WorldCom stock and watched it become worthless, was finally fed up so he worked to oust Bernie and take the CEO spot. Max says some of the information in the article is untrue and is upset at other board members and executives who he says fed the article to the press to harm him. At one Audit Committee meeting, he becomes emotional and leaves.

Meanwhile, the temporary CFO continues to stop by to deliver messages, always with an edge: You still need to move your department; certain executives in Washington aren't happy about some of Internal Audit's findings; top executives are upset that some members of your team have spoken to the press. You're not to talk to the press.

"Who is sending these messages?" I ask.

"I'm not going to say," he responds explaining that it doesn't matter who it is. "They just want to make sure you get the message." I don't understand why they won't call and tell me themselves. Soon, a member of the press tells my attorney that two top executives still with the company are working the phones to criticize and discredit me in the media. Which of the people I have worked with for years wants to disparage me?

One day, I'm in a meeting with my team when my administrative assistant interrupts. "Cynthia, Bob Muse is on the line and he says it's important." Every day, I brace myself for what strange and surreal event will happen next, but what he's about to say is a real shocker.

"Cynthia, I've just gotten a call from a well-respected reporter who says that two of the very highest executives still with the company are calling around to different members of the press telling them that you blew the whistle because you are a scorned lover." Since there is no truth to it, it is never printed. There are only a few top executives who are still with the company. I try to guess which of them would say such a thing and why, but I soon block it from my mind and refocus on my work.

It is disquieting not knowing who you can trust and realizing some unidentified people are working behind the scenes against you. Some on my team are even fearful for our safety. It's obvious that someone is coming into our offices at night. We return in the morning to find items rearranged, and doors and drawers unlocked. We have some of the locks re-keyed, and one of my staff even leaves a piece of tape across the door to see if it is disturbed the next day. One afternoon, several of my team members and I return from a funeral to find a team of investigators hired by the Board of Directors rummaging, unannounced, through our file room.

"Don't stay up here anymore late at night by yourself," one of my directors tells me. "I don't want to scare you, but you never know. You need to be very careful." Gene tells me, "When I was here late one night by myself, I jumped several feet each time I heard a noise or someone opened the doors in our area. It was usually just the security guard or cleaning people making their rounds."

It's late in the evening. The WorldCom parking lot is empty and my car is out toward the back. I walk quickly with my keys in my hand across the vacant expanse of blacktop. I look over my shoulder several times, but see no one. Next time I'll get someone from security to walk me out, I think. It's easy to become paranoid in this type of environment, but I want to guard against it. I've received no overt threats.

As we continue to work late, my mother sometimes calls for food orders. My father serves as the delivery man. Most of the time we get sandwiches. One night we're blessed with a home-cooked meal of chicken, vegetables, my mother's cornbread, and home-grown tomatoes.

The Clinton office has become extremely tense. The sea of empty cubicles outside my office grows every day. Our once thriving office has grown still. There are times when I think I'm going to suffocate if I don't get out of this environment. But I want to do my part and stay with my team at least for awhile. I can tell by the political winds that if I leave too soon, everyone in my group who works out of Clinton will almost certainly lose their jobs. My management team and I decide the key is to try and maintain a positive attitude and to keep ourselves and our staff busy. Many of my staff are worried. It won't be easy for them to replace their jobs in the Jackson area. Despite everything going on, the auditors in my group have been courageous. With so much out of our control, we try to stay focused and depend on each other for support. If we don't do well one day, we try again the next.

Tonia and Gene, two internal auditors who worked on the capital expenditure audit, are also being called by various groups for interviews. When Gene asks WorldCom's legal department to cover fees so he can engage his own personal attorney to guide him through the morass, he is told no. Instead, they offer counsel from a firm working with World-Com's legal department. He's informed that attorneys from this firm can prepare and accompany him to any interviews. But after the experiences Glyn and I have had with in-house legal, Gene isn't comfortable. He appeals to WorldCom's Board of Directors and is again declined. Gene is becoming increasingly frustrated. I speak to one of the Board members on Gene's behalf and am told the decision is final. Employees below the director level must use in-house legal.

While I've reported to John Sidgmore since Scott was fired four months ago, we've still not spoken. Finally, I run into him at a dinner party in Washington hosted by KPMG, our external auditor. Max Bobbitt is also present, and there are still more than a few bad feelings between the two. John shakes my hand as I enter. "I want to talk with you later," he says. He's warm and friendly.

True to his word, after a few minutes, he makes his way across the room. "Come on, let's go find a place to sit and talk for a minute. Watch, this will make Max mad," he says as he ushers me past the Audit Committee Chair. "He'll wonder what I'm talking to you about." We sit just outside the room where everyone is milling around before dinner.

"How have you been?" he asks.

"Good," I say.

"No, how are you really?" he repeats, with a look of sincere concern.

"It's been difficult," I say. "How are you doing?"

"It's been very hard for me, too. My wife says that if I don't get away from here soon, I'll either end up dead because of the stress or in prison," he says jokingly. John explains he hasn't contacted me because he just didn't feel comfortable. Perhaps his discomfort is because I report directly to the Audit Committee Chair with whom he is having conflict. I'm also beginning to get the feeling that many people are simply uncomfortable with whistleblowers. Maybe it is just a natural part of human nature. I'm not sure. I let the comment pass without delving.

"You know, I would have bet everything that Scott would never do something like this," John adds, shaking his head.

This will be the last conversation I ever have with John Sidgmore. He'll leave the company in December when WorldCom hires a new CEO. Later, Scott Sullivan will testify that he told John about the fraud before Internal Audit identified it, soon after John became CEO, but John will not have an opportunity to respond. Tragically, John's words to me that night will prove prophetic. On December 11, 2003, John dies, leaving his wife and a 12-year-old son. He was 52 years old.

The *Journal*'s Article

It's late October, 2002. My father, an incessant worrier, had frequently warned my mother: Please don't talk to any reporters. Every time, she assured him she wouldn't. And we might have never learned about her slip-up if she hadn't given herself away by accident.

When the *Wall Street Journal* publishes an article by Susan Pulliam and Deborah Solomon discussing how Internal Audit identified the fraud at WorldCom, it includes a reference to Farrell Malone's kind reminder to keep things in perspective that afternoon in the office. But I don't remember discussing it with anyone outside my family. The article says that Farrell pointed out the sunset from a balcony at WorldCom's headquarters.

"Who would have told them that?" I ask my mother. "There was no balcony. We just looked out the window."

"Oh, I thought you saw it from a WorldCom balcony," she says.

"Did you tell them that?!"

"Well . . . " she says, smiling. I just shake my head in disbelief.

"Whatever you do, don't tell your Dad. It'll just get him going and I'll never hear the end of it. Let's send him to get us all something to eat, and I'll tell you about it." Since my dad is known to come back into the house for one thing or another before finally heading out, we wait in silence to hear the car go up the drive.

"What did they ask you?" I ask.

"Well, one of them said she heard you had a bodyguard."

"A bodyguard? You've got to be kidding!"

"I told her it wasn't true."

"I opened the door and there they were," my mom continues. "Poor things looked so pitiful standing there in the heat. And, besides, it would have been rude not to invite them in. So I did. And they were such nice young ladies. One of them reminded me of you."

"Oh, mama."

Finally, when my dad comes home, my mother comes clean with him as well. The article titled "Uncooking the Books," is part of a series on accounting scandals for which the *Journal's* staff will receive the 2003 Pulitzer Prize for explanatory reporting. It has a lasting impact on Farrell, too. A few of his colleagues at KPMG take to calling him "Sunset Malone," even flashing an image of a sunset at one of the company's meetings.

An Inspiring Meeting

It's November, 2002. When I check my voice-mail one morning, I have a message from Amanda Ripley, a reporter from *Time* Magazine. Because I have intentionally stayed out of the press so far, I ask my attorney Bob Muse to return *Time's* phone call. Bob calls me back several days later.

"Cynthia, *Time* is looking to do an article for their December edition on you, Sherron Watkins, and Coleen Rowley," he says, referring to the

Enron and FBI whistleblowers. "I think you should give this interview."
While I'm very reluctant, Bob believes that it's a tremendous opportunity
to meet two other women who've faced similar challenges. My husband,
Lance, is also encouraging me to do the interview. He thinks it will benefit
people to hear all three of these personal stories.

After talking with my family, I call Bob back. "I'll do it only if the
others agree to the interview," I tell him. As it happens, I'm not the only
one who wants to make sure the others are on board before signing on.
We're all three reluctant, especially Coleen. While Sherron has resigned
from Enron, Coleen is still an attorney in the FBI's Minneapolis office,
and has less than two years until retirement.

The reporters work back and forth with the three of us until everyone
agrees to the interview. They must move quickly to meet tight deadlines.
Amanda Ripley, one of the *Time* reporters, is coming to Mississippi to
interview my family and me over several days. She's professional, warm
and congenial; any uncertainty I once had about reporters quickly
dissipates. Two other reporters are interviewing Sherron and Coleen
separately at their homes, and then all six of us will get together for a
group interview. I'm eager to meet Sherron and Coleen. I know their
names through the press, but little about their personal stories. I don't
remember ever meeting a whistleblower before. I wonder if our experiences will be similar. Will we have anything in common?

It's early December, 2002. I'm flying to Minneapolis, where Coleen
lives. Sherron is flying in from Texas. The three of us will have dinner with
the reporters. In the morning, we'll have a roundtable discussion and a
photographer will take our picture. "I hope I've made the right decision
about going through with this interview," I tell my husband before
leaving.

As Amanda and I walk into the hotel restaurant, Sherron is already
waiting. She rises to greet me. We hug and have an instant casual rapport.
Though we've never met, I feel somehow as if I already know her. After a
few moments, Coleen arrives. Her demeanor is friendly but more formal,
what I would expect from an FBI agent. We shake hands instead, and
depart for dinner. I'm equally fascinated about meeting the three *Time*

reporters, all women. As we sit at dinner, the conversation is easy and informal.

Sherron, 43, and Coleen, 48, are several years older than I am. They both seem more outspoken, but there's an immediate connection between us. While our stories and personalities are different, many of our experiences and challenges are similar. We will become friends and share advice based on what we went through. It's been only five months since this nightmare started for me, but Sherron has been living it longer.

Sherron was a vice president in Enron's Finance department when she warned Ken Lay, Enron's CEO, about shady accounting. Soon after, her boss Andy Fastow, Enron's CFO, seized the hard drive from her computer. She was moved out of her executive suite into a smaller run-down office with an old desk. Behind the scenes, executive management looked into firing her. As an e-mail by Enron's outside counsel to an Enron executive, written just two days after Sherron spoke to Ken Lay, stated, "Per your request, the following are some bullet thoughts on how to manage the case with the employee who made the sensitive report. . . . Texas law does not currently protect corporate whistle-blowers. The Supreme Court has twice declined to create a cause of action for whistle-blowers who are discharged." Fearful for her personal safety, Sherron spoke with company security personnel about protection. She once received a call from someone blaming her for the fact that a senior Enron executive had taken his life shortly after the company's scandal broke. After less than a year, feeling isolated and frustrated that she was being given only busywork, Sherron left the company.

After the September 11 attacks, Coleen wrote a 13-page letter to then-FBI Director Robert Mueller. She also gave a copy of the letter to two Senators on the Senate Committee on Intelligence. The letter indicated that her office in Minneapolis had forwarded information to higher-ups related to a French-Moroccan, who had registered for flight school in the area, and that the information had not been properly addressed.

Coleen seems to have had a particularly difficult time. Disclosing internal FBI issues to Congress didn't go over well within the halls of the FBI. Loyalty is important in any organization, but especially so in law enforcement. She received nasty letters and phone calls, some that could be construed as threatening. One of Coleen's co-workers warned her that senior FBI personnel were talking about filing criminal charges against her. Coleen found herself faced with colliding values: loyalty to her superiors against what she believed was right and the obligation she felt to the American public. As she will say in her *Time* interview, "Loyalty to whoever you work for is extremely important. The only problem is, it's not *the* most important thing." Coleen will stay with the FBI until retirement, but before she leaves, she voluntarily takes a demotion, giving up her position as an attorney for her field office.

We all loved where we worked and had a strong belief in the value of our organizations. Sherron and I were both at the vice president level and had each been with our companies for around eight years. Coleen had worked with the FBI her entire career. She even dreamed of working as an FBI agent as a child when she organized her 5th grade girlfriends into a spy club. As an elementary school girl, she wrote the FBI for more information and soon learned that females weren't allowed to be agents. No matter, she was sure she would one day work for them anyway. By the time she grew up, the rules had changed, but she was one of the trailblazers, as there were still few female agents.

The photo shoot is the next morning. Coleen is a tri-athlete who is typically toting a gun wherever she goes. Wearing dresses and make-up is not her thing. But today, she agrees to make an exception. The hotel's racquetball court has been turned into a temporary studio. The photographer takes picture after picture, Coleen in the middle, Sherron and I to her sides. As he snaps away, he instructs us not to smile. I agree—the topic is too serious, and it would seem inappropriate. We're all surprised by the extent of the photo shoot. "I thought this was just going to be a snapshot for an article in the magazine," Coleen says as we leave.

It's early one Saturday morning in late December. I'm still in a deep sleep when the phone rings. Thinking it likely a family member, I roll over trying to shake the fog from my brain and pull the phone to my ear. "Cynthia, this is Jim Kelly with *Time* Magazine." I try to compose myself and mask the fact I have just been awakened, as I listen to him say that we will be the 2002 Persons of the Year and that it will be announced first thing tomorrow morning. It is a call I will not forget. For an average citizen who has never been in the public eye, it is an incredibly humbling part of my journey. Beneath our photo, *Time* prints "The Whistleblowers," a term I don't much care for until my mother calls to tell me what one of the news stations is saying: Three snitches were named Persons of the Year. Maybe "whistleblower" isn't so bad after all, I think.

When *Time*'s December issue comes out, the managing editor will write that the reporters were worried the night before the three of us met—"How would Rowley, famous for her fanny pack and 20-year-old-suits, get along with Watkins, who was bemoaning a lost airline bag containing a Hermes scarf? Would Cooper, who had stayed fiercely private since her name was leaked over the summer, have anything to say to anyone?" But he went on to note that the "worries were groundless." I admire these women for their tenaciousness and perseverance through tough times. Meeting them, I finally feel less alone. Lance will tell me that I returned from the meeting changed, "The person who left for Minneapolis isn't the same person who came home," he says.

From a personal perspective, meeting Sherron, Coleen and the *Time* reporters will be an incredible step forward for me. After the articles, my team and I receive many letters of encouragement. It will help me look beyond my own circumstances and begin to see how sharing this story might help others. What happened to Sherron, Coleen and me in our places of employment could have happened to anyone. In fact, most people have at one level or another identified wrongdoing or, like Betty Vinson and Troy Normand, felt pressured to do something they didn't believe was right. What happened to people in many companies involved in recent scandals will happen again, to other people, in other companies.

The Whistleblower Phenomenon

Before being labeled a whistleblower, I hadn't given much thought to whistleblowers or what they go through, but now, I want to learn more. Are my experiences shared by others? I query whistleblowers on the

Internet and find a multitude of articles, studies and books. I finally decide on a book titled *Whistleblowers: Broken Lives and Organizational Power* by C. Fred Alford.

"Your book came today," Lance says. On its cover is a school of fish swimming in one direction with one fish swimming in the opposite. I read the back cover to Lance. "Alford argues that few whistleblowers recover from their experience, and that, even then, they live in a world very different from the one they knew before their confrontation with the organization." That's not encouraging.

I don't read far before it's clear that whistleblower studies offer a bleak outlook. "Of the several dozen whistleblowers I have talked with, most lost their houses," Alford writes. "Many lost their families. It doesn't happen all at once, but whistleblowers' cases drag on for years, putting a tremendous strain on families. Most whistleblowers will suffer from depression and alcoholism. Half of the whistleblowers examined by one study went bankrupt." Alford continues, "Most whistleblowers will be unable to retire. A typical fate is for a nuclear engineer to end up selling computers at Radio Shack."

A number of studies have shown that 50 to 66% of whistleblowers lose their jobs. For the most part, people who blow the whistle will leave their place of employment within a year. As Alford writes, "usually the whistleblower is not fired outright. The organization's goal is to discon-nect the act of whistleblowing from the act of retaliation, which is why so much legislation to protect the whistleblower is irrelevant. The usual practice is to demoralize and humiliate the whistleblower, putting him or her under so much psychological stress that it becomes difficult to do a good job." And whether someone goes outside their organization or blows the whistle internally makes almost no difference in terms of retaliation.

Whistleblowers are typically shocked by how they are treated, and many say they wouldn't do it again. Everything I read is extremely negative. Is this destined to be my future?

"Will you stop reading that book?" Lance says.

"No." I read on. The reading is tough, but for me, the book is an enormous relief and empowerment. I realize that there's probably not a whistleblower alive who hasn't experienced what I've been through. Put a hundred other ordinary citizens in my place, and they would likely experience the same things. There is definitely some sort of a whistle-blower phenomenon—step over the "invisible line," and you will experience it. There are many lessons within these pages. I realize I can either let these events continue to have a negative impact on my life or find a way to move in a positive direction.

I will continue to meet many other whistleblowers—some high-profile cases, others that received little or no public attention. Not one has a positive story to tell me about what happened to them afterward. Because some people view them as loose cannons, troublemakers whose loyalty is questionable, one of the biggest problems is finding new employment.

Late one afternoon at the office, a gentleman calls me and begins weeping uncontrollably. He says he devoted his career to his company, often at the expense of his wife and children, only to be laid off after blowing the whistle. "I've lost everything," he says. I encourage him as best I can and will later hear he is doing better.

After preparing a speech for some students, I walk through it with several friends. Each person cautions me not to discuss the trials of whistleblowers.

"It's too negative," one says.

"If you say some whistleblowers suffer from alcoholism or depression, people may think you suffer from alcoholism or depression," another says. "I would just leave it out."

I continue to include the consequences of bringing forward wrong-doing in my speeches because I think understanding is important to changing behavior. Laws will only go so far in protecting whistleblowers from being isolated, "laid off," or pressured. In fact, I've come to believe a free press can offer a balance of power and as much protection for whistleblowers as any law may provide. I also believe knowledge is empowering to people who may be contemplating blowing the whistle, and a relief to those who have. My advice to whistleblowers is to educate yourself about what may happen once you come forward, know who you are at your core, avoid looking to others for self-worth, and move your life in a different direction if necessary.

Back and Forth to Washington and New York

For over two and a half years, Glyn and I will travel to Washington and New York assisting the Justice Department and giving interviews related to the various and often redundant investigations. Fortunately, the company has agreed to cover our attorney fees. Sometimes we go to the offices of high-powered law firms where the accommodations are plush and caterers serve unbelievable spreads of food. At other times, we are at the offices of the Justice Department, a stark contrast, where rows of boxes and metal filing cabinets crowd walkways, and we are often crammed into small conference rooms. I once heard my attorney Bob Muse ribbing someone at Justice that "you can't even get a cup of coffee or donut" there. "At least no one can say they are wasting taxpayer dollars," I tell Bob.

My friend Stephen Martin was right about the benefits of retaining an attorney in the thick of things in Washington and New York. Bob Muse moves between these milieus—FBI agents, Justice prosecutors, the SEC, investigators hired by WorldCom's Board and appointed by the bankruptcy court, congressional committee staff—with ease and grace. Bob and Bill Corboy, his colleague, will become our dear and trusted friends. They have a long-time partnership. They complement each other, seem to anticipate one another's moves, and even have a collective approach to asking questions, one picking up where the other leaves off. Bill zones in on details. Bob has an uncanny ability to see the big picture and anticipate where matters will go as we prepare for various proceedings. Among Bob's great contributions is simply to build confidence. He quickly absorbs complicated issues, reassures that the events before us are manageable, and helps us understand our relationship to each party with whom we might interact. Later Bill will accompany Bob when the latter becomes chief Democratic counsel to the Senate Committee investigating Hurricane Katrina.

One day, I ask Bob why Bill quit his job as a homicide detective and changed professions. "He blew the whistle on police corruption," Bob says. "He was a real Serpico. Bill finally got tired of the way he was being treated and decided to leave the force." While some people dismiss the repercussions I'm experiencing as a whistleblower, Bill never does. He's lived it himself.

Whenever Glyn and I are in Washington, Bob invites us over to his home. Everyone loves "The House" as Bob calls it, a hub of constant activity brimming with great charm and warmth. The second of 11 children, Bob thrives on activity. As we sit on the front porch that wraps around his three-story Victorian-style home with a white-picket fence, which lies in the shadow of the National Cathedral, friends of Bob's sons stop to chat as he asks about their day and offers fatherly advice. In fact, you never know who'll come walking up. On any given evening, you're sure to have a number of acquaintances and friends wander up for a visit on the porch, even members of Congress. It's these friendships that make Bob's life so full and interesting. Divorced and the father of three, Bob has made a wonderful home for his sons, and spending time with them always comes first, followed by his career.

A New Team

It's December, 2002. WorldCom has become a game of musical chairs with board members and executives leaving and new ones coming in. As I sit in the December Audit Committee meeting, it is strange to look around and realize that all of the faces around the table are new. The entire board has resigned. Michael Capellas has been appointed as the new CEO. Michael served as the Chief Information Officer, and from 1999 to 2001 as the CEO, of Compaq, one of the country's largest manufacturers of personal computers. Though Clinton is still technically headquarters, Michael and many of the new executives will work out of the Ashburn,

Virginia office. Richard Breeden, the former Chairman of the Securities and Exchange Commission, has been assigned by the United States District Court for the Southern District of New York to serve as Corporate Monitor. As such, he sits in on each Audit Committee and Board Meeting. Denny Beresford, Jack Rogers, and Nicholas Katzenbach have been appointed as the new Audit Committee members.

Each of the Audit Committee members is highly qualified. Jack Rogers is the former Chairman and CEO of Atlanta-based Equifax, one of the country's largest consumer credit reporting agencies. Denny Beresford, the new Audit Committee Chairman, is an accounting professor at the University of Georgia in Athens and a former Ernst & Young partner who once chaired the Financial Accounting Standards Board—a body that sets accounting standards for public companies in the United States. I now report functionally to Denny. He's been immediately supportive and has flown to Clinton several times to meet with my team and me. Just as importantly, he always has a kind word of encouragement, gives my directors positive feedback about their work, and seems to appreciate the challenges we face. Maybe, finally, things will get better.

When Nicholas Katzenbach was appointed the 65th Attorney General of the United States by President Johnson, Bernie Ebbers was still in college, and I hadn't even had my first birthday. Born in 1922, he now uses a cane to walk, but he has an extremely quick wit and his mind is sharp as ever. He participated in some of the most historic events and trying times in our nation's history. In the 1960s, he testified before the Warren Commission that investigated President Kennedy's assassination; met with Martin Luther King and President Johnson to talk about voting legislation; brought in federal troops in 1962 to confront Mississippi's Governor Ross Barnett and accompany James Meredith, the first African American admitted to the University of Mississippi, as he registered; and stood across from then Governor George Wallace of Alabama in the "Stand at the Schoolhouse Door," when the Governor tried to fight desegregation at the University of Alabama.

The former Attorney General will soon deliver a speech at the University of Mississippi in his first visit since he arrived with federal troops

41 years before. In between talking about corporate governance, I am eager to hear his views on the country's progress on equal opportunity. "This university should take great pride in what it has accomplished by way of racial diversity," he will say in his speech. "I congratulate you, Mr. Chancellor, on your truly remarkable accomplishments to date and the doors you have flung open to an even greater academic future." Last year, the University of Mississippi dedicated a memorial to James Meredith. "We cannot undo the misdeeds of the past," said Chancellor Robert Khayat. "We can express our heartfelt regret that equal rights and equal opportunity were once long denied to a large segment of our state's population. Out of the tragedy of 1962, this university has risen to lead the way in racial reconciliation. It is time for the nation to see us as we are today, not as we were 40 years ago."

Everyone in my group is excited about the new executive team and the promise of a fresh start. Our optimism and hopes are high. It will be interesting to compare this team's approach and management style to the former executives. What will they do to change the tone at the top and the corporate culture? Will they be able to turn WorldCom around, or is the state of telecom such that revenues will continue to decline no matter what? As my former boss Charles believed so many years before, I cannot see how WorldCom can survive without merging with a large local carrier. I wonder if this executive team's plan is to pull WorldCom out of bankruptcy and flip the company in a sale. Many of the new executives come from industries other than telecom. They will face tremendous challenges in moving this company out of bankruptcy. They are entering an industry that has experienced a historic boom and bust, in size as well as the speed with which it occurred. The sector has lost $2 trillion in market cap, twice that of the dot.com bubble; and in just two years, over 500,000 telecom workers have lost jobs.

The telecom implosion was so severe that WorldCom's stock price had already fallen from its high of $64 to $0.83 before the company announced that it was restating its financial statements due to the fraudulent accounting entries. Neither the fraud nor the discovery of the fraud caused the downfall of WorldCom. The fraud simply masked the true state of the business. WorldCom should have gone into bankruptcy long before it did.

The new executive team will be forced to deal with the same powerful market forces that have plagued the industry to this point. Like the railroad companies of the 1800s, telecom has simply overbuilt. Within the five years following the passage of the Telecom Act of 1996, millions of miles of fiber optic cable were buried in the ground. Jack Grubman's theory—no matter how large the attic, it will get filled—did not hold. The tremendous glut of telecom capacity has resulted in scores of companies going bankrupt and fiber buried all over the world that won't be used for years. Excess supply and telecom companies fighting for market share have dramatically driven down rates for telecom services. Web hosting, dot.com, and start-up telecom companies cancelled orders with World-Com and other large players that, in turn, cancelled orders with telecom equipment and fiber-optic manufacturers. The telecom industry fell like a circle of dominoes.

Deregulation, Internet mania, conflicts of interest, delusions of quick riches, and low interest rates created the perfect storm. Can society take the hard-earned lessons of what happened in the telecom industry and keep history from repeating yet again? In the future, can the Fed reduce the flow of capital invested in the markets enough to stop additional bubbles of this scale without slowing innovation and progress? How does one find the proper balance between deregulating to encourage growth and free markets and the regulation needed to protect capital markets and prevent conflicts of interest? What role did quarterly earnings guidance and excessive use of stock options with short vesting periods play in executive decision making?

"[W]e were too trapped into the mantra of deregulation, mindlessly stripping back on regulation," Joe Stiglitz, winner of the 2001 Nobel Prize for Economics and former Chairman of the White House Council of

Economic Advisers, writes in his book *The Roaring Nineties*. "Deregulation of the telecommunication sector paved the way for the over-investment bubble, which then burst so resoundingly in 2001. Deregulation of the electricity market led to the market manipulation that hurt the California economy, the heart of so much of America's innovation. Deregulation of banking—notably the repeal of the Glass-Steagall Act—opened up new opportunities for conflicts of interest, when what was needed was stronger regulations to address extant and growing conflicts of interest which would eventually do so much to undermine confidence in our securities markets. Lax regulation of the accounting sector provided opportunities and incentives to proffer misleading or wrong information."

While analysts, industry experts, and government reports were stating as late as 2002 that Internet traffic was doubling every quarter, it turned out to be nothing more than a myth. "The markets bought lock, stock and barrel that Internet traffic would double every three months forever," says FCC Chairman Reed Hundt. "There was just no way there was enough traffic to justify all of these huge networks."

Andrew Odlyzko, a professor at the University of Minnesota and former researcher for AT&T Labs, has traced the start of the Internet myth back to statements made in 1996 and early 1997 by several WorldCom executives, including John Sidgmore. Odlyzko writes that "most of the WorldCom claims about astronomical growth rates of their network were about network capacity, not [Internet] traffic . . . . One of the remaining mysteries of this story is how it was that claims about network capacity were universally interpreted and passed on as claims about network traffic. . . . The memory of this brief period of manic growth (starting when the Internet was tiny) appears to have led to a perception that doubling every quarter was normal for the Internet." He adds that "myths are very persistent . . . [and] people are extremely credulous, especially when the message they hear confirms their personal and business dreams (as the Internet growth myth did, by offering the prospects of huge growth in telecom and effortless riches for participants in the game)."

The Clinton office has in many ways become a pariah. It seems that the WorldCom headquarters has been tainted by the fraud, and Mississippi is fighting old stereotypes. We listen as some of the high-level company executives in other locations make derogatory comments about Clinton and Mississippi. Legacy MCI employees move into many of the top executive positions. The fact that the different factions of WorldCom have never felt united becomes more apparent than ever. Long-time legacy WorldCom executives are laid off one by one across the company. The company's name is changed from WorldCom to MCI. "We're taking our company back," one legacy MCI executive says. "My company was not founded in a motel coffee shop," another employee writes in an e-mail being forwarded throughout the company. Headquarters is moved from Clinton to the campus WorldCom built in Ashburn, Virginia, just outside Washington, DC. Employees in groups such as Accounts Payable, Payroll, and Accounting are moved out of Clinton to Atlanta and Ashburn. While in some major cities, losing jobs may have been less important to the local economy, here they will be difficult to replace. "Management wants to make a statement in the location where the fraud occurred," one board member tells me.

After so many years of fighting to build the Internal Audit department, and prove the competence of our group, the importance of internal controls, and the value of a strong internal audit function, I find myself at square one with a new management team. Jon Mabry, the first auditor I ever hired, has come back to Internal Audit. When he was faced with being laid off as a Senior Director in Marketing, I hired him. The group is much more established than when Jon left 6 years ago: Over 90 percent of my staff have at least one professional certification and many have multiple designations and years of telecom audit experience. I remember the days when Jon and I worked so hard to get support for Internal Audit. I wonder if we will have to do it all over again? I am no longer naïve to the challenges my team and I face. It has been and will continue to be a rough road.

There is now a new executive team and board, as well as contract employees and investigators. Though the faces around the table have changed, the politics continue. The pressure to move out of bankruptcy is intense. Hundreds of millions of dollars are at stake, and many stand to make fortunes in a short period of time. The *Wall Street Journal* writes a piece that mentions the strained atmosphere. On a couple of occasions, Denny Beresford, the Chair of the Audit Committee, becomes exasperated and threatens to resign. Fortunately, he decides to stay on. While some executives include my department as part of the team, others do not, sometimes making for an extremely difficult working environment. Some of the internal auditors find the situation too stressful and decide to leave the company.

I soon turn around to find that I'm the only corporate vice president left in Clinton. As one after another of Clinton's top executives lose their jobs, the Facilities group continues to go down the list giving the next employee in line the right to a space in the small executive parking area where Bernie and Scott once parked. When the offer comes to me, I decline.

There have been those times when I couldn't hide my feelings of sadness about the devastation all around me. Once, at a company dinner soon after the Board resigned, the speaker joked that the company put all of the former Board members on a bus and sent them away together. The room erupted in laughter. I sat solemn, looking forward. "It's OK to laugh," one of the new executives leaned over and whispered.

CHAPTER 27

A Visit to Federal Court

Walking Through a Graveyard

It's November, 2004. The double glass doors to the executive suite are locked. I peer through the glass to see drops of water leaking from the ceiling in several spots and a dimly-lit room, many of the lights burned out and the remaining ones flickering, a ghostly symbol of the fall of a company and an executive team that once seemed invincible.

Several members of Internal Audit and I are giving Bob Blakely, the CFO, a tour of the Clinton building. In April, 2003, some ten months after Scott Sullivan was fired, the Board hired Bob to replace the temporary CEO. Bob works out of the Ashburn headquarters and has played a key role in helping the company exit bankruptcy. His team of Controllers and hundreds of accountants have worked tirelessly to restate the company's financial statements.

The company successfully emerged from bankruptcy on April 20, 2004. "A lot of people didn't think we could get it done," Denny Beresford told *CFO* Magazine. "It was a Herculean effort to get to that point." In all, MCI spent around $800 million in professional fees to various consultants, attorneys, and accountants, including $351 million for required audits.

The audit "is the hardest thing I have done in my career," says Bob, who led the finance team in recreating prior-year financial statements and reviewing the accounting related to previous acquisitions. At one point, he was overseeing as many as 1,500 people (500 to 600 company employees, and nearly a thousand additional hires from KPMG and Deloitte & Touche). The restatement required the team to make over three million accounting entries. It was "the largest and most complex financial restatement ever undertaken," Bob tells the press.

I've reported to Bob for the past year and a half, but this is his first visit to Clinton. He wants to see the executive suite where Bernie and Scott once worked. Because it is sealed, as there are no remaining senior executives, we're accompanied by a security guard. The suite is eerily silent. Not so long ago, this place was full of activity, the epicenter of negotiations for many a deal.

At 63, Bob looks as if he just stepped off the pages of a men's fashion magazine, always dressed in the finest suits accompanied by the perfect selection of tie and cufflinks. With an MBA from Cornell University and a PhD from Massachusetts Institute of Technology, he has a wealth of experience. In 1998, he received *CFO* Magazine's CFO Excellence Award for Capital Structure Management. After serving as a managing director at Morgan Stanley and 18 years as CFO of Tenneco, a $4.4 billion Fortune 500 company that manufactures automotive emission and ride control products, he was enjoying retirement and a long-standing passion for motorcycles when he received a call from an executive recruiter about the WorldCom job. He might have done well to hang up the phone, but Bob is a risk-taker who likes a good challenge. He used to race motorcycles for sport. When his wife finally managed to persuade him to quit, he took up sponsoring racers.

While I recently left the company as a full-time employee, I'm continuing to manage Internal Audit on a contract basis until my replacement is hired. I stayed for over two years, until WorldCom successfully emerged from bankruptcy. I'm proud of the contribution my team has made. They continued to be dedicated in the face of numerous obstacles. Many of the internal auditors have now found good jobs with other companies.

I'm also ready for a fresh start. It's time to get on with my life. Several people have graciously asked if I would be interested in positions with their organizations, but I think I'm ready for a different direction and to be on my own for awhile. I've studied WorldCom and other fraud cases—commonalities, what went wrong, what I would have done differently, and what can be done to prevent and detect frauds more quickly. I want to share the lessons I've learned. My mother is encouraging me to write a book that could be used by parents and teachers. While the business lessons are important, I find myself also thinking about what personal lessons I want to share with my own children. But where in the world does someone who isn't a writer and knows nothing about publishing start with such a project?

The guard unlocks the doors to the executive suite, and we file in. Brown cardboard boxes are everywhere, hundreds of them, stacked from wall to wall, each labeled with the name of a former WorldCom executive whose work products are presumably stored inside. There is barely room to walk. "The Justice Department is requiring us to keep these boxes locked up," the security guard explains. We nod our heads in acknowledgment. It feels as if we're somehow trespassing on private property. I read the names of people I used to work with as we slowly walk through, as if strolling through an old graveyard, reading the dates of life and death on the headstones. I think of lost retirements, ended relationships and camaraderie with peers, and years of dedication and hard work for thousands of employees. What had once been an inspiring experience has vanished into the ether.

"Can we look at Bernie's office?" Bob asks.

"Sure," the guard says, weaving in and out of the maze of boxes. Bernie's office is completely empty, not even a hook on the wall, as if the Grinch has been through. The huge mahogany desk, meeting table, chairs, pictures, and bronze statues that once adorned the room are all gone.

"This is a great office," Bob says, his voice echoing off the barren walls.

Bob appreciates the adobe fireplace, the pine-plank floors, the lake view just outside. He can't know the sadness we're feeling as we enter the room. He doesn't have the history, has never met Bernie. He has no memories of sitting here talking with members of WorldCom's management team during happier times. We do, and the sense of loss runs deep.

Except for 19 auditors and a few stragglers from other departments, the entire floor where my department works is empty. In an attempt to camouflage the devastating impact on employee morale in the Clinton location, just before Bob's visit, several Internal Audit Directors hung large company banners with new corporate objectives in front of the cubicles on our floor. "I just hope he doesn't look behind the signs and see that there is nothing but empty cubicles," Jon Mabry said.

Bernie's criminal trial is scheduled to begin in just a few months. I'll likely be subpoenaed to testify, and here I stand in his old office for the first time since he left over two and a half years ago. Being here brings back a rush of the sadness I felt so acutely in the months after the fraud was announced.

Walking to the window, I stare down at the lake. I see the walking trail where Bernie once complained employees spent too much time. He must have gazed out of the same window hundreds of times. I've tried to imagine what it would be like to reach the apex of success and then awaken in a dark valley—freedom hanging in the balance; wealth replaced by hundreds of millions in debt; respect, prestige, and power gone; the object of much disdain and anger. I cannot.

Preparing to Testify

Many are anxiously awaiting Bernie's trial. The question on everybody's mind is: Did Bernie know about the fraud? The public hasn't yet heard from Bernie or Scott. What will Scott say on the stand? Will Bernie testify? Does the Justice Department have direct evidence tying Bernie to the fraud? At this point, I don't know whether Bernie did or did not know about the fraud, and I want to keep an open mind. While nothing in Internal Audit's testing pointed to Bernie, my team and I are eager to learn through the trial whether or not Bernie was aware of or involved in the fraud.

I had expected to be called by the prosecution in Scott Sullivan's criminal trial. But in March, 2004, just over a month before Scott's trial was scheduled to begin, he pled guilty and agreed to cooperate with the government in its case against Bernie. Immediately after the plea, Attorney General John Ashcroft announced that Bernie had been charged with three counts related to the WorldCom fraud. The indictment was later amended to include nine counts: one count of conspiracy, one count of securities fraud, and seven counts of filing false statements with the SEC— one for each quarter's financial statements during the time the government alleges fraud.

For a while, it looked like the prosecution would call me to testify at Bernie's trial, but the dynamics have changed. "It doesn't look like the prosecution is going to subpoena you for Bernie's trial, but the defense is," Bob, my attorney, explains. The defense is hoping to demonstrate that Internal Audit's investigation didn't turn up evidence that Bernie knew about the fraud.

"There's no way you're getting out of this one. There are very few people the defense can even call to the stand. The government has tied up three people who the defense wanted to call."

"What do you mean 'tied up?'" I ask.

"The defense has asked the government to grant immunity to several former employees who have been named unindicted coconspirators, but the government won't do it. If the defense calls them, they'll be forced to take the Fifth because they could have some exposure to government prosecution."

It's January 25, 2005. Bernie's trial begins today. Witnesses for the prosecution are streaming into Manhattan to take the stand. All five people who have pled guilty—Scott, David, Buddy, Betty, and Troy— have agreed to cooperate with the prosecution against Bernie in hopes of a reduced sentence. All but Buddy will be called to the stand.

Dan Reingold, the Wall Street analyst who was always tentative on WorldCom, sits in on the trial. He will write that he saw Bernie in the restroom.

"How are you holding up, Bernie?" Dan will later recall asking.

"Fine, Dan," Bernie replies, according to Dan. "Dan, I know one thing. I just have to stand in front of my God, whenever that comes. I know I didn't do anything wrong."

"Bernie, based on what I've heard in the opening arguments, I don't see evidence that you knew what Scott was doing."

"Dan, perhaps I should have known, but I didn't. It's just a shame, a damn shame. This whole thing is so sad."

Because the Federal Sentencing Guidelines recommend sentences that are computed on a point-based system, with the most significant portion computed on often rough calculations of what investors lost, the Judge could impose extremely long prison sentences. If they had not pled guilty and agreed to cooperate with the government, Scott Sullivan could have been facing as many as 25 years behind bars; David Myers, 20 years; Troy Normand and Betty Vinson, each 15 years. Mark Abide, the mid-level manager who made some of the entries, signed a non-prosecution agreement to cooperate with the government and tell the truth. If he does not, he could be prosecuted. Each of these employees will be called to the stand to testify. After Bernie's trial, the government will write a letter to the judge explaining each witness's level of cooperation and requesting a reduction of the sentence. But it is the judge who will make the final decisions on sentencing, and there are no guarantees.

Judge Barbara Jones presides over the trial. She is a former assistant U. S. Attorney for the Southern District of New York—she prosecuted members of the Mafia in the 1970s and 1980s—and is well-known, among both prosecutors and defense attorneys, for being evenhanded. Occasionally, she breaks the tension of the proceedings with her deadpan sense of humor. Reid Weingarten, Bernie's lawyer, argues during a private meeting that, based on one fund manager's droning testimony, additional investors shouldn't be allowed to testify. Reid quips that "every minute of [his] testimony I wanted to hang myself." Judge Jones parries: "That's a fascinating argument, Mr. Weingarten."

As the date for my testimony approaches, I mentally prepare myself by envisioning the jury, the judge, the attorneys, the press, and Bernie. I've never even stepped into a courtroom and have no idea what to expect. The whole notion is unnerving. But that's selfish. I owe it to the jury to be prepared, show up in a professional manner, and answer the questions. I try to picture myself standing with my right hand raised. I try to tune out extraneous noise about the trial, whether from the media or people making comments.

Arriving in Washington to prepare for the trial, I stay at a hotel just across the street from Bob Muse's office. Bob, Bill Corboy, and Ron Kovner, another colleague, describe the courtroom, what makes a good witness—someone who's credible, consistent, understandable, logical, and whose manner the jury can respect—and drill me with potential questions. Every day, my attorneys obtain a transcript of the day's proceedings, but they don't let me read it so that my testimony won't be impacted by what other witnesses have said.

It's two days before my testimony. I've gotten sick and feel horrible. My attorneys have helped me find a physician in Washington, and I'm taking antibiotics. Sitting in Bob's conference room with trial documents, I begin crying. It still feels as if I'm trapped in someone else's nightmare.

"What's wrong?" Bob asks when he walks in.

"I'm just so tired and stressed. I'm sick and I have to testify in two days."

"I want you to fly home today and see your family before you go to New York," Bob says.

"I can't. I have to keep preparing. I don't feel ready yet," I say, gesturing to the work-strewn table in front of me.

"You're ready. Trust me. I know what I'm talking about. You need to go home and see your husband and children even if it's just for a day. I absolutely insist that you do it."

Bob books a flight home, and I head for the airport.

The Bridge Builder

As I board my connecting flight in Atlanta, a distinguished African-American gentleman sits next to me. I feel like I've seen him before but can't place him. He seems to know half the people who board the plane, greeting them by name and with a warm smile as they pass. How does he know so many people? And what does he do? He must be a pastor, I guess from his warm demeanor.

"Are you a minister?" I ask after we start chatting.

"A minister of sorts," he says, smiling. "I'm a bridge builder."

"A bridge builder?"

"I work for a non-profit organization called Mission Mississippi," he says, explaining that he works through Mississippi churches to promote reconciliation and unity between blacks and whites. "I'm Dolphus Weary," he says, shaking my hand.

I instantly recognize his name. I've heard a great deal about the positive influence he's making. For the next hour, I forget about my troubles and become engrossed in Dolphus's story. It's a welcome escape. I ask him why the churches are still so segregated, how he feels about the progress Mississippi has made toward unity and healing, what still needs to be done, and what we can do to change the unfairly negative image many in other parts of the country seem to still have of Mississippi.

Traveling throughout the country has made me realize that many people have views of Mississippi that are outdated. As a child and young adult, the Mississippi-born actor Morgan Freeman will write that he "wanted to leave Mississippi and never return." But when he left, he will write in *Proud to Call Mississippi Home,* he was confronted with a more "deceptive" form of racism—more concealed, but just as virulent. "Mississippi is in fact no more or no less racist than the rest of the country," he came to realize. After more than 25 years away, he moved back to Mississippi, making a home in Clarksdale. "It is a source of pride for me to reclaim my state," he will write. "I had left for greener pastures, found them, and mined them. In time I discovered that my parents owned the greenest pasture right here in our ancestral home, the Mississippi

Delta. . . . one of the smartest moves I have made in life is to come back home. Mississippi is the first place I felt truly embraced as a professional and as a friend."

Dolphus was raised in a small Mississippi town where he and his seven siblings lived in a three-room shotgun house with his mother. He writes in his autobiography that as a young child, he spent much of his time picking cotton during the harvest season. The family struggled to make enough to survive. They had no running water, no plumbing, and no closets. Clothes had to be hung on nails jammed into the wall.

Like Morgan Freeman, Dolphus left Mississippi in the 1960s, dreaming of a better life. "Lord, I am leaving Mississippi, and I ain't never coming back," he said to himself as he left to attend a predominately white college, where he received a basketball scholarship, in California. But then, Dolphus, like many African-Americans, decided to come back to the South. Listening to Dolphus and seeing how he has chosen to live his life has lessons that go beyond issues of race. His strong sense of purpose reminds me of what matters. He was faced with a choice. He could have remained bitter and angry about injustices, or he could forgive, focus on the positive, and work to make a difference.

"You go home and get some rest and you'll do fine with the testimony," Dolphus tells me. "I'm going to be praying for you." What a blessing it is to have met such a special person. Never was there a time when I more needed someone like him to sit next to me. Suddenly, I feel restored and more hopeful. Here is a man who overcame extreme hardship and strives to make a better place for the next generation.

Raise Your Right Hand

My attorney was right. I needed to have some time with Lance and my daughters, even if only for a day. Lance offers to go with me to New York, but I just feel like this is something I have to do by myself. Sitting in the back of a cab as I head to the hotel in New York, I rub my fingers across the inscription on the pewter bracelet my father gave me over two years ago: "What lies behind you and before you is a tiny matter, compared to what lies within you. Ralph Waldo Emerson." I've worn the bracelet often throughout these last years. It is in the small things that I have found strength.

On the morning of my testimony, I'm tense, but feel ready. My attorneys and I take a cab to the United States Courthouse for the Southern District of New York at Foley Square in lower Manhattan. It's hovering in the mid-20s, unfortunate considering that the cab has to drop us off a long way from the courthouse, and I forgot my coat and gloves.

"Just like a Southerner to show up in New York without a coat," Bob teases.

When we walk in, I'm awed by the elaborateness of the courthouse. "During the Great Depression, the U. S. Government subsidized artists and builders who built these ornate and elaborate palaces of justice across the country," Bob says. The architecture is clearly intended to leave one with respect for the justice system. The walls and floors are made of gray and white marble, the ceilings are high, and the expansive hallways ring with a hollow echo when you speak.

Bob and I sit just outside the courtroom on long wooden pews like the ones I sat in at church as a child. Hours pass as we wait for the prosecution to wrap up and for me to be called. Finally, people begin to pour out of the courtroom for a lunch break. We walk to a small deli nearby. As we eat, we watch as an array of diverse people come and go with their sandwiches. New York is an amazing place to people-watch.

After lunch, we make our way back to the courthouse. I'm starting to wear down, tired from the stress of waiting. I walk down to the restroom just outside the courtroom. Bang, bang, bang! It sounds like someone's trying to break down the door. I open it to see Bob.

"Come on, hurry up, they're looking for you," he calls. The Judge has sent out a search team—apparently, I was supposed to be in a witness holding room on the other side of the building.

There's one problem. Neither of us knows how to get around to the front, near the judge, where witnesses enter. Bob opens the courtroom door and we look in. It suddenly feels as if the entire room turns at once, staring at us. I can see Bernie looking toward me from the defense table.

Bob shuts the door, and someone quickly comes out to escort us to the other side.

I take a deep breath, walk in, and step up to the witness stand. I can see Bernie out of the corner of my eye, sitting next to his attorneys. It's been over two and a half years since I've seen him. I can see him watching me but I don't look his way during my two days of testimony. I want to maintain my focus on testifying.

I expect the courtroom to be packed, standing-room only, but there are many empty seats. One of the wonderful things about our justice system is that every courtroom is open, and any citizen can observe a trial. "There are retired people who go from case to case, watching trials," Bob has told me. "Sometimes, they know more about the case than the attorneys."

After being sworn in, I take my seat. My mouth feels dry, just as it did in my first interview with prosecutors and FBI agents. Brian Heberlig, one of the defense attorneys, begins asking questions. The first round concerns my background. The intent is to make the witness comfortable and ease into substantive discussions. More general questions about my role at WorldCom follow.

I look at the attorney as he asks questions, but when I answer, I look at the jurors. They're the ones who have to analyze the facts and make the final judgment. The pool of 12 jurors and 4 alternates includes 10 women and 6 men. They are—teachers, transit workers, bank employees, a nurse, an administrative assistant, a housewife—average American citizens who must sort through weeks of testimony.

At the last minute, the government decided not to call an Audit Committee member who was on its witness list. Now, the defense is left with no way to enter Arthur Andersen's presentations—submitted to the Audit Committee and forwarded to Bernie Ebbers—as evidence, except through my testimony. Since I attended the Audit Committee meetings, the Judge decides to allow it. The defense hopes to show that Bernie, like the Audit Committee, relied on Arthur Andersen's representations. Bernie's attorney hands me report after report showing that Arthur Andersen found no irregularities in WorldCom's financial statements and represented that internal controls supporting line costs and capital expenditures were operating effectively.

The judge dismisses us for a break. In the hallway, I see Bob talking with someone.

"Cynthia, I'd like to introduce you to Susan Pulliam," the *Wall Street Journal* reporter who wrote about WorldCom. She is sitting in on parts of the trial. I've wanted to meet her since I first learned that she spoke with my mother several years ago. Over the past few years, Susan and her colleagues have written a number of WorldCom articles that not only break down the mechanics of the fraud but illuminate the human aspects of the story. As I travel the country speaking to students, many professors tell me they use these articles in the classroom as teaching tools.

After only a few minutes, I'm motioned back to the witness room. It's time for another round of questions. At the end of the first day, the judge instructs me not to discuss the case with anyone, even my attorneys. We head off to Little Italy for dinner. As we walk up and down a street lined with restaurants, employees coax customers to choose their establishment. The competition seems fierce. Some restaurants are packed, some almost empty. Better to stick with a packed one, we think. The restaurant is small and loud, with elbow-to-elbow tables. A man walks around the room singing old Johnny Mathis songs as a tip basket circulates.

Bob tries to make conversation, but I'm preoccupied. The anticipation of going back to court preys on my mind. After apologizing for not being very good company, I sit quietly wishing tomorrow wouldn't come and replaying the day's testimony in my mind over the sounds of Johnny Mathis.

A Sense of Peace

It's Day 2. As we enter the courthouse, Reid Weingarten, Bernie's attorney, rushes by, clearly preoccupied as he looks for a folder. Bob escorts me past the milling crowd to the "witness room" where I will sit until the judge calls. Bob quickly shuts the door and leaves. The room is stark. It has no pictures, just a dark wood table with a few chairs, a window, and a coat rack. There's nothing to do here but wait and stare at the walls.

I feel my heartbeat quicken and try to breathe slowly to relax. I walk around the room. I hear jurors coming down the hall talking and laughing as they enter the holding room next to mine. I sit in one of the chairs. I pray.

After a long time and still no word, I open the door and glance down the hall. The marshal is standing just outside my door. "We're still waiting for a few jurors," he says, and instructs me to stay in the room. I pace back and forth and then make my way to the window. Looking out, I see paper cut in the shape of a cross and taped to the inside of two windows in an adjacent building. Below is an elevated patio that holds a small statue of a woman. It must be a church, I think. I feel a sudden sense of peace and wonder if the crosses were hung intentionally to comfort those who find themselves in these cold, barren rooms, waiting to testify. How many people have looked out this window with fear and anxiety?

People I know, as it turns out. As I will later read, David Myers stood in what may have been the same witness room and found solace as he looked out the window at a cross. The building is, in fact, a church—the Church of Saint Andrew.

The marshal finally knocks on the door. It's time.

As testimony progresses, the questions become more focused on how Scott Sullivan conducted himself and what Bernie may or may not have known.

I can feel the jurors perk up as I describe what Scott was like as a colleague. But at other times, I notice that several jurors have closed their eyes. In fact, two keep their eyes closed for much of my testimony. I testify about my interactions with Scott and how he moved from cordial to hostile over time. Bernie's attorney asks questions to show that Scott tried to mislead Internal Audit, that no one we interviewed indicated Bernie was involved with the entries, and that Bernie's name was nowhere on the audit trail. He also asks questions that draw out the fact that Scott, not Bernie, was hostile toward me during the Wireless internal audit.

The government's cross-examination is brief. While there was nothing in our internal audit work that pointed to Bernie knowing about the fraud, the Assistant United States Attorney asks questions pointing to the fact that Internal Audit's focus was on operational auditing. Rounding up accomplices was not part of our investigation, and while no one we spoke with implicated Bernie, we didn't specifically ask the co-conspirators whether Bernie was aware of or involved in the fraud.

"You're dismissed," the judge says. I rise and exit out the back, making my way around to the front of the courtroom, where Bob is waiting for me. "I'm surprised the government didn't cross-examine you much," he says, "but then again, there was nowhere for them to go."

Bob goes back into the courtroom to hear Bert Roberts, the former Chairman of the Board, testify. As I sit waiting just outside on the wooden benches, a woman with long hair approaches. "I thought you might want to see this," she says, holding up a painting of me on the witness stand. The judge is to my right, one of Bernie's attorneys is leaning forward as if in the middle of a question, and Bernie is in the lower left-hand corner.

"Wow. When did you do this?"

"My mother and I were both working on it today while you testified." They are the court artists.

"Really? I never saw you."

"We were right in front of you," she replies with a smile. "Look, I even painted your earrings. If you give me your e-mail address, I will send you a copy." Just before walking off, she adds, "Today, during your testimony, is the first time through the entire trial that I have seen a sparkle in Bernie's eye." I guess a sparkle in the eye is something an artist would pick up on. I can see why Bernie may have felt a bit of hope. My testimony was probably more favorable to him than anything he'd heard for weeks from witnesses called by the prosecution.

Bob comes out and says Bert Roberts' testimony contradicts Scott's claims. After the fraud was exposed, Bert says he asked Scott if Bernie had known about the irregularities. "Scott's answer to me was, 'Bernie did not know of the journal entries,'" Bert says. But during cross-examination prosecutors ask questions that imply Bernie could still have known of the fraud without knowing about the "journal entries."

Within half an hour, people stream out of the courtroom for the morning break. "Cynthia, Bernie will be coming back from his break soon," Bob whispers in my ear. "Do what you want to, but people are running from him, and his life is spiraling out of control. You may want to go over and talk to him."

What should I do? I could look the other way. No, why would I do that? I will look back with regret if I don't speak. I don't know whether Bernie did or didn't know about the fraud, but I don't take any pleasure in another's pain. Since we identified the fraud, I have found myself turning to my faith to sort through issues of justice, mercy, forgiveness, and compassion.

I turn to see Bernie returning from his break. He's still as tall as I remember, but his commanding presence has faded. Now his face shows sadness and fatigue. I make my way toward him.

Bernie sees me and walks to meet me. He gives me a brief hug and a smile.

"Hey, Cynthia."

"How are you, Bernie?"

"Okay," he answers, "So what are you up to these days?"

"I've left the company. I have my own business now," I reply, pausing in search of something to say. "I spend a lot of time talking with students."

"That's great," he says. With nothing else to say, we stand for several seconds in awkward silence. I feel a profound sense of sadness at the moment.

"Well, it's good to see you," Bernie finally says.

I never said goodbye to Bernie when he left WorldCom because he simply vanished one day. I want to tell Bernie that I'll be praying for him, but he's already turning back toward the courtroom, his eyes moist. It's the last time I will see Bernie Ebbers.

"Bernie shouldn't take the stand," Bob says as we leave the courthouse. "But it's always a tough call."

"Why shouldn't he testify?" I ask as we walk.

"It's often a mistake for a defendant to testify. The jury can end up focusing on how the defendant comes across, as opposed to whether the prosecution has proven its case beyond a reasonable doubt. None of Internal Audit's work implicated Bernie. Overall, your testimony was favorable for Bernie. Bert Roberts testified that Scott personally told him Bernie didn't know about this. That should be the end of testimony."

"Knowing Bernie, he'll take the stand," I say. And he does. For a man who has taken risks all his life, it will likely be his biggest gamble yet. Will the jury believe him? Or will they, as my attorney suggested, begin to focus more on his personality and demeanor?

CHAPTER 28

United States of America Versus Bernard J. Ebbers

> I just want you to know you aren't going to church with a crook. . . . No one will find me to have knowingly committed fraud.
>
> —Bernie Ebbers speaking to his church congregation just after the fraud was reported

The Government's Case

Bernie is about to take the stand. The government has already presented their case. The prosecution contends that Bernie knew of and directed the WorldCom fraud beginning in the third quarter of 2000, when the telecom bubble burst, and continuing through the first quarter 2002. In addition to fraudulently reducing expenses, the government holds that Bernie and some of his top lieutenants had a process called "close the gap," whereby they would compare quarterly revenue to Wall Street expectations, analyze potential items they could record to make up the difference, and book revenue items that had not been booked in the past. The government alleges that this additional revenue should have been separately disclosed to investors as being outside the normal business process. The defense argues that Bernie knew nothing of the fraudulent expense

338

reductions, and that while he was involved each quarter with discussing potential items that could be booked as revenue, it was a legitimate process, and none of the revenue booked was fraudulent.

Scott Sullivan, the former CFO, has spent some 400 hours helping the prosecution build their case and testified on the stand for eight days. Some believe the government's case is thin because it is built on circumstantial evidence and depends heavily on Scott's testimony. Bernie was known not to use e-mail and there is no "smoking gun" that directly ties him to the fraud. Scott testified that he "falsified the financial statements of the company to meet analysts' expectations," and that for each of the seven quarters—from the third quarter 2000 through the first quarter 2002—he told Bernie about the fraudulent adjustments.

Even though Bernie wasn't an accountant, Scott indicated "Bernie had a grasp of financial information that surpassed the level of chief operating officers and even some chief financial officers at companies we were acquiring." Scott described Bernie's management style as "micromanaging" and "very hands-on" and testified that Bernie could be "very intimidating." Scott said his interaction with Bernie was "very good" until 2000 when WorldCom's results began to suffer. "It was very tough. There was a lot of stress," he said. He added that Bernie "would make comments to [him] in the presence of other people. 'We'll just get a new CFO, that's what we'll do.' . . . He said it in a kidding way, but I didn't take it as a joke."

Scott testified that when he tried to get Bernie to warn Wall Street that WorldCom wouldn't hit third-quarter 2000 earnings expectations, Bernie said, "Scott, we can't issue an earnings warning to the marketplace until we tell them what we are going to do about it. We can take down guidance for the fourth quarter, but . . . we have to hit our numbers." After having his accountants make fraudulent adjustments, Scott said he told Bernie, "we made adjustments that had nothing to do with the business," that it "wasn't right," and that Bernie "looked at the information. He looked up after a period of time and he [said], 'We have to hit our numbers this quarter.'" Scott testified that quarter after quarter, Bernie continued to tell him that "we have to hit the numbers."

"You took his words [we have to hit the numbers] as a command to go out and commit accounting fraud?" Reid asked.

"Yes, I took that as an order to make adjustments and hit the earnings per share number, yes. He said we had to hit the numbers."

"[Y]ou were a member of the board. . . . You have been awarded . . . CFO of the year by *CFO* Magazine. . . . And you cashed in some $30 million worth of stock. . . . And you felt you had no choice but to interpret Mr. Ebbers's words, we have to hit the numbers, as [a command] to go out and commit accounting fraud. Is that your testimony?" Reid asked.

"Yes, that is my testimony."

After third-quarter 2000 earnings were announced, WorldCom did in fact reduce earnings guidance, but Scott said it should have been even lower. Scott testified that Bernie didn't want to go below 15% revenue growth because of his belief that Wall Street would no longer value WorldCom as a growth company. Scott also testified he told Bernie that two staff level accountants were talking about quitting over the entries, and that Bernie responded, "We shouldn't be making adjustments. We've got to get the operations of this company going. We shouldn't be putting people in this position."

The prosecution is also relying on WorldCom controller David Myers' claim that Bernie apologized to him "that you were asked to do what you were asked to do" when they ran into each other just outside the executive suite after the third quarter in 2000, when the first falsifications had been made. Bernie "gave me his word that we would never have to do that again," David says. Bernie went on, according to David: "Scott and I have had a conversation. He told me about the fact that you were having some problems with your staff, and that is something you [and they] should not have been put in the position to do. . . ." David says he never again discussed the adjustments with Bernie, but that he went to Troy and Betty afterward and told them of Bernie's apology. But Bernie's attorney will counter that the apology from Bernie simply never took place and that David made it up because he was potentially facing 20 years in prison and was simply telling the prosecution what they wanted to hear. Reid will also point out that neither Betty nor Troy said on the stand that David told them about this conversation with Bernie.

Scott testified that when he again inquired about reducing earnings guidance after the fourth quarter 2000 showed no improvement, Bernie told him, "We can't lower our guidance. We're sticking with our revenue and expense guidance this quarter, and we have to make our numbers. Get to work on it."

According to Scott, during a March, 2001 dinner at a Morton's steakhouse in Washington, he again told Bernie that expenses were increasing faster than revenues, and WorldCom was not on target to meet guidance given to Wall Street. "I told [Bernie] that we are going to have to do something drastic if we are going to stay with our guidance for the quarter," Scott said. After suggesting capitalizing expenses, he said he told Bernie "[t]hat it wasn't right, that it was a shortcut to earnings and that we would do it this one time" because he expected revenue to grow next quarter. According to Scott, Bernie simply commented on the need to "get our revenue going" and "cut our expenses."

Scott said he showed Bernie two separate versions of the first quarter 2001 income statement, with and without the adjustments. "I told Bernie that we had made an adjustment . . . [and that] it was the only way I knew of to get our earnings number for the first quarter." He recalled Bernie saying, "We have to grow our revenue and we have to cut our expenses, but we have to hit our numbers this quarter." Bernie "asked me how were we doing it and what effect did it have, where was the adjustment going? . . . I told him . . . we were going to treat it as a capital asset of the company."

Scott said that in August, 2001, when Verizon's CEO was talking to Bernie about buying WorldCom, he told Bernie he was concerned Verizon could find the bad accounting if they looked at WorldCom's records. According to Scott, Bernie said: "You're right. . . . [T]his probably isn't a good time to be talking to Verizon anyhow because our stock price isn't where it should be. . . . " Ivan Seidenberg, the CEO of Verizon Communications Inc., testified that discussions fizzled because of disagreement over a purchase price.

Bernie's loans and margin calls were laid out as the pressure that drove him to commit fraud. Prosecutors argued that Bernie worried if World-Com didn't meet earnings forecasts, his personal investments could be decimated. Scott told the jury that as WorldCom's stock price dropped at the end of 2000 and into 2001, Bernie regularly demanded that he tell him why it was declining. "He was angry more often," Scott said. "He was frustrated. He was in a bad mood. He was distracted by the stock price. . . . The change that I saw is in the 1990s, Bernie Ebbers drove the stock market. In . . . the later half of 2000, the stock market was driving Bernie Ebbers."

On cross-examination, Bernie's attorney, Reid Weingarten, questioned Scott.

"Was there ever an occasion where you said, numbers be damned, I'm just not booking it?" Reid asked.

"No, because I went along with hitting the earnings per share number," Scott replied.

"And hitting the earnings per share number was more important to you than your obligations to follow the law?" Reid asked.

"I knew it was wrong and I knew it was against the law, but I thought we were going to get through it in a short period of time. And that didn't make it right . . . I had no excuse for what I did."

Reid showed e-mails with Scott and David using aggressive language with employees to show they weren't people who would have been easily intimidated by Bernie. In one e-mail, David demands that an accounting employee immediately book an entry. Reid argued that Scott and David were being dishonest because they were facing long prison sentences if they didn't cooperate. When asked about the number of years he was facing in prison when he agreed to cooperate with the prosecution, Scott replied, "It was a very, very bad situation."

Reid worked to impeach Scott's testimony by showing how he deceived others. Scott admitted that he lied to auditors, the Audit Committee, in-house legal, his co-workers, WorldCom's board, and even to the U. S. Government. (In the 1990s and as late as 2001, Scott testified that he used cocaine on occasion though he was dishonest about it on a government security clearance application he once completed while working at WorldCom.)

"So, if you believe something is in your interest, you are willing and able to lie to accomplish that . . . ?" Reid asked after Scott admitted misleading WorldCom's Board of Directors when they finally confronted him about the fraudulent entries.

"On that date, yes, I was lying," Scott says.

"And you looked those 12 people right in the eye and you lied your head off?" Reid asks, seemingly making a correlation to the twelve members of the jury. "Mr. Weingarten," Judge Jones admonishes.

Reid also highlighted the fact that no one can confirm any of the times Scott said he told Bernie of the fraud. "In any of these conversations . . . was anyone else present?" Reid asked. Scott responds that the conversations were only between Bernie and himself.

Scott and David testified that they were successful in keeping the fraud hidden from external audit, the board, internal audit, analysts and investors until internal audit discovered it in June, 2002. Scott testified that he lied to my team and me and instructed his staff to do the same. David also said he limited my department's accounting system access, told others to withhold information from us at Scott's instruction, and sent e-mails to stall and mislead us. David testified that he was dishonest when he told internal auditors in a prior operational review of capital expenditures that portions of the capital additions represented corporate accruals—a common accounting concept. In fact, some of the amounts were related to the fraudulent adjustments.

Scott went on about his actions. "Do not give her [Cynthia] the total picture. . . ." Scott e-mailed one of his direct reports related to company revenue reports. "I don't know that I berated [Cynthia] . . . ," Scott said regarding his reaction to me during the Wireless audit, but "there were times where I was not nice to her, yes."

"So is it fair to say the sum of your interview with Cynthia Cooper was you were lying to her and you just wanted the interview to be over?" Reid asked referring to the meeting where I questioned Scott about prepaid capacity.

"That's pretty much it," Scott answered.

After eight days of testimony, Scott is dismissed. "Mr. Sullivan was a compelling and calm witness who spoke in great detail and appeared to show remorse for his crimes," wrote the *New York Times*. But will the jury view him as a credible witness?

Other than Scott's testimony and David's account of an apology in the hall, no other witnesses testified that they spoke to Bernie about the fraud. The mid-level accounting managers, Betty Vinson and Troy Normand, who participated in the fraud testified they never spoke with Bernie about the entries. Betty testified that when she and Troy were thinking about resigning and met with Scott, he said "Bernie knew that there was a problem with some accountants not wanting to make entries but that [Bernie] didn't want to lower [earnings] expectations . . . so that we needed to make the entry. . . . he asked us to kind of go along with everything, that this would be a one-time entry, we would get over the hump, things would be better. He told us not to jump out of the plane. . . . Just hang in there and help him get through the situation." But Troy only corroborated that Scott told them Bernie didn't want to lower earnings guidance.

Betty said she was afraid that if she didn't make the entries, Scott or David would fire her. She said David told her to "use any accounts that would make the current quarter's expense look like the prior quarter's expenses." She said David assured her that neither KPMG nor Andersen would find the entries, and that she booked amounts to accounts she believed would be less detectable by the external auditors.

Bernie Takes the Stand

When Bernie takes the stand in his own defense, he insists that he didn't know about the fraud. He says he learned of it only when Mike Salsbury, WorldCom's general counsel, contacted him in June to tell him about it and that he was "shocked."

"[I] never thought anything like that had gone on . . . ," he says. "I put those people in place. I trusted them. . . . " Reid points out that Bernie isn't well-versed in accounting. "The closest thing I ever had to an accounting course is a preliminary course in economics," Bernie says. To try and show that Bernie is financially astute, the prosecutors counter by asking questions that require Bernie to discuss financial terms he used on analyst calls or in evaluating companies for acquisition.

"I wasn't advised by Scott Sullivan of anything ever being wrong," Bernie says. "He has never told me he made an entry that wasn't right. If he had, we wouldn't be here today." Regarding the conversation David says he had with Bernie after the third quarter in 2000, Bernie says that it simply never took place. "I didn't have anything to apologize for. I don't have any recollection of that conversation. I don't know what I would have been apologizing for."

The defense describes Bernie as the coach who relied on his team. They will say that his primary area of focus in the company was on sales and every day expense items like rent and utilities. Bernie's description of his management style and level of expertise is similar to comments he has made in the press throughout his career. He says he relied heavily on his executive team and hired competent finance employees. "I know what I don't know," he says. "To this day, [I] don't know technology, and [I] don't know finance or accounting. I always thought I was a pretty good coach, and . . . supervising sales . . . and marketing people is really like coaching, and so I focused on the area I thought I could handle."

The prosecution used the fact that Bernie would question small expenditures like coffee. The line of reasoning goes—If he questioned small amounts, how could he not know about large amounts? One witness testified that Bernie got rid of the free coffee for employees because he noticed that there were "more coffee filters than coffee bags," so people must have been stealing; and that he had the security guards covertly fill empty water bottles in the Washington offices with tap water to save money. "The employees didn't know the difference," one employee remembered Bernie saying. "Does it make any sense that the guy who counts coffee bags doesn't notice $732 million?" the prosecutor will later ask the jury.

As I read press accounts of the trial, I go back and forth in my mind. On the one hand, is it possible that Bernie focused on areas of the company he understood, just as he did in the motel business when he counted towels and made sure the tomatoes were sliced thin to cut costs? My former boss Charles will say that Bernie would focus on the price of a shingle on the house he was building while ignoring the overall cost; and that while Bernie would complain about someone who overspent by a few hundred dollars, Charles couldn't get him to review or approve billion dollar budgets. There does seem to have been something impulsive and random about Bernie's focus in the workplace as well as the way he acquired personal assets. Is it possible that Scott was calling the shots by himself when it came to the financial statements? On the other hand, how could the CEO not know about this fraud, especially during a time when his personal fortune was on the line? I'm always left in the same spot, not knowing for certain one way or another.

When Assistant U.S. Attorney David Anders asks Bernie if he is "detail-oriented," he responds, "It depends on what the topic is." When asked about his propensity to focus on immaterial issues like coffee and water, Bernie says cutting coffee saved $4 million. "I don't consider when you're playing with shareholders' money that $4 million is a small number. . . . if you look after the pennies, the dimes will take care of themselves." But, he adds, he didn't come up with many of the cost-cutting ideas mentioned by prosecution witnesses. He asked some of his staff for "unusual cost savings [ideas] that we don't typically look at." The list came back with "things like what time do we turn the lights off in the buildings at night, what time do we turn down the heat or air at night. A big bill was Growing Green, which is they maintain plants, and a lot of companies were starting to go to plastic plants." Bernie says he simply took the recommendations, thought they sounded like good ideas, and approved them.

Bernie says almost all of his family, including siblings and parents, had everything invested in WorldCom stock. He adds that he once owned WorldCom stock worth over $1 billion. He held it until it went down to zero and he was left owing WorldCom $350 million. When asked why he continued to hold his stock when he could have sold at one point and walked away with a billion dollars, Bernie replied: "Through all of my history with WorldCom I had been absolutely committed to try and not sell stock, and . . . Well, [it was a] matter of pride. I was the CEO of the company, the founder of the company. I don't think it would have sent a good signal to the shareholders." Regarding the personal investments he made by borrowing from banks and using the stock as collateral, he said his strategy was to stick with "low-risk" investments like land; and that his goal was to one day form a foundation to help young people. He believed his choice of timberland was sound, "trees grow, and if you have enough acreage, you cut the growth each year, and you pay off your note through the growth. . . . "

In addition to the stock he held, the defense attorneys also bring out the fact that between May 23 and May 31, 2002—after Bernie left the company but before the fraud was identified—he purchased three million additional shares of WorldCom stock for $5.3 million. "I used . . . almost all of the money I had available," to buy WorldCom stock. When asked why, Bernie replies: "I believed that WorldCom was a great company. I believed that they were going through some difficult times. I believed very strongly that they would come out of them in good shape, and I needed to do something to try and help pay off my note [to WorldCom], and so I invested in the best company I knew." Why would someone who knew of a massive fraud keep buying stock? The defense argues that holding and buying more stock is "utterly inconsistent" with someone committing a fraud. But the prosecution will remind jurors: "Bear in mind that when Ebbers bought those shares, WorldCom was trading at an all-time historical low, and . . . those purchases cannot erase the evidence that Ebbers knew about and directed the fraud."

While the prosecution witnesses testified that several monthly budget variance reports that showed line costs fluctuating by hundreds of millions of dollars were forwarded to Bernie's office, Bernie says, "I did not notice that. If I would have noticed it, we would not be here. I just didn't see it." With some of the reports, Bernie says he either never looked at them or may have even thrown them in the trash.

The Summation

William Johnson, the Assistant United States Attorney, delivers a powerful closing argument on behalf of the government. He appeals to the jury's logic and common sense, urges them to ask themselves some basic questions, and gives the jury a list of the "top ten" reasons Bernie is guilty. Scott's testimony is number one on the list. Four other items on the list, such as the failed discussions with Verizon, also hinge on Scott's testimony.

"We all know money can corrupt people," William Johnson says. "Power can corrupt people. Pressure can corrupt people. Any of those things is enough, but all those at once is like the perfect storm of corruption. Money, power, and pressure corrupted and motivated Bernard J. Ebbers to commit fraud on a billion dollar scale. . . . When it all started in October 2000, Ebbers stood at a crossroads. . . . Ebbers faced a choice of admitting the truth about WorldCom's true financial performance or lying to cover it up. But the truth would have caused the price of WorldCom stock to drop; the truth would have wiped him out financially. He chose to commit a crime, to cover up WorldCom's bad business with fraud."

"The question for you is simple: Who put this fraud in motion?" William asks, "Who had the greatest motive to fool WorldCom's investors? Was it Troy Normand? Betty Vinson? David Myers? Scott Sullivan? Or Bernard Ebbers? . . . You have been fed the 'aw shucks, I'm just not that sophisticated' defense. . . . Why on earth would Scott Sullivan do this all on his own without involving his demanding and controlling boss?" He adds that Bernie, not Scott, was the one under extreme financial pressure and therefore, Bernie had the "real motive" to commit the fraud. He reminds the jury that according to Scott, Bernie told him over and over throughout the time of the fraud that "we have to hit the numbers."

"Ebbers ordered his troops into battle, knowing full well that the battle plan was fraud," Johnson says.

Bernie's attorney, Reid Weingarten, says Scott is "the chief cook and bottle washer" as well as the prosecution's 'snitch.'" He reminds jurors that there are no witnesses to the conversations Scott says he had with Bernie. "How could you possibly believe a word [Scott] says?" Reid asks, "He is facing 25 years. He's got one ticket down and that's a departure [from the sentencing guidelines through cooperating with the prosecution]. . . . His life, his whole life turns on what that letter [from the prosecutors in exchange for his cooperation] says. He has every incentive in the world to tell them what they want to hear."

Reid says David just wanted to get a "go-home" letter from the government, and to do so had to exaggerate events. He also reviews e-mails between Scott and David discussing the fraud. "When you see Sullivan and Myers doing their thing, you won't see any cc's to Bernie Ebbers . . . ," he says. "There is no smoking gun. We don't have any. . . . It's just Scott Sullivan's word and I think at this point we know what that's worth."

Regarding Scott's testimony that Bernie didn't want to lower guidance, Reid points out that guidance is simply an estimate and that from November 2000 through April, 2002 WorldCom lowered guidance and or issued earnings warnings five times—"once in 2000, twice in 2001 and twice in 2002."

While the prosecution alleges that Bernie employed an "aw shucks, I'm not sophisticated defense," Reid says otherwise. "We are not now and have never held him out as a moron. . . . But that doesn't make you a sophisticated financial analyst." Reid tells jurors, "Obviously he was the CEO. . . . In that sense, he is responsible" for the fall of WorldCom. But, Reid argues "this is a criminal case" and Bernie "should not be convicted" if he was unaware of the fraud.

I continue to be unsure about whether Bernie did or didn't know about the fraud. Members of my team debate the issue. How could he not have known? But maybe he didn't know. The fact that there is no direct evidence tying Bernie to the fraud makes it difficult. Everyone seems to have an opinion on the matter, but the ones that count in carrying out justice and determining Bernie's future are those of the jury and the judge. They heard the entire testimony, saw all of the evidence submitted in trial, and were able to observe demeanor and assess credibility of the witnesses. What will they decide?

CHAPTER 29

The Judgment

The Verdict

Day after day, the jury deliberates. One week moves into the next as the public, employees, former shareholders, Bernie, and his family wait. Instead of staying in his hotel room, Bernie spends each day in the courtroom, waiting for the verdict. Meanwhile, the jury sends out notes asking for copies of various testimony, and, one day, tiring of the cafeteria options, a request for pizza. On Friday, March 11, after six days of deliberation, the jury asks for a flip chart, markers, WorldCom press releases, and my testimony.

It's Day 8 of jury deliberations. My sister-in-law Rachel calls. "Cynthia, turn on the television. The news says the jury has come back with a verdict." I stare at the television as the commentator reads the verdict for each count. "Guilty," he repeats nine times.

News accounts will note that as the verdict is read, Bernie's step-daughter and wife, Kristie, begin to cry. Bernie goes over to console them. It is a long walk from the courthouse to the street. Bernie holds on to his wife's hand leading her through the crowd of cameras and reporters who have gathered outside the courthouse. The two walk in silence, hail a cab, and disappear in the distance.

After the verdict is given, a number of jurors talk to the press about the difficulty they had reaching a verdict and what finally swayed them. After seven days of deliberation, four of the twelve jurors still weren't

351

persuaded that Bernie was guilty. The tough part, one of those four told the *Wall Street Journal,* was that while it was obvious Scott and his employees colluded in a specific plan, there was no clear connection to Bernie.

On day seven, after hours of debate, one juror moved from not guilty to undecided. Ms. Evans, the forewoman, encouraged the four who were unsure to spend time thinking about their decision. In the deliberation room, one juror prayed. Another looked pensively through the court-house window. Twenty minutes passed with no one speaking. Then, the jurors were each given a piece of paper to once again write down where they stood. This time, each juror voted guilty. When Ms. Evans announced that they had a consensus, there was silence. Then, several jurors broke down in tears.

"He was the man who was in charge. It's just kind of hard to sit there and think he didn't know what was going on," juror number seven, a Manhattan bus driver, told the *Wall Street Journal.* "I truly believe [Bernie] wanted to save his company. We'd probably be very surprised about how many companies do the exact same thing, and then the economy turns around and they are able to correct the changes that they do," says juror number eight, a bank administrator.

A number of jurors said they didn't find Scott Sullivan credible enough to convict Bernie solely on his testimony. "The most difficult thing was to find the evidence that supported the conviction without relying on Scott Sullivan," says juror number ten, a school teacher. Because Scott "had his own agenda," juror number eight says she didn't put much credence in his testimony. "I didn't care for him," she adds, "Everything he said was too laid out for me, too scripted."

In the end, the jurors went back to documents that witnesses testified were forwarded to Bernie's office. One juror says the reports were "very important" in the decision. "At the end, the people who were not leaning toward guilty, they had to step back and take another look at the reports, because they weren't going by testimony, and they weren't believing Scott." Juror number eight says, "the reports that Mr. Ebbers himself said he had received" weighed heavily. Because some jurors were less finan-cially astute, the discussions were extremely time-consuming. Juror number ten says, "It was frustrating to see other people being slow in understanding those financial and corporate terms."

Some jurors believed that Bernie hurt his case by taking the stand. "Before he testified, I could be swayed either way," one juror says. Another says she was impacted by the difference in Bernie's persona on the stand versus the confident, knowledgeable, strong personality in videos played for the jury during the trial. "I think Ebbers pretty much hung himself," says juror number four, "How could he be up that high in a company that he started and then he says I didn't know anything?" Juror number eight concludes, "I find it hard to believe that someone who started a company and built it up like he did would suddenly pull away and let other people run it."

The *Wall Street Journal* reports that the decision ultimately came back to a CEO's accountability. "If I have an accountant doing my taxes, he does it, I sign it," one juror says. "I don't look over it carefully, but if it goes to the IRS and they find a problem, I'm the person that has to pay a penalty—not my accountant. I still have to be accountable."

The Sentencing

More than three years after we identified the fraud, Judge Jones decrees the sentences.

Troy Normand is sentenced to three years' probation. He was "at the very bottom" of the chain of employees who pled guilty, says federal prosecutor David Anders. "I made decisions at WorldCom that today I wish I definitely hadn't made," Troy says. "My head was telling me one thing; but my heart was telling me another."

Betty Vinson is sentenced to five months in prison and five months of house arrest. "Had Ms. Vinson refused to do what she was asked," Judge Jones says, "it's possible this conspiracy might have been nipped in the bud." At her sentencing, Betty says, "I never expected to be here, and I certainly won't do anything like this again."

Buddy Yates is sentenced to one year and one day. A sentence of greater than a year is required to allow Buddy an opportunity to serve a reduced sentence for good behavior. "I failed my family and loved ones, the employees and investors at WorldCom, myself, but most importantly my God," Buddy says. "I chose the easy way out. There are no words to describe my shame and humiliation." The judge calls him "perhaps the least useful" of those who cooperated with the prosecution, though she adds "[h]e did not instigate this scheme. He did not think it up."

One of the most unexpected parts of this journey is how my emotions have been pulled in so many different directions. I live in a small community where many know one another through church and school activities. As my husband, youngest daughter, and I picked up candy and beads thrown from the floats at the high school homecoming parade almost two years after the fraud was announced, I glanced up to suddenly see Buddy Yates, who had already pled guilty. He was driving a trailer carrying the high school football team. Our eyes met for the few seconds it took him to slowly drive by, my thoughts turning to his son, sitting on the float with his friends.

On Sunday in church, I would often see Buddy sitting by himself. As I began to give speeches around the country, someone who once attended and knows Buddy asked me to give him a note she had written to let him know she was thinking of him and his family. I carried it in my Bible, but each time I saw him at church and tried to make my way towards him, my eyes welled up with tears. I'll try again next Sunday, I would tell myself, tucking the note back between the pages of my Bible. But one Sunday, he was no longer sitting there. He was in prison, the note still not given.

The next school year, as announcers call out the members of the high school's sports teams, a fall ritual, my thoughts are on my daughter, who's being introduced as a member of the cross country team, until Buddy's son is introduced as a starting player on the senior football team. As he steps forward, my joy quickly turns to sadness for this young man whose father is not in the stands. I have grieved for the innocent people who lost jobs and life savings, and I have also grieved for the families of the people involved in the fraud.

David Myers is also sentenced to one year and one day. He tells Judge Jones that he deeply regrets his role in the fraud scheme and that it will stay with him for the remainder of his life. "At the time I consider to be the single most critical character-defining moment of my life, I failed." He said, "As I teach my children what is right and what is wrong, I've got to acknowledge that I did something that was not just wrong, but horribly wrong."

"[Myers'] cooperation is a significant reason to greatly reduce his sentence," Judge Jones says. "Myers was more sophisticated than Yates, Vinson, and Normand but he did not say 'no' to Mr. Sullivan or Mr. Ebbers. On the other hand, he did not instigate the scheme." The Judge adds that David's sentence was reduced in part because he received much less compensation through bonuses and stock options than Bernie and Scott.

Scott Sullivan is sentenced to five years in prison. Scott voluntarily relinquished most of his assets—proceeds from the sale of his Boca Raton mansion as well as the remainder of his retirement savings—toward civil-suit settlements. He was a "model cooperator" and "the key factor" in the succesful prosecution of Bernie, the government stated in a 13-page letter to Judge Jones on Scott's behalf. "Without this type of information, Ebbers could not have been charged, let alone convicted, of the conduct in this case."

"My actions are inexcusable," Scott says. "I'm sorry for the hurt that has been caused by my cowardly behavior." He reads his statement, explaining that he's gotten only a few hours' sleep in the past several days and is too distraught to talk without notes.

Judge Jones calls Scott the fraud's "architect." "You are fortunate that this case presented you with an opportunity to cooperate," she tells him. "You would have faced a substantial sentence had you not cooperated." The Judge says Scott was "detailed . . . candid . . . an excellent witness," and that "his value to the prosecution is enormous." In sentencing, Judge Jones gave "great weight" to the fact that his wife Carla is severely ill with diabetes and needs help to take care of their 4-year-old daughter. She has been to the hospital nine times in the past year alone.

Legal scholars discuss the message of Scott's sentence. "When you reward the architect of a fraud with five years, you are sending a strong message: Cooperate or else," Thomas Connolly, a former federal prosecutor, tells the *Wall Street Journal* soon after the trial. "The message is: Don't ever go to trial, because the consequences are so severe. That is a frightening message, because prosecutors are generally honorable, but there are occasions when they overreach."

In determining Bernie's sentence, his attorneys ask Judge Jones to consider Bernie's extensive philanthropy and the fact that he has ongoing health problems related to a heart disorder. In addition, Judge Jones has received 169 letters from people writing on Bernie's behalf, discussing his character, good deeds in the community, and charitable giving.

Judge Jones sentences Bernie to 25 years in prison saying she is giving a slight downward departure from what the sentencing guidelines recommend (30 years to life). For a 63-year-old, it's virtually a life sentence, and one of the harshest penalties ever imposed for a white-collar crime. Though the judge suggests a minimum-security facility in Yazoo City, Miss., close to Bernie's family, the Federal Bureau of Prisons will assign him to a medium-security prison in Oakdale, La., 200 miles from his home, a rarity for a first-time white-collar offender.

As I read of the sentences, I'm struck by the disparity in sentencing between Bernie and the others involved in the fraud. Bernie's defense team files an appeal with the United States Court of Appeals for the Second Circuit. A panel of three judges will study the case. Regarding Bernie's sentence of 25 years, the appeal holds that it is too disparate with the other sentences given in this case, is unreasonably long, and that the investor loss amount, the primary factor used to compute the sentence, wasn't accurate.

"There are many violent criminals who don't get 25 years in prison," Judge Cabranes, one of the appellate judges, says at the oral hearing. "Twenty five years does seem like an awfully long time." The U.S. Assistant Attorney reminds the panel that the fraud "affected literally millions of people." Bernie's attorney says "it shocks the conscience" that while Scott was given five years and David one, Bernie was sentenced to 25. "I understand that prosecutors need to encourage snitches to snitch," says Reid Weingarten, Bernie's attorney, referring to Scott's having received a much lighter sentence in exchange for cooperation, "but [the differences between Bernie's and Scott's sentences] simply cannot be reconciled with fairness, and they create overwhelming incentives for snitches to fabricate evidence against superiors."

Based on the current Sentencing Guidelines, it is easy for public-company financial frauds to lead to longer prison sentences than many violent crimes. In 1984, Congress passed the Sentencing Reform Act to eliminate unjustifiable sentencing disparities for similar crimes, impose minimum sentences, and make sentences more predictable by abolishing parole. Federal inmates must now serve their full sentence with the exception of being eligible for a 15% reduction by earning "good behavior" credits. Based on the Act, federal judges were required to sentence by Sentencing Guidelines and a Table, which dictates sentence ranges based on the number of points attributed to the crime and the individual. After 18 years of mandatory use and just prior to Bernie's trial, the Supreme Court ruled that sentencing by the Guidelines and Table was no longer mandatory. However, many judges still rely on them, and Bernie's sentence was largely based on the guidelines.

Computation of amounts lost by investors due to the fraud is a primary factor contributing to Bernie's sentence. Critics argue that, for public companies, prosecutors are able to put forward rough calculations of investor loss based on drops in stock price times outstanding shares, and assign the full amount to the convicted felon without accounting for factors other than the fraud that could have contributed to stock price declines. The highest investor loss threshold in the Sentencing Table is $100 million, an amount easily met by even small stock price declines. As the appellate court reviewing Bernie's case will note, "a 15 cent decline in share price in a firm with only half the number of outstanding shares that WorldCom had would constitute a loss of $200 million," well above the highest threshold in the Table.

On July 28, 2006, the three-judge panel reviewing Bernie's case upholds the conviction and the sentence commenting that Bernie's life had "an element of tragedy." They conclude that Bernie's sentence is "harsh but not unreasonable." The court holds there are valid reasons for differences between sentences given to Bernie and other co-conspirators. Because Bernie was the CEO and the others were his subordinates, Bernie "had primary responsibility for the fraud." Also, the fact that Bernie didn't cooperate or plead guilty as the others did is "a reasonable explanation of the different sentences."

"Twenty-five years is a long sentence for a white collar crime, longer than the sentences routinely imposed by many states for violent crimes, including murder, or other serious crimes such as serial child molestation," the Court writes. "However, Congress has directed that the Guidelines be a key component of sentence determination. Under the Guidelines, it may well be that all but the most trivial frauds in publicly traded companies may trigger sentences amounting to life imprisonment—Ebbers' 25-year sentence is actually below the Guidelines level."

The Appellate Court acknowledges that there are problems with the way investor losses are computed. For instance, factors other than the fraud could have contributed to the drop in WorldCom's stock price after the fraud was announced. But even if you adjust for such factors, the court says the loss easily exceeds the highest threshold for sentencing under the current Guidelines.

The court discusses implications of investor loss computations attached to long sentences dictated by the Tables. "Even the threat of indictment on wafer-thin evidence of fraud may therefore compel a plea. . . . No matter how many reasons other than the fraud may arguably account for the decline [in stock price], a potential defendant would face an enormous jeopardy, given the present loss table. . . . " Nevertheless, the Court states that "the Guidelines reflect Congress' judgment as to the appropriate national policy for such crimes . . . Given Congress' policy decisions on sentences for fraud, the sentence is harsh but not unreasonable."

In a WorldCom-related civil suit against a number of investment banks, Arthur Andersen, and the Board, the plaintiffs' lawyers set a record, recovering $6.1 billion, almost twice that of the prior record of $3.2 billion recovered in a class action suit related to Cendent Corporation, a company which falsely inflated revenue by $500 million over three years. The investment banks prove to have the deepest pockets, with Citigroup settling for $2.57 billion, J.P. Morgan Chase for $2 billion and Bank of America for $461 million. Many other banks are able to settle for lesser amounts, and Arthur Andersen, on its last leg, settles for $65 million. The twelve board members who served during the time of the fraud will settle for $55 million. Of that amount, the directors will agree to pay $25 million out their own pockets. Amounts to be paid personally are based on approximately one fifth of each director's net worth.

In addition to the civil suits, the Securities and Exchange Commission will eventually obtain a judgment against WorldCom for $750 million, the largest in history against a public company. The judgment will include $500 million in cash and $250 million in stock of the new company once it emerges from bankruptcy.

A New Beginning

After MCI exited bankruptcy, the company was sold to Verizon. Many of my former staff had already left the company, and those who remained elected to accept severance packages. "Who will be the one to turn out the lights?" we joked as our numbers dwindled. For each employee who left, the remaining Audit Directors organized a going-away luncheon. "The last one to leave won't have a very nice luncheon," someone teased. For several months in 2006, Elaine Saxton, an Internal Audit director and the second employee I hired, came to work to a deserted workplace, the last auditor remaining in Clinton. In April, 2006, she closed her office door and "turned out the lights" for the last time, more than ready for a new beginning.

Each of the former WorldCom internal auditors were able to find good jobs. Elaine now works as the Accounting Director for a privately held business. Jon Mabry works as a contractor, helping to provide grants to Hurricane Katrina victims in Mississippi on behalf of Governor Haley Barbour's administration. Ten former WorldCom internal auditors work with Jon. Glyn Smith accepted an Internal Audit Director position with Blockbuster in Texas. Gene Morse and Tonia Buchanan, two auditors who worked on the capital expenditure audit, were able to find finance positions with other employers in the Jackson area. Dean Taggart moved to Birmingham and is Vice President of Internal Controls, in charge of Sarbanes-Oxley compliance at HealthSouth, helping to restore the company after its fraud. Lisa Smith is also at HealthSouth in Birmingham, where she serves as Director of Internal Controls.

Since I left WorldCom, I've spent much of my time sharing the lessons of its spectacular rise and fall, not only with corporations and professional groups, but also with high-school and college students. As I recall those trying times, I think of a small group of auditors who stood together during a company's darkest hours; a priest who held my hands and said "You can be a wounded healer"; a friend who paused amid the chaos and turned my attention to a beautiful sunset, reminding me that tomorrow the sun would set again.

When I think about these past years, I remember a husband's love and understanding, a family's unwavering support, a daughter's notes of encouragement, and a child's comic antics, making my family laugh in spite of it all.

These blessings, held in my heart, tell me clearly I did not walk alone on this journey.

For me, this has been a story of heartbreak, but also of hope and healing, a faith journey of growth and moving forward. I've come to appreciate that while we can't always choose our circumstances, we can choose how to react to them. Amanda Ripley, the *Time* Magazine reporter who interviewed me, once mailed me a quote by pastor and educator Charles Swindoll:

The longer I live, the more I realize the impact of attitude on life . . . Attitude, to me, is more important than facts. It is more important than the past, than education, than money, than circumstances, than failures, than successes, than what other people think or say or do. It is more important than appearance, giftedness or skill. It will make or break a company . . . a church . . . a home. We cannot change our past . . . we cannot change the fact that people will act in a certain way. We cannot change the inevitable. The only thing we can do is play on the one string we have, and that is our attitude . . . I am convinced that life is 10% what happens to me and 90% how I react to it.

We all face the various storms of life sooner or later—death of a loved one, divorce, illness, loss of a job. While none of us would ask for adversity, it can make us stronger, and we can use our experiences to reach out to others who may face similar struggles. It is my prayer that this book will give hope to those who may find themselves in the midst of a dark time or standing at a crossroads, faced with tough choices.

Epilogue

Shaping the Next Generation

Train up a child in the way he should go, and when he is old, he will not depart from it.

Proverbs 22:6

In many ways this story is about human nature, about people and choices. It shows how power and money can change people, and how easy it is to rationalize, give in to fear, and cave under pressure and intimidation. It speaks of the importance of living a life of integrity and making decisions we can look back on without regret. It illuminates the value of developing strong boundaries, keeping our paths straight, and guarding against the temptations and trappings of material success.

Going through these events has made me more aware of the importance of teaching values to my own two daughters, now 18 and 6, and sharing this story with the next generation of leaders. "Good habits formed at youth make all the difference," wrote Aristotle. I want to make sure my children are able to recognize an ethical dilemma and make the right choices. When I share this story with high-school and college students, I encourage them to put themselves in the shoes of others, think about the decisions they may have made, and envision how these events might have impacted their family, friends, and co-workers. What would you do, if like Betty Vinson or Troy Normand, your boss pressured you to do something you didn't believe was right? What if you were a high-level executive, like Scott Sullivan or Bernie Ebbers, used to being at the top of your profession, and your company wasn't going to meet quarterly earnings unless you fudged the numbers—just this once?

Most of the people who participated in the WorldCom fraud were ordinary, middle-class Americans. They had no prior criminal records and never imagined they would be confronted with such life-altering choices. They were mothers and fathers who went to work to support their families, spent their weekends going to their children's activities and to church, and were respected within their communities. *Wall Street Journal* reporter Susan Pulliam once told me that she was drawn to write about the WorldCom fraud because the people involved seemed so ordinary.

Often, I'm asked: "Were these bad people, or basically good people who made bad decisions?" Most people are honorable and want to do the right thing. But sometimes it's tough, even when the line between right and wrong is clear. I believe most of the employees who participated in the fraud were basically good people. But each of us is capable of making bad decisions. "We're all like clay pots that are cracked," Chip Henderson, my pastor says. "Not one of us is a perfect pot with no flaws or cracks." So how do good people lose their way so easily? "Think of a swimmer," Chip tells me. "In the pool, the lines on either side help him swim straight. But a tri-athlete swimming on the open water has no lines. He must pick a landmark and regularly look up at it to check his direction. If he doesn't, he'll easily find himself off-course."

There are many reasons people make poor choices. Betty Vinson and Troy Normand felt pressured and afraid that they would lose their jobs if they didn't go along. They also began to rationalize—if their boss told them to do it, it must be okay, and besides, they were just following orders. I think David Myers, the Controller, felt a sense of loyalty to his boss Scott Sullivan. Scott rationalized that he was trying to save the company. The employees involved initially told themselves the fraudulent entries would be a one-time thing and that there was likely an error that would correct itself. Once down the path, they felt trapped. Top-level executives, used to seeing their company win, felt a sense of pride, and didn't want WorldCom to fail on their watch. Greed may have been a factor for the executives who had their personal fortunes on the line.

I have come to believe that WorldCom outgrew the man most responsible for building it. The entrepreneur who builds a company is often not the best person to lead it as the company matures. But entrepreneurs sometimes have difficulty letting go and drawing a clear line between themselves and the company they've helped build. What does this story teach about leadership? About the influence executives at the top of a company have on the corporate culture? About the line between being an aggressive capitalist and committing fraud? If you overextend your personal investments, like Bernie Ebbers, how will it affect your ability to lead?

Young people may find it hard to imagine that they will ever find themselves in a position such as the employees who took part in the WorldCom fraud. Hopefully they won't. But we all face ethical choices and pressures daily: Give the money back to the cashier who gave too much change or keep it? Cheat on an exam or take it honestly? Fudge an expense report or tax return or file it truthfully? Keep our word or break a promise? The list is endless. "Every time you make a choice," wrote C. S. Lewis, "you are turning the central part of you, the part that chooses, into something a little different than it was before." The foundation of our character is laid brick by brick, decision by decision, in how we choose to live our lives.

We spend a lot of time teaching students math, science, and history, but we must also spend time teaching ethics and leadership. Some argue that you can't teach ethics at the high school or college level because values are primarily instilled at a young age. But character is not static. People can and do change throughout their lives, and by incorporating ethics into the curriculum, we can challenge students to think and help make sure they have the tools to recognize an ethical dilemma, think it through, and make the right decision.

As I talk to my children and students, I share what I've learned from this story and from talking with professors, ministers, and business professionals about what each of us can do to help sort through tough issues and make the right choices.

1. Know what you believe is right and wrong. Write down the values you will live by and what you will do if your values collide. Is your moral compass pointed in the right direction? Are your priorities in the right order? Goethe once wrote, "Things which matter most must never be at the mercy of things which matter least." Our priorities impact the choices we make.

2. When making decisions, apply the Golden Rule: Treat other people the way you would want to be treated. "If you lived each day as though it were your last, what would you do differently?" my pastor recently asked a group, "Would you speak more kindly? Love more deeply? Forgive more freely?" It is easy in the rush of the business world to forget the humanity of our daily encounters. The Golden Rule endures because it is such a central tenet of our existence. It comes as close as any value to being universally accepted, and, though worded differently, is incorporated in each of the world's major religions.

3. Guard against being lulled into thinking you're not capable of making bad decisions. Each of us is imperfect and must protect against giving in to temptation. Keep in mind that what is legal and what is ethical are sometimes different. For example, giving the WorldCom CEO loans to cover personal debt was legal at the time, but was it the right decision?

4. Ask yourself: Would I be comfortable with my decision landing on the front page of a newspaper? Would I be okay with my parents, professors, and mentors knowing about my choice? What are the potential consequences of my actions?

5. Practice ethical decision making every day. "Good and evil both increase at compound interest," wrote C.S. Lewis. "That is why the

little decisions you and I make every day are of such infinite importance." Ask yourself, did the decisions I made today coincide with my values?

6. Discuss tough ethical dilemmas with others you respect—a professor, a parent, a friend. David Myers, the Controller, didn't share the pressure he was under at work with his wife or family. He kept it to himself. Since people often rationalize their decisions, it's important to get opinions from others who are removed from the situation.

7. Find your courage. Most people want to be part of a team. But groupthink can be dangerous, and the team can be like a herd of bison that follow one after another over the cliff's edge. A man once wrote a letter to me and said he and his wife try to teach their children that courage is not without fear. Courage is acting in the face of fear. If we practice finding our courage in smaller matters each day, we'll stand a better chance of keeping the courage of conviction when we come to the crossroads of more critical decisions.

8. Apply the same code of ethics whether at home, work, school, or a house of worship. Compartmentalizing can result in acting different ways in different environments instead of being one unified self.

9. Pay attention to your instincts. If something doesn't feel right, it may not be. Stop, step back, and re-evaluate the situation. Betty and Troy initially felt uncomfortable with what their bosses asked of them, even writing resignation letters, but they didn't act on those initial instincts.

10. Above being loyal to your superiors, be loyal to your principles. Don't assume that what superiors are telling you is right just because they are in positions of authority. Scott Sullivan assured Betty and Troy that they wouldn't get in trouble because they were just doing what they were told.

People are fascinated by the WorldCom story and the characters involved, but if we fail to focus on its lessons, apply them in our lives, and share them with our children and grandchildren, the story is of little value. The many recent corporate scandals are a backdrop for timeless lessons. Next month and next year, the company, cast of characters, and circumstances will be different, but the ethical dilemmas will continue.

In the end, life is about choices. Our challenge is to choose well. "There are really only two important points when it comes to ethics," the author John C. Maxwell writes. "The first is a standard to follow. The second is the will to follow it." We each have an opportunity to make a real difference in our world, whether through mentoring a child, teaching ethics in the classroom, sharing the lessons of our own experiences, or instilling values in our children so the next generation may benefit from what we've learned. Doing this is not merely a responsibility. It is a privilege, a gift of caring and guidance.

Notes

Much of the information in this book is based on interviews, my recollection of events, contemporaneous notes, internal memos, documents released by the New York State Attorney General's office, e-mails, court testimony and WorldCom-related reports. The following proved to be valuable resources: Lynne Jeter's book *Disconnected: Deceit and Betrayal at WorldCom,* provided insight into the early years of LDDS. Dan Reingold's *Confessions of a Wall Street Analyst: A True Story of Inside Information and Corruption in the Stock Market*, and Charles Gasparino's *Blood on the Street: The Sensational Inside Story of How Wall Street Analysts Duped a Generation of Investors* provided fascinating accounts of Wall Street during the bubble years. Om Malik's *Broadbandits: Inside the $750 Billion Telecom Heist* provided valuable information on the rise and fall of the telecom industry. C. Fred Alford's *Whistleblowers: Broken Lives and Organizational Power* documented the experiences of whistleblowers. Thank you also to Susan Pulliam, Deborah Salomon and their colleagues at the *Wall Street Journal;* Amanda Ripley and her colleagues at *Time;* Seth Shiesel of the *New York Times;* Peter Elstrom and Charles Haddad of *Businessweek;* Brooke Masters of the *Washington Post* and each of the writers credited for their insightful coverage of the WorldCom story and bubble years of the late nineties.

Introduction

The quotes from Lynne Jeter, *Disconnected Deceit and Betrayal at WorldCom,* John Wiley and Sons, Copyright © 2003 by Lynne Jeter. Used with permission.

Page vii: WorldCom was the fifth most widely held stock. Charles Haddad, "WorldCom's Sorry Legacy," *Businessweek,* June 28, 2002.

Page viii: Bernie "was an outsider...", "Today, he's considered one of the industry's..." Lynn Haber, "Here's a Look at the 15 Most Important People, Inventions and Events that Shaped Our Networked World," *Network World,* March 26, 2001.

Page viii: Scott is the highest paid CFO in the country. Linda Gorman, "As Good As It Gets," *CFO.com,* November 1, 1998.

Page viii: "[Scott] walked on water." Jayne O'Donnell, "A Couple of Bad Apples Spoiled 'CFO' Award," *USA Today,* May 5, 2004.

Page x: Alford discusses an "invisible line" that whistleblowers step over. Fred Alford, *Whistleblowers: Broken Lives and Organizational Power.* Ithica, NY: Cornell University Press, 2001.

Chapter 1   A Dark Cloud

Pages 3–4: David played basketball in high school and his stock option value of $15 million. Susan Pulliam, "Crossing the Line: At Center of Fraud, WorldCom Official Sees Life Unravel," *Wall Street Journal,* March 24, 2005.

Page 7: Scott invites Betty and Troy to his office. Susan Pulliam, "Over the Line: A Staffer Ordered to Commit Fraud Balked, Then Caved—Pushed by WorldCom Bosses, Accountant Betty Vinson Helped Cook the Books—A Confession at the Marriott," *Wall Street Journal,* June 23, 2003.

Page 8: Betty Vinson is concerned about entering the job market as a middle-aged executive. Ibid.

Page 10: Under increasing strain at work, David feels that he cannot leave WorldCom, becomes depressed and contemplates taking his life. Susan Pulliam, "Crossing the Line" *Wall Street Journal,* op. cit.

Page 10: "You're somewhere else..." Ibid.

Pages 10–11: A description of David's interaction with his wife, David would like to leave and start his own business, David fears that if the fraud is discovered, the path will lead back to him. Ibid.

Chapter 2   Graduation Day

Page 20: "Be kind and compassionate to one another..." *The Holy Bible, New International Version*, Grand Rapids, Michigan, 2002.

Page 20: "Love your neighbor as yourself." Matthew 22:39, Ibid.

Page 20: "Do to others as you would have them do to you." Luke 6:31, Ibid.

Page 20: "Love is patient, love is kind." 1 Corinthians 13:4, Ibid.

Page 20: The Parable of the Good Samaritan, Luke 10:30, Ibid.

Chapter 3   New Beginnings

Page 26: Murray Waldron prays in a Mississippi hotel room. Lynne Jeter, *Disconnected: Deceit and Betrayal at WorldCom.* Hoboken, NJ: John Wiley & Sons, 2003.

Page 26: "My life hadn't been..." Ibid.

Page 27: Murray Waldron's previous occupations are highlighted by "The Wall Street Fix" Frontline, *PBS,* May 22, 2003.

Page 27: Murray and William visit the Hattiesburg Chamber of Commerce. Jeter, Disconnected, op. cit.

Pages 27–28: Murray and William Rector's plan for a new business; and Bill Fields recruits David Singleton who then turns to Bernie Ebbers for investment capital. Kelli Langlois, "LDDS Phones Home," *Daily Leader,* April 27, 1995.

Pages 27–28: "There was not that kind of money around in my world..." Jeter, *Disconnected,* op. cit.

Page 28: "I didn't fully understand..." Ibid.

Page 28: There was no running water in Bernie's home as a young child. Susan Pulliam and Almar Latour, "Lost Connection: Trial of WorldCom's Ebbers Will Focus on Uneasy Partnership," *Wall Street Journal,* January 12, 2005.

Page 28: "We didn't have much..." Thomas J. Neff and James M. Citrin, *Lessons from the Top: The 50 Most Successful Business Leaders in America—and What You Can Learn From Them.* New York: Doubleday: 1999.

Page 29: "Our work ethic came from our father...," Reed Branson, "WorldCom's Ebbers Builds Mississippi Muscle," *Commercial Appeal,* November 9, 1997.

Pages 28–30: Information about Bernie's early life and college years. Court transcripts and Jeter, *Disconnected,* op. cit.

Page 30: "Delivering milk day to day..." John Greenwald, "Bernie's Deal," *Time,* June 24, 2001.

Page 31: "Jackson will no longer be..." Carroll Brinson, Jackson/A Special Kind of Place. Jackson: City of Jackson, 1977.

Page 32: Bernie arrives in Mississippi with little more than a pair of jeans and a few dollars. Jeter, *Disconnected,* op. cit.

Page 32: "Told him, 'Boy, shut that door...'" Branson, *Commercial Appeal,* op. cit.

Page 33: "We didn't have a very good basketball team..." "Bernie did a darn good job..." Jeter, *Disconnected,* op. cit.

Page 33: "He enjoys being in charge..." "He has always had plenty of nerve..." "He got the most out of that..." Branson, *Commercial Appeal,* op. cit.

Page 33: "Bernie was painfully shy..." Jeter, *Disconnected,* op. cit.

Page 33: The only way he'll leave the state is "in a box." Charles Haddad, "WorldCom Laying It on the Line," *Businessweek,* November 2000.

Page 34: Bernie meets fellow Little League coach, Lamar Bullard who offers him a job. Jeter, *Disconnected,* op. cit

Page 35: Bernie considers opening a Slack Shack. David Faber, "The Big Lie: Inside the Rise & Fraud of WorldCom," *CNBC,* September 9, 2003.

Page 35: "like a band of gypsies..." Jeter, *Disconnected,* op. cit.

Page 35: "I remember driving down..." Ibid.

Pages 36: "You owe it to me ..." Ibid.

Page 36–37: Description of BestWestern purchase; Bernie's net worth; early investors purchasing a switch for $450,000; and initial split of LDDS shares. Ibid.

Page 39: LDDS is approximately $1.5 million in debt when Bernie becomes CEO. MCI WorldCom Inc., *International Directory of Company Histories*, Vol. 27. St. James Press, 1999.

Page 39: "My vision was simple ..." Neff and Citrin, op. cit.

Page 40: "It just kept on growing ..." "The Wall Street Fix" Frontline, op. cit.

Chapter 5   The Turnaround

Page 50: "This may sound hokey ..." Will Pinkston, "WorldCom Sits on Hold—For Now," *Clarion-Ledger*, September 10, 1995.

Page 52: "Bernie took a big risk ..." Lynne Jeter, *Disconnected: Deceit and Betrayal at WorldCom*. Hoboken, NJ: John Wiley & Sons, 2003.

Page 53: "You run into a lot of CEO's ..." Ibid.

Chapter 7   Building A New Life

Page 73: "If we'd ever dreamed ..." Will Pinkston, "WorldCom Sits on Hold—For Now," *Clarion-Ledger,* September 10, 1995.

Chapter 8   King of the Resellers

Page 83: A biography of Francesco Galesi is available at (http://www.mshventures.com/galesi.html).

Page 83–84: A synopsis of Scott Sullivan's early career can be found in "Scott Sullivan: Master of the Mega Merger," *Oswego,* Spring/Summer 1999.

Page 85: Jack Grubman's childhood as highlighted by Amy Feldman and Joan Caplin, "What Would It Take to be the Worst Analyst Ever?" *Money,* May 2002.

Page 85: "I am a blue-collar guy ..." Peter Elstrom, "Jack Grubman: The Power Broker," *Businessweek,* May 15, 2000.

Pages 85–86: "We both came from the wrong side ..." Kevin Maney, "Small Town Exec Strikes Big Deal: Down to Earth Style is Secret to His Success," *USA Today,* August 28, 1996.

Page 86: Jack Grubman's college and early career, Charles Gasparino, *Blood on the Street: The Sensational Inside Story of How Wall Street Analysts Duped a Generation of Investors.* New York: Free Press, 2005.

Page 86: "Jack basically said the emperor ..." Anita Raghavan, "For Salomon, Grubman Is Big Telecom Rainmaker," *Wall Street Journal*, March 25, 1997.

Page 86: Wall Street searches for telecom analysts after the AT&T breakup. Dan Reingold and Jennifer Reingold, *Confessions of a Wall Street Analyst: A True Story of Inside Information and Corruption in the Stock Market.* New York: HarperCollins, 2006.

Page 86: After 8 years Jack leaves AT&T for Paine Webber. Gasparino, *Blood on the Street,* op. cit.

Page 87: A biography of John Kluge is available at (http://www.ketupa.net/metromedia.htm#kluge).

Page 88: Jack Grubman and Dan Reingold are opposites in demeanor leading the press to dub them the "Siskel and Ebert of Telecom." Mark Landler, "The Siskel and Ebert of Telecom Investing," *New York Times,* February 4, 1996.

Page 88: Information about Jack's negative report on MCI. Reingold and Reingold, *Confessions of a Wall Street Analyst,* op. cit.

Page 88: "There are precious few..." Landler, *New York Times,* op. cit.

Page 88: Dan recounts analyst interest in LDDS stock, LDDS's stock increase since Jack initiated coverage and Dan's visit to Mississippi. Reingold and Reingold, *Confessions of a Wall Street Analyst,* op. cit.

Page 88: "Singapore Airlines it ain't." Ibid.

Page 88: "indirectly there was the hope..." Ibid.

Page 89: "forlorn," "dingy headquarters," "It looked more like..." "seedy, sorry-looking Holiday Inn," Ibid.

Page 89: "It was probably the best..." Ibid.

Page 89: "He was so different from..." Ibid.

Page 89: "The book was full of those..." Ibid.

Pages 89–90: "For each potential acquisition..." Ibid.

Page 90: "country boy's dream," "The Wall Street Fix" Frontline, *PBS,* May 22, 2003.

Page 90: Description of Dan Reingold's WorldCom stock coverage and relationship with Bernie. Reingold and Reingold, *Confessions of a Wall Street Analyst,* op. cit.

Chapter 9   The Hottest Company in Town

Page 93: "This company can go..." Adam Levy, "Company Spotlight: LDDS Prime for Buyout, After Years of Buying," *Bloomberg*, May 13, 1994.

Page 94: "We don't intend to slow down..." Adam Levy, "LDDS Expects Revenue to Grow 25% in 1994 with Acquisitions," *Bloomberg*, April 12, 1994.

Page 95: LDDS has become "prime for buyout" and an "enticing takeover target." Adam Levy, *Bloomberg*, op. cit.

Page 95: "We never had an offer..." Reuters Information Service, "LDDS CEO Says Company Not "Quarreling" with Q2 EPS Forecast of $0.25," May 26, 1994.

Page 95: "If it will help them call ..." with Bernie adding that he'd like to be fishing in a few years. Levy, *Bloomberg,* op. cit.

Page 96: "WilTel is the only asset..." Caleb Solomon, "LDDS's Offer Means William's Fiber Will Be Tested," *Wall Street Journal,* May 17, 1994.

Page 97: Sudikoff begins his company with a $15,000 car loan, also his personal net wealth. Daniel Taub, "Satellite King Lands In Court—IDB Communications Group Inc.'s CEO Jeffrey Sudikoff," *Los Angeles Business Journal,* February 15, 1999.

Page 97: In 1993 IDB was the fourth largest international long distance carrier and had annual revenues exceeding $300 million. Gautam Naik, "LDDS in Talks to Acquire IDB, A Phone Carrier—Deal May Be All for Stock, Totaling $700 Million," *Wall Street Journal,* July 14, 1994.

Page 97: "record revenue and earnings," also a description of Deloitte's resignation from the engagement. Daniel Taub, "Satellite King Lands In Court—IDB Communications Group Inc.'s CEO Jeffrey Sudikoff," *Los Angeles Business Journal,* February 15, 1999.

Page 97: On June 1, after the controversy, IDB's stock has a record fall. Colleen M. McElroy, "IDB Communications Shares Rise Amid Acquisition Talks," *Bloomberg*, July 14, 1994.

Page 97: IDB stockholders file suit alleging that executives sold over $37 billion in stock before IDB's "improper financial practices" are exposed. Ibid.

Page 98: Description of Dan's view on IDB, his participation in the IDB analyst call and subsequent downgrade of the stock, also "Jeffrey Sudikoff and..." Dan Reingold and Jennifer Reingold, *Confessions of a Wall Street Analyst: A True Story of Inside Information and Corruption in the Stock Market.* New York: HarperCollins, 2006.

Page 98: Sudikoff gives a differing account of Deloitte withdrawing from the IDB engagement. Kathleen Murray, "LDDS Communications Seen Courting IDB," *New York Times,* July 14, 1994.

Page 98: Bernie makes a $936 million stock offer for IDB. McElroy, *Bloomberg*, op. cit.

Page 98: "If both deals went through..." Ibid.

Page 98: The IDB acquisition gives LDDS licenses to operate in over 40 countries. Ibid.

Page 98: "They [LDDS] have to keep ..." "Street Talk" The Money Wheel, *CNBC*, July 28, 1994.

Page 98: "Ebbers is intent on building..." Ibid.

Page 98: "We don't comment..." Reuters Information Service, "LDDS Rises Sharply On Takeover Rumors," August, 17, 1994.

Page 99: Bringing WilTel's profit margin into line with LDDS's will add to earnings. Levy, *Bloomberg,* op. cit.

Pages 99–100: A description of WilTel's Executive Suite. Solomon, *Wall Street Journal,* op. cit.

Page 101: "Who invented a tie..." Will Pinkston, "WorldCom Sits on Hold—For Now," *Clarion-Ledger*, September 10, 1995.

Page 104: Description of indictments related to IDB executives. Taub, *Los Angeles Times,* op. cit.

Page 104: Description of the settlement related to IDB executives. Litigation Release no. 16663, August 28, 2000. Available at (www .sec.gov/litigation).

Chapter 10   Nowhere To Go But Up

Page 112: "Michael Jordan came and asked..." Kelly Ingebretsen, "WorldCom Chief Quells Rumors of Relocation," *Mississippi Business Journal,* April 29, 1996.

Page 113: "As someone who knows what it takes..." WorldCom, Inc. (December 18, 1995). *Basketball Superstar Michael Jordan Joins WorldCom, Inc. Management Team.* Press Release.

Page 113: NBA playoffs are viewed in millions of homes. Will Pinkston, "Superstar Gets Super Results for WorldCom," *Clarion-Ledger,* May 26, 1996.

Page 115: "It can be hard to know . . ." Seth Schiesel, "The Re-engineering of Bernie Ebbers; After Buying Spree, WorldCom Chief Must Learn to Run What He Has Built," *New York Times,* April 27, 1998.

Page 116: "Bernie was a paradox..." Lynne Jeter, *Disconnected: Deceit and Betrayal at WorldCom.* Hoboken, NJ: John Wiley & Sons, 2003.

Page 117: "Somebody who worked for us..." Ibid.

Chapter 11   A New Era

Page 123: "Anyone in this industry..." Kevin Maney, "Small Town Exec Strikes Big Deal Down-to-Earth Style is Secret to His Success," *USA Today,* August 28, 1996.

Page 123: "The Telecom Act is . . ." GTE. (February 8, 1996). *GTE Chairman Praises Prompt Enactment of Telecom Bill.* Press Release.

Page 123: "We only have 5 percent . . ." Lynne Jeter, *Disconnected: Deceit and Betrayal at WorldCom.* Hoboken, NJ: John Wiley & Sons, 2003.

Pages 123–124: Bills to regulate the telecom industry have failed in the past. Dan Reingold and Jennifer Reingold, *Confessions of a Wall Street Analyst: A True Story of Inside Information and Corruption in the Stock Market.* New York: HarperCollins, 2006.

Page 124: The idea of one-stop shopping becomes popular. "One Bill Fits All," *WashingtonTechnology,* September, 26, 1996.

Page 124: AT&T employees sent to Washington to protest telecom bill. Reingold and Reingold, *Confessions of a Wall Street Analyst,* op. cit.

Page 125: Dan Reingold and Jack Grubman disagree on which companies will succeed in the new telecom environment. Mark Landler, "The Siskel and Ebert of Telecom Investing," *New York Times,* February 4, 1996.

Page 125: "starry-eyed," "bull-headed," "nuts," Ibid.

Page 125: "I bet you that in college ..." Ibid.

Page 125: "Before making conclusions ..." Ibid.

Page 126: "[WorldCom] now sits at the head ..." Emory Thomas, Jr., "Shareholder scoreboard: Which companies stood out for better or worse: Best 10-year performer: WorldCom Inc.," *Wall Street Journal,* February 29, 1996.

Page 126: Bernie's "dumb as a fox approach." Ibid.

Page 126: "Don't let the toothpick ..." Ibid.

Pages 126–127: "I strongly concur with John ..." Bernard J. Ebbers, "Paper Ignoring Positive Business News," *Clarion-Ledger*, March 9, 1996.

Page 127: "Our goal is not ..." Amy Barrett and Peter Elstrom, "Making WorldCom Live Up to Its Name," *Businessweek,* July 14, 1997.

Page 127: Bernie's comparison of a $100 investment between AT&T, MCI and Sprint, Cassandra Townsend, "Training Important to Industry, Says Ebbers," *Daily Leader,* July 26, 1996.

Page 127: WorldCom joins the S&P 500. Standard & Poor's. (March 25, 1996). *Standard & Poor's Announces Index Changes.* Press Release.

Page 127: Bernie is ranked among Corporate America's Most Powerful People by Forbes magazine in their May 20, 1996 issue.

Page 127: Providing flyaway Earth stations to The Summit of the Peacemakers, WorldCom, Inc. (March 14, 1996). *IDB Systems Provides Earth Stations for Egypt's Arento to Support Anti-Terrorism Summit.* Press Release.

Page 127: "I don't rule anything out." Will Pinkston, "Tough, Successful WorldCom Chief Eyes Politics," *Clarion-Ledger,* April 9, 1996.

Page 128: "Let's be honest ..." Ibid.

Page 128: "We never had an approach ..." Staff and Wire Reporters, "WorldCom Stock Rises to $24.50, Up $2.38," *Clarion-Ledger,* July 31, 1996.

Page 128: "realized long ago that ..." Thomas, Jr., *Wall Street Journal,* op. cit.

Page 129 "people that have problems ..." Seth Schiesel, "The re-engineering of Bernie Ebbers; After Buying Spree, WorldCom Chief Must Learn to Run What He Has Built," *New York Times,* April 27, 1998.

Page 129: "You don't have to be ..." "Ebbers One-on-One with Bert Case" *WLBT,* April 30, 2002.

Page 129: "I'm the coach ..." Schiesel, *New York Times,* op. cit.

Page 129: "Almost instantly, Scott D. Sullivan ..." Ibid.

Page 129: "He is one of the brightest ..." Joseph McCafferty, "Scott Sullivan—WorldCom Inc.," *CFO Magazine,* September 1, 1998.

Page 130: Salomon Smith Barney's recruiting of Jack Grubman. Charles Gasparino, *Blood on the Street: The Sensational Inside Story of How Wall Street Analysts Duped a Generation of Investors.* New York: Free Press, 2005.

Page 131: "I was mystified..." Reingold and Reingold, *Confessions of a Wall Street Analyst,* op. cit.

Page 132: "I swallowed deep..." Barrett and Elstrom, *Businessweek,* op. cit.

Page 132: "He's organically smart..." Maney, *USA Today,* op. cit.

Page 132: "He doesn't believe in management..." Ibid.

Page 132: Nineteen of 24 analysts covering WorldCom have a "buy" or better rating and none with sell ratings. Staff writers, "Brave New WorldCom," *Red Herring,* November 1, 1997.

Page 132: Dan concedes that the acquisition "made tremendous strategic sense..." Also, his rating of LDDS stock. Reingold and Reingold, *Confessions of a Wall Street Analyst,* op. cit.

Page 133: When *Institutional Investor* creates a category for telcom start-ups, Jack is the top rated analyst. Ibid.

Page 133: Jack helps win $60 million in banking fees for Salomon, brings in $7.5 million on the MFS deal and has a 1996 salary of $3.5 million. Gasparino, *Blood on the Street,* op. cit.

Page 133: Information about WorldCom's building plan in downtown Jackson. Will Pinkston, "WorldCom Tower Will Dwarf Its Neighbors," *Clarion-Ledger,* June 6, 1996.

Page 134: "Coup of the century..." Maybelle G. Cagle, "WorldCom move 'coup of the century,'" *The Clinton News,* September 12, 1996.

Page 134: "Today, we begin a new phase... Mississippi College," Also, a description of the Mississippi College announcement. "A New Dawn," *The Beacon,* Spring 1997.

Page 134: "It gives me great pleasure..." Ibid.

Page 134: "I've been where those kids..." Jeter, Disconnected, op. cit.

Page 135: Highlights of Greenspan's "irrational exuberance" dinner speech, and discussions at the FOMC meeting, Peter Hartcher, *Bubble Man: Alan Greenspan & The Missing 7 Trillion Dollars.* Melbourne: Black, Inc., 2005.

Page 135: "It was not a shot-from-the-hip..." Ibid.

Page 135: "We thought long and in detail..." Ibid.

Page 135: "What worries me..." Federal Open Market Committee Meeting Transcripts, September 24, 1996.

Pages 135–136: "I recognize..." Ibid.

Page 136: "I guarantee..." Ibid.

Page 136: "You know I've always been..." Hartcher, *Bubble Man,* op. cit.

Page 136: "People said, 'How dare you...'" Ibid.

Chapter 12   The Glass Sieve

Page 139: "That's just the fun part..." Seth Schiesel, "The Re-engineering of Bernie Ebbers; After Buying Spree, WorldCom Chief Must Learn to Run What He Has Built," *New York Times,* April 27, 1998.

Page 139: "I'm not a technology dude." Tim Padgett, "The Rise and Fall of Bernie Ebbers," *Time,* May 5, 2002.

Page 140: "In this business..." Kate Gerwig, "No Worrying Over the Dress Code," *Internetweek,* December 7, 1998.

Pages 141–142: A description of Francesco Galesi's mansion. Blair Golson, "Dragon's Curse," *New York Observer,* August 12, 2002. Also see, T.J. Clemente, "Chesterton," Danshamptons.com, May 18, 2007.

Chapter 13   The Tide Comes In

Page 148: "No one has ever seen..." Morino Institute, "In the Digital Age," *Netpreneur Exchange,* November 12, 1997.

Page 148: "I went to the State..." Jeremy M. Brosowsky, "Is Less More for Sidgmore?" *Business Forward,* December 2000.

Page 148: "I drink 20 cups..." Ibid.

Chapter 14   The Minnow Swallows the Whale

Page 151: "Every time there is another..." "Scott Sullivan: Master of the Mega Merger," *Oswego,* Spring/Summer 1999.

Page 151: "We will not be..." Lynne Jeter, *Disconnected: Deceit and Betrayal at WorldCom.* Hoboken, NJ: John Wiley & Sons, 2003.

Page 152: "if the price is right." Amy Barrett and Peter Elstrom, "Making WorldCom Live Up to Its Name," *Businessweek,* July 14, 1997.

Page 152: If BT buys MCI it will be the largest foreign acquisition of a U.S. company in history. Steven Lipin, "British Telecom and MCI Unveil $20.88 Billion Merger Agreement," *Wall Street Journal,* November 4, 1996.

Page 152: "I bet I could get you..." Anita Raghavan, "For Salomon, Grubman Is Big Telecom Rainmaker," *Wall Street Journal,* March 25, 1997.

Page 152: "swashbuckling deal broker," Ibid.

Page 152: "Jack has veto power..." Ibid.

Page 152: "Jack of all trades," "Grubman from the analyst pack," Ibid.

Page 152: "There are no hard and fast rules..." Ibid.

Page 153: "It really is a question..." Ibid.

Page 153: MCI's losses in the second half of 1997 are much higher than anticipated. Peter Elstrom, "The New World Order," *BusinessWeek,* October 13, 1997.

Page 153: Description of Dan Reingold's participation on the MCI conference call, view on whether the MCI/BT deal will be renegotiated, and his advice to BT. Dan Reingold and Jennifer Reingold, *Confessions of a Wall Street Analyst: A True Story of Inside Information and Corruption in the Stock Market.* New York: HarperCollins, 2006.

Page 153: "With one exception..." Ibid.

Page 153: British Telecom holds three seats on MCI's board and 20% of its stock. Seth Schiesel, "From Wimp to a Kingmaker in Battle for MCI," *New York Times,* October 17, 1997.

Page 153: BT reduces its offer for MCI to $19 billion. Seth Scheisel, "The Battle for MCI: The Offer; MCI accepts offer of $36.5 billion; Deal Sets Record," *New York Times,* November 11, 1997.

Pages 153–154: A description of Jack Grubman and the Salomon arbitrage department. Charles Gasparino, *Blood on the Street: The Sensational Inside Story of How Wall Street Analysts Duped a Generation of Investors.* New York: Free Press, 2005.

Page 154: Scott runs into Eduardo Mestre at the airport. Joseph McCafferty, "Scott Sullivan—WorldCom Inc.," *CFO Magazine,* September 1, 1998.

Page 154: "We might be able…" Ibid.

Pages 154–155: Scott crunches the numbers on his flight home to see if an MCI deal is possible. Ibid.

Page 155: WorldCom versus MCI revenues and WorldCom's stock premium. Peter Elstrom, "The New World Order," *BusinessWeek,* October 13, 1997.

Page 155: Salomon's arbitrageurs lose an estimated $100 million in the failed MCI/BT deal. Gasparino, *Blood on the Street,* op. cit.

Page 155: "We were exuberant…" Joseph McCafferty, "Scott Sullivan—WorldCom Inc.," *CFO Magazine,* September 1, 1998.

Page 155: "WorldCom's bold takeover…" Reingold and Reingold, *Confessions of a Wall Street Analyst,* op. cit.

Page 155: "The man from Mississippi," Lynn Haber, "Here's a Look at the 15 Most Important People, Inventions and Events that Shaped Our Networked World," *Network World,* March 26, 2001.

Page 155: Bernie calls Sprint CEO Bert Roberts to make an unsolicited bid for the company. Elstrom, *BusinessWeek,* op. cit.

Page 156: AT&T was our "other choice…" but they "didn't know who we were," Ibid.

Page 156: "After we get our deal…" Ibid.

Page 156: "A little bit earlier…" Ibid.

Page 156: "I'm putting the likelihood…" Ibid.

Page 156: GTE also makes an offer for MCI valued at $28 billion, Schiesel, *New York Times,* op. cit.

Page 156: "Some investors and analysts…" Ibid.

Page 157: WorldCom offers $36.5 billion for MCI and buys out BT's portion of the company. Schiesel, *New York Times,* op. cit.

Page 157: "Executives close to the…." Ibid.

Page 157: Bernie refers to Bert Roberts as "boss man." Ibid.

Page 157: WorldCom and MCI officially merge… WorldCom, Inc. (September 14, 1998). *WorldCom Completes Merger with MCI.* Press Release.

Page 157: "Mr. Ebbers will release . . ." Reed Branson, "WorldCom's Ebbers Builds Mississippi Muscle," *Commercial Appeal,* November 9, 1997.

Page 157: "I think the world changed . . ." Elstrom, *BusinessWeek,* op. cit.

Page 157: "[Bernie] was an outsider . . ." Ibid.

Page 157: "He's the Ted Turner . . ." Branson, *Commercial Appeal,* op. cit.

Page 158: "[Bernie] has proven to be . . ." Ibid.

Page 158: "Ten years ago . . ." Elstrom, *BusinessWeek,* op. cit.

Page 158: "That's what makes [Bernie] . . ." Ibid.

Page 158: "[The MCI deal has become] the stuff of legends." McCafferty, *CFO Magazine,* op. cit.

Page 158: "WorldCom is here to stay." *Time,* "1998 Top 50 Cyber Elite."

Page 158: "Master of the Mega Merger" "Scott Sullivan" *Oswego,* op. cit.

Page 158: Scott's 1997 compensation. Linda Gorman, "As Good As It Gets," *CFO.com,* November 1, 1998.

Page 158: "I'm willing to lay it all . . ." Ibid.

Page 158: Scott "walked on water . . ." Jayne O'Donnell, "A Couple of Bad Apples Spoiled 'CFO' Award," *USA Today,* May 5, 2004.

Page 159: "He has no peer . . ." McCafferty, *CFO Magazine,* op. cit.

Page 159: "Scott's intimate knowledge . . ." Reingold and Reingold, *Confessions of a Wall Street Analyst,* op. cit.

Page 159: Salomon closes its arbitrage division. Gasparino, *Blood on the Street,* op. cit.

Page 159: The advantages of the MCI purchase. Henry Goldblatt and Nelson D. Schwartz, "Telecom in Play as British Telecom, WorldCom, and GTE Vie for MCI," *Money,* November 10, 1997.

Page 159: "We put in a lot of . . ." Also, description of facilities, Sarah Schafer, "For 2 Companies, Playful Coexistence," *Washington Post,* June 8, 2000.

Pages 159–160: How MCI's decline in revenue and prices affect WorldCom, Toni Mack, "Grand Illusions," *Forbes.com,* July 6, 1998.

Page 160: "When John Sidgmore . . ." John Wohlstetter, "The Rise and Fall of the Ebbers Empire," *National Review Online,* June 28, 2002.

Page 160: "within 24 hours . . ." Ibid.

Page 162: "Unloading the planes . . ." Nelson D. Schwartz, "How Ebbers Is Whipping MCI WorldCom Into Shape: No Planes, No Limos, No Fancy Hotels," Fortune, February 1, 1999.

Page 162: "I always take a cab . . ." Ibid.

Page 162: "I look at every single . . ." Ibid.

Chapter 15   Finding Balance

Page 164: Miss McCarty's biography and donation are profiled by Sharon Wertz, "Oseola McCarty Donates $150,000 To Southern Miss," June 26, 1995. (http://www.usm.edu/pr/oolamain.htm)

Chapter 16   Top of the Mountain

Page 167: WorldCom is the country's fifth most widely held stock and has a market capitalization of $115 billion. Charles Haddad, "WorldCom's Sorry Legacy," *Businessweek,* June 28, 2002.

Page 168: Ten IPOs jump by over a thousand percent. Peter Hartcher, *Bubble Man: Alan Greenspan & The Missing 7 Trillion Dollars.* Melbourne: Black, Inc., 2005.

Page 169: Traditional ways of valuing a company... "page views," and "engaged shoppers." Gretchen Morgenson, "How Did They Value Stocks? Count the Absurd Ways," *New York Times,* March 18, 2001.

Page 169: There's a glut of new publications..., also CNBC viewership. Hartcher, *Bubble Man,* op. cit.

Page 169: CEOs see a significant increase in compensation during the 1990s. Ibid.

Page 169: "Like the attic of a house gets filled..." Yochi Dreazen, "Fallacies of the Tech Boom," *Wall Street Journal,* September 26, 2002.

Page 169: There are now over 3000 telecommunication companies in the United States. Bill Mann, "WorldCom's Hairy Ride," *The Motley Fool,* April 24, 2002.

Page 170: From 1998 to 2000, the telecom sector will add $ 323 billion... Ken Belson, "Industry Picks Up Pieces as Ebbers Trial Begins," *New York Times,* January 18, 2005.

Page 170: Over $1.2 trillion will be spent in the telecom sector. Mann, *Motley Fool,* op. cit.

Page 170: Claims about Internet growth and the growth of Internet commerce. "The Emerging Digital Ecomony," April 15, 1998.

Page 170: "We've always been bandwidth junkies..." "Cable Guy," *New York Magazine,* January 24, 2000.

Pages 170–171: Description of the nineteenth century railroad industry. "Boom and Bust" The Online NewsHour with Jim Lehrer, *PBS,* August 31, 2001.

Page 171: "Conventional economics is dead..." Thomas Petzinger, "So Long, Supply and Demand," *Wall Street Journal,* January 1, 2000.

Page 171: "The Tinker Bell approach..." Warren Buffett and Carol Loomis, "Mr. Buffett on the Stock Market," Fortune, November 22, 1999.

Page 171: Jeff Bezos, who coined the phrase "dot-com," is Time's Person of the Year. Hartcher, *Bubble Man,* op. cit.

Page 172: "They're beginning to put..." Amy Barrett and Peter Elstrom, "Making WorldCom Live Up to Its Name," *Businessweek,* July 14, 1997.

Chapter 17   A Double-Edged Sword

Page 174: "The thing that has helped me..." Tim Padgett, "The Rise and Fall of Bernie Ebbers," *Time,* May 5, 2002.

Page 177: "[Bernie's] a monarch..." Charles Haddad, "WorldCom Laying it on the Line," *Businessweek,* November 20, 2000.

Page 178: Scott refers to Bernie as "the milkman" and "red-necked hillbilly," Susan Pulliam and Almar Latour, "Lost Connection: Trial of WorldCom's Ebbers Will Focus on Uneasy Partnership," *Wall Street Journal,* January 12, 2005.

Page 179: "Bernie and Scott were like..." Ibid.

Page 179: "We have mega-merger-mania..." David McGuire, "FCC & FTC Raise Concerns About Telecom Mergers," *Newsbytes.com,* November 8, 1999.

Page 179: "just a merger away..." Peter S. Goodman, "FCC Chairman Wary of MCI-Sprint Union," *Newsbytes.com,* October 1, 1999.

Page 179: "American consumers are enjoying..." Ibid.

Page 179: "The opportunity—in fact..." "MCI WorldCom CEO Announces 'All-Distance' Service, Open Access to All Network Services," *Cambridge Telecom Report,* January 17, 2000.

Page 180: Bernie defends the proposed Sprint merger against anti-competition concerns, including that there's "too much competition and too much capacity." Ibid.

Page 180: The Telecom Act results in a "flood" of fiber capacity and description of the telecom industry. Ibid.

Page: 180: "Mr. President, we're very pleased..." David Faber, "The Big Lie: Inside the Rise & Fraud of WorldCom" *CNBC,* September 9, 2003.

Pages 180: "We live in a time..." The White House. (March 1, 2000) *Remarks by the President to UUNET and WorldCom Employees.* Press Release.

Pages 180–181: Ebbers' retirement plans, borrowing and personal assets are highlighted by Susan Pulliam, Deborah Solomon and Carrick Mollenkamp, "Former WorldCom CEO Built An Empire on Mountain of Debt," *Wall Street Journal,* December 31, 2002.

Page 181: At the stock's height, Bernie's personal fortune is worth $1.3 billion. Greg Farrell, "Convicted Executives Forced to Sell Homes," *USA Today,* November 12, 2006.

Page 182: Ebbers brings a hockey team to Mississippi. Joe Culpepper, "Bandits' Roller-Coaster Ride Began in 1998 in Capital City," *Clarion-Ledger,* April 6, 2003.

Page 182: The history behind the Bandits of the Natchez Trace as documented by, Barbara Lazear Ascher, "An Old World the Mississippi Left Behind," *New York Times,* November 25, 1984.

Page 182: In the last month alone... 27 IPOs, Peter Hartcher, *Bubble Man: Alan Greenspan & The Missing 7 Trillion Dollars.* Melbourne: Black, Inc., 2005.

Page 183: Bank of America provides lead financing for the purchase of Wiltel. Pulliam, Solomon and Mollenkamp, *Wall Street Journal,* op. cit.

Page 183: Bank of America administers WorldCom's revolving credit facility. Revolving Credit Agreement among WorldCom, Inc., Borrower, Bank of America, N.A. and the Chase Manhattan Bank, Co-Administrative Agents, June 8, 2001.

Page 183: Salomon Smith Barney collects over $100 million in fees while doing business with Bernie Ebbers. Andrew Ross Sorkin, "Turmoil at WorldCom: The Bankers; Salomon Brothers May Face WorldCom Shareholder Suits," *New York Times,* June 29, 2002.

Page 183: "He almost played with reckless abandonment…" Reed Branson, "WorldCom's Ebbers Builds Mississippi Muscle," *Commercial Appeal,* November 9, 1997.

Chapter 18   A Titan Stumbles

Page 184: "It's only when the tide goes out…" Peter Hartcher, *Bubble Man: Alan Greenspan & The Missing 7 Trillion Dollars.* Melbourne: Black, Inc., 2005.

Page 184: "Would he ever trash…" Peter Elstrom, "Jack Grubman: The Power Broker," *Businessweek,* May 15, 2000.

Pages 184–185: Jack would make derogatory comments about AT&T during presentations. Charles Gasparino, *Blood on the Street: The Sensational Inside Story of How Wall Street Analysts Duped a Generation of Investors.* New York: Free Press, 2005.

Page 185: Jack's history with AT&T stock upgrade can be found in Eliot Spitzer's investigation of Jack Grubman and conflicts of interest among the banking industry. Attorney General of the State of New York Bureau of Investment Protection, *In the Matter of Jack Benjamin Grubman. Assurance of Discontinuance Pursuant to Executive Law Section 63 (15).* April 28, 2003.

Page 185: "The *Wall Street Journal* tried…" "Cable Guy," *New York Magazine,* January 24, 2000.

Page 185: "that this is a brave new world…" Ibid.

Page 185: "turning the roles of the stock…" Elstrom, *Businessweek,* op. cit.

Page 185: "What used to be a conflict…" Ibid.

Page 185: "Someone like me…" Ibid.

Page 186: "Objective, The other word for it is uninformed." Ibid.

Page 186: Jack's view on the growth of the telecom sector… Ibid.

Page 186: "He has had a thesis…" Ibid.

Page 186: Companies will spend $35 billion to lay 100 million miles of fiber, "more than enough…" Simon Romero, "Once-Bright Future of Optical Fiber Dims," *New York Times,* June 18, 2001.

Page 186: "He can move billions…" Elstrom, *Businessweek,* op. cit.

Page 186: "I'm sculpting the industry…" " I get feedback from…" Ibid.

Page 186: Jack's fluctuating recommendation on AT&T from Attorney General of the State of New York Bureau of Investment Protection, *In the*

Matter of Jack Benjamin Grubman. Assurance of Discontinuance Pursuant to Executive Law Section 63 (15). April 28, 2003.

Page 186: "deficiencies in data strategy," Attorney General of the State of New York Bureau of Investment Protection, *In the Matter of Citigroup Global Markets Inc. (formerly known as Salomon Smith Barney Inc.). Assurance of Discontinuance Pursuant to Executive Law Section 63 (15).* April 28, 2003.

Pages 186–188: Discussion of Jack Grubman and the 92nd Street Y, Attorney General of the State of New York Bureau of Investment Protection, *In the Matter of Jack Benjamin Grubman. Assurance of Discontinuance Pursuant to Executive Law Section 63 (15).* April 28, 2003.

Page 186: "fresh look," Attorney General of the State of New York Bureau of Investment Protection, *In the Matter of Jack Benjamin Grubman.* op. cit.

Page 187: "AT&T and the 92nd Street Y..." Ibid.

Page 187: "On another matter..." Ibid.

Page 187: "You know everyone thinks..." Ibid.

Page 188: "The biggest thing that [angered me]..." Gasparino, *Blood on the Street*, op. cit.

Page 188: "I always viewed [AT&T]..." Attorney General of the State of New York Bureau of Investment Protection, *In the Matter of Jack Benjamin Grubman.* op. cit.

Page 188: "The claims..." "The notions that used..." "and important cultural institution..." "In asking Grubman to take..." "it was clear that I never ..." the 92nd Street Y's importance to New York and Citigroup's philanthropic pledge to the Y, Sandy Weill and Judah S. Kraushaar, *The Real Deal: My Life in Business and Philanthropy.* New York: Hachette Book Group USA, 2006.

Page 189: "I hear [Focal] complained..." Ibid.

Page 189: "If anything the record shows..." Ibid.

Page 189: "If [a senior investment banker]..." Ibid.

Page 189: "legitimate concern about the objectivity..." Attorney General of the State of New York Bureau of Investment Protection, *In the Matter of Citigroup Global Markets Inc.,* op. cit.

Page 189: A presentation by the head of Salomon's Global Equity Research Management showed that out of 1,179 stocks rate by the firm, none were rated "sell" and only one "under-perform." Ibid.

Page 189: "We're not trying to be..." D. Victor Hawkins, "LDDS It Happened Right Here In Mississippi," *The Jackson Journal of Business,* February 1988.

Page 189: "This merger threatens..." Department of Justice. (June 27, 2000). *Justice Department Sues to Block WorldCom's Acquisition of Sprint.* Press Release.

Page 190: "Likely collapse of the..." United States District Court Southern District of New York, WorldCom Securities Litigation is available at (http://fl1

.findlaw.com/news.findlaw.com/hdocs/docs/worldcom/nyworldcom101402cacmp
.pdf).

Page 192: "In Washington, we have..." Kate Gerwig, "No Worrying Over
the Dress Code," *Internetweek,* December 7, 1998.

Page 192: "You have to wear something..." Sarah Schafer, "For 2
Companies, Playful Coexistence," *Washington Post,* June 8, 2000.

Page 192: "You can't show..." Ibid.

Page 192: "WorldCom was smart enough..." Ibid.

Page 192: "It's a matter of pride..." Ibid.

Page 192: WorldCom and UUNET sales departments compete with each
other. Andrew Backover and Michelle Kessler, "Internal Rifts Threaten
WorldCom," *USA Today,* August 27, 2002.

Page 192: When WorldCom's stock drops $13, Bernie's net worth decreases
by almost half. United States Southern District of New York, "Third and Final
Report of Dick Thornburg, Bankruptcy Court Examiner," January 26, 2004.

Page 193: "He was trying to do..." Susan Pulliam, Deborah Solomon and
Carrick Mollenkamp, "Former WorldCom CEO Built An Empire on Mountain
of Debt," *Wall Street Journal,* December 31, 2002.

Page 193: Many investors who had dumped dot.com stocks, transferred their money into the telecom sector. Om Malik, *Broadbandits: Inside
the $750 Billion Telecom Heist.* Hoboken, NJ: John Wiley & Sons, 2003.

Page 193: Information about WorldCom's Compensation Committee and
loans made to Bernie by WorldCom's Board of Directors is detailed by the
Special Investigative Committee of the Board of Directors of WorldCom, Inc.,
March 31, 2003.

Page 193: Amount of stock Stiles Kellett holds. Pulliam, Solomon and
Mollenkamp, *Wall Street Journal,* op. cit.

Page 196: WorldCom Compensation Committee members go with Bernie to
Bank of America, WorldCom's Board of Directors are detailed by the Special
Investigative Committee of the Board of Directors of WorldCom, Inc., March
31, 2003.

Page 196: Salomon agrees to guarantee all future loan risk and convinces
Citibank to raise the threshold for margin calls. United States Southern District
of New York, "Third and Final Report of Dick Thornburg, Bankruptcy Court
Examiner," January 26, 2004.

Page 196: "[Bernie] is associated with..." Ibid.

Page 196: Jack continues to issue a "buy" rating on WorldCom's
stock, calling it "dirt cheap" and WorldCom issues more loans to Bernie. Ibid.

Page 197: "I've let you as investors..." Charles Haddad, "WorldCom
Laying it on the Line," *Businessweek,* November 20, 2000.

Page 197: WorldCom announces the use of tracker stocks. WorldCom, Inc.
(November 1, 2000). *WorldCom to Realign Businesses, Creating Two Tracking
Stocks.* Press Release.

Page 197: "high cash flow" and "The new structure..." Ibid.

Page 197: WorldCom stock drops 20% to below $19 in the wake of lowered earnings estimates. Charles Haddad, "WorldCom Laying it on the Line," *Businessweek,* November 20, 2000.

Page 197: "On the strength of..." United States Southern District of New York, "Third and Final Report of Dick Thornburg, Bankruptcy Court Examiner," January 26, 2004.

Page 197: The full Board is informed of Bernie's loans and the rationale for approving the loans. Special Investigative Committee of the Board of Directors of WorldCom, Inc., March 31, 2003.

Page 198: "Is there a bandwidth glut?" Gasparino, *Blood on the Street,* op. cit.

Page 198: "Analyst said gloomy outlooks..." Tiffany Kary, "Gloom on the Horizon for Long-Distance Giants," *CNET News.com,* January 26, 2001.

Page 198: "the 15 most important people..." Lynn Haber, "Here's a Look at the 15 Most Important People, Inventions and Events that Shaped Our Networked World," *Network World,* March 26, 2001.

Page 198: "Ebbers has demonstrated how..." Ibid.

Page 199: "The U.S.'s number two..." Roy Mark, "WorldCom's Net Income Plunges," *dc.internet.com,* October 25, 2001.

Page 199: Bernie refuses Verizon's offer to buy WorldCom. Charles Haddad with Steve Rosenbush, "Woe is WorldCom," *Businessweek,* May 6, 2002.

Page 199: Many telecom executives sell their stocks as the industry collapses. Dennis K. Berman, "Before Telecom Bubble Burst, Some Insiders Sold Out Stakes," *Wall Street Journal,* August 12, 2002.

Page 200: "Hundreds of telecom executives..." Ibid.

Page 200: "seven points of light" Charles Haddad with Steve Rosenbush, "Woe is WorldCom," *Businessweek,* May 6, 2002.

Page 200: "Bernie is running a $40 million company..." Ibid.

Page 200: Bernie discontinues free coffee for employees. Ibid.

Pages 200–201: "A goal of this hearing..." House Subcommittee on Capital Markets, "Analyzing the Analysts," June 14, 2001.

Page 201: "I am distressed..." Ibid.

Page 201: Eliot Spitzer highlights the conflict between analysts, bankers and brokers, including internal report card comments by brokers. Attorney General of the State of New York Bureau of Investment Protection, *In the Matter of Jack Benjamin Grubman.* op. cit.

Page 201: "Mr. Grubman should decide..." Attorney General of the State of New York Bureau of Investment Protection, *In the Matter of Citigroup Global Markets Inc.,* op cit.

Page 201: "Jack Grubman has lost..." Attorney General of the State of New York Bureau of Investment Protection, *In the Matter of Jack Benjamin Grubman.* op cit.

Page 201: "His cheerleading..." Ibid.

Page 201: "I realize that Jack..." Ibid.

Page 201: "Not all four letter words..." Will Leitch, "Endpiece: From the Mouths of Brokers," *Registered Rep,* June 1, 2003.

Page 201: "In my 16 years in the retail..." Will Leitch, "Endpiece: From the Mouths of Brokers," *Registered Rep,* June 1, 2003.

Page 201: "Please do not fire Jack..." Ibid.

Chapter 19   The Rule of Ten

Page 211: Women and men express frustrations differently. Barbara Annis, *Same Words, Different Language.* Toronto: Penguin Group, 2003.

Chapter 20   What is Prepaid Capacity?

Page 217: Bernie borrows over $900 million. Susan Pulliam, Deborah Solomon and Carrick Mollenkamp, "Former WorldCom CEO Built An Empire on Mountain of Debt," *Wall Street Journal,* December 31, 2002.

Page 218: Bernie and WorldCom's loan to him are discussed by the Special Investigative Committee of the Board of Directors of WorldCom, Inc., March 31, 2003.

Page 218: Bernie resists selling personal assets to pay off loans. Pulliam, Solomon and Mollenkamp, *Wall Street Journal,* op cit.

Page 218: Bernie signs a separation agreement with WorldCom. Special Investigative Committee of the Board of Directors of WorldCom, Inc., March 31, 2003.

Pages 218–219: Discussion of Board conflict over CEO position. Charles Haddad, "How Ebbers Kept the Board in His Pocket," *Businessweek,* October 14, 2002.

Page 219: "I feel like crying..." "Ebbers One-on-One with Bert Case" *WLBT,* April 30, 2002.

Page 219: "I have had an incredible..." Ibid.

Page 219: "You wonder sometimes why people..." Ibid.

Page 219: "I'm just going back..." Ibid.

Page 220: WorldCom, Inc. (June 5, 2002) *WorldCom, Inc. Announces Intention to Exit Wireless Resale Business.* Press Release.

Page 220: WorldCom, Inc. (May 21, 2002) *WorldCom, Inc. Announces It Will Eliminate Tracking Stock Structure.* Press Release.

Pages 220–221: Discussion of whistleblower Kim Emigh. Gales Reaves, "Accounting for Anguish," *Fort Worth Weekly,* May 16, 2002.

Chapter 23   The Confrontation

Page 262: Betty, Troy and Buddy meet with government officials. Susan Pulliam, "Ordered to Commit Fraud, A Staffer Balked, Then Caved," *Wall Street Journal,* June 23, 2003.

Page 262: Scott and David's flight to Washington is tense. Susan Pulliam, "Crossing the Line: At Center of Fraud, WorldCom Official Sees Life Unravel," *Wall Street Journal*, March 24, 2005.

Page 264: David's job isn't as secure as he believed and he has to retain his own counsel. Ibid.

Page 264: David's wife tells him "he is a good man..." Ibid.

Chapter 24   A Desperate Search for Counsel

Page 266: WorldCom Inc. (June 25, 2002). *WorldCom Announces Intention to Restate 2001 and First Quarter 2002 Financial Statements.* Press Release.

Page 266: "I'm concerned about the..." The White House. (June 27, 2002) *U.S., Russia Continue Joint Efforts to Fight Terrorism.* Press Release.

Page 266: "What happened at WorldCom..." Harvey L. Pitt, "Speech by SEC Chairman: Remarks before the Economic Club of New York," June 26, 2002.

Page 267: WorldCom stock falls to $0.09 before trading is halted. Reuters Information Service, "The Rise and Fall of WorldCom," *USA Today,* July 21, 2002.

Chapter 25   Washington Attorneys Visit the Deep South

Page 287: "Do not be anxious..." *The Holy Bible, New International Version*, Philippians 4:6–7, Grand Rapids, Michigan, 2002.

Page 287: "For no sooner has the sun..." Scripture taken from the New King James Version. Copyright © 1982 by Thomas Nelson, Inc. Used by permission. All rights reserved.

Page 288: "When all the activities at WorldCom..." House Committee on Financial Services, "Wrong Numbers: The Accounting Problems at WorldCom," July 8, 2002.

Page 288: "Although I would like..." Ibid.

Page 289: "I don't think it's right..." Jonathan Krim and Christopher Stern, "2 Key WorldCom Witnesses Silent," *Washington Post,* July 9, 2002.

Page 289: While it's pointed out that Andersen has been the external auditor of many failed audits, Melvin Dick defends Andersen's testing procedures. House Committee on Financial Services, "Wrong Numbers: The Accounting Problems at WorldCom U.S. House of Representatives, Committee on Financial Services," July 8, 2002.

Page 289: "On each occasion..." Ibid.

Page 290: When questioned by Congressman Oxley, Jack Grubman defends his WorldCom's ratings as being consistent with his business philosophy. Ibid.

Page 290: "The newer, more nimbler companies..." Ibid.

Page 290: "Based on the financial statements..." Ibid.

Page 290: "Their only real competitor..." Ibid.

Chapter 26   Navigating the Storm

Page 296: When filing bankruptcy, WorldCom lists $41 billion in debt and $107 billion in assets. "WorldCom Files Largest Bankruptcy in US History," *People's Daily Online,* July 23, 2002.

Page 297: Statistics on fraud detection in the workplace. "2002 Report To The Nation Occupational Fraud And Abuse," *Association of Certified Fraud Examiners,* Copyright 2002.

Page 298: "The most far-reaching reforms..." Elisabeth Bumiller, "Corporate Conduct: The President; Bush Signs Bill Aimed at Fraud in Corporations," *New York Times,* July 31, 2002.

Page 298: President Bush establishes a Corporate Fraud Task Force and calls for increased support of the SEC and longer sentences for white collar crimes. Edwin Chen and Richard Simon, "Bush Urges Tougher Laws to Fight Fraud," *Los Angeles Times,* July 10, 2002.

Pages 298–299: After his "perp walk" David stands outside a locked car. Susan Pulliam, "Crossing the Line: At Center of Fraud, WorldCom Official Sees Life Unravel," *Wall Street Journal,* March 24, 2005.

Page 299: "I came to believe these..." Stephen Taub, "Four Down, Ebbers to Go," *CFO.com,* October 11, 2002.

Page 299: Betty Vinson's demeanor during questioning, Susan Pulliam, "How Following Orders Can Harm Your Career," *CFO.com,* October 3, 2003.

Page 299: Betty talks to her daughter about the possibility of prison. Susan Pulliam, "Over the Line: A Staffer Ordered to Commit Fraud Balked, Then Caved—Pushed by WorldCom Bosses, Accountant Betty Vinson Helped Cook the Books—A Confession at the Marriott," *Wall Street Journal,* June 23, 2003.

Page 299: David Myers' young son gives him a prized toy. Pulliam, *Wall Street Journal,* Op. Cit.

Page 299: WorldCom, Inc. (August 8, 2002). *WorldCom Announces Additional Changes To Reported Income For Prior Periods.* Press Release.

Page 300: Description of Jack being hounded by press. Dan Reingold and Jennifer Reingold, *Confessions of a Wall Street Analyst: A True Story of Inside Information and Corruption in the Stock Market.* New York: HarperCollins, 2006. Also see Blair Golson, "Grubman Giveaway?" *The New York Observer,* November 25, 2002.

Page 300: Descriptions of Jack Grubman's severance package from Salomon, Attorney General of the State of New York Bureau of Investment Protection, *In the Matter of Jack Benjamin Grubman. Assurance of Discontinuance Pursuant to Executive Law Section 63 (15).* April 28, 2003.

Page 300: From 1999 to 2002, Jack's compensation and the banking fees from telecom companies Jack followed. United States District Court for the Southern District of New York, *SEC vs. Jack Benjamin Grubman,* April 28, 2003.

Page 300: "The relentless series of negative statements..." Om Malik, *Broadbandits: Inside the $750 Billion Telecom Heist.* Hoboken, NJ: John Wiley & Sons, 2003.

Page 300: Eliot Spitzer uncovers the practice of "spinning" stocks. Office of the New York State Attorney General. (September 30, 2002). *State Suit Seeks Repayment of IPO and Stock Option Profits of Corporate Executives.* Press Release.

Page 300: "It was simple..." "The Wall Street Fix: Interviews: Eliot Spitzer" Frontline, *PBS,* May 8, 2003.

Page 300: "The evidence was overwhelming." Ibid.

Pages 300–301: "What we found was that analysts..." Ibid.

Page 301: Spitzer believes that Wall Street's problems are so pervasive that he opts to not criminally indict and firms or individuals. Ibid.

Page 301: "I believe that there are theoretical..." Ibid.

Page 301: Spitzer announces a settlement with Jack Grubman, a global settlement fining investment firms and reforms to the investment banking industry. Office of the New York State Attorney General. (April 28, 2003). *Conflict Probes Resolved at Citigroup and Morgan-Stanley.* Press Release. Also see, Office of the New York State Attorney General. (April 28, 2003) *Statement by Attorney General Eliot Spitzer regarding the "Global Resolution" of Wall Street Investigations.* Press Release.

Pages 302–303: "Bernie's Boys," "Ebbers' Loyalists," "current and former WorldCom directors and executives," and "spearheaded." Charles Haddad, "How Ebbers Kept the Board in His Pocket," *Businessweek,* October 14, 2002.

Page 309: Sherron Watkins' experience and comments as a whistleblower as highlighted by Jodie Morse and Amanda Bower, "The Party Crasher," *Time,* December 30, 2002.

Page 309: "Per your request..." Ibid.

Pages 309–310: Coleen Rowley's experience and comments as a whistle-blower as highlighted by Amanda Ripley and Maggie Sieger, "The Special Agent," *Time,* December 30, 2002.

Page 310: "Loyalty to whoever you work for..." Ibid.

Page 311: "How would Rowley..." James Kelly, "The Year of the Whistle-Blowers," *Time,* December 30, 2002.

Page 311: "Alford argues that..." Fred Alford, *Whistleblowers: Broken Lives and Organizational Power.* Ithica, NY: Cornell University Press, 2001.

Page 312: "Of the several dozen..." Ibid.

Page 312: "Usually the whistleblower..." Ibid.

Page 312: And whether someone goes to the press... Ibid.

Page 312: Whistleblowers are typically shocked by the way they are treated. Ibid.

Page 313: Alford discusses an "invisible line" that whistleblowers step over. Ibid.

Page 317: "This University should take..." First International Conference on Race: Racial Reconciliation, "Opening Address by Nicholas Katzenbach," October 1, 2003.

Page 317: "We cannot undo the misdeeds..." Bill Maxwell, "The Man Behind Mississippi's Sea Change," *St. Petersburg Times,* February 19, 2003.

Page 317: The telecom sector loses $2 trillion in market cap and 500,000 jobs. Glenn Bischoff, "USTA Repeats Call for End of UNE-P and TELRIC," *TelephonyOnline,* October 23, 2002.

Pages 317–318: WorldCom's stock has fallen from its height to .83 when the fraud is announced. Jane Black, "Pitt vs. Ebbers: This Time, It's Personal," *Businessweek,* July 1, 2002.

Pages 318–319: "[W]e were too trapped..." Joseph E. Stiglitz, *The Roaring Nineties: A New History of the World's Most Prosperous Decade.* New York: W. W. Norton & Company, Inc., 2003.

Page 319: "Deregulation of the telecommunications..." Ibid. Also see, Peter Hartcher, *Bubble Man: Alan Greenspan & The Missing 7 Trillion Dollars.* Melbourne: Black, Inc., 2005.

Page 319: "The markets bought lock, stock and barrel..." Yochi Dreazen, "Fallacies of the Tech Boom," *Wall Street Journal,* September 26, 2002.

Page 319: "There was no way there was enough traffic..." Ibid.

Page 319: "Most of the WorldCom claims..." Andrew M. Odlyzko, "Internet traffic growth: Sources and Implications," is available at (http://www.dtc.umn.edu/~odlyzko).

Page 320: "My company was not founded..." Andrew Backover and Michelle Kessler, "Internal Rifts Threaten WorldCom Deteriorating Worker Morale, Customer Service Could Be Lethal," *US Today,* August 27, 2002.

Chapter 27   A Visit to Federal Court

Page 322: "A lot of people..." "It was a Herculean effort..." "is the hardest thing..." a description of the resources required to complete the audit and the number of accounting entries. Joseph McCafferty, "Extreme Makeover," *CFO Magazine,* July 1, 2004.

Page 323: "the largest and most complex financial restatement..." "MCI Restatement Wipes Out $74bn," *BBC News,* March 12, 2004.

Pages 326–327: Dan's conversation with Bernie as related in *Dan Reingold and Jennifer Reingold, Confessions of a Wall Street Analyst: A True Story of Inside Information and Corruption in the Stock Market.* New York: HarperCollins, 2006.

Page 327: Judge Barbara Jones as profiled by Ken Belson, "In a High-Profile Trial, Quick Rulings and the Leavening of Humor," *New York Times,* March 16, 2005.

Page 327: "Every minute of [his] testimony..." Ibid.

Page 329: "wanted to leave Mississippi and never return," and "deceptive." *Mogran Freeman Proud To Call Mississippi Home.* Germantown, Tennessee: Image Publishing, Inc., 2006.

Page 329: "Mississippi is in fact no more..." also, "It is a source of great pride..." Ibid.

Page 329: Dolphus Weary recounts his childhood. Dolphus Weary, *I Ain't Never Coming Back.* Carol Stream, Illinois: Tyndale House, 1990.

Page 330: "Lord, I am leaving Mississippi..." Ibid.

Page 334: David finds comfort as he waits to testify. Susan Pulliam, "Crossing the Line: At Center of Fraud, WorldCom Official Sees Life Unravel," *Wall Street Journal*, March 24, 2005.

Chapter 28 United States Versus Bernard J. Ebbers

Page 338: Scott spends over 400 hours assisting the prosecution. Carrie Johnson, "Ex-WorldCom CFO Gets 5-Year Term," *Washington Post,* August 12, 2005.

Page 338: "Falsified the financial statements..." Ken Belson, "Witness Links Ebbers to Fraud At WorldCom," *New York Times,* February 8, 2005.

Page 338: "Bernie had a grasp..." Ibid.

Page 338: Scott describes Bernie's management style as "micromanaging." Kevin McCoy, "Witness Links Ebbers to Fraud," *USA Today,* February 7, 2005.

Page 339: Scott describes Bernie's management style as "very hands-on." Belson, *New York Times,* op. cit.

Page 339: Scott says that Bernie can be "very intimidating." Ibid.

Page 339: Interaction with Bernie was "very good," Brooke A. Masters, "Ebbers Called Hands-On," *Washington Post,* February 8, 2005.

Page 339: "It was very tough..." Ibid.

Page 339: Bernie "would make comments..." Brooke A. Masters, "Conflicting Portraits Of Ebbers Drawn at Trial," *Washington Post,* March 2, 2005.

Page 339: "We made adjustments that..." Brooke A. Masters, "Ex-CFO Says He Told Ebbers About Fraud," *Washington Post,* February 9, 2005.

Page 340: "You took his words..." Brooke A. Masters, "Defense Questions Sullivan On Lies," *Washington Post,* February 17, 2005.

Page 340: "Yes, I took that as an order..." Ibid.

Page 340: "We shouldn't be making..." Masters, *Washington Post,* op. cit.

Page 344: "Mr. Sullivan was a compelling..." Ken Belson, "Ebbers May Testify, But Should He?" *New York Times,* February 27, 2005.

Page 345: David Anders questions if Bernie is "detail oriented..." "Ebbers Denies Knowledge of Earnings Alert," *Bloomberg,* March 2, 2005.

Page 346: "It depends on what..." Ibid.

Pages 347–348: "I did not notice..." Masters, *Washington Post,* op. cit.

Chapter 29   The Judgment

Page 351: Jurors request markers, a flip chart and Cynthia Cooper's testimony. Brooke A. Masters, "No Verdict in Ebber's Trial," *Washington Post,* March 12, 2005.

Pages 351–352: Jury deliberations are highlighted by Almar LaTour, Shawn Young and Li Yuan, "Held Accountable, Ebbers Is Convicted In Massive Fraud," *Wall Street Journal,* March 16, 2005.

Page 352: "He was the man . . ." Ibid.

Page 352: "I truly believe . . ." "Ebbers Juror Says Data Led to Conviction." *Bloomberg,* March 17, 2005.

Page 352: "The most difficult thing . . ." LaTour, Young and Yuan, *Wall Street Journal,* op. cit.

Page 352: "had his own agenda," "I didn't care for him. Everything was . . ." " Ebbers Juror Says," *Bloomberg,* op. cit.

Page 352: The documents were "very important" in Bernie's conviction. Jesse Drucker and Li Yuan, " 'How Could He Not See?': Documents Swayed Ebbers Jury," *Wall Street Journal,* March 17, 2005.

Page 352: "At the end, the people who . . ." Ibid.

Page 352: "The reports that Mr. Ebbers . . ." "Ebbers Juror Says" *Bloomberg,* op. cit.

Page 353: "It was frustrating to see . . ." Jesse Drucker and Li Yuan, " 'How Could He Not See?': Documents Swayed Ebbers Jury," *Wall Street Journal,* March 17, 2005.

Page 353: "Before he testified . . ." Ibid.

Page 353: "I think Ebbers . . ." LaTour, Young and Yuan, *Wall Street Journal,* op. cit.

Page 353: "I find it hard to believe . . ." "Ebbers Juror Says Data Led to Conviction," *Bloomberg,* March 17, 2005.

Page 353: "If I had an accountant . . ." Drucker and Yuan, *Wall Street Journal,* op. cit.

Page 353: "at the very bottom . . ." Staff and Wire Reporters, "2 Ex-execs Sentenced in WorldCom Scandal," *Clarion-Ledger,* August 6, 2005.

Page 353: "I made decisions at WorldCom . . ." Ibid.

Page 353: "Had Ms. Vinson refused . . ." Ibid.

Page 353: "I never expected to be here . . ." Ibid.

Page 354: "I failed my family . . ." Erin McClam, "WorldCom Sentencing Continues," *CBSNews.com,* August 9, 2005.

Page 354: "I chose the easy way . . ." Associated Press, "Ex-WorldCom Accounting Director Gets 1 Year in Prison," *USA Today,* August 9, 2005.

Page 354: "perhaps the least useful . . ." Ibid.

Page 354: "he did not instigate . . ." Ibid.

Page 355: "At the time I consider . . ." Associated Press, "Former WorldCom Exec Gets Prison," *CBSNews.com,* August 10, 2005.

Page 355: "[Myers'] cooperation is a significant reason..." Ana Radelat, "1 Year, 1 Day For Controller," *Clarion-Ledger,* August 11, 2005.

Page 355: "Myers was more sophisticated..." Ibid.

Page 355: Scott Sullivan relinquishes personal assets. Erin McClam, "Sullivan Forfeits Mansion, Retirement Under Deal," *USA Today,* July 28, 2005.

Page 355: Scott is a "model cooperator," Carrie Johnson, "Leniency Sought for WorldCom's Sullivan," *Washington Post,* July 28, 2005.

Page 355: Scott was "the key factor" in winning the prosecution's case. Ibid.

Page 355: Prosecutors write a 13-page letter to Judge Jones. Ibid.

Page 355: "Without this type of information..." Ibid.

Page 355: "My actions are..." and Scott's demeanor as he reads his statement. Shawn Young, Dionne Searcey and Nathan Koppel, "Cooperation Pays: Sullivan Gets Five Years," *Wall Street Journal,* August 12, 2005.

Page 355: Scott is the fraud's "architect," Ibid.

Page 355: "You are fortunate..." Ibid.

Page 355: Judge Jones gives "great weight" to Scott's family situation in determining his sentence. Ibid.

Page 355: Scott was "detailed...candid...an excellent witness," Carrie Johnson, "Ex-WorldCom CFO Gets 5-Year Term," *Washington Post,* August 12, 2005.

Pages 355–356: "When you reward the architect..." Young, Searcey and Koppel, *Wall Street Journal,* op. cit5.

Page 356: "The message is..." Ibid.

Page 356: Bernie's lawyers cite his philanthropy and medical condition. Greg Farrell and Jayne O'Donnell, "Judges Often Deaf to Good Deeds," *USA Today,* July 12, 2005.

Page 356: Bernie is forced to serve his sentence in a medium security prison regardless of Judge Jones' recommendation. Carrie Johnson, "Ebbers Must Serve Time in Medium-Security Prison," *Washington Post,* August 25, 2005.

Page 356: Bernie's defense team appeals his conviction, with a panel of judges reviewing the appeal. Brooke A. Masters, "Ebbers Prosecutors Questioned On Tactics," *Washington Post,* January 31, 2006.

Page 356: "There are many violent criminals..." Ibid.

Page 356: "Twenty-five years does seem..." Stephen Taub, "Ebbers Has Reason for Hope," *CFO.com,* January 31, 2006.

Page 356: "affected literally millions..." Brooke A. Masters, "Ebbers Prosecutors Questioned On Tactics," *Washington Post,* January 31, 2006.

Pages 356–357: "it shocks the conscience..." Ibid.

Page 356: "I understand that prosecutors..." Young, Searcey and Koppel, *Wall Street Journal,* op. cit.

Page 357: Discussion of federal Sentencing Guidelines. Craig McCann, "Rethinking Sentencing Guidelines in Criminal Securities Frauds," Securities Litigation and Consulting Group, Inc., 2005.

Page 357: "a 15 cent decline in share price..." United States Court of Appeals for the Second Circuit, "United States v. Bernard J. Ebbers," Argued: January 30, 2006, Decided: July 28, 2006.

Page 358: Bernie's life had "an element of tragedy." Ibid.

Page 358: Bernie's sentence is "harsh but not unreasonable." Ibid.

Page 358: Bernie "had primary responsibility for the fraud."

Page 358: "A reasonable explanation..." Ibid.

Page 358: "Twenty-five years is a long sentence..." Ibid.

Page 358: "However, Congress has directed..." Ibid.

Page 358: "Even the threat of..." Ibid.

Page 358: "The Guidelines reflect Congress' judgement..." Ibid.

Page 359: Descriptions of settlements made regarding WorldCom class action lawsuits, Office of the New York State Comptroller. (April 26, 2005). *Arthur Andersen, Final WorldCom Defendant Settles.* Press Release.

Page 359: WorldCom Directors contribute personal funds towards settling class action claims. Office of the New York State Comptroller. (March 18, 2005). *Hevesi Revives Historic Settlement, Former WorldCom Directors to Pay from Own Pockets.* Press Release. Also see, Office of the New York State Comptroller. (March21, 2005). *Hevesi Announces Settlement With Former WorldCom Chairman Bert Roberts.* Press Release.

Page 359: Description of the SEC settlement against WorldCom. Unites States Securities and Exchange Commission, Litigation Release No. 182219, July 7, 2003.

Index